Kare Kano

his and her circumstances

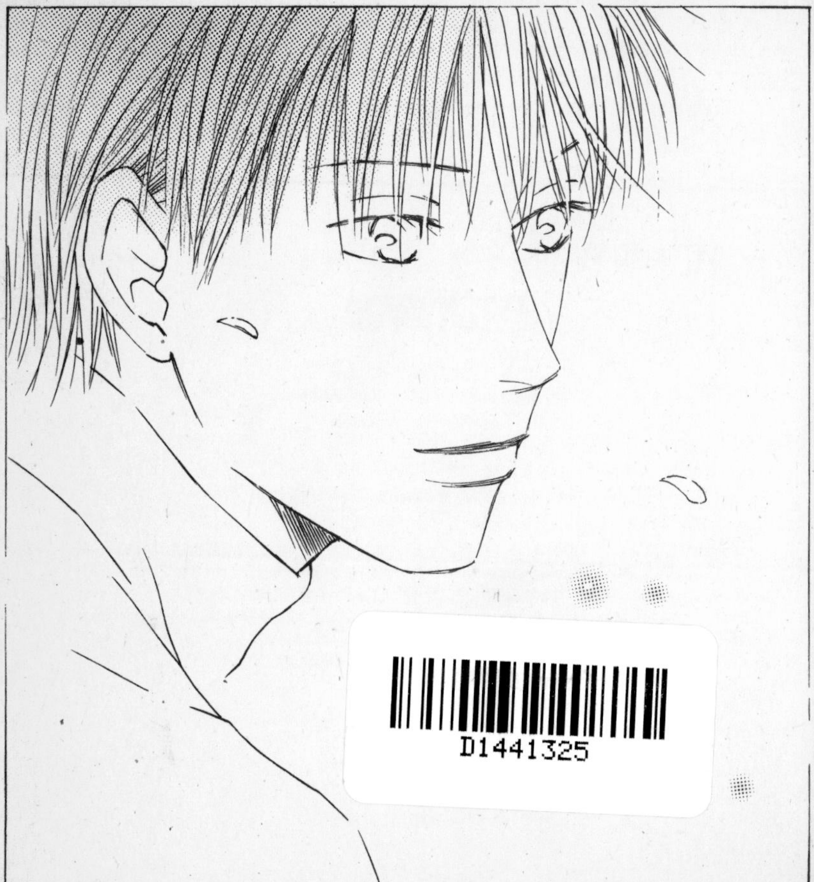

Kare Kano Vol. 20
Created by Masami Tsuda

Translation - Michelle Kobayashi
English Adaptation - Darcy Lookman
Copy Editor - Hope Donovan
Retouch and Lettering - Alyson Stetz and Jennifer Carbajal
Production Artist - Mike Estacio
Cover Design - Joe Macasocol, Jr.

Editor - Carol Fox
Digital Imaging Manager - Chris Buford
Production Manager - Elisabeth Brizzi
Managing Editor - Sheldon Drzka
Editor in Chief - Rob Tokar
VP of Production - Ron Klamert
Publisher - Mike Kiley
President and C.O.O. - John Parker
C.E.O. and Chief Creative Officer - Stuart Levy

A  Manga

TOKYOPOP Inc.
5900 Wilshire Blvd. Suite 2000
Los Angeles, CA 90036

E-mail: info@TOKYOPOP.com
Come visit us online at www.TOKYOPOP.com

ISBN: 1-59816-183-0

First TOKYOPOP printing: August 2006
10 9 8 7 6 5 4 3 2
Printed in the USA

kare kano

his and her circumstances

volume twenty

by Masami Tsuda

HAMBURG // LONDON // LOS ANGELES // TOKYO

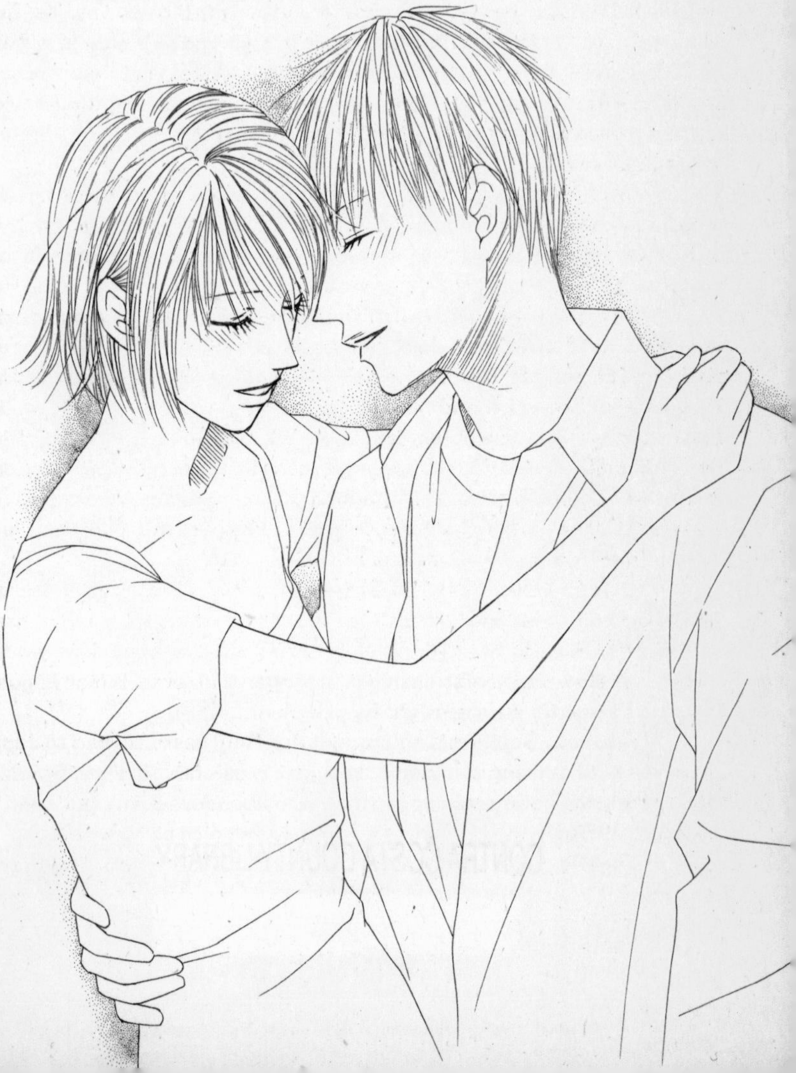

KARE KANO: THE STORY SO FAR

Yukino Miyazawa seemed like the perfect student: kind, athletic and smart. But in actuality, she was the self-professed "queen of vanity"--her only goal was to win the praise and admiration of others, and her sacred duty was to look and act perfect during school hours. Only at home would she let down her guard and let her true self show.

But when Yukino entered high school, she met her match: Soichiro Arima, a handsome, popular, ultra-intelligent guy. At first when he stole the top seat in class from her, Yukino saw him as a bitter rival. But over time, she learned that she and Soichiro had more in common than she had ever imagined. As their love blossomed, the two made a vow to finally stop pretending to be perfect and simply be true to themselves.

Still, they had plenty of obstacles. Jealous classmates tried to break them up, and so did teachers when their grades began to suffer as a result of the relationship. Yet somehow Yukino and Soichiro's love managed to persevere. But their greatest challenge was yet to come.

For although Soichiro's life seemed perfect, he'd endured a very traumatic childhood...and the ghosts were coming back to haunt him. His father left him early, and his mother was so abusive that his uncle adopted him and raised him as his own. But when Soichiro started to get nationwide attention for his high school achievements, his birth mother resurfaced, hoping to cash in. Soichiro met with her a few times to learn more about the family that abandoned him...until he realized she had nothing for him but more abuse and lies. With that (and a little help from his friends), he severed contact.

Soichiro had been keeping the family drama secret from Yukino, afraid it would destroy everything they'd worked for in their relationship. But she finally broke down his walls and made him tell her everything. Now their relationship is stronger than ever. Which is good, because Yukino thinks she might be pregnant...

And now, Soichiro's delinquent dad Reiji has returned to Japan after years of touring the world as a jazz musician. At first Soichiro has very mixed feelings about the man who abandoned him, but soon he finds himself enjoying his father's company in spite of himself.

That is, until Reiji levels a loaded gun at Soichiro's birth mother...

kare kano
volume twenty

TABLE OF CONTENTS

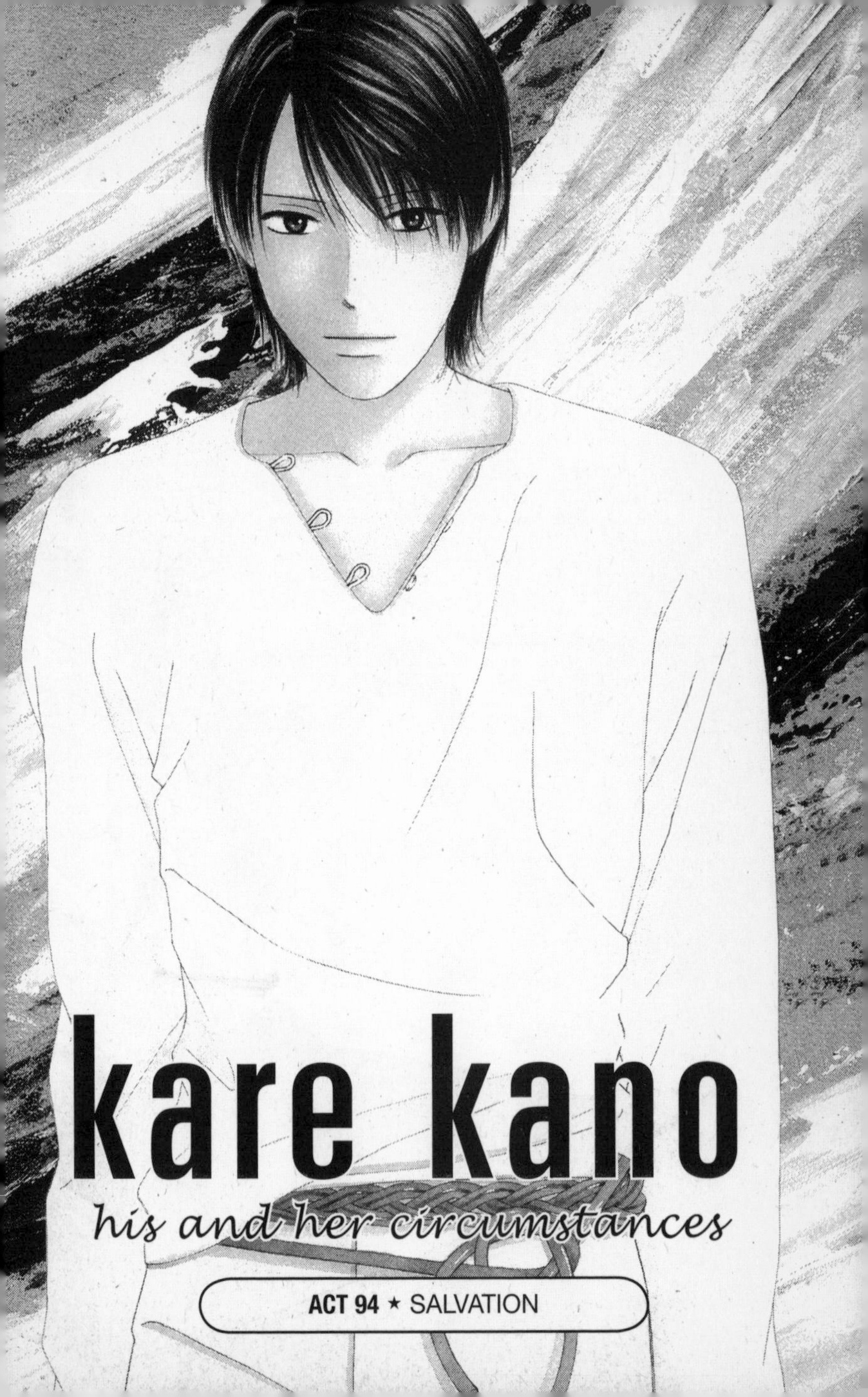
kare kano
his and her circumstances
ACT 94 ★ SALVATION

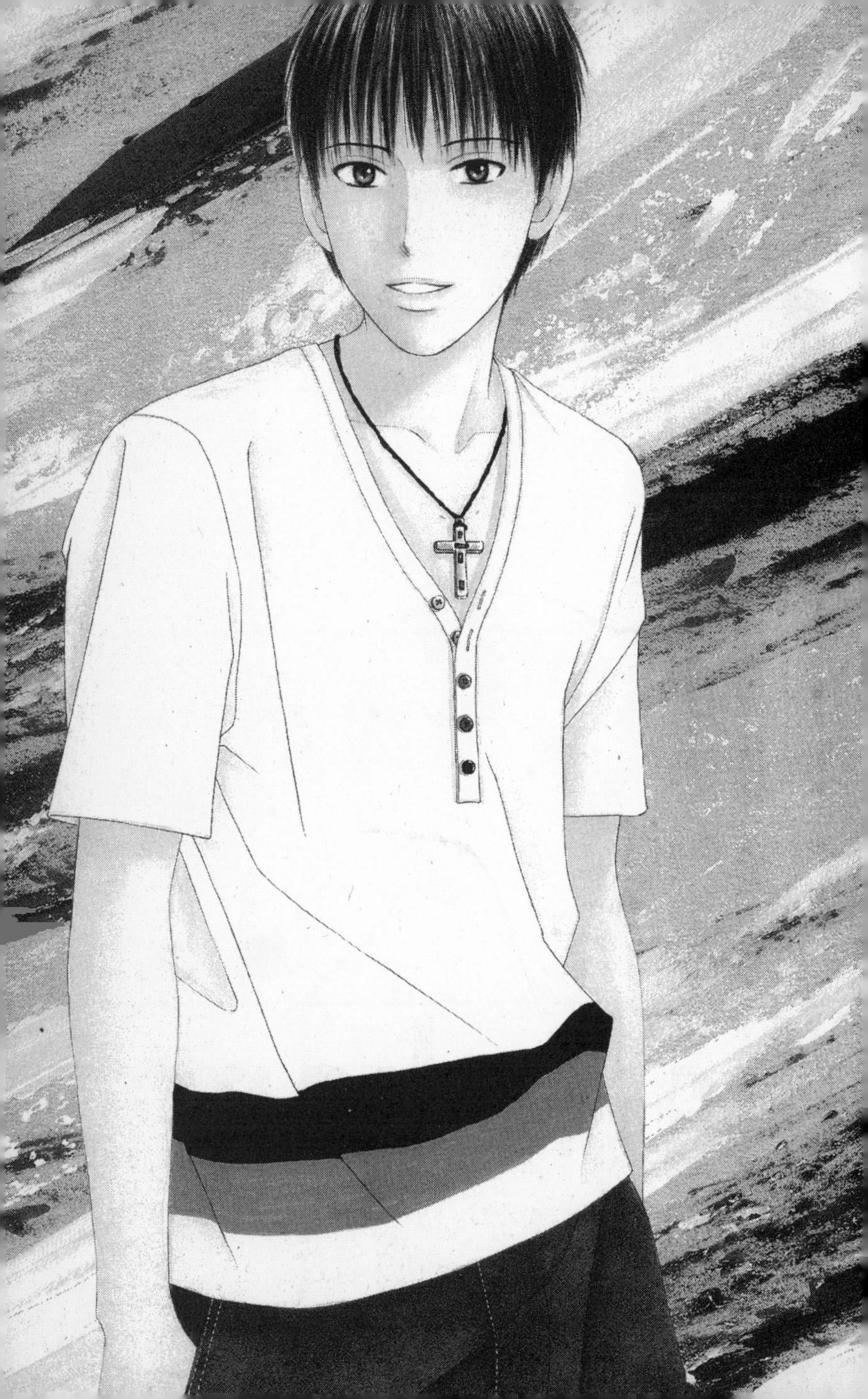

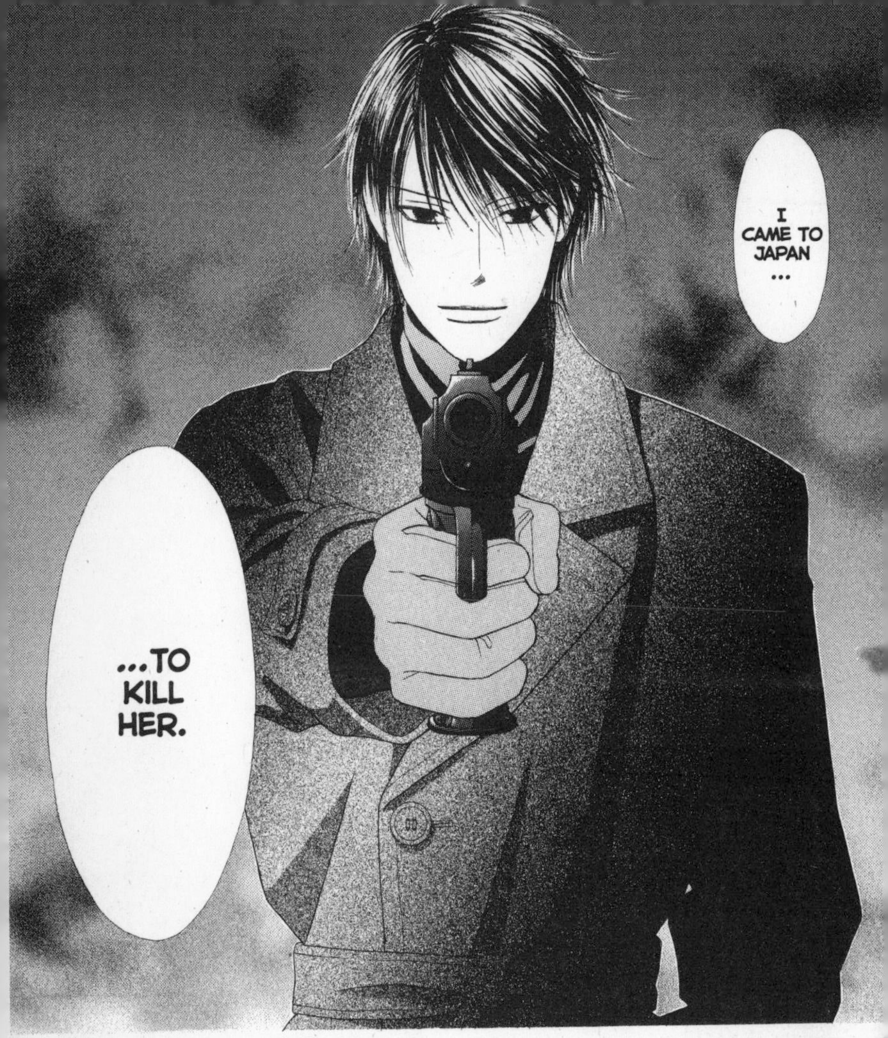
I CAME TO JAPAN ...
...TO KILL HER.

Human Anatomy

I've gotten interested in human anatomy lately. I've watched lots of kabuki and ballet, and the Olympic games, too. I've even started to watch martial arts matches. In my line of work, I don't get to use my body much, but I love looking at people who have made a profession out of developing theirs. They're gorgeous!

I figure I should do a little something with my body, too, so I stretch. I feel so good when I do it in the morning.

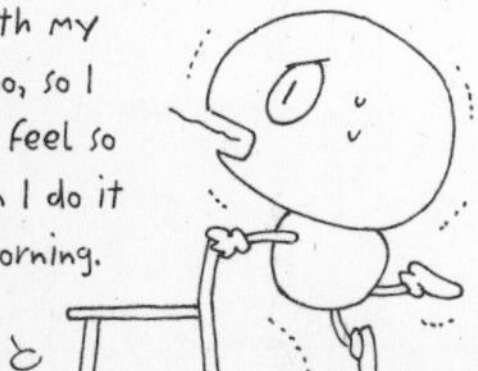

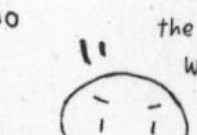

I've even been to the "Body Worlds" exhibit.

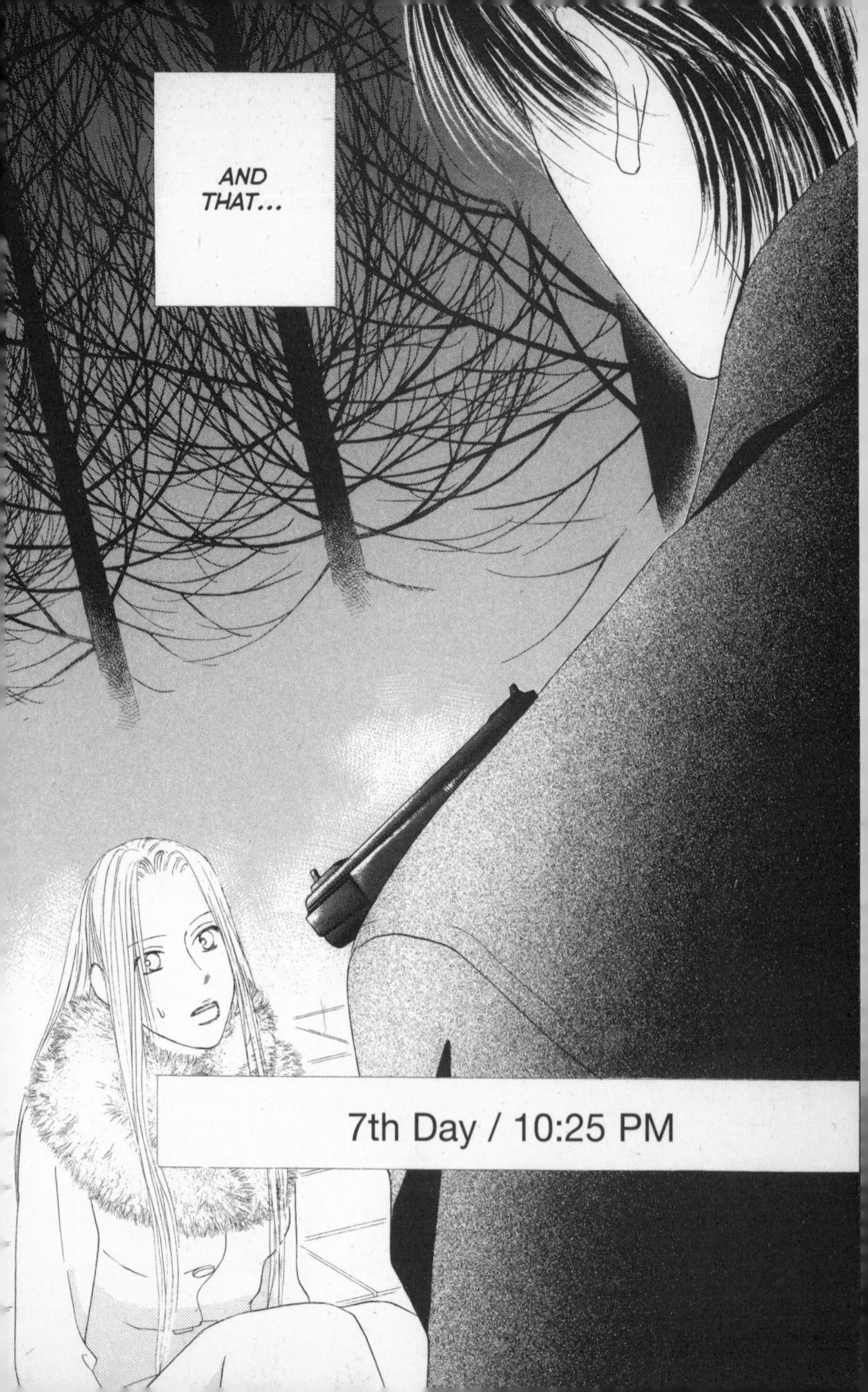
AND THAT...
7th Day / 10:25 PM

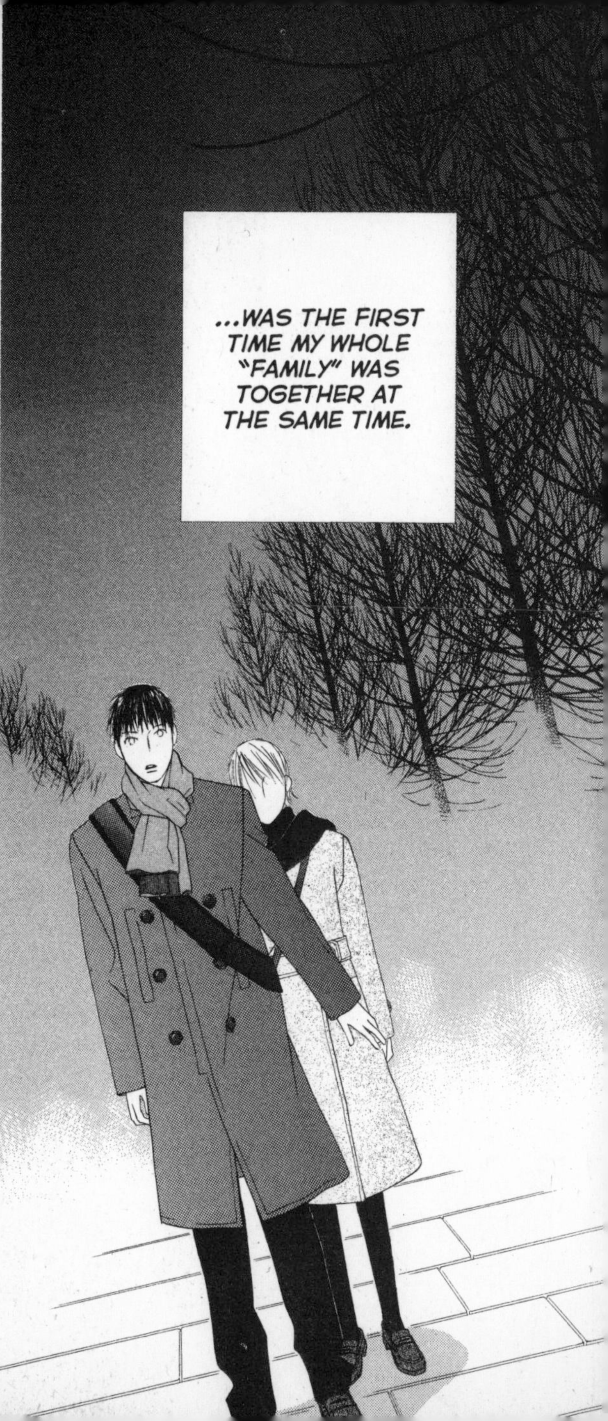
...WAS THE FIRST TIME MY WHOLE "FAMILY" WAS TOGETHER AT THE SAME TIME.

1

Hello!
This is Kare Kano Volume 20.

VOLUME 20!

Thanks to everyone out there who is reading this!

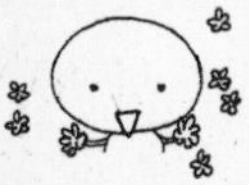

I'm writing this at the beginning of 2005, and this year's theme is "Beauty"!

So anyway, I'm going to try to make things beautiful! Up until now, I've been more of the neutral-color type. I've never really bothered decorating the things around me, but now I think it's time to add splashes of color to my life!

I'll start by putting flowers on my desk.

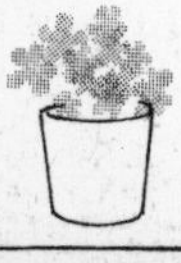

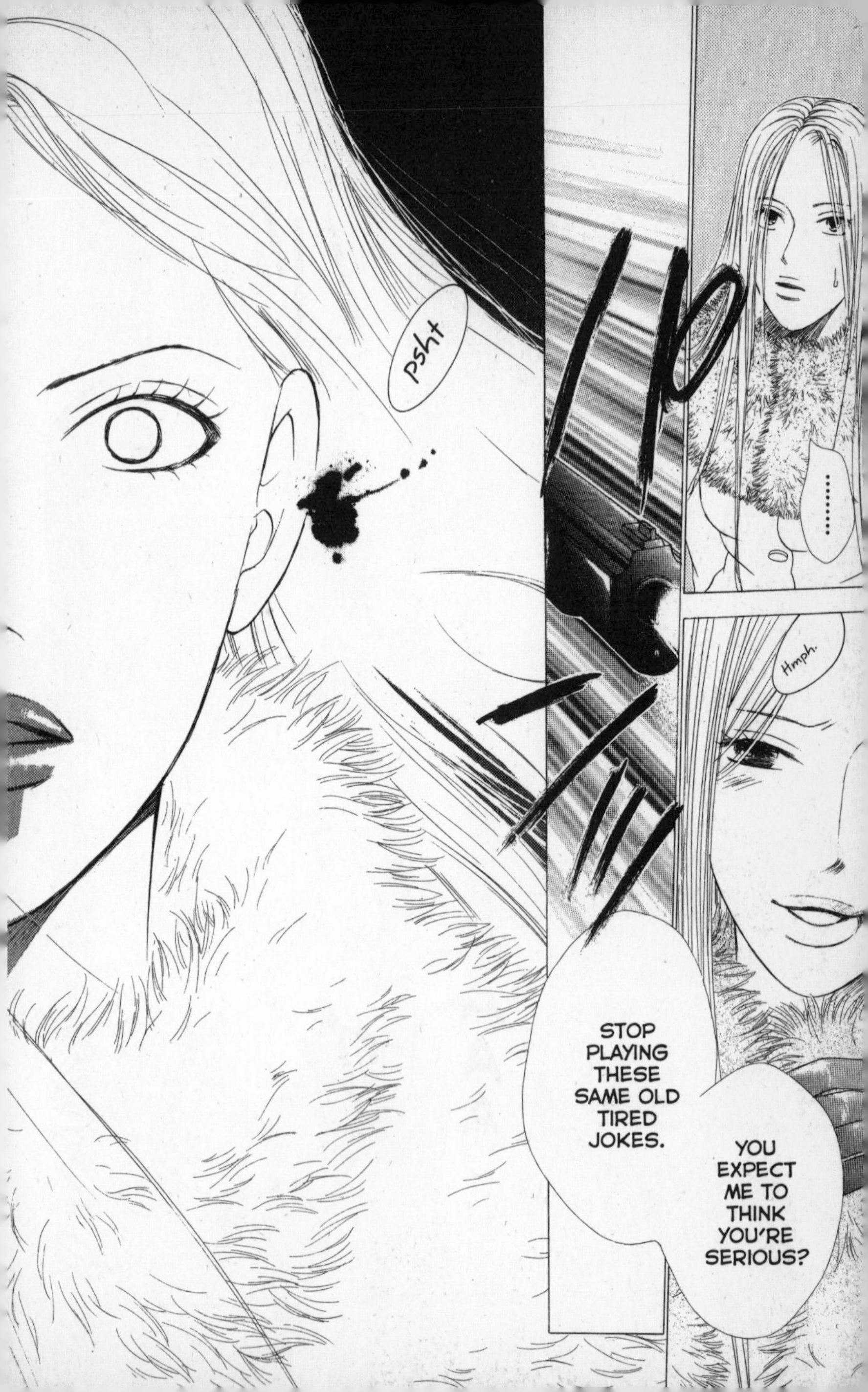
......
Hmph.
YOU EXPECT ME TO THINK YOU'RE SERIOUS?
STOP PLAYING THESE SAME OLD TIRED JOKES.
psht

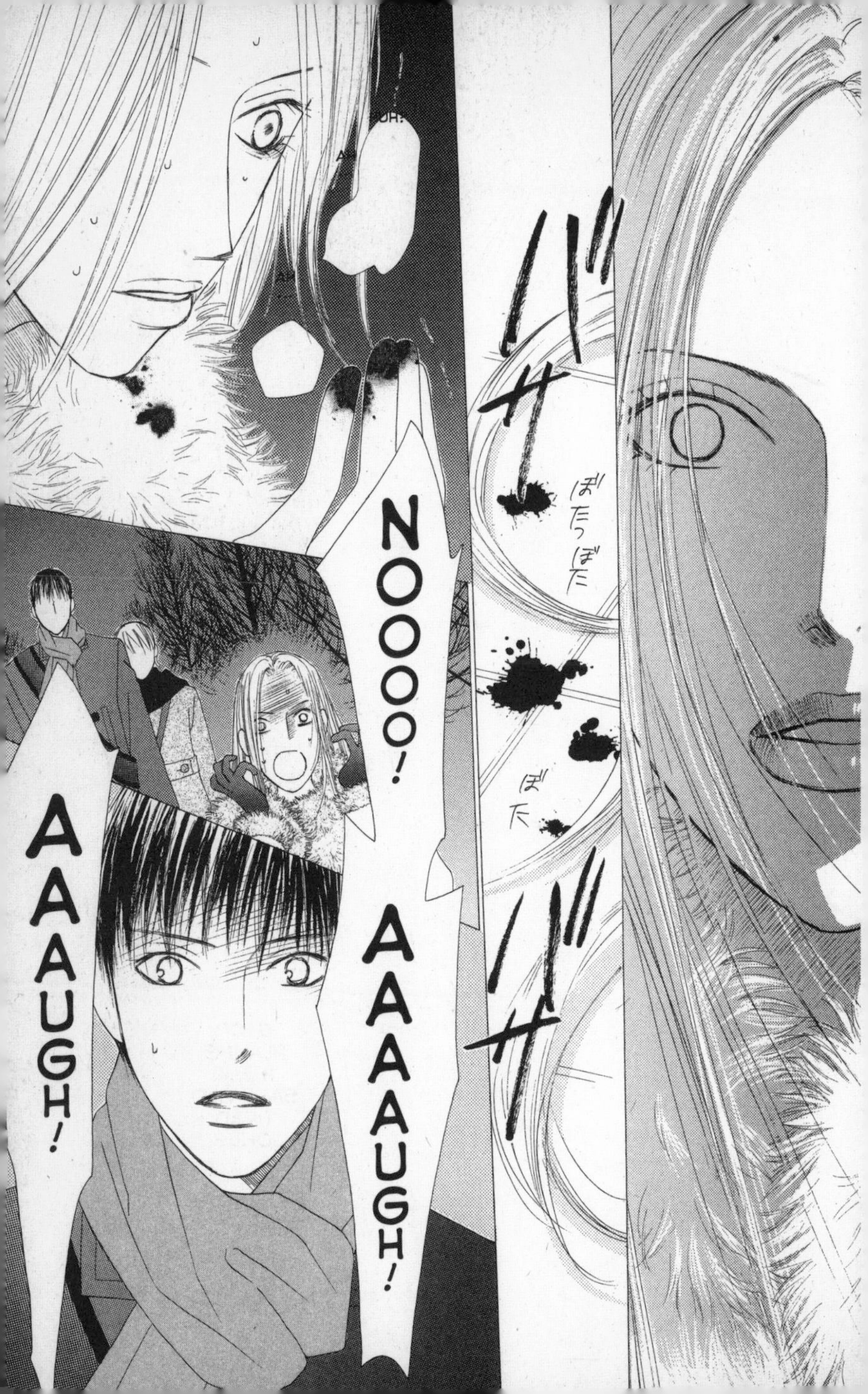
バサ
ぼたっぼた
ぼた
バサ
NOOOO! AAAAAUGH!
AAAUGH!

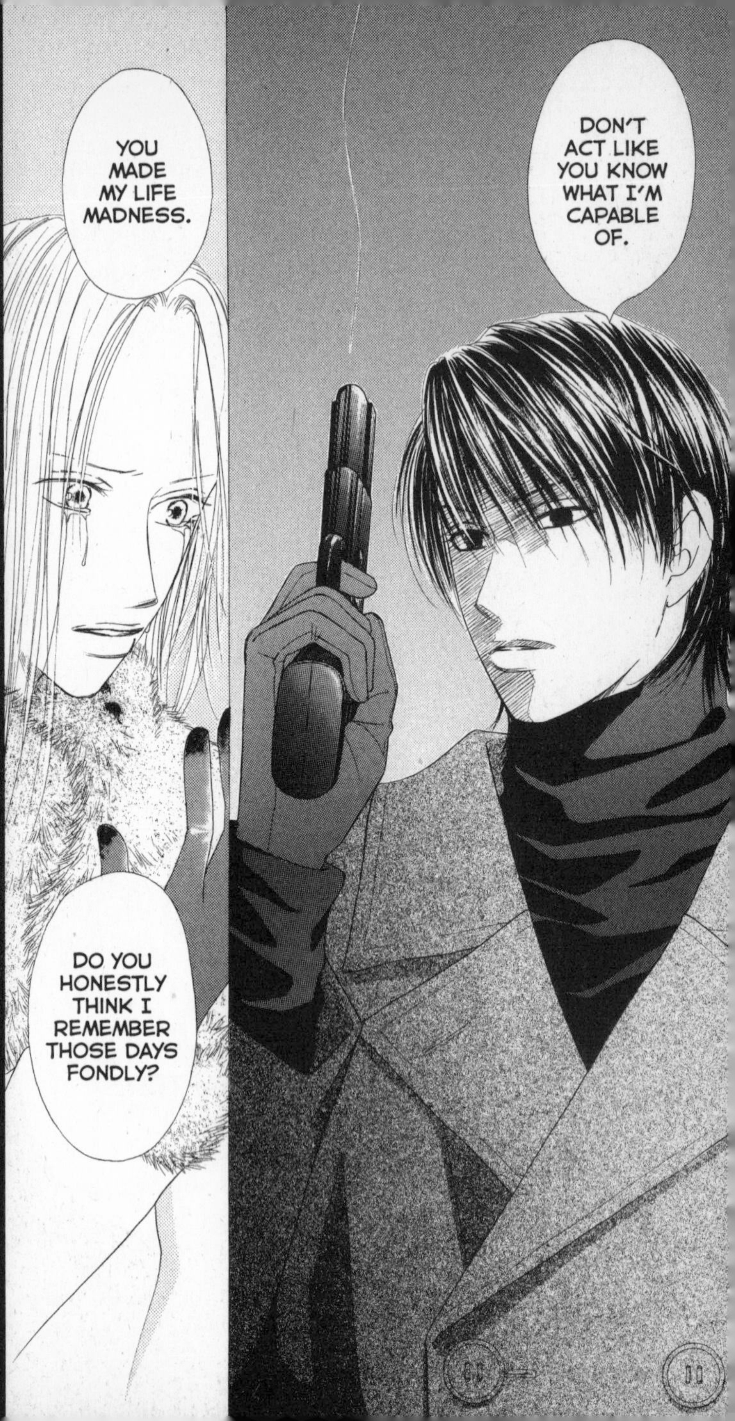
DON'T ACT LIKE YOU KNOW WHAT I'M CAPABLE OF.
YOU MADE MY LIFE MADNESS.
DO YOU HONESTLY THINK I REMEMBER THOSE DAYS FONDLY?

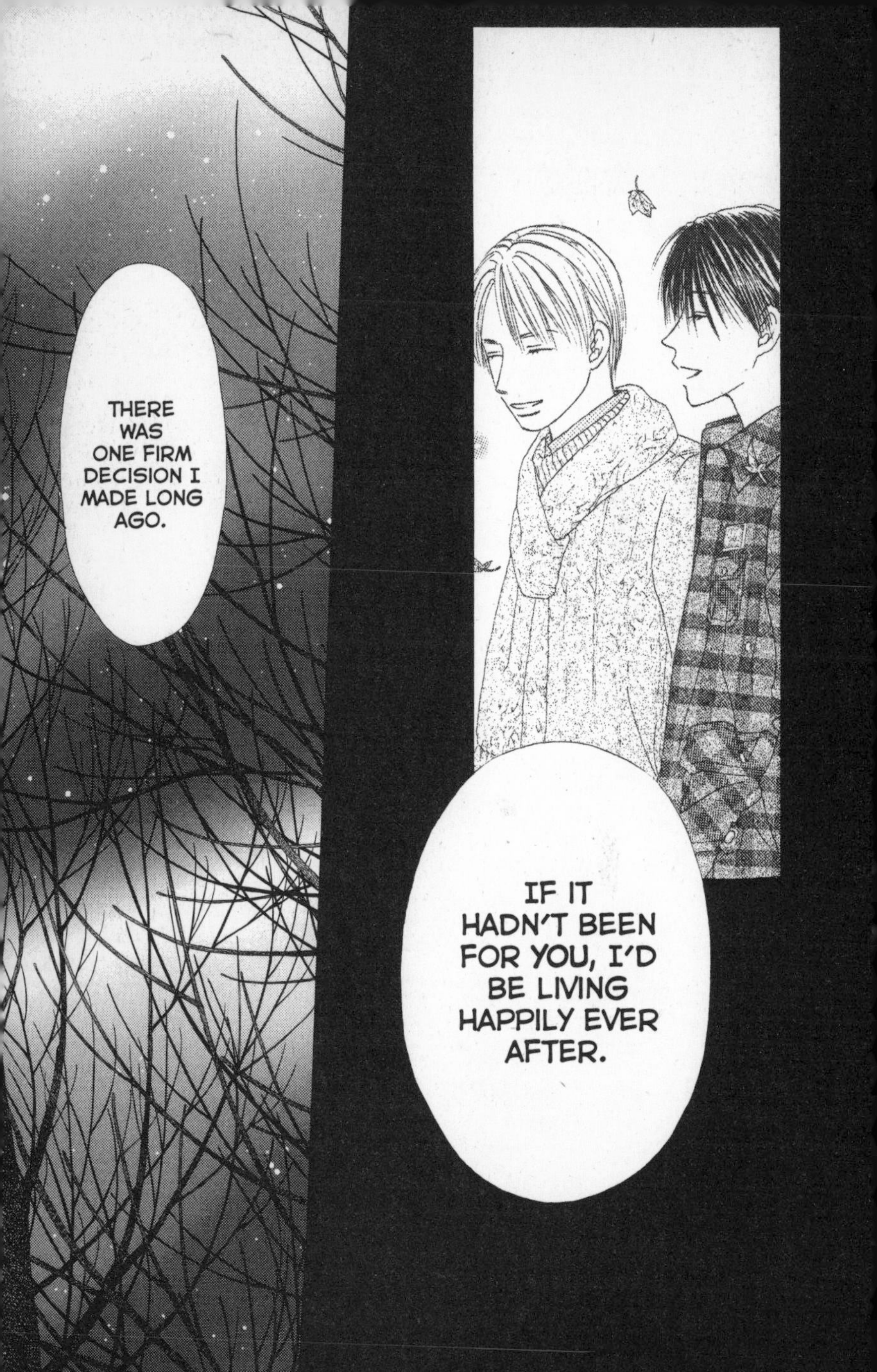
IF IT HADN'T BEEN FOR YOU, I'D BE LIVING HAPPILY EVER AFTER.
THERE WAS ONE FIRM DECISION I MADE LONG AGO.

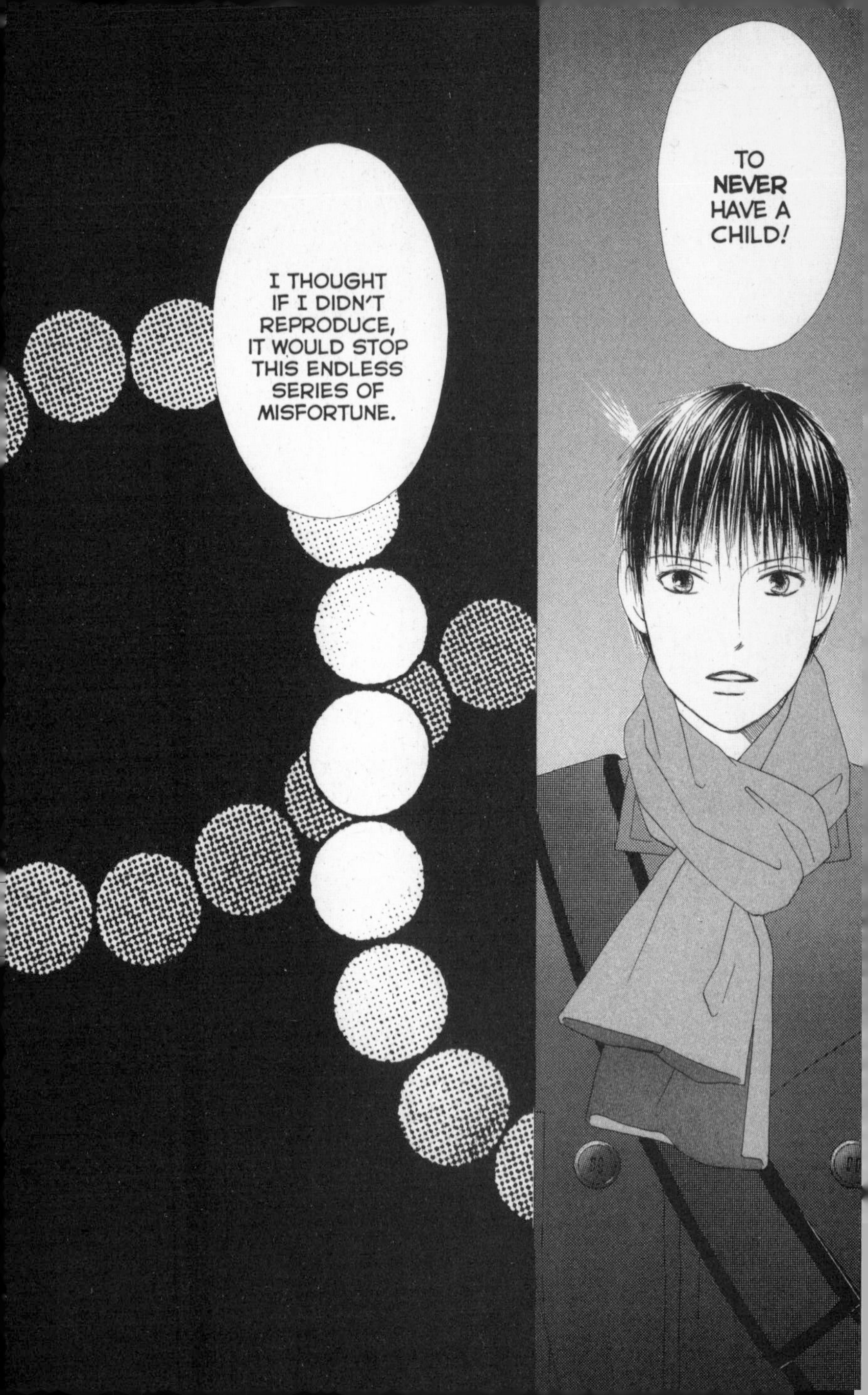
TO NEVER HAVE A CHILD!
I THOUGHT IF I DIDN'T REPRODUCE, IT WOULD STOP THIS ENDLESS SERIES OF MISFORTUNE.

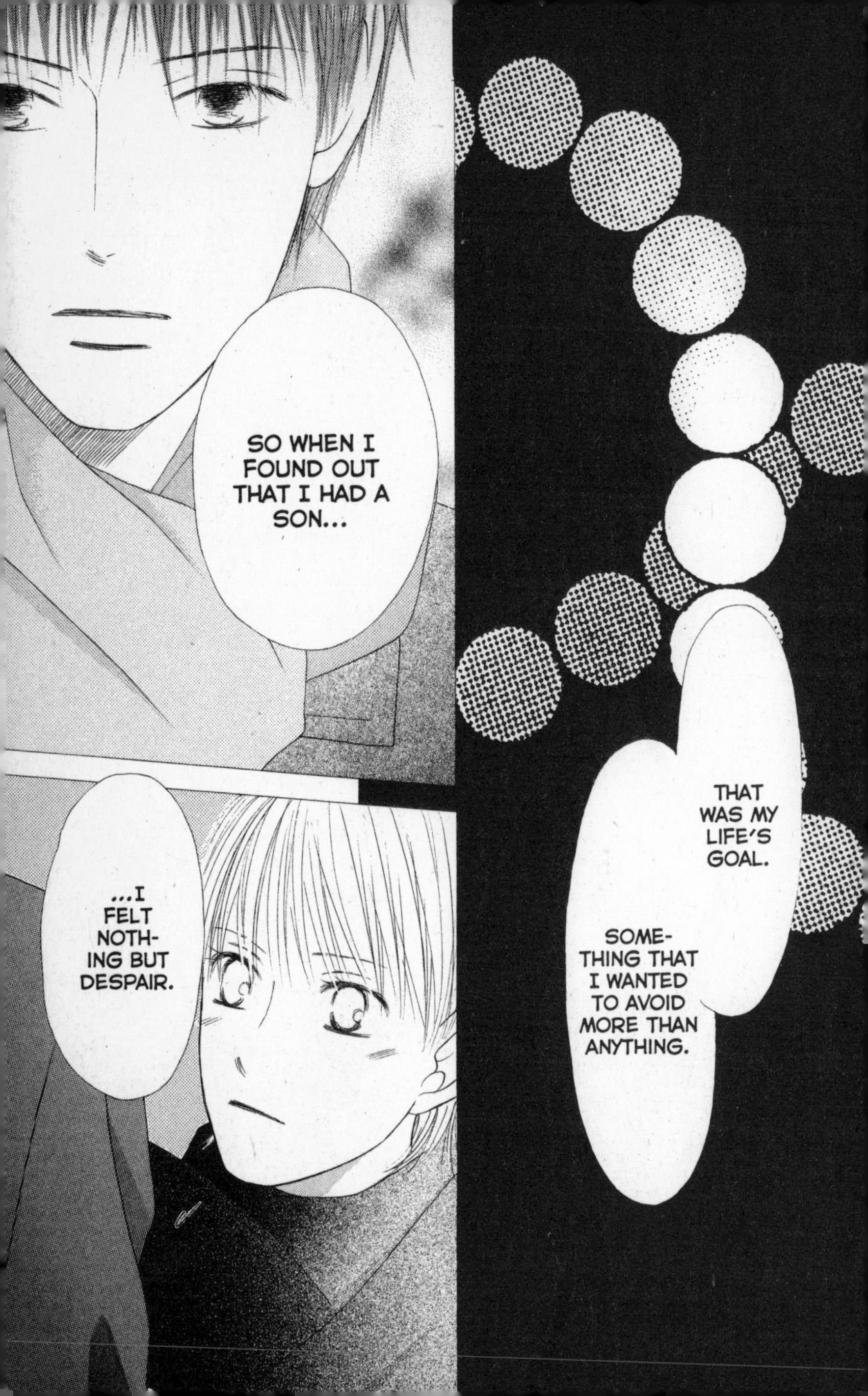
THAT WAS MY LIFE'S GOAL.
SOME-THING THAT I WANTED TO AVOID MORE THAN ANYTHING.
SO WHEN I FOUND OUT THAT I HAD A SON...
...I FELT NOTH-ING BUT DESPAIR.

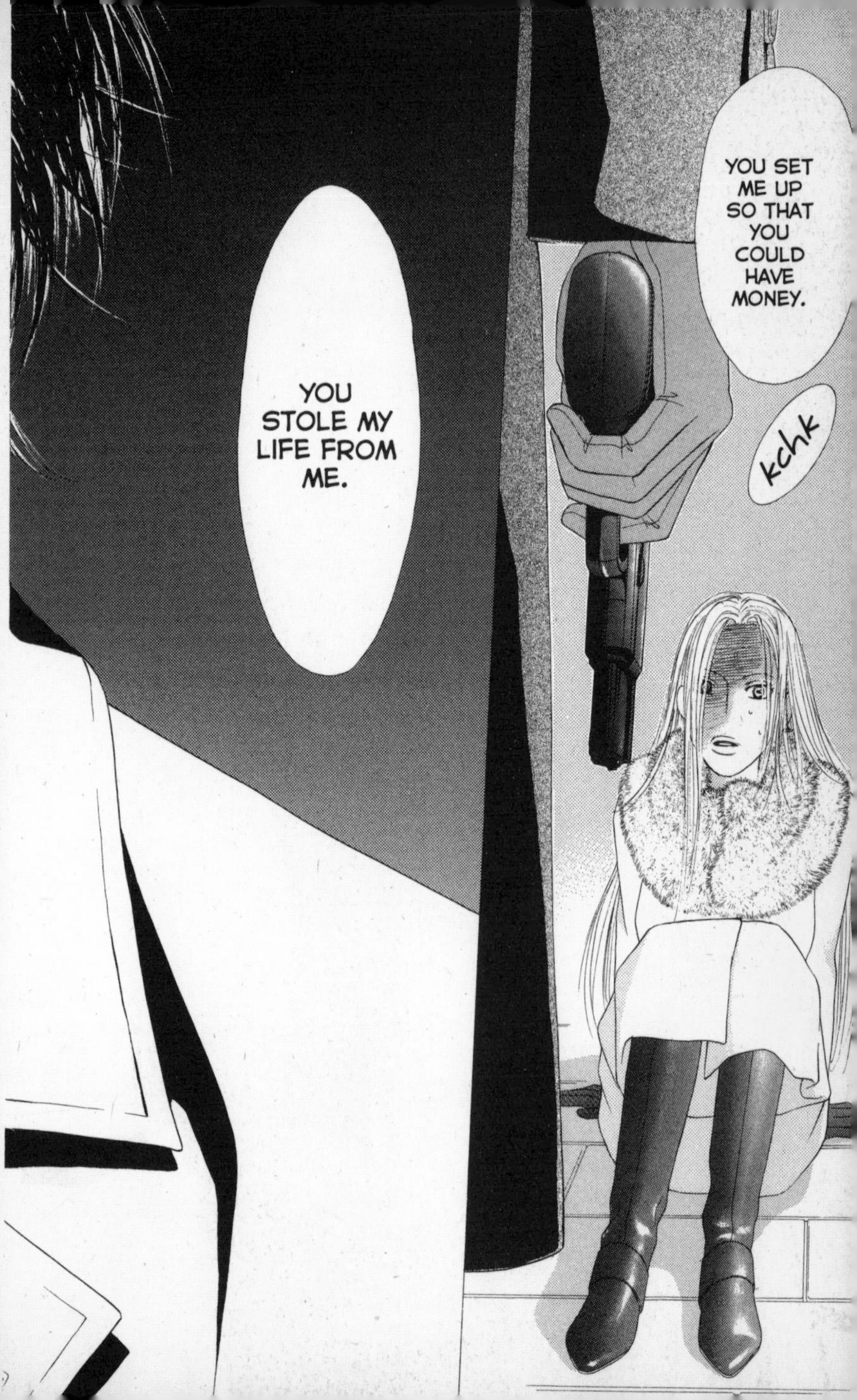
YOU SET ME UP SO THAT YOU COULD HAVE MONEY.
kchk
YOU STOLE MY LIFE FROM ME.

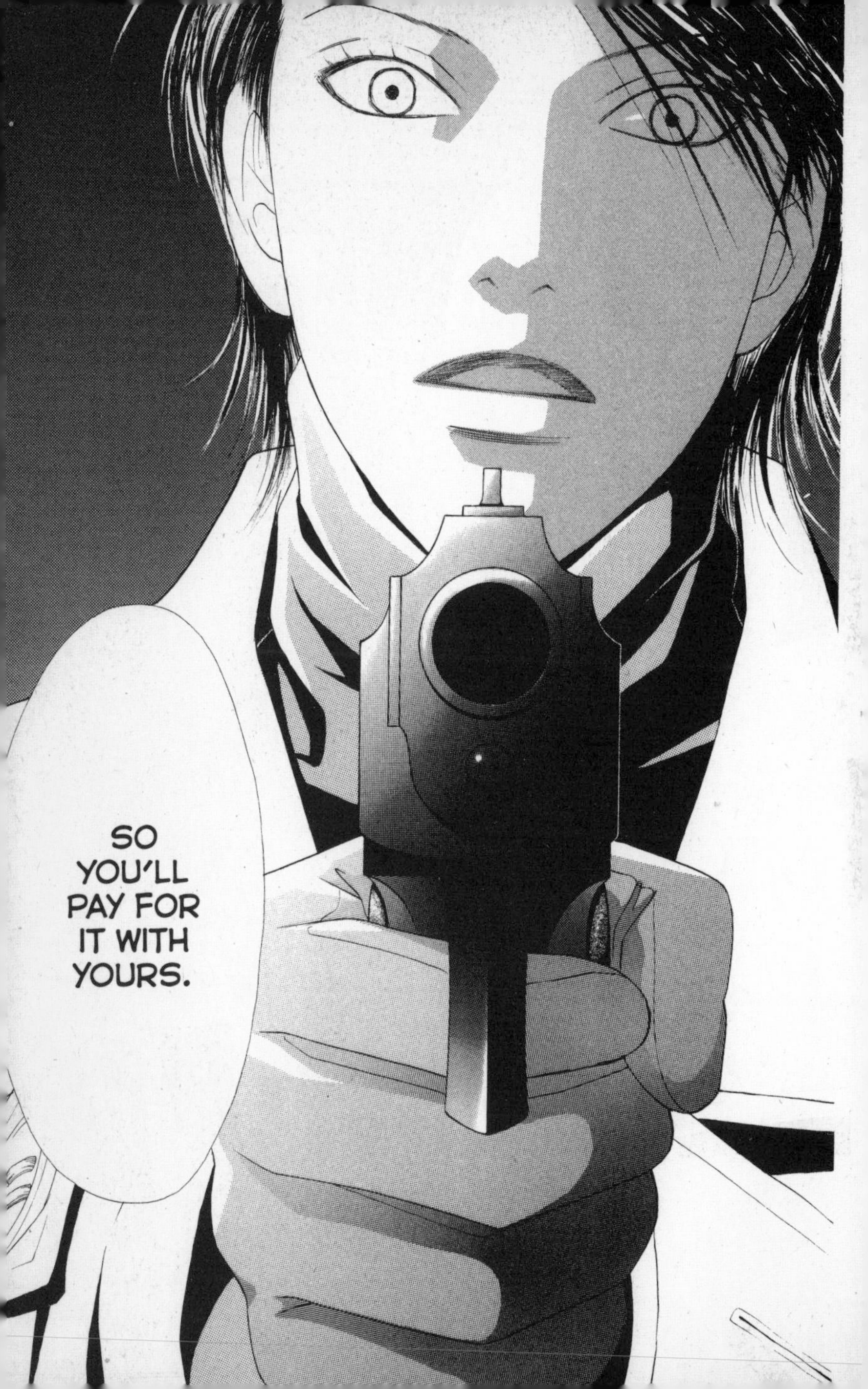
SO YOU'LL PAY FOR IT WITH YOURS.

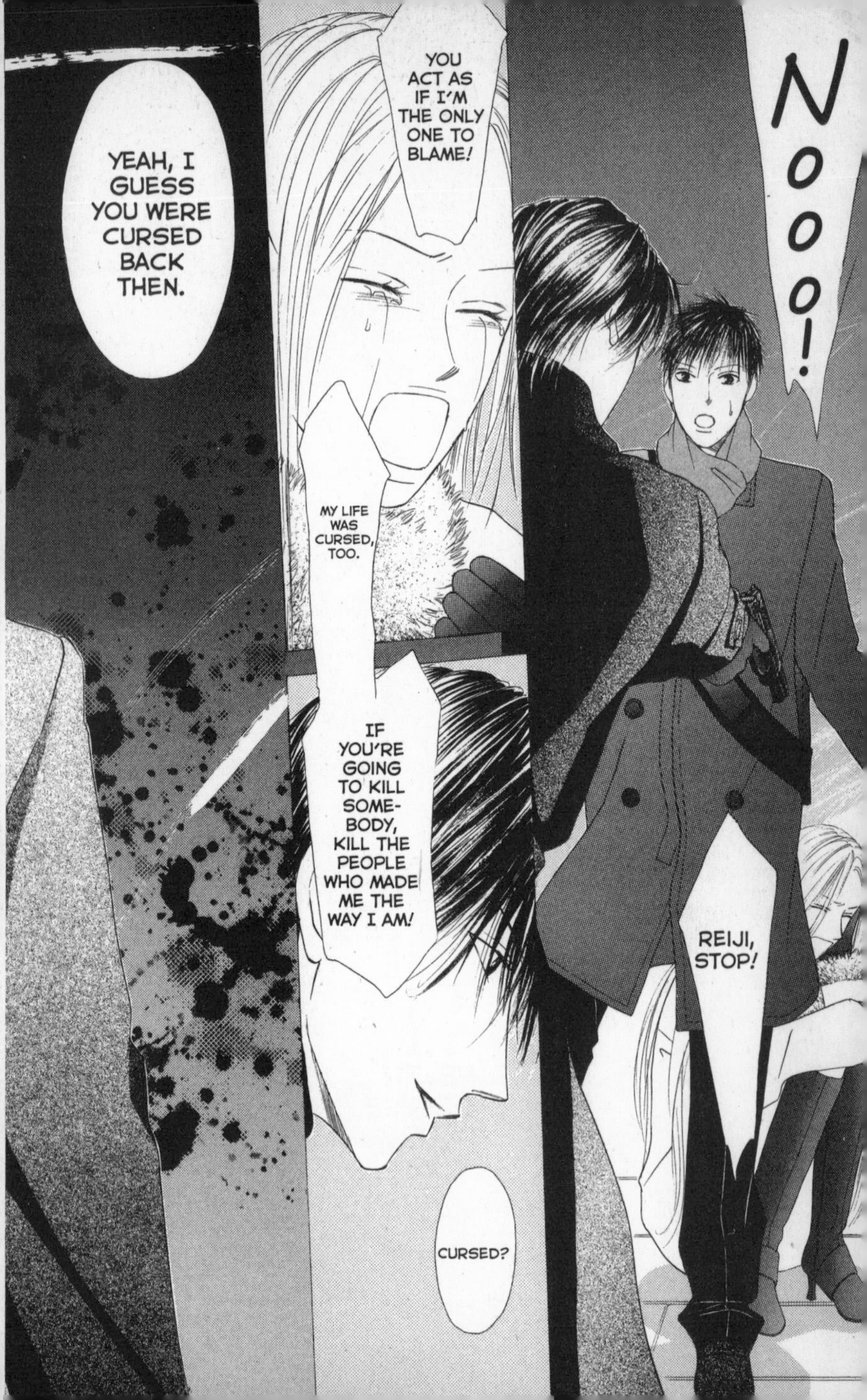
NOOO!
REIJI, STOP!
YOU ACT AS IF I'M THE ONLY ONE TO BLAME!
MY LIFE WAS CURSED, TOO.
IF YOU'RE GOING TO KILL SOMEBODY, KILL THE PEOPLE WHO MADE ME THE WAY I AM!
CURSED?
YEAH, I GUESS YOU WERE CURSED BACK THEN.

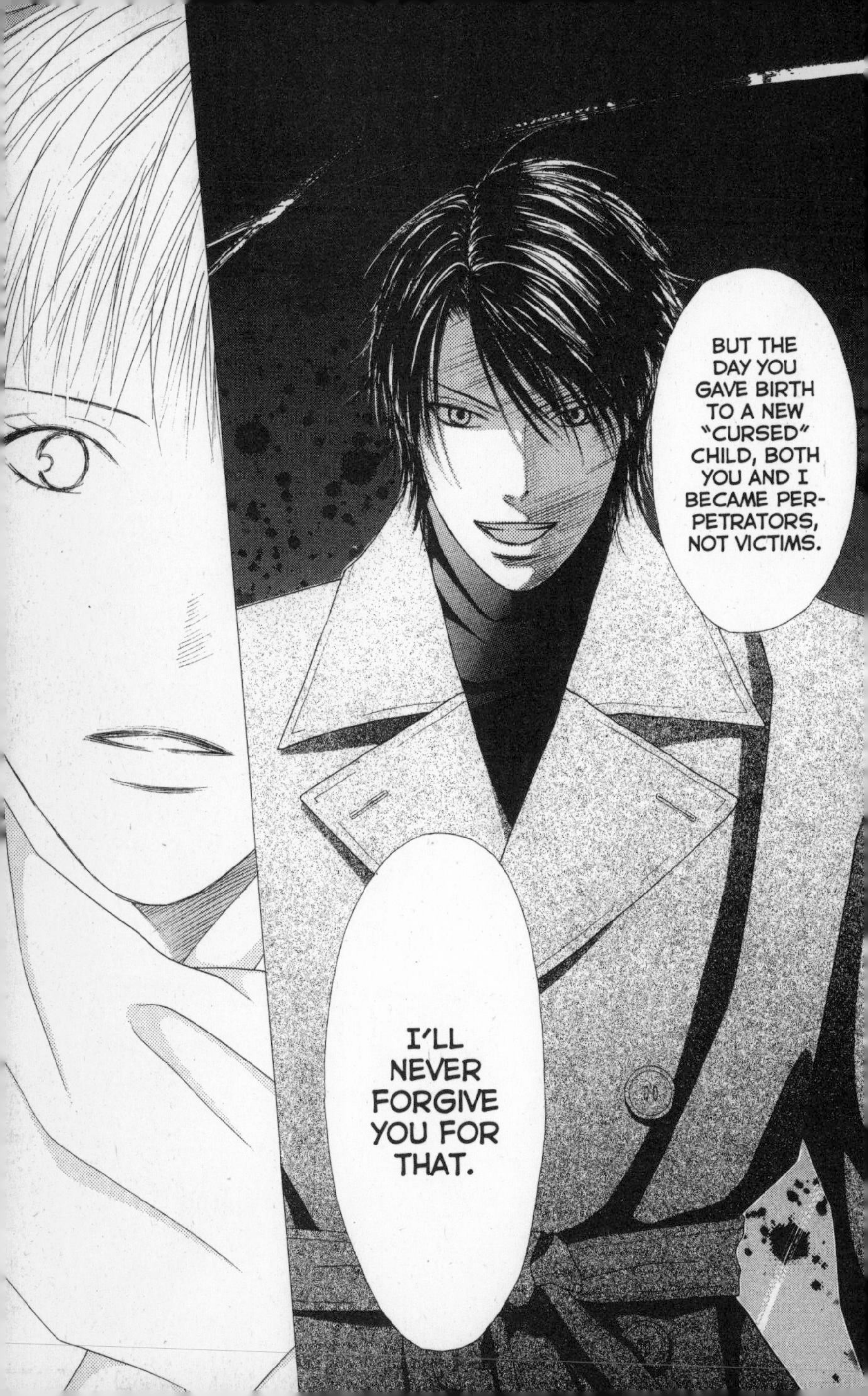
BUT THE DAY YOU GAVE BIRTH TO A NEW "CURSED" CHILD, BOTH YOU AND I BECAME PER-PETRATORS, NOT VICTIMS.
I'LL NEVER FORGIVE YOU FOR THAT.

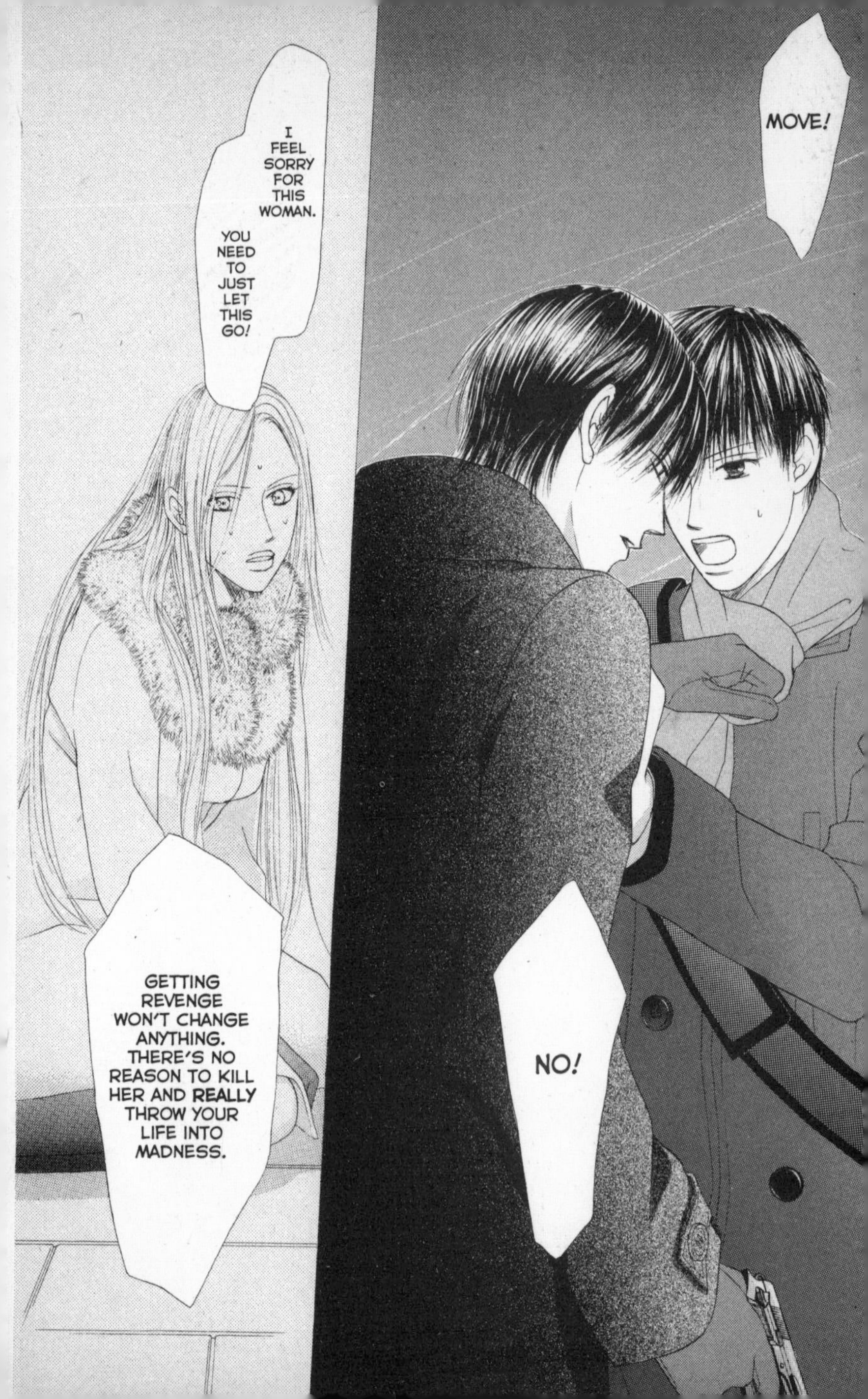
MOVE!
NO!
I FEEL SORRY FOR THIS WOMAN.
YOU NEED TO JUST LET THIS GO!
GETTING REVENGE WON'T CHANGE ANYTHING. THERE'S NO REASON TO KILL HER AND REALLY THROW YOUR LIFE INTO MADNESS.

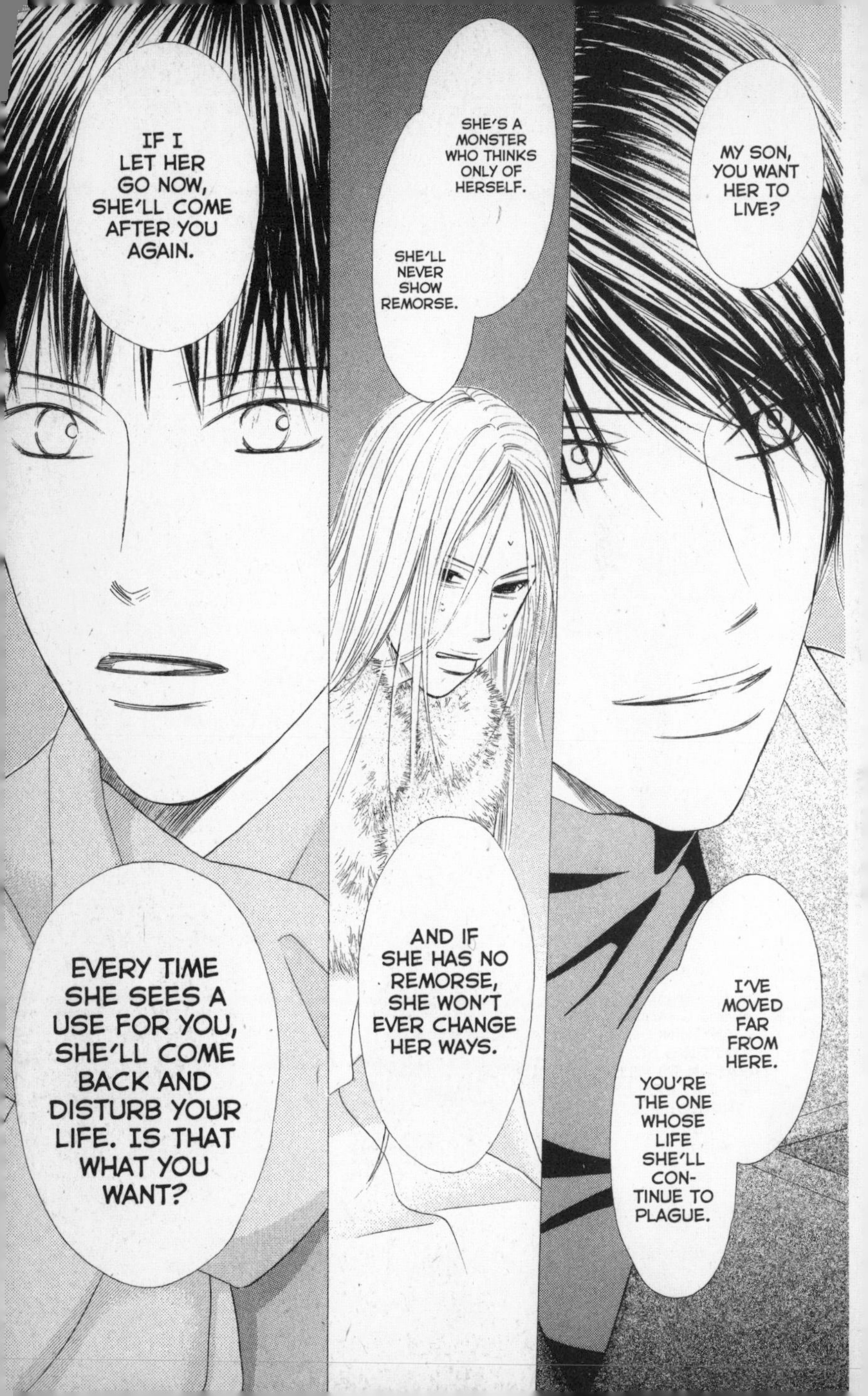
MY SON, YOU WANT HER TO LIVE?
I'VE MOVED FAR FROM HERE.
YOU'RE THE ONE WHOSE LIFE SHE'LL CON-TINUE TO PLAGUE.
SHE'S A MONSTER WHO THINKS ONLY OF HERSELF.
SHE'LL NEVER SHOW REMORSE.
AND IF SHE HAS NO REMORSE, SHE WON'T EVER CHANGE HER WAYS.
IF I LET HER GO NOW, SHE'LL COME AFTER YOU AGAIN.
EVERY TIME SHE SEES A USE FOR YOU, SHE'LL COME BACK AND DISTURB YOUR LIFE. IS THAT WHAT YOU WANT?

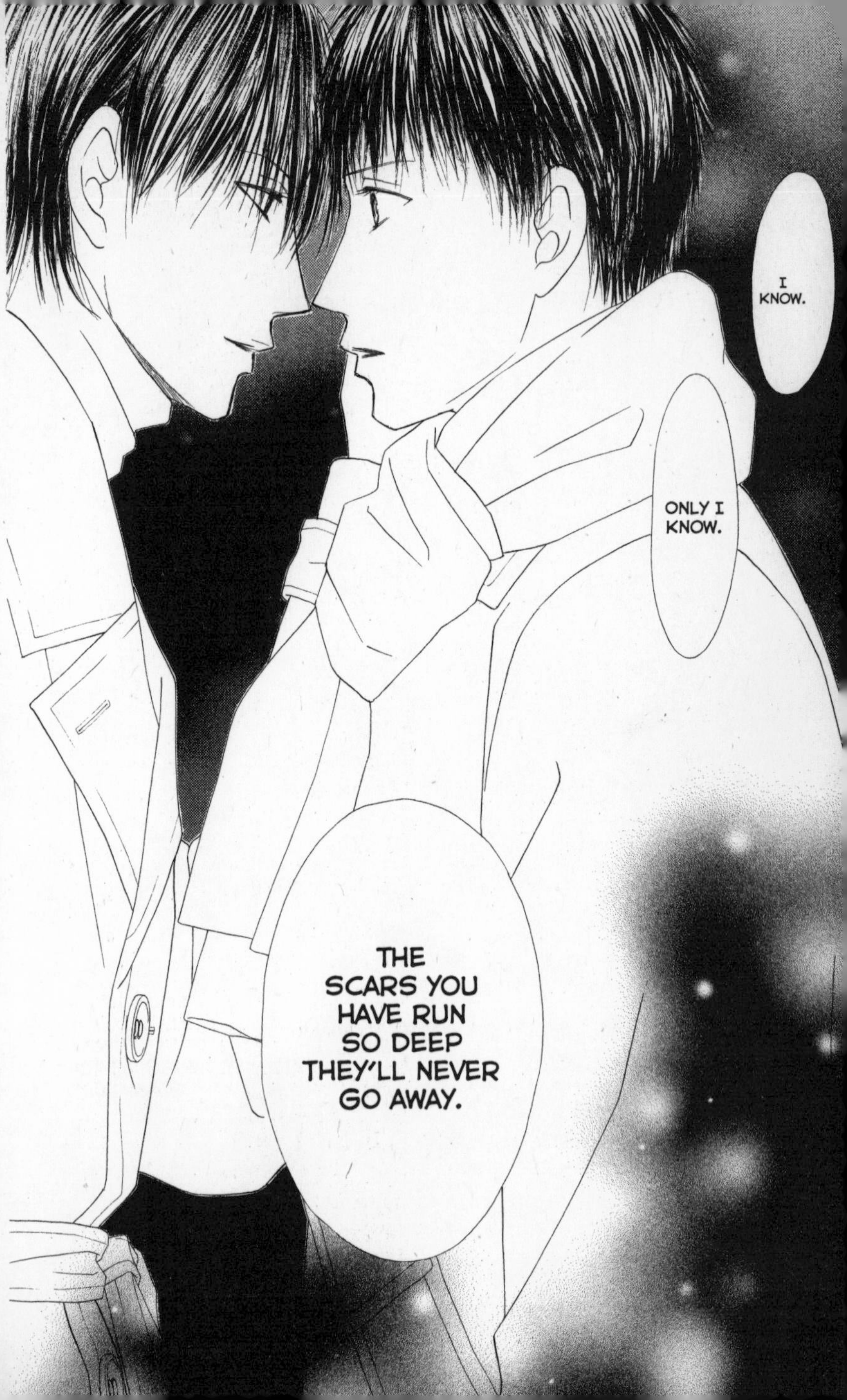
I KNOW.
ONLY I KNOW.
THE SCARS YOU HAVE RUN SO DEEP THEY'LL NEVER GO AWAY.

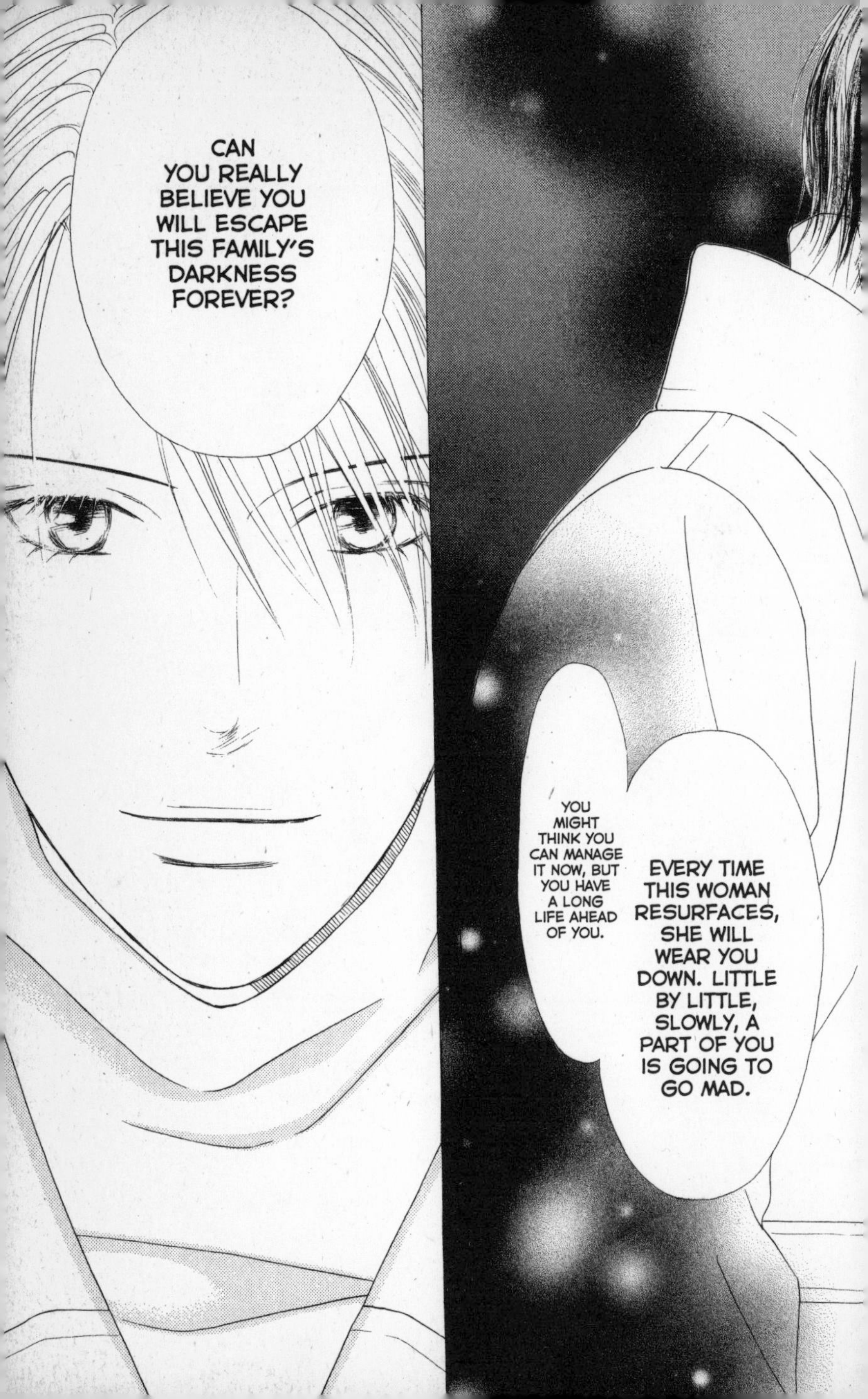
EVERY TIME THIS WOMAN RESURFACES, SHE WILL WEAR YOU DOWN. LITTLE BY LITTLE, SLOWLY, A PART OF YOU IS GOING TO GO MAD.
YOU MIGHT THINK YOU CAN MANAGE IT NOW, BUT YOU HAVE A LONG LIFE AHEAD OF YOU.
CAN YOU REALLY BELIEVE YOU WILL ESCAPE THIS FAMILY'S DARKNESS FOREVER?

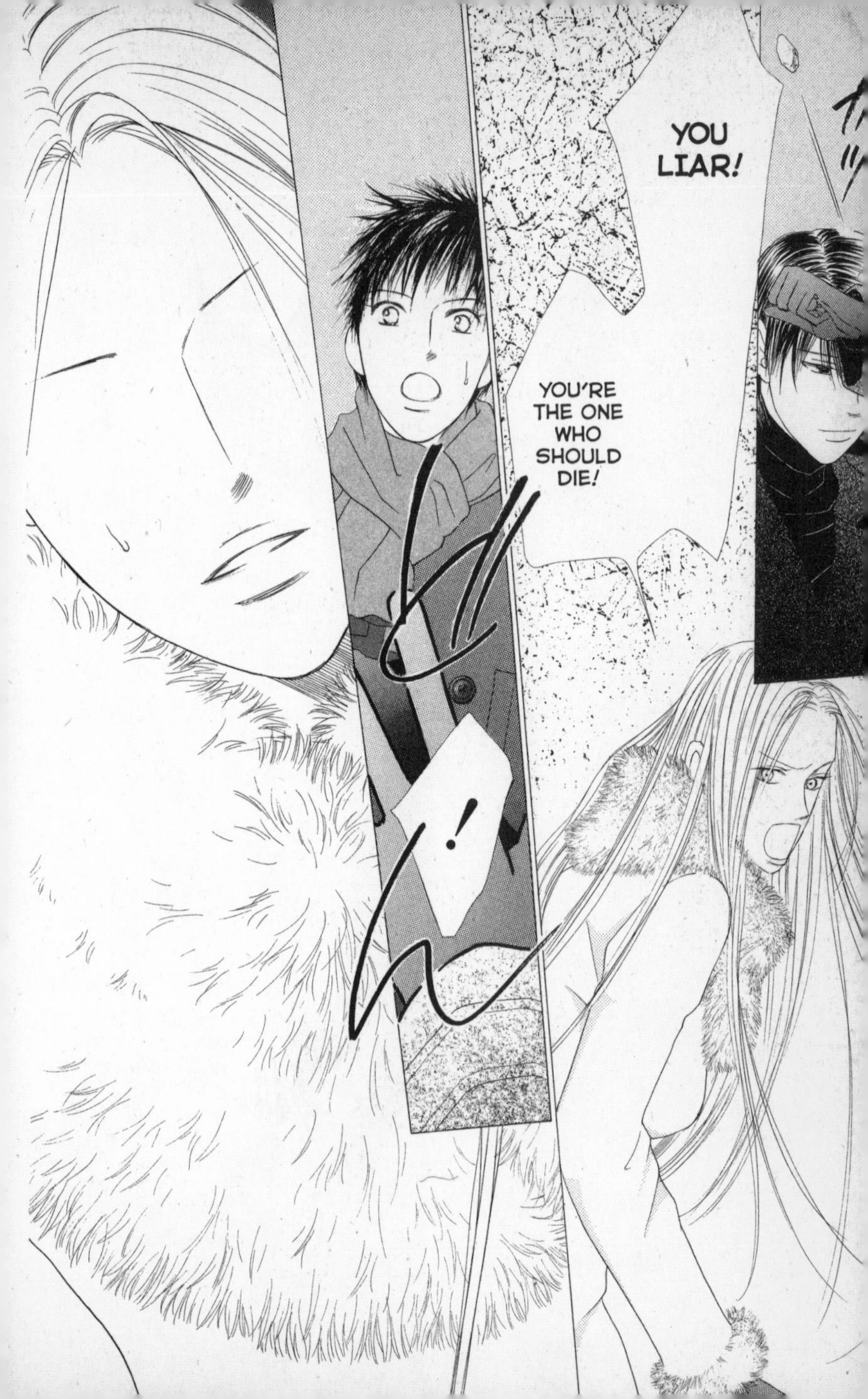
YOU LIAR!
YOU'RE THE ONE WHO SHOULD DIE!
!

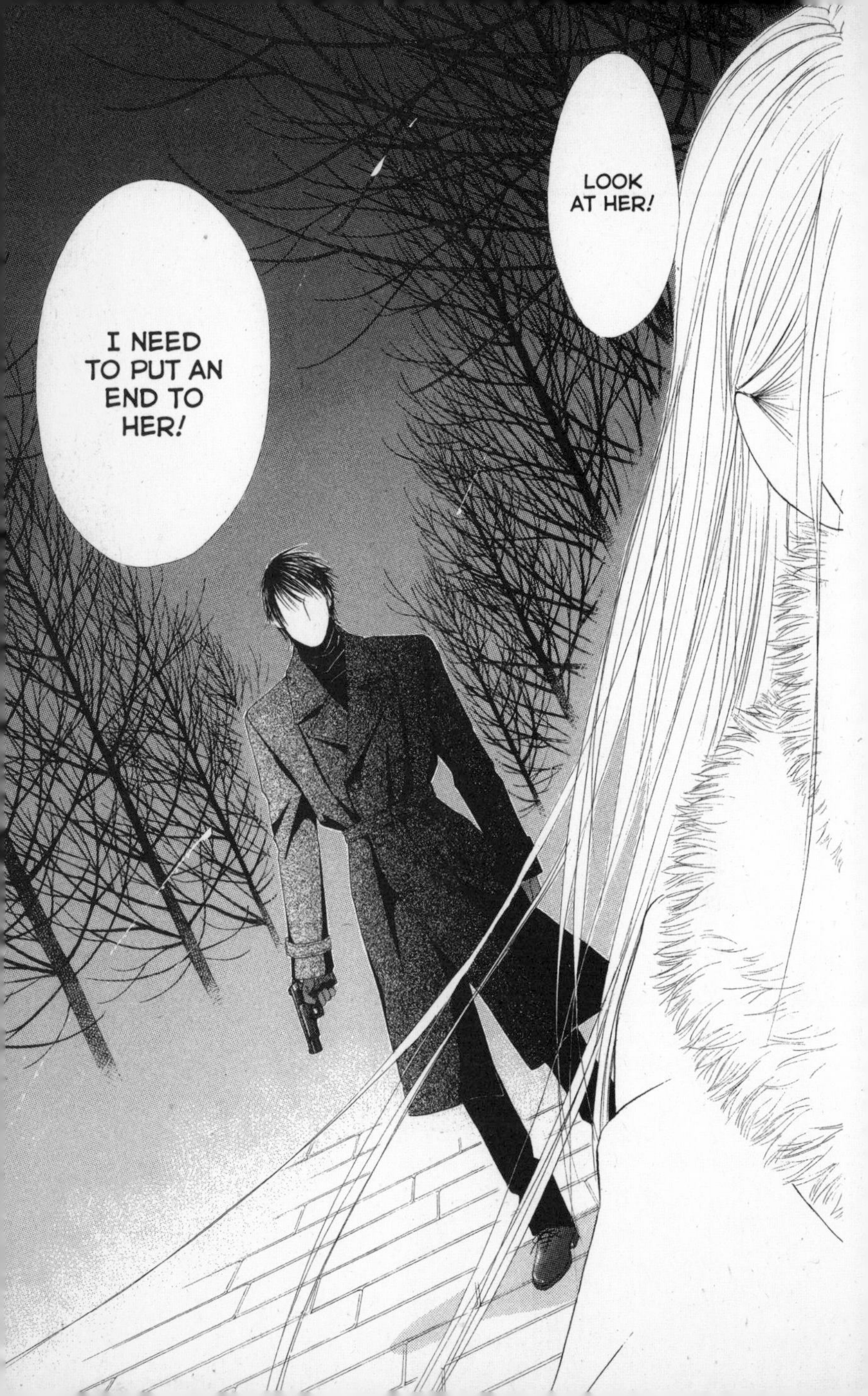
LOOK AT HER!
I NEED TO PUT AN END TO HER!

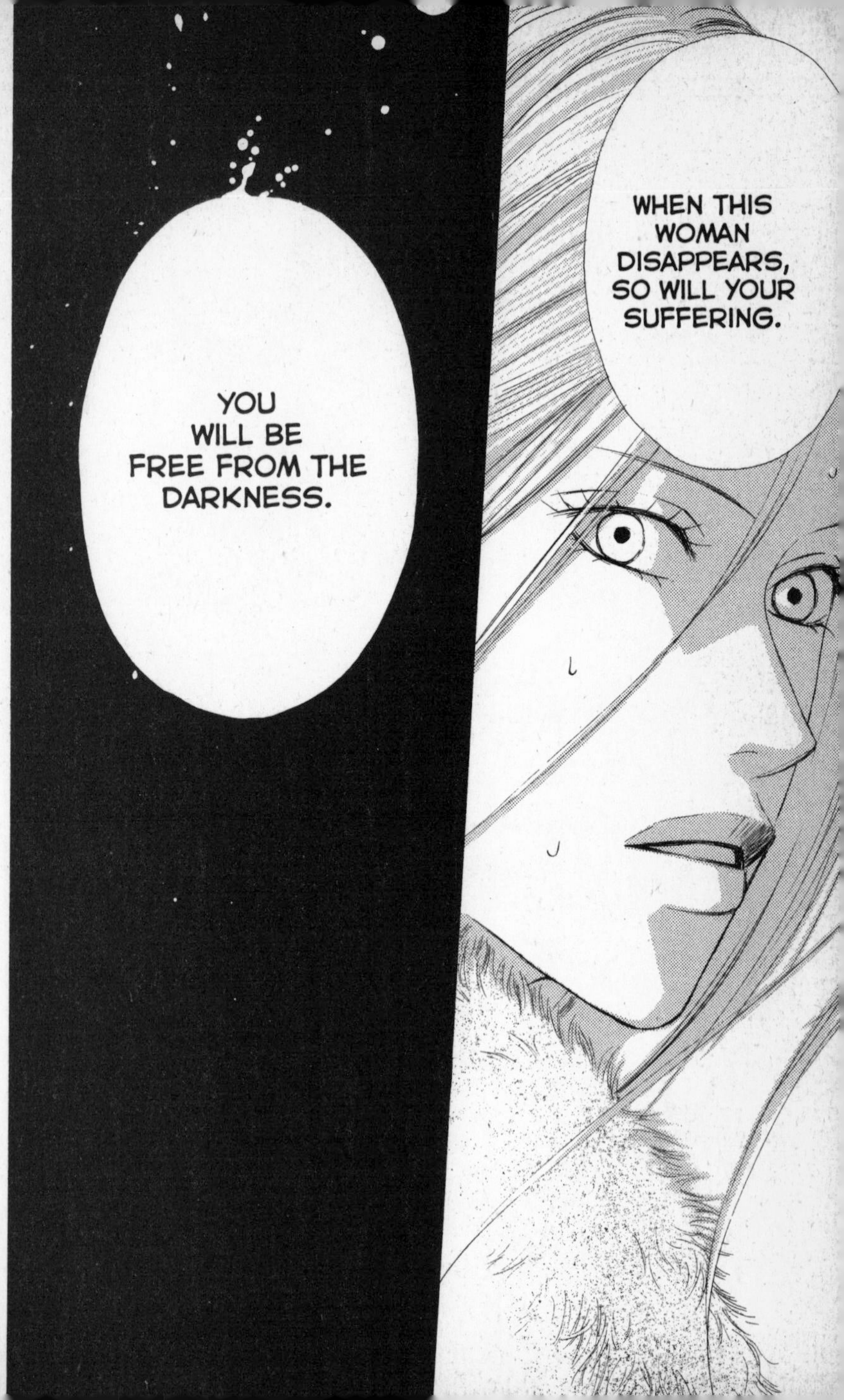
WHEN THIS WOMAN DISAPPEARS, SO WILL YOUR SUFFERING.
YOU WILL BE FREE FROM THE DARKNESS.

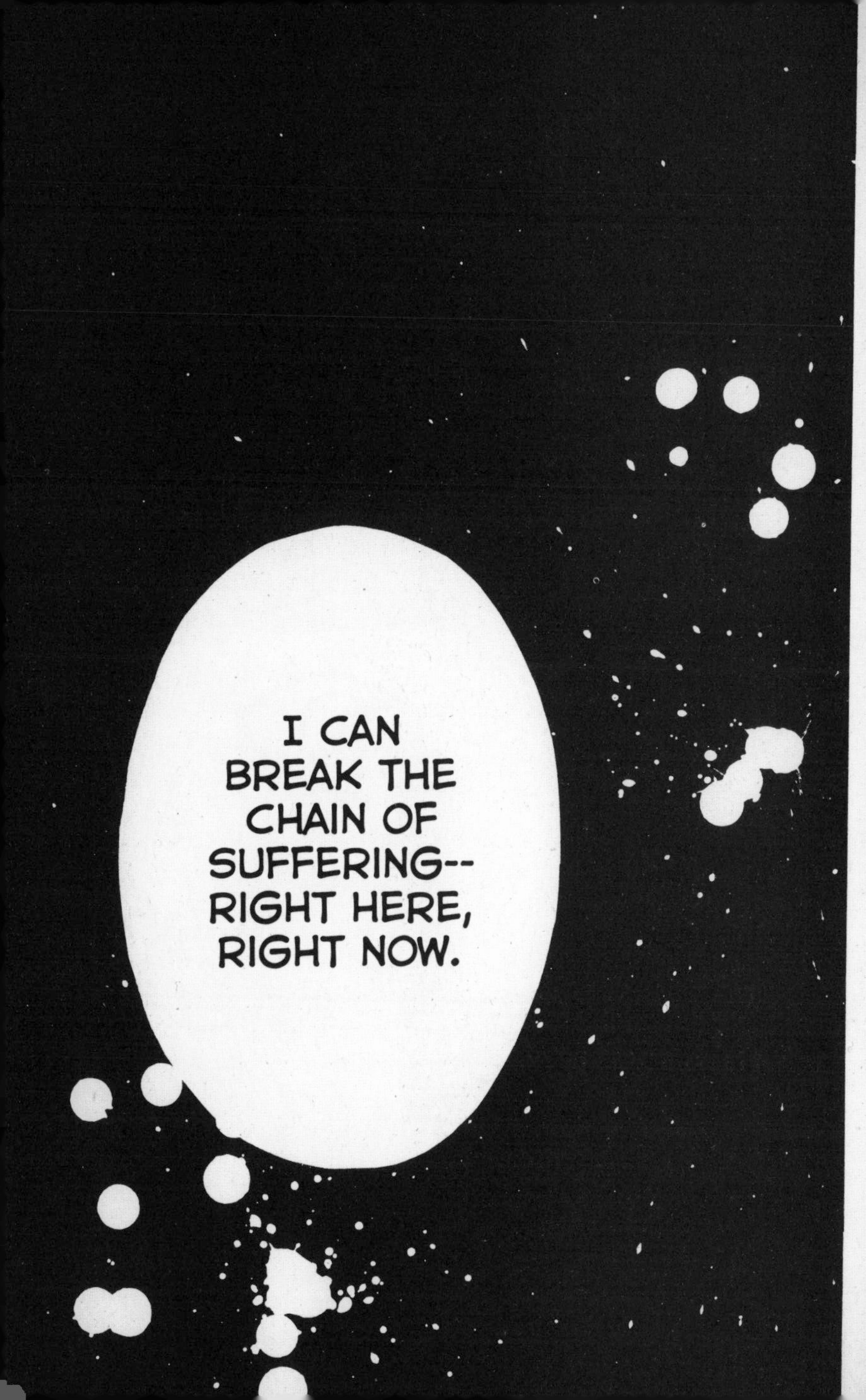
I CAN BREAK THE CHAIN OF SUFFERING-- RIGHT HERE, RIGHT NOW.

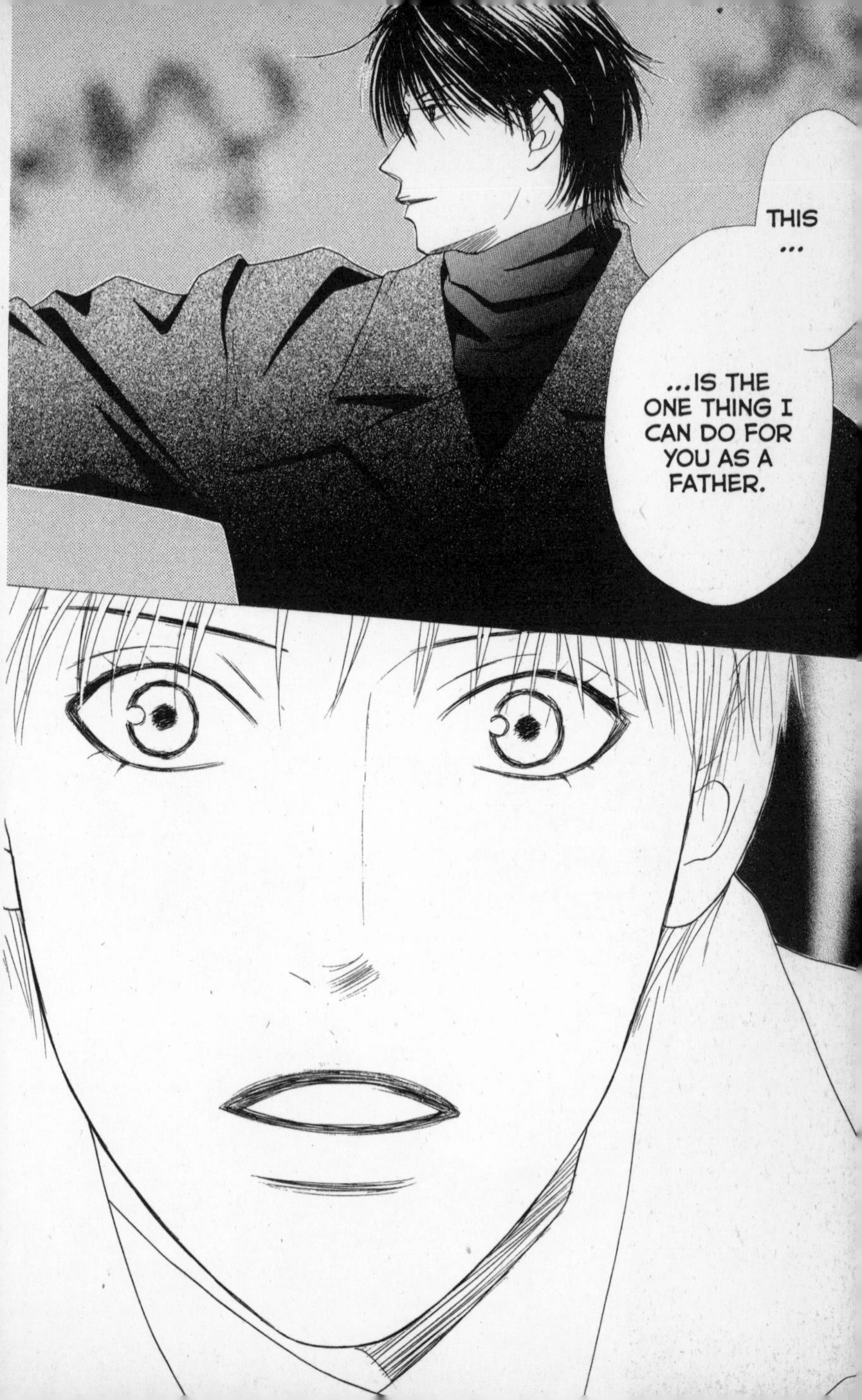
THIS ...
...IS THE ONE THING I CAN DO FOR YOU AS A FATHER.

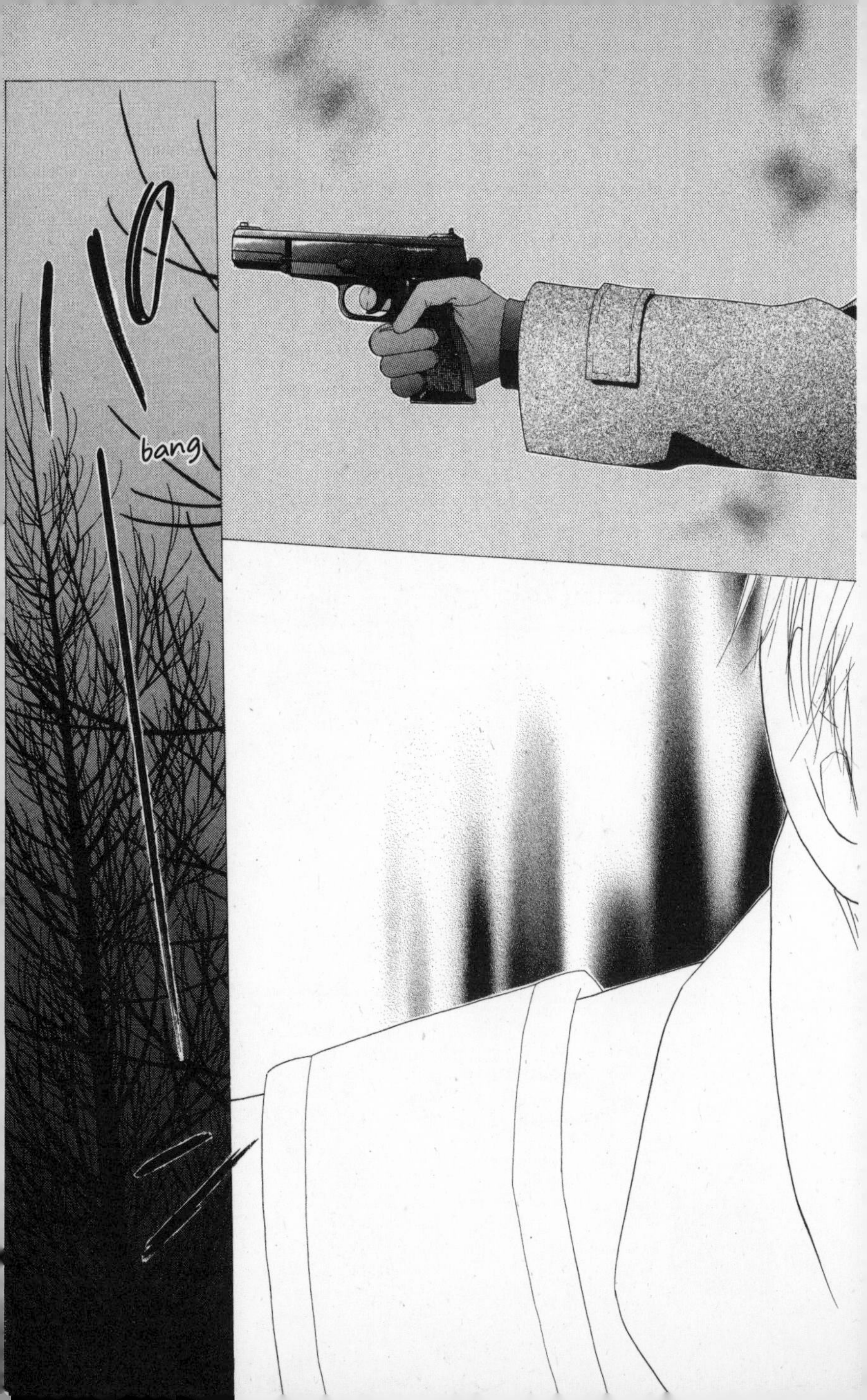
bang

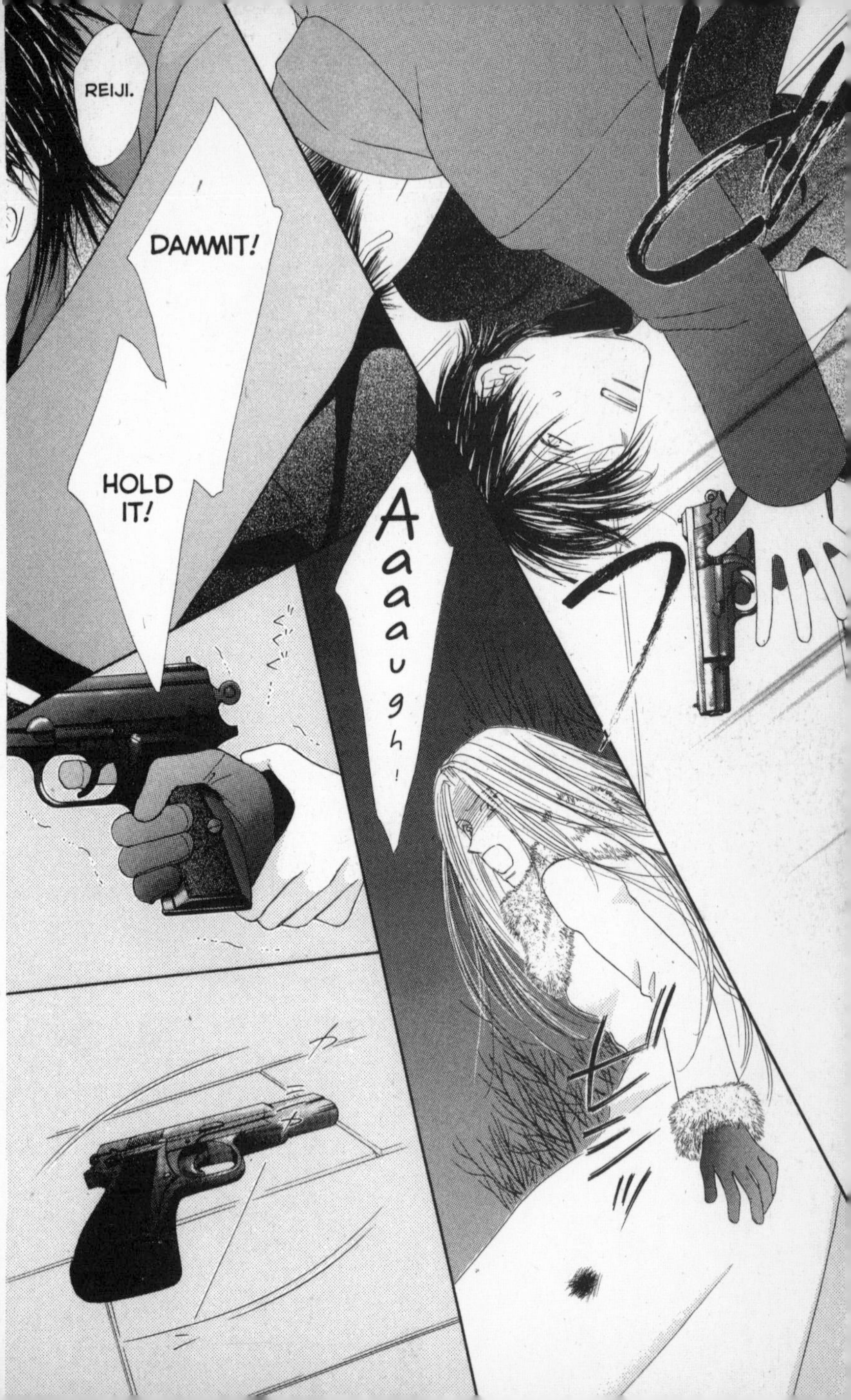
Aaaaugh!
REIJI.
DAMMIT!
HOLD IT!

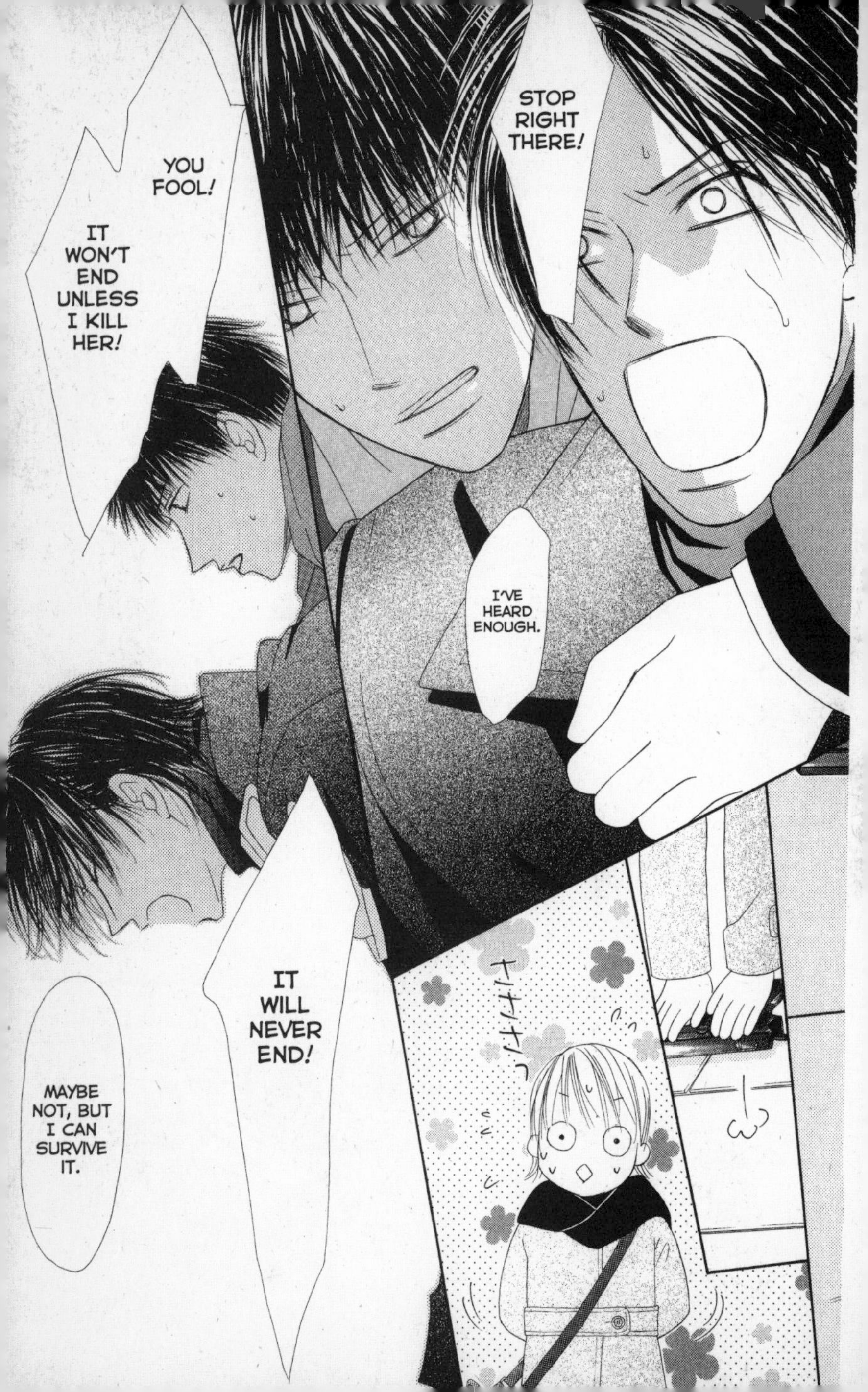
STOP RIGHT THERE!
YOU FOOL!
IT WON'T END UNLESS I KILL HER!
I'VE HEARD ENOUGH.
IT WILL NEVER END!
MAYBE NOT, BUT I CAN SURVIVE IT.

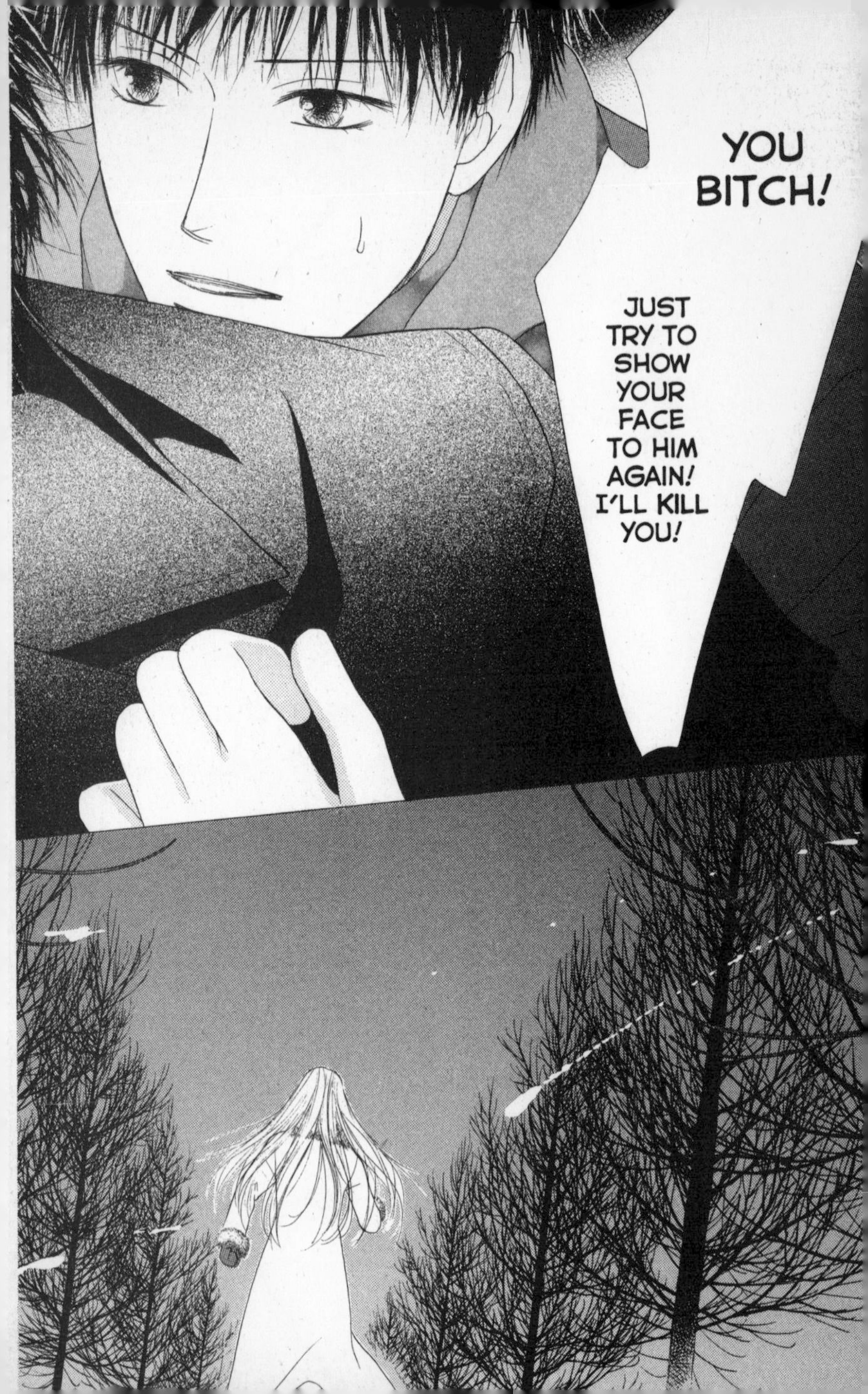
YOU BITCH!
JUST TRY TO SHOW YOUR FACE TO HIM AGAIN! I'LL KILL YOU!

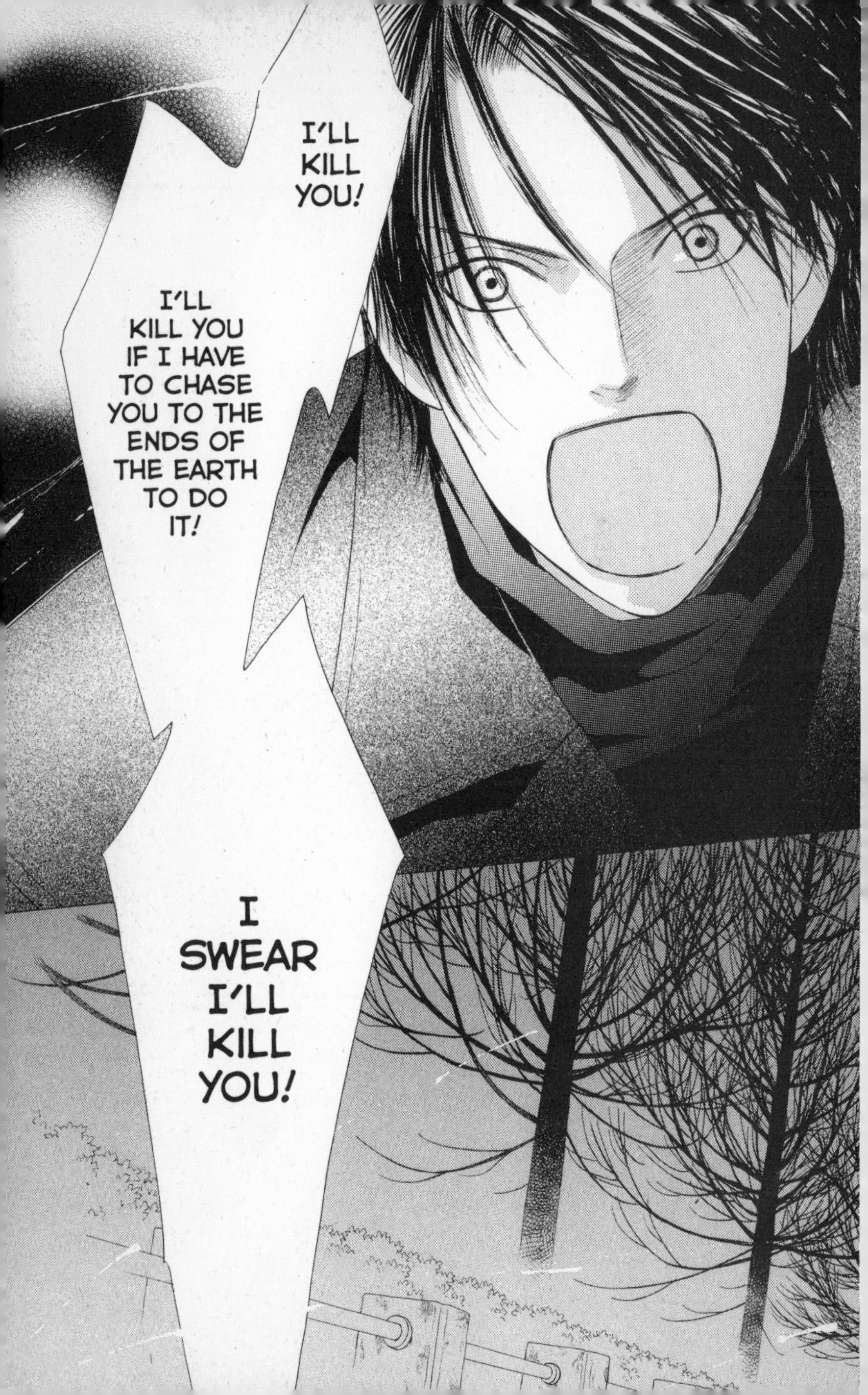
I'LL KILL YOU!
I'LL KILL YOU IF I HAVE TO CHASE YOU TO THE ENDS OF THE EARTH TO DO IT!
I SWEAR I'LL KILL YOU!

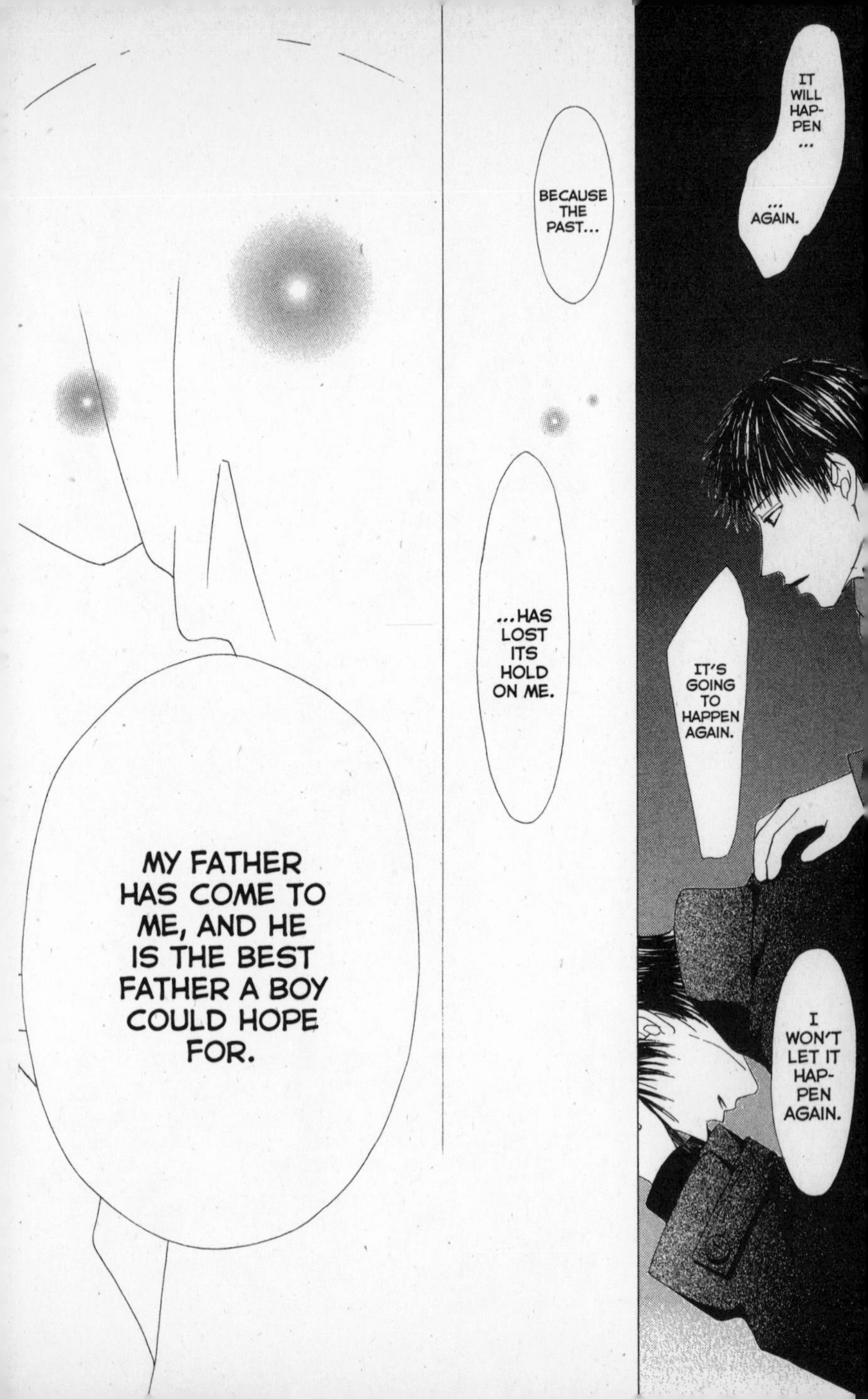
IT WILL HAP-PEN... ...AGAIN.
IT'S GOING TO HAPPEN AGAIN.
I WON'T LET IT HAP-PEN AGAIN.
BECAUSE THE PAST...
...HAS LOST ITS HOLD ON ME.
MY FATHER HAS COME TO ME, AND HE IS THE BEST FATHER A BOY COULD HOPE FOR.

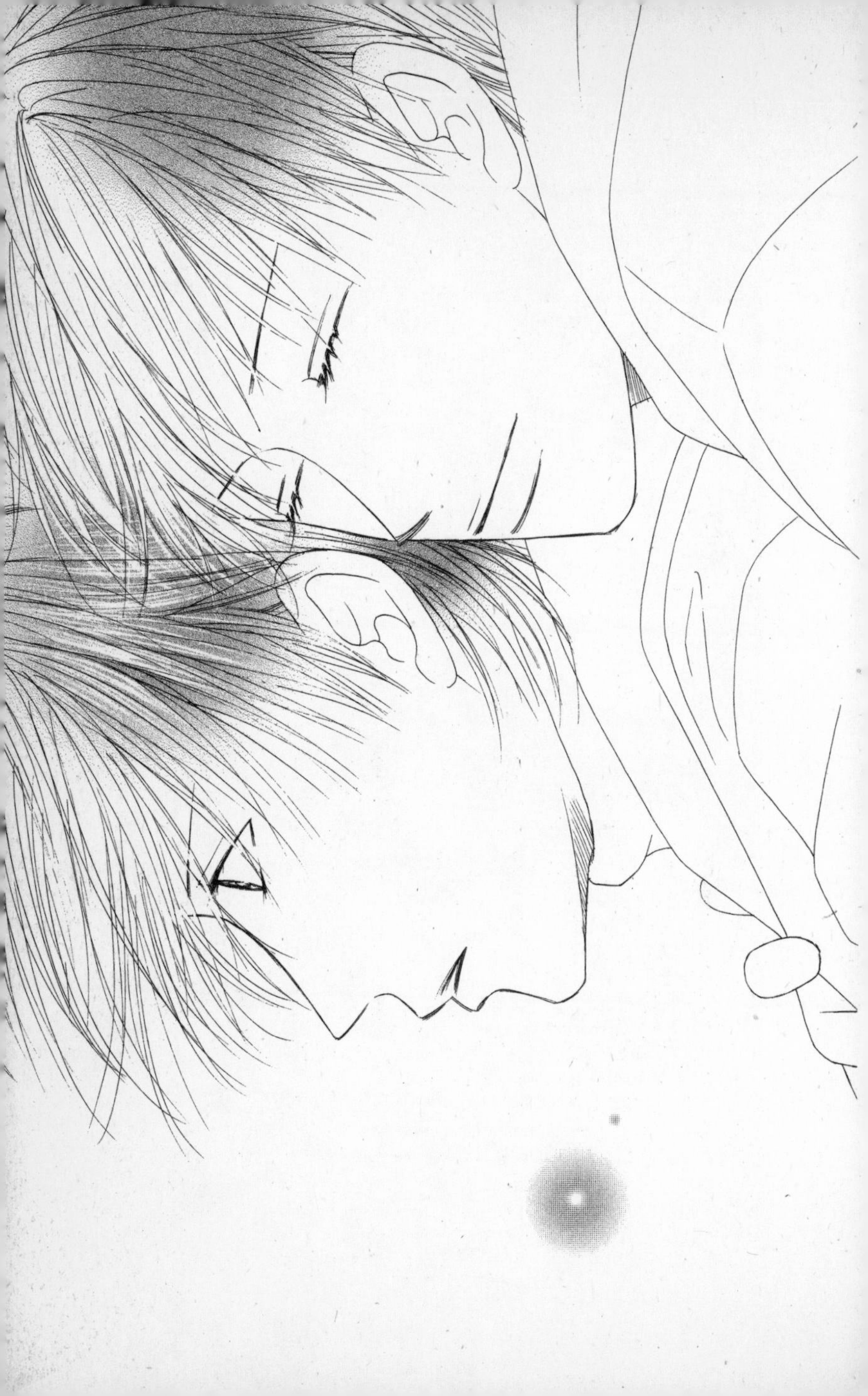

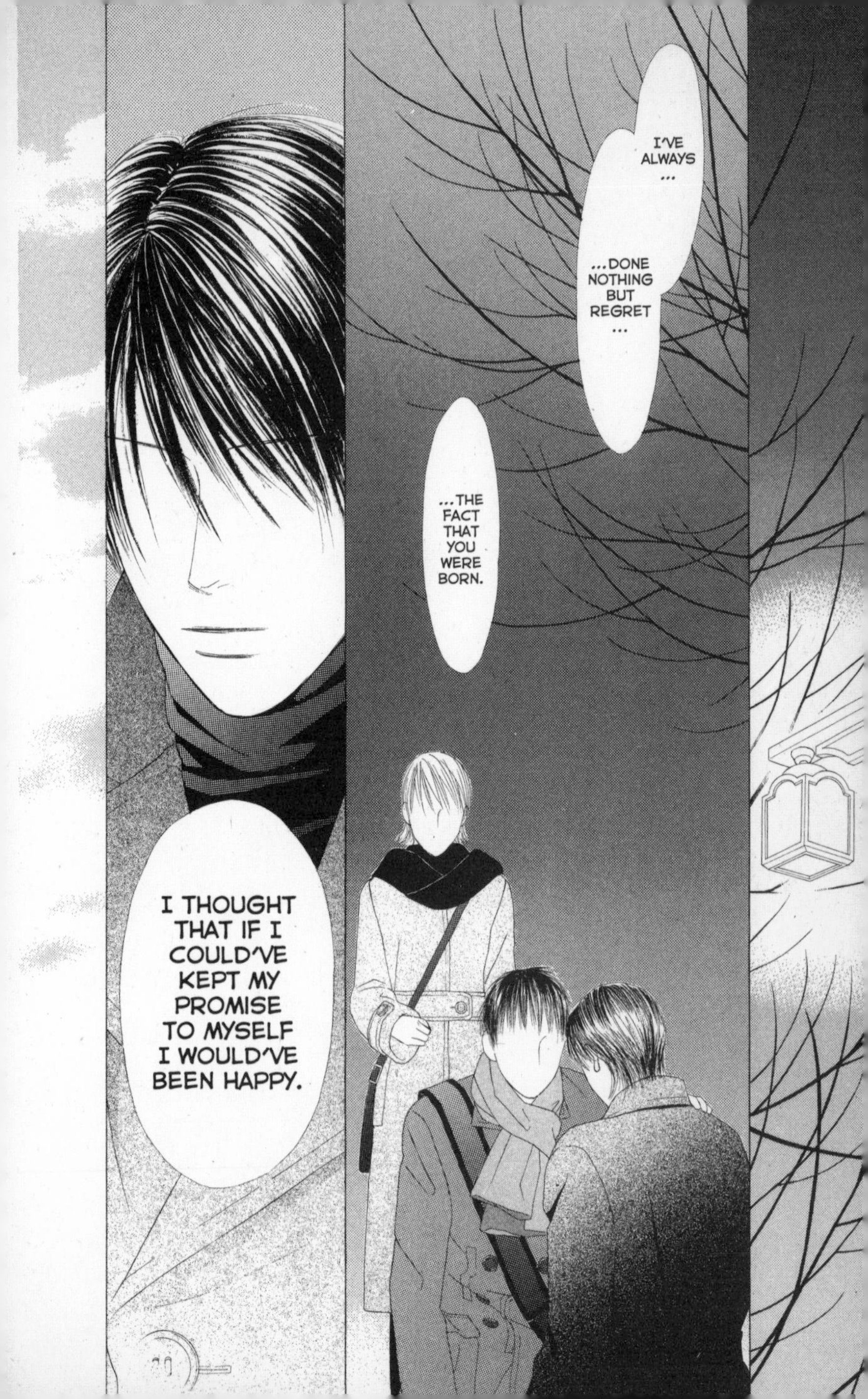
I'VE ALWAYS ...
...DONE NOTHING BUT REGRET ...
...THE FACT THAT YOU WERE BORN.
I THOUGHT THAT IF I COULD'VE KEPT MY PROMISE TO MYSELF I WOULD'VE BEEN HAPPY.

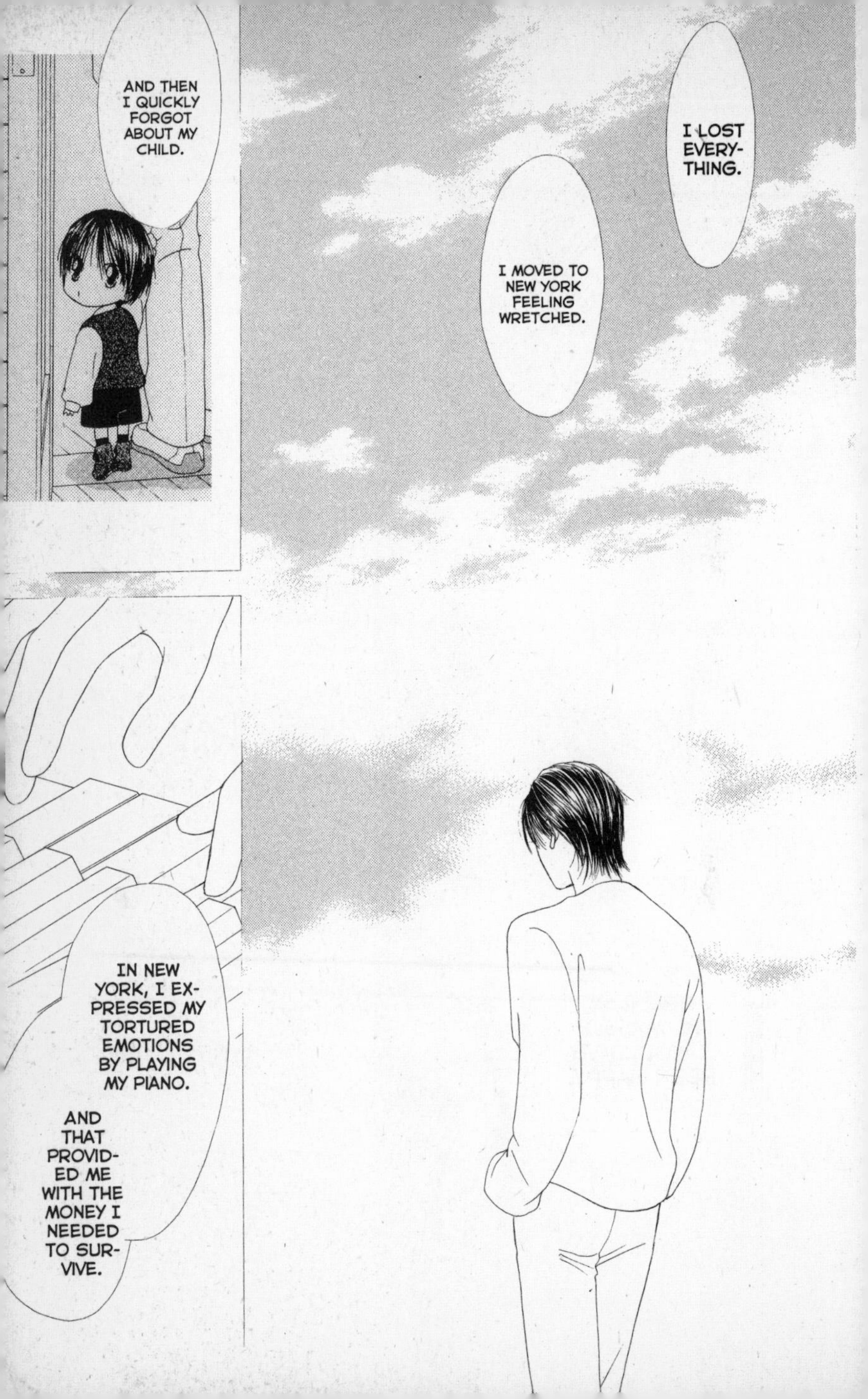
I LOST EVERY-THING.
I MOVED TO NEW YORK FEELING WRETCHED.
AND THEN I QUICKLY FORGOT ABOUT MY CHILD.
IN NEW YORK, I EX-PRESSED MY TORTURED EMOTIONS BY PLAYING MY PIANO.
AND THAT PROVID-ED ME WITH THE MONEY I NEEDED TO SUR-VIVE.

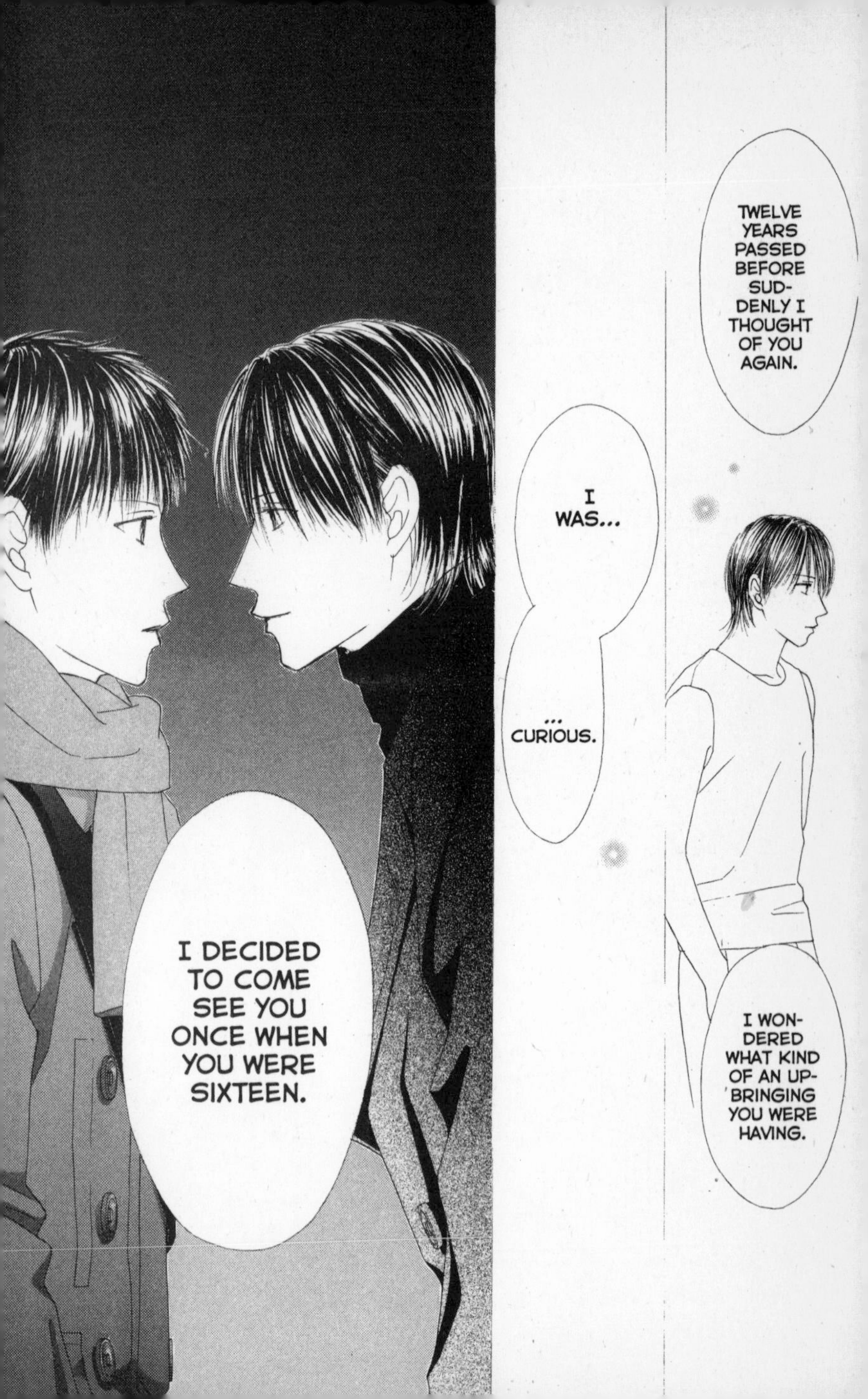
TWELVE YEARS PASSED BEFORE SUD-DENLY I THOUGHT OF YOU AGAIN.
I WAS...
...CURIOUS.
I WON-DERED WHAT KIND OF AN UP-BRINGING YOU WERE HAVING.
I DECIDED TO COME SEE YOU ONCE WHEN YOU WERE SIXTEEN.

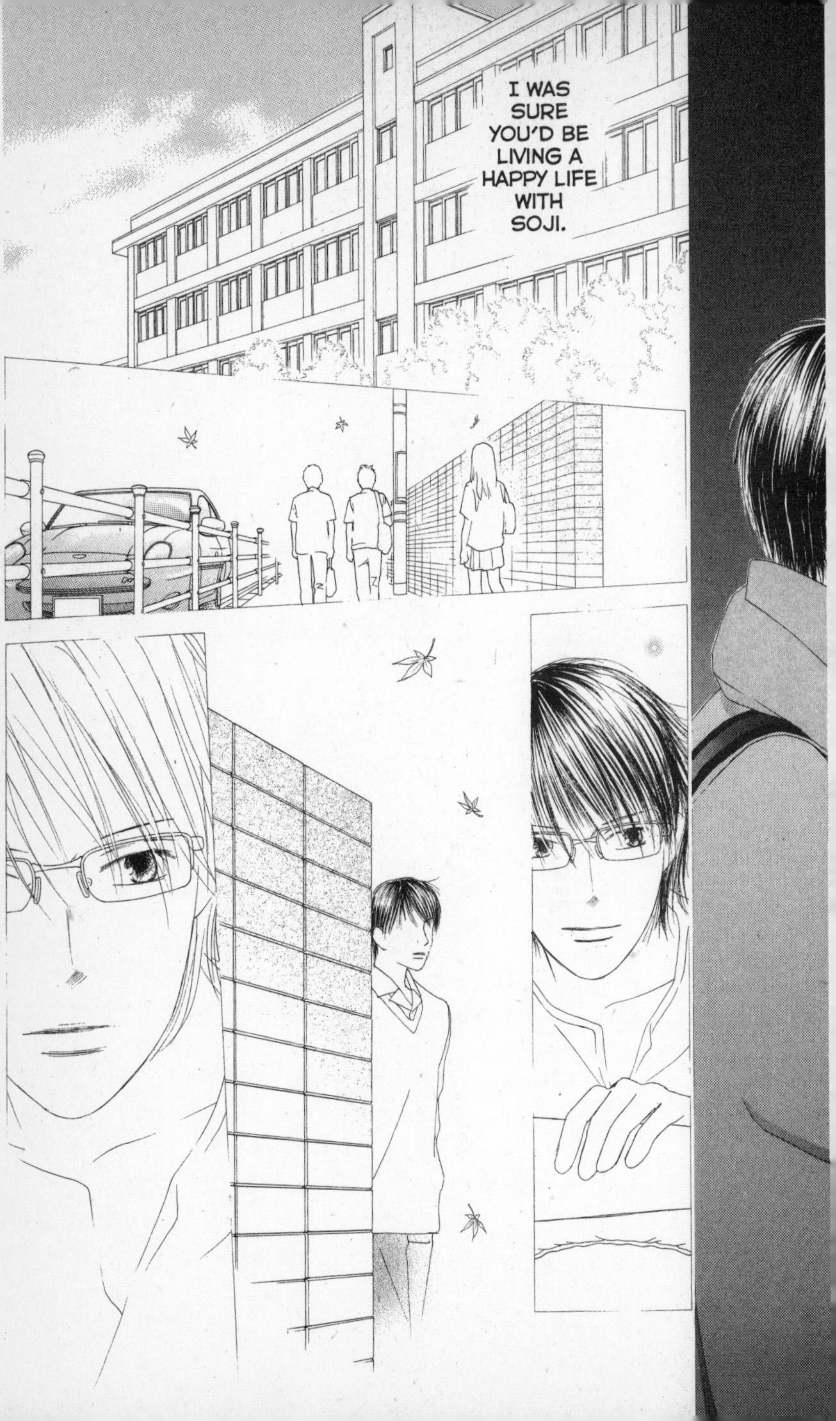
I WAS SURE YOU'D BE LIVING A HAPPY LIFE WITH SOJI.

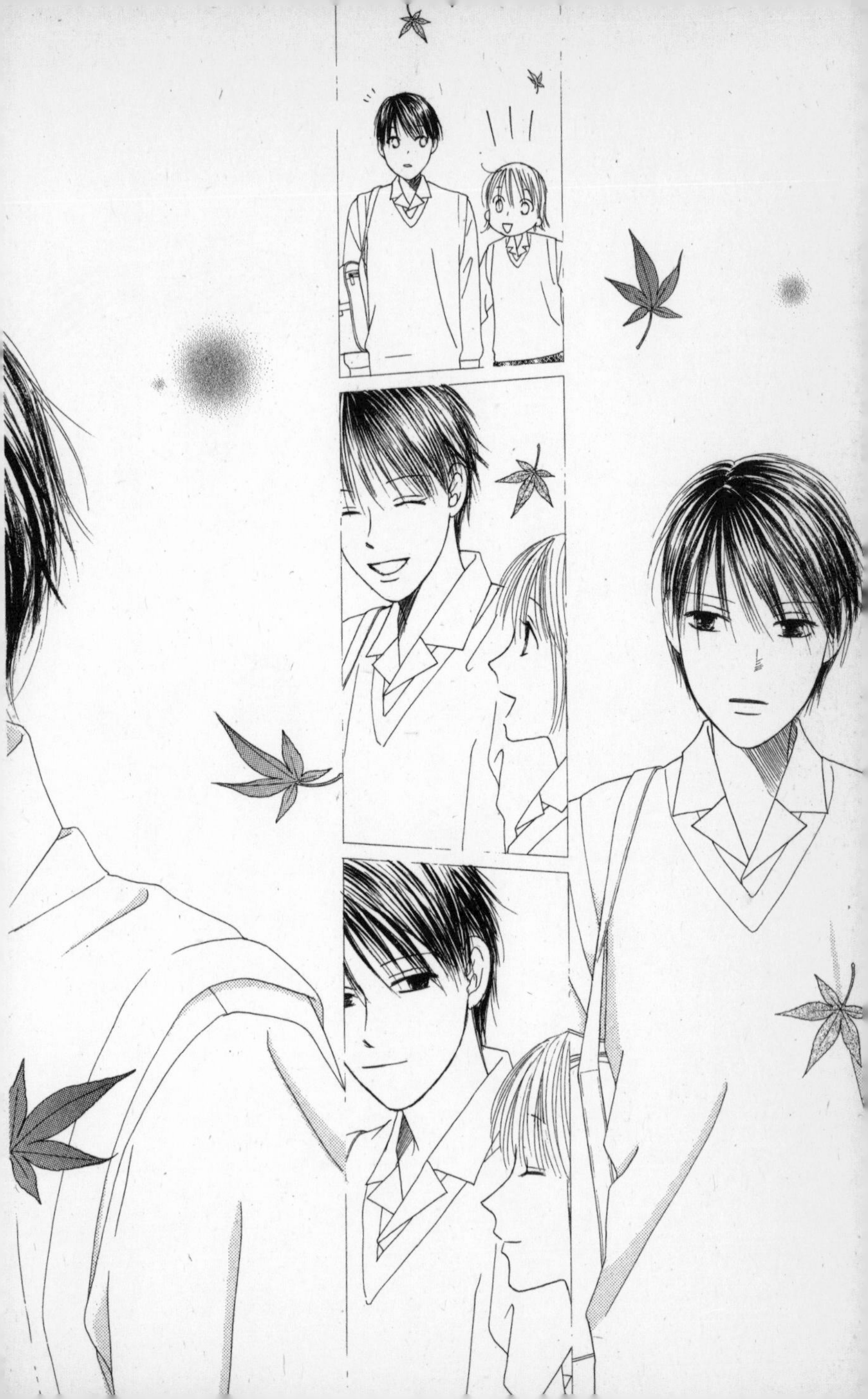

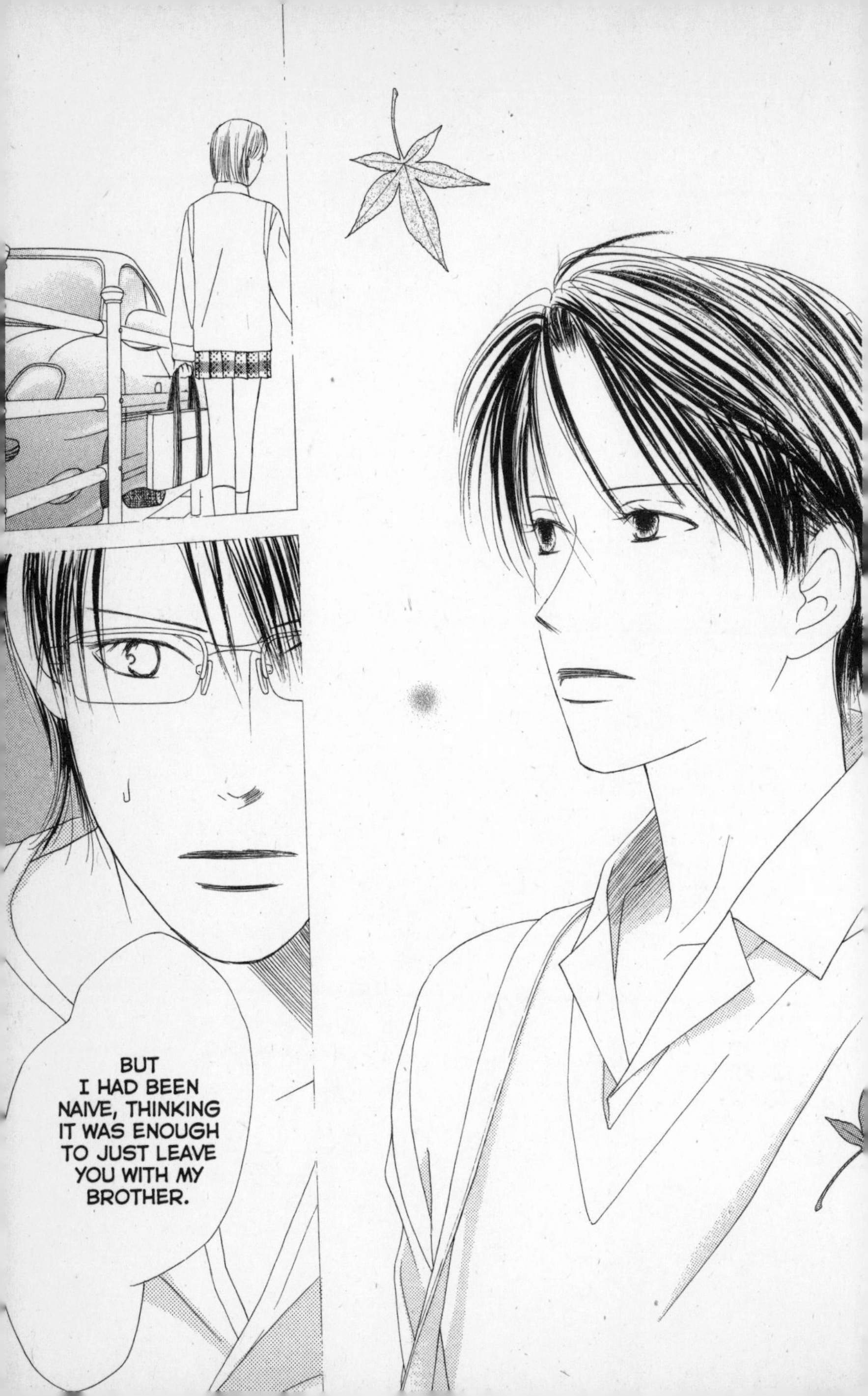
BUT I HAD BEEN NAIVE, THINKING IT WAS ENOUGH TO JUST LEAVE YOU WITH MY BROTHER.

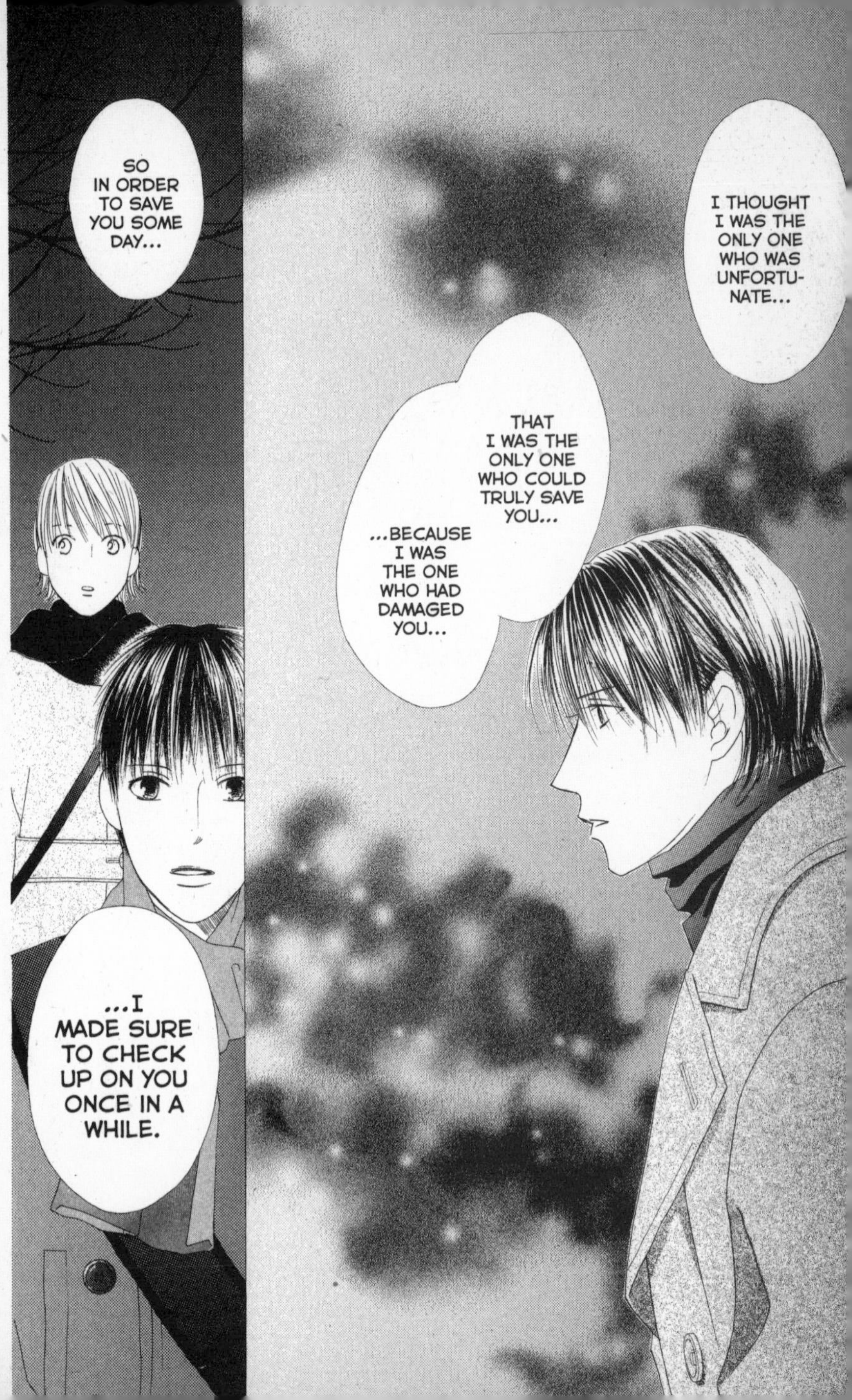
I THOUGHT I WAS THE ONLY ONE WHO WAS UNFORTU- NATE...
THAT I WAS THE ONLY ONE WHO COULD TRULY SAVE YOU...
...BECAUSE I WAS THE ONE WHO HAD DAMAGED YOU...
SO IN ORDER TO SAVE YOU SOME DAY...
...I MADE SURE TO CHECK UP ON YOU ONCE IN A WHILE.

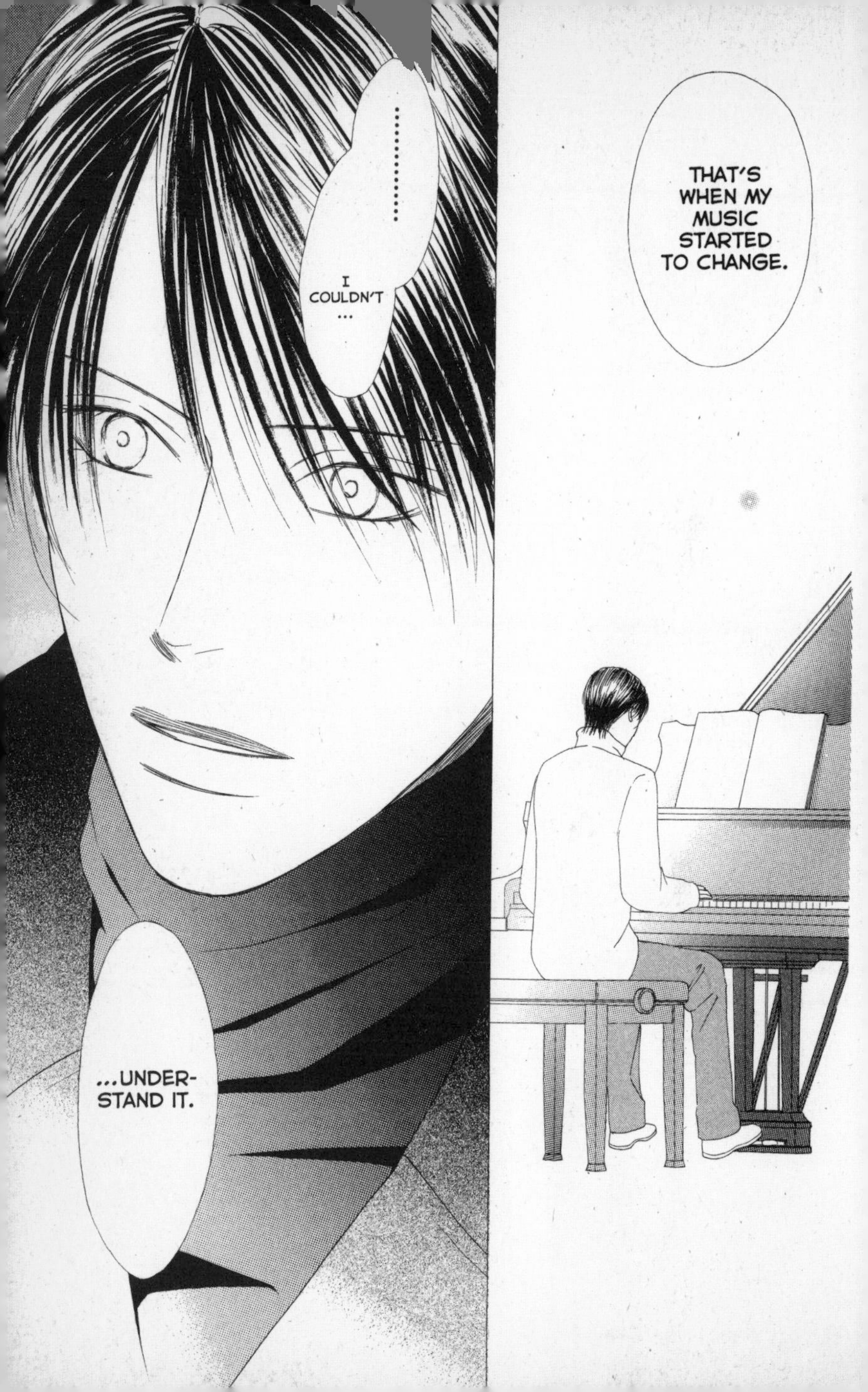
THAT'S WHEN MY MUSIC STARTED TO CHANGE.
....
I COULDN'T ...
...UNDER-STAND IT.

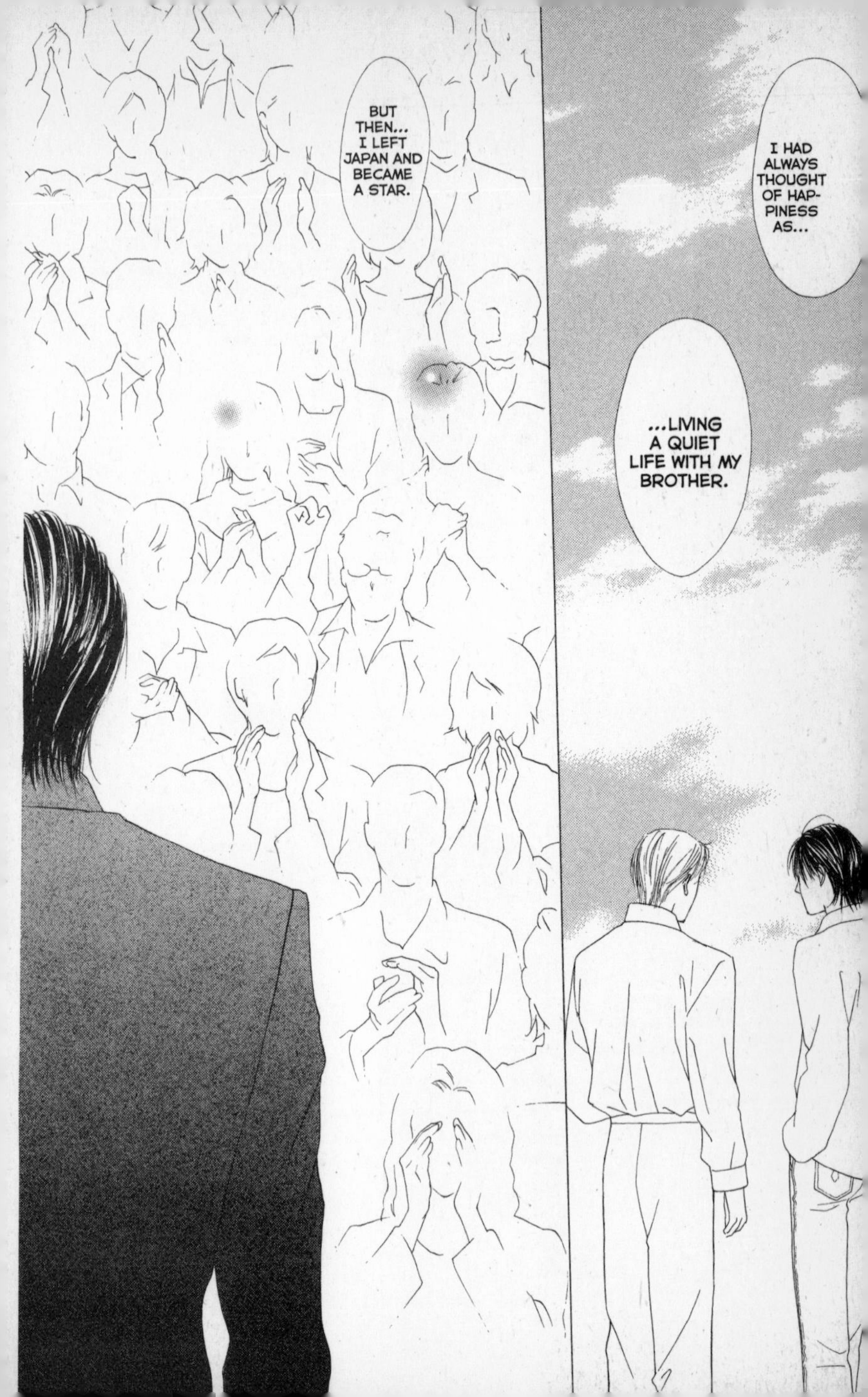
I HAD ALWAYS THOUGHT OF HAP-PINESS AS...
...LIVING A QUIET LIFE WITH MY BROTHER.
BUT THEN... I LEFT JAPAN AND BECAME A STAR.

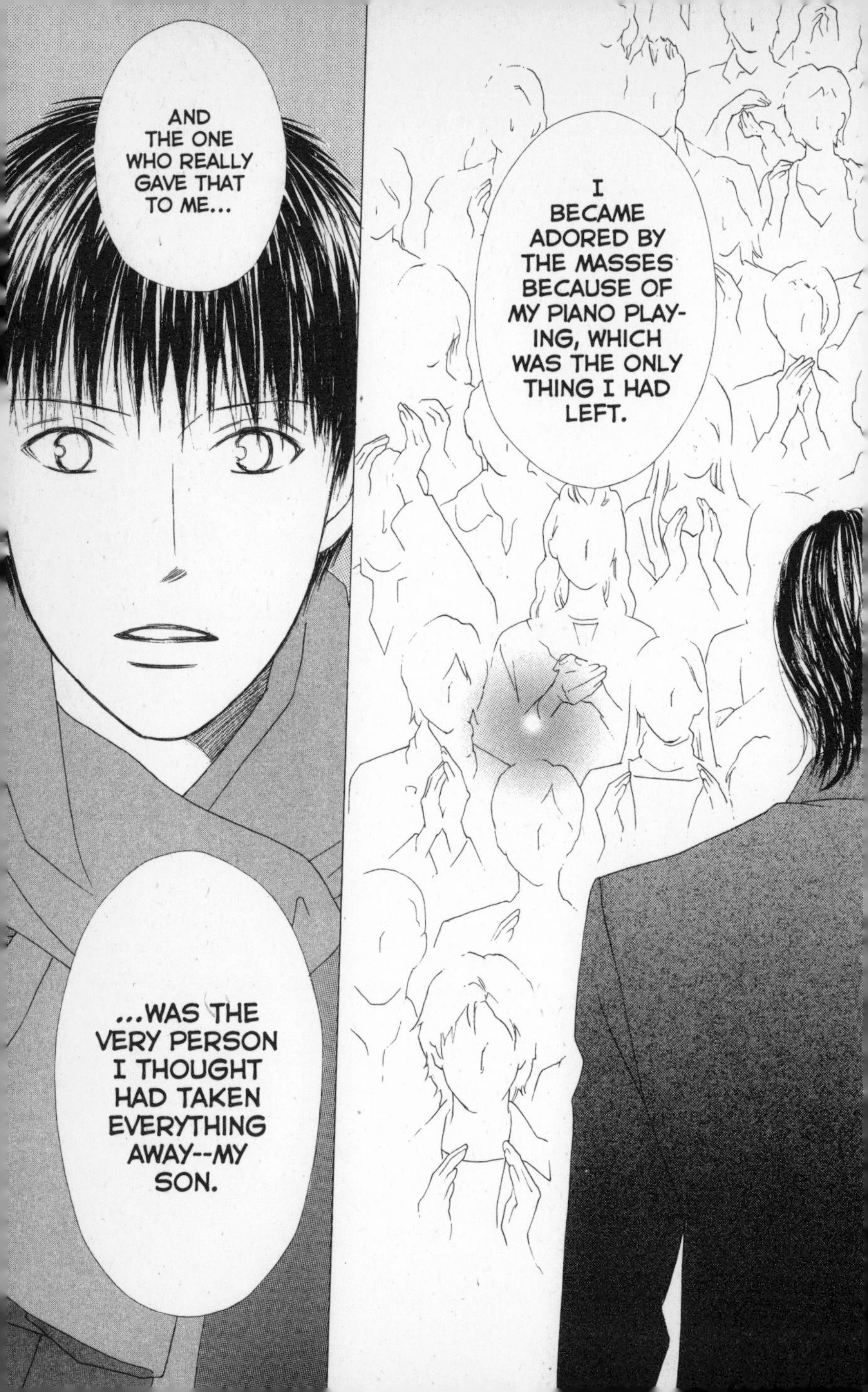
I BECAME ADORED BY THE MASSES BECAUSE OF MY PIANO PLAY-ING, WHICH WAS THE ONLY THING I HAD LEFT.
AND THE ONE WHO REALLY GAVE THAT TO ME...
...WAS THE VERY PERSON I THOUGHT HAD TAKEN EVERYTHING AWAY--MY SON.

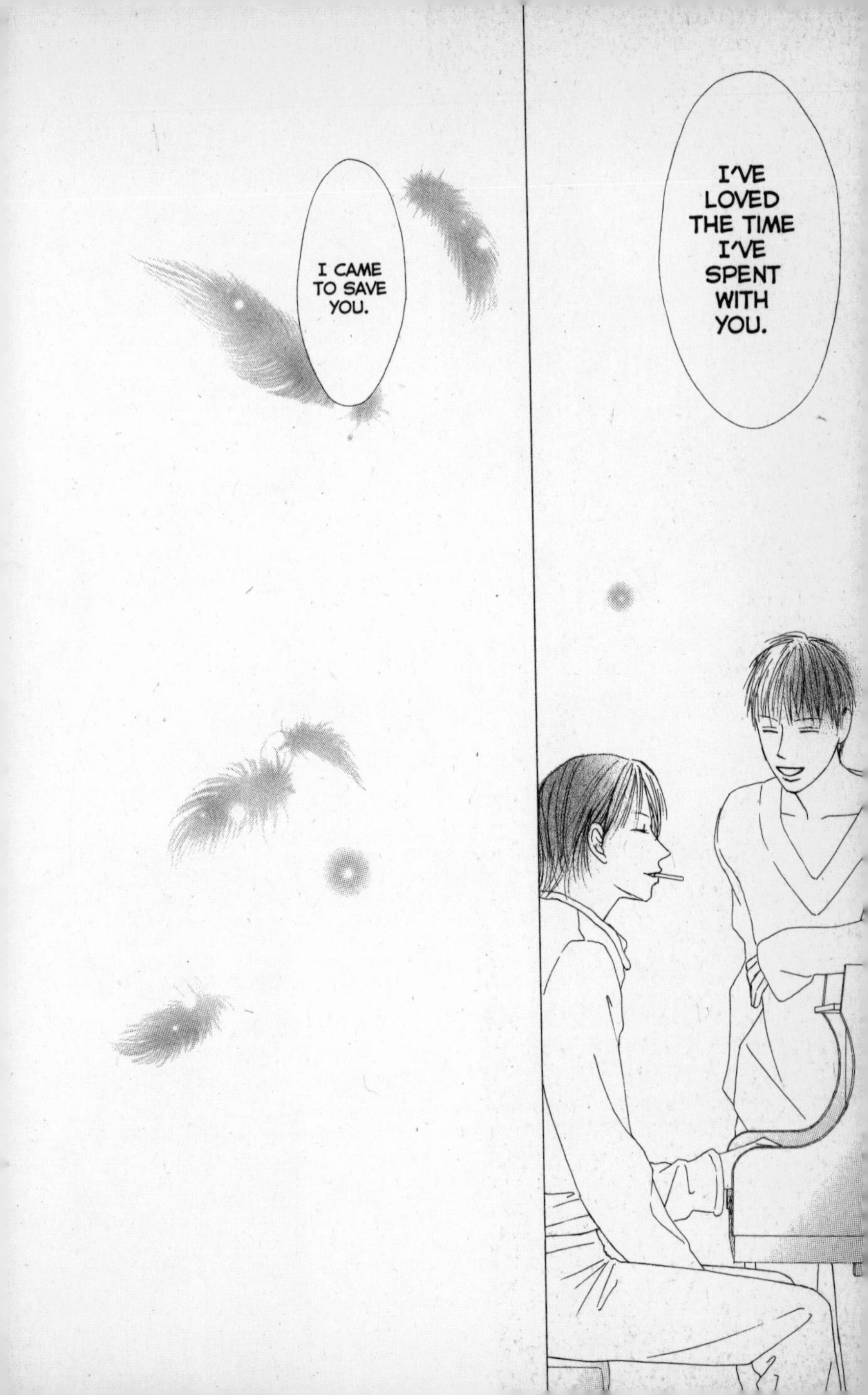
I'VE LOVED THE TIME I'VE SPENT WITH YOU.
I CAME TO SAVE YOU.

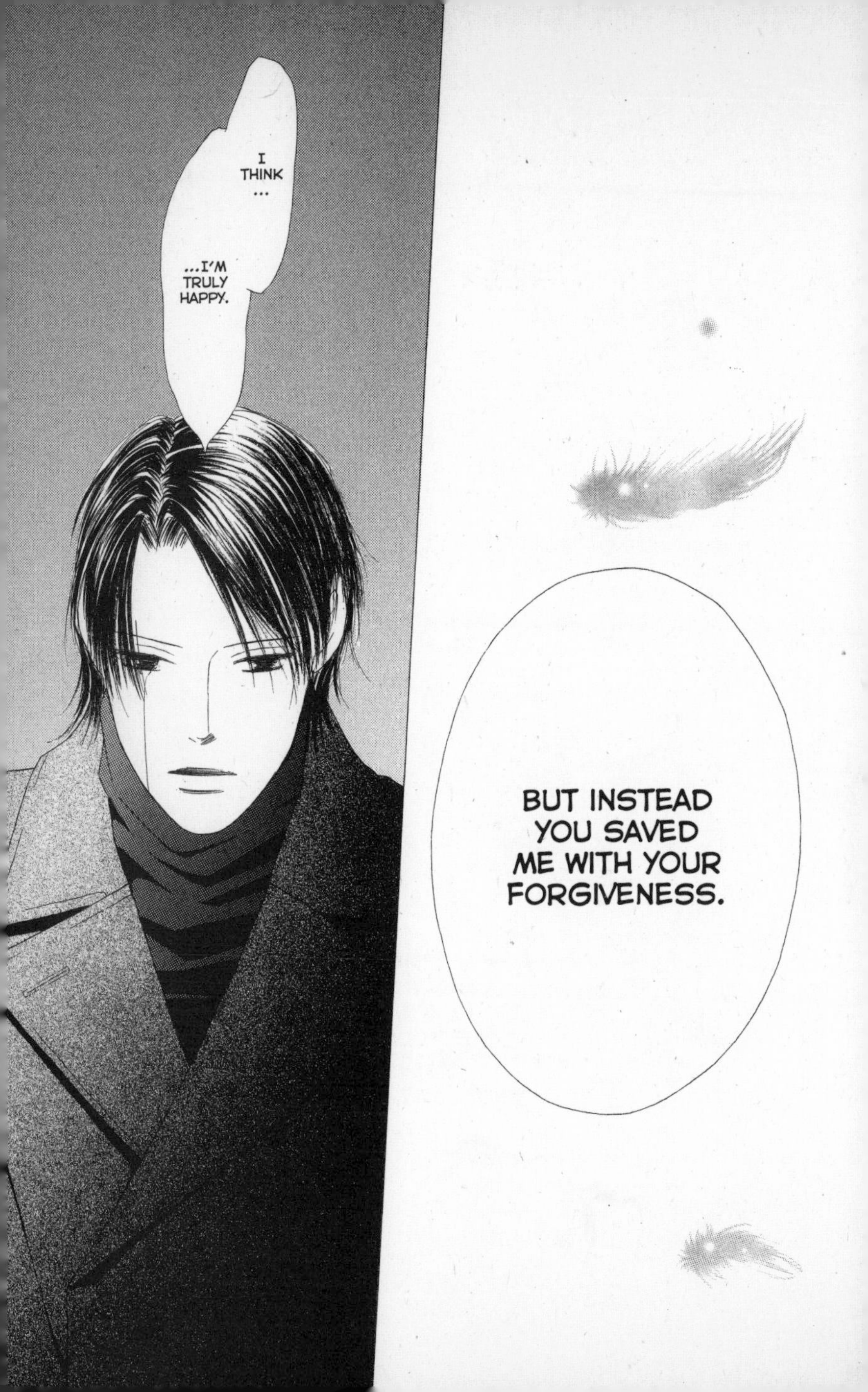
BUT INSTEAD YOU SAVED ME WITH YOUR FORGIVENESS.
I THINK ...
...I'M TRULY HAPPY.

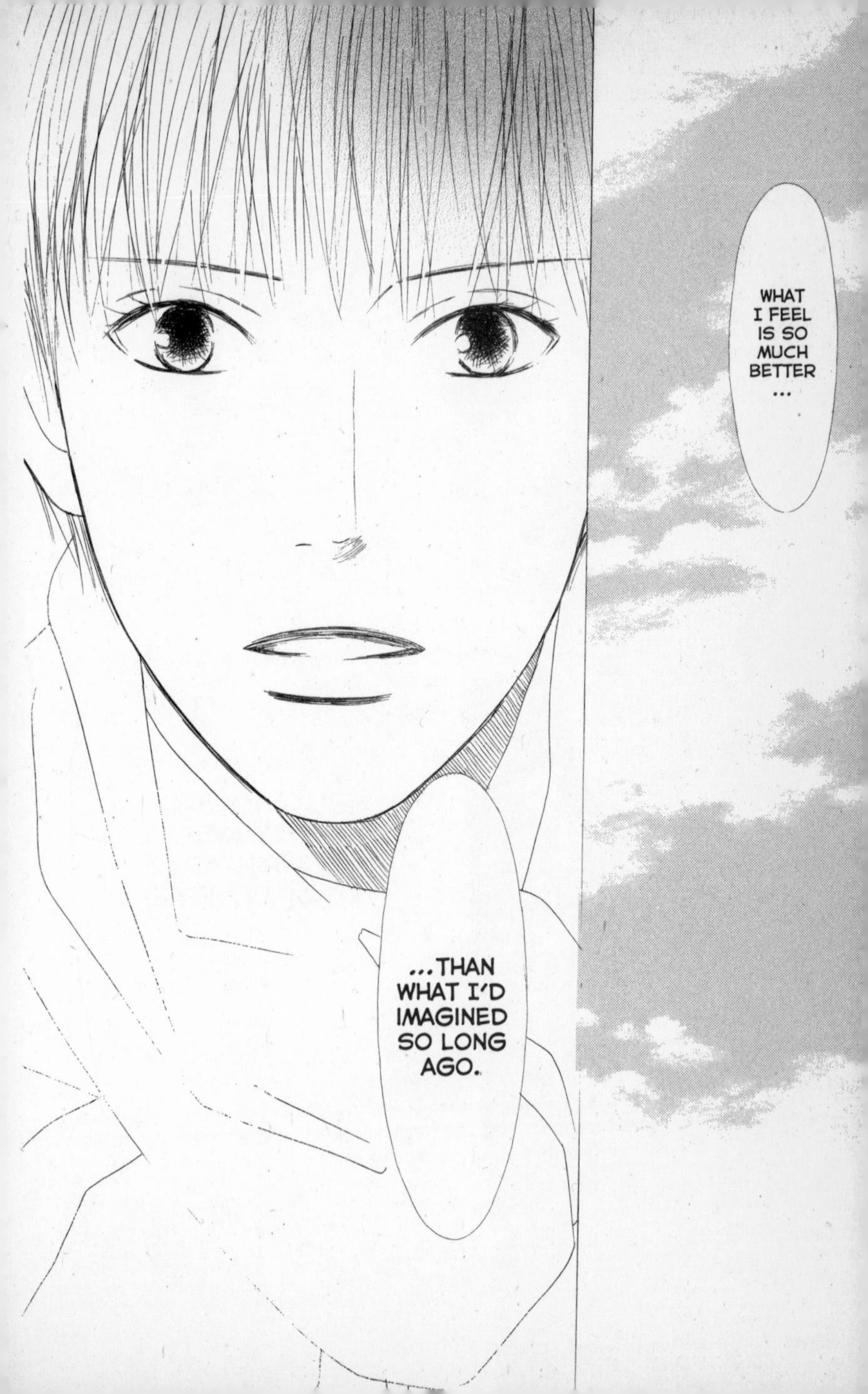
WHAT I FEEL IS SO MUCH BETTER ...
...THAN WHAT I'D IMAGINED SO LONG AGO.

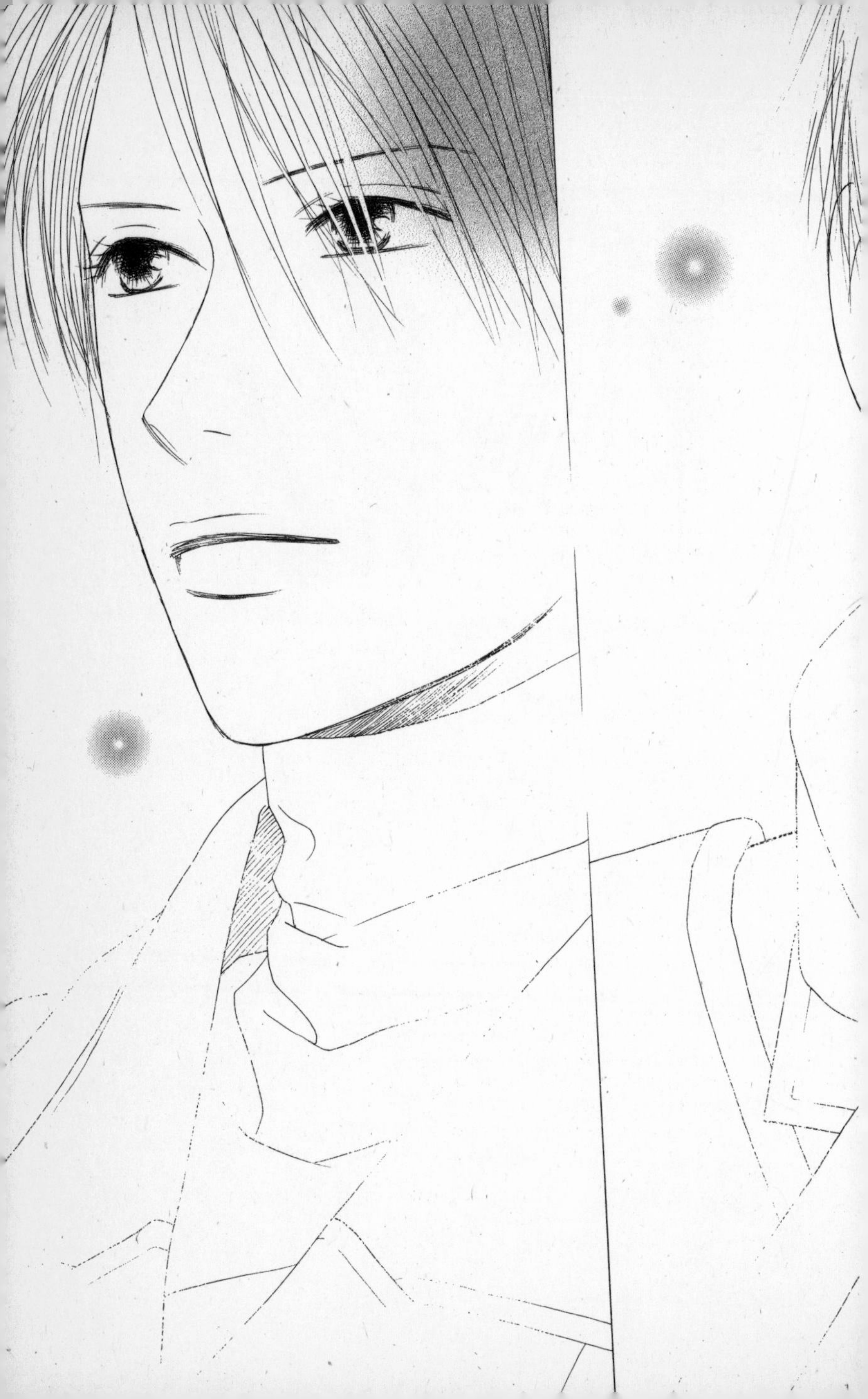

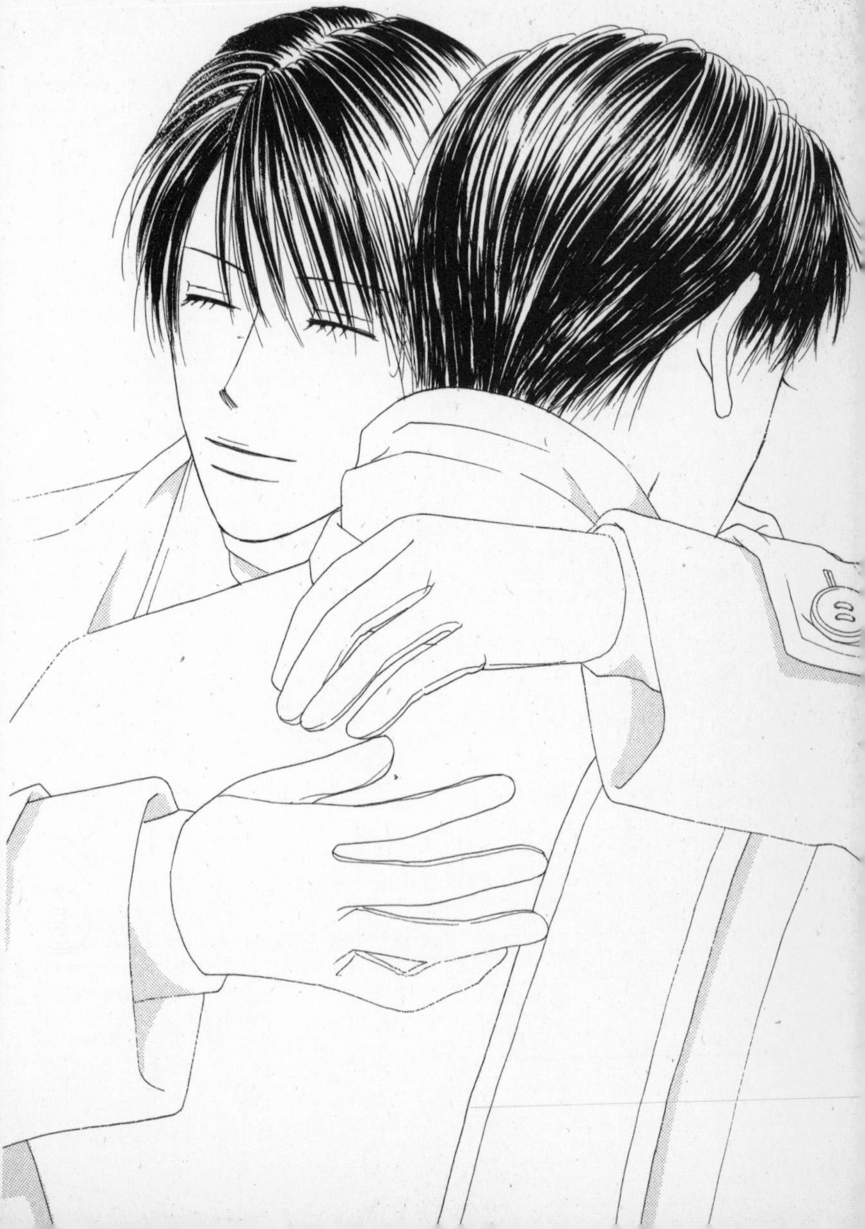

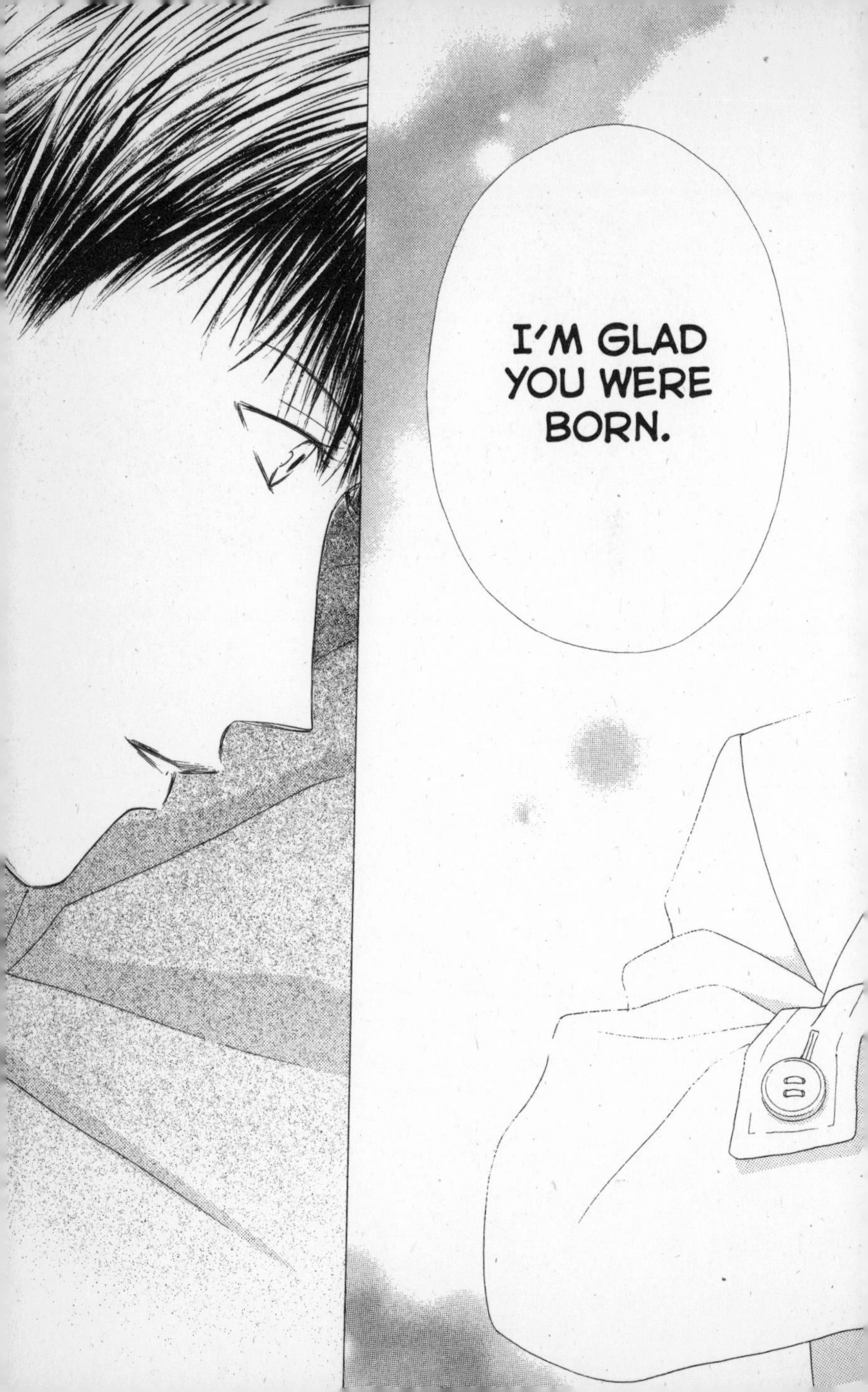
I'M GLAD YOU WERE BORN.

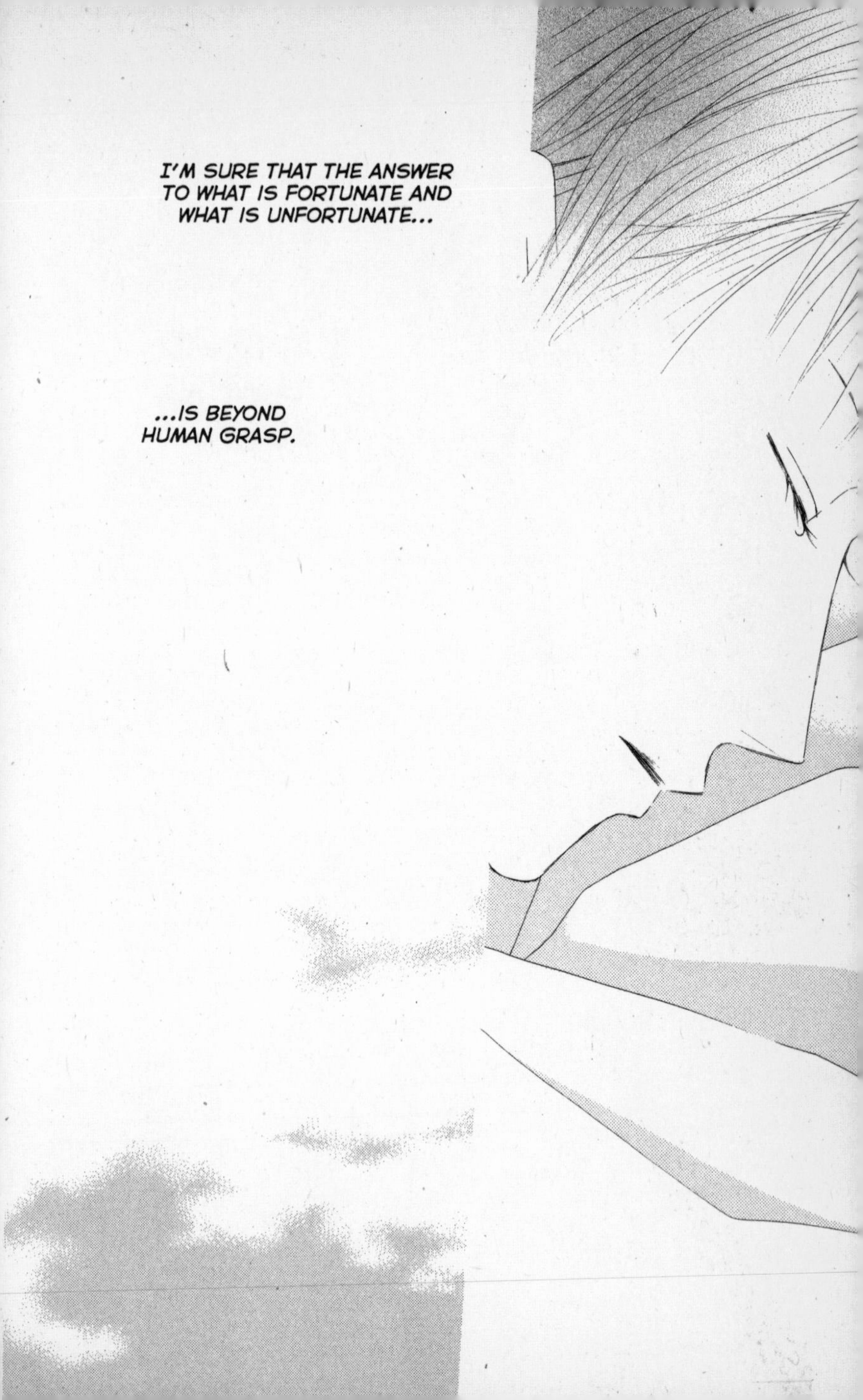
I'M SURE THAT THE ANSWER TO WHAT IS FORTUNATE AND WHAT IS UNFORTUNATE...
...IS BEYOND HUMAN GRASP.

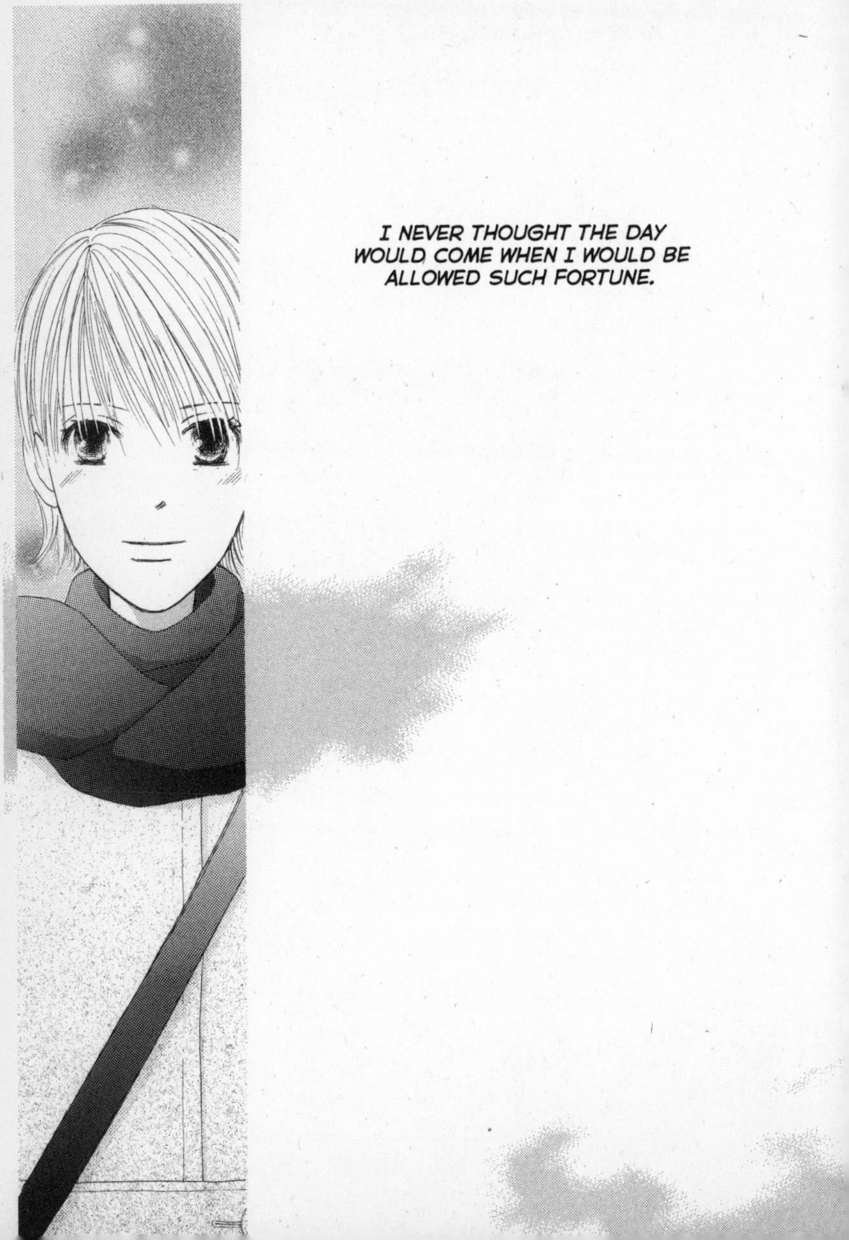
I NEVER THOUGHT THE DAY WOULD COME WHEN I WOULD BE ALLOWED SUCH FORTUNE.

ON THAT DAY, WE WERE SET
FREE FROM OUR LONG SUFFERING.

THERE'S NO REASON TO FEAR THE DARKNESS ANYMORE.

BECAUSE OUR HEARTS HAVE BEEN FILLED.

ACT 94 ★ SALVATION / END

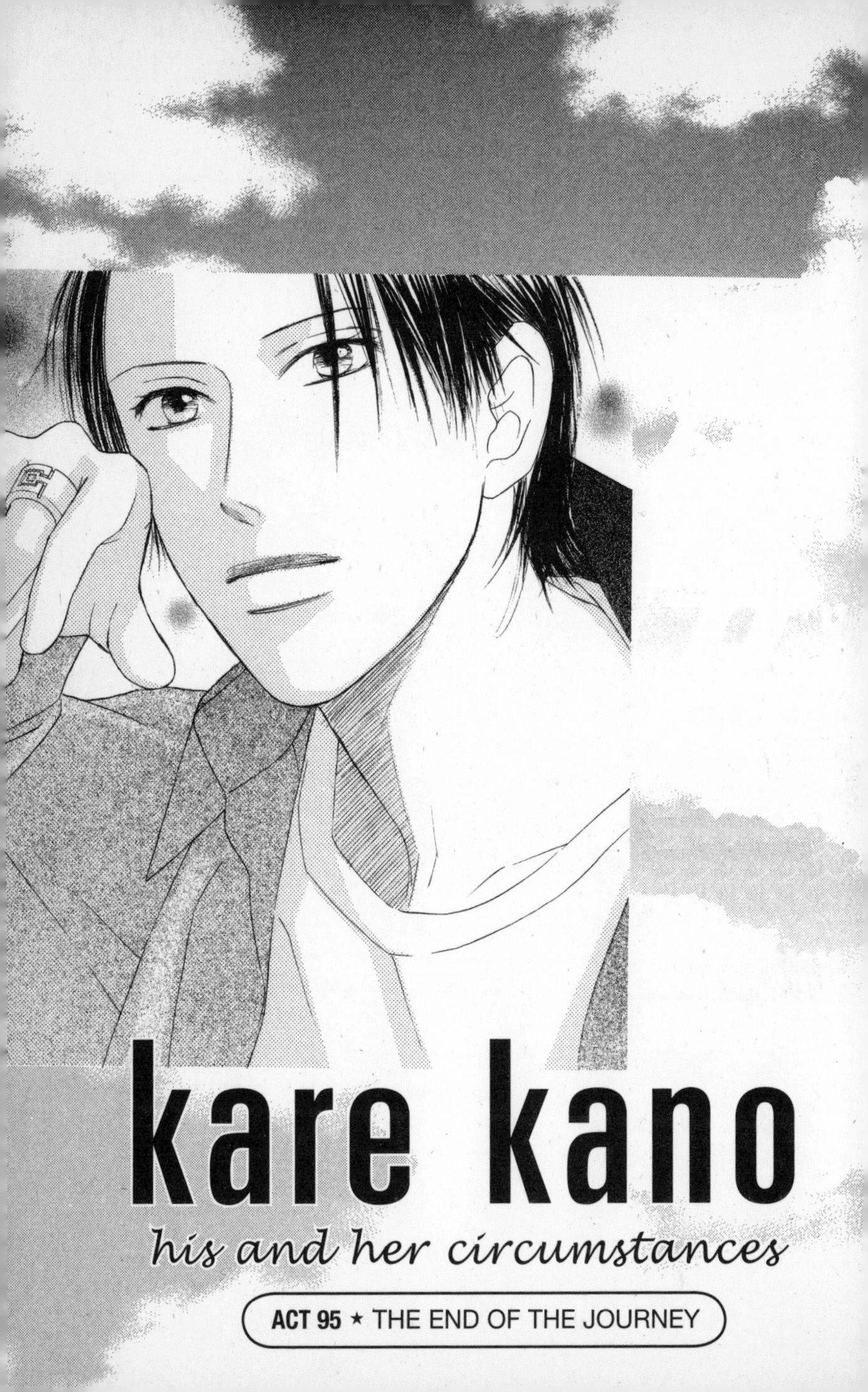
kare kano
his and her circumstances
ACT 95 ★ THE END OF THE JOURNEY

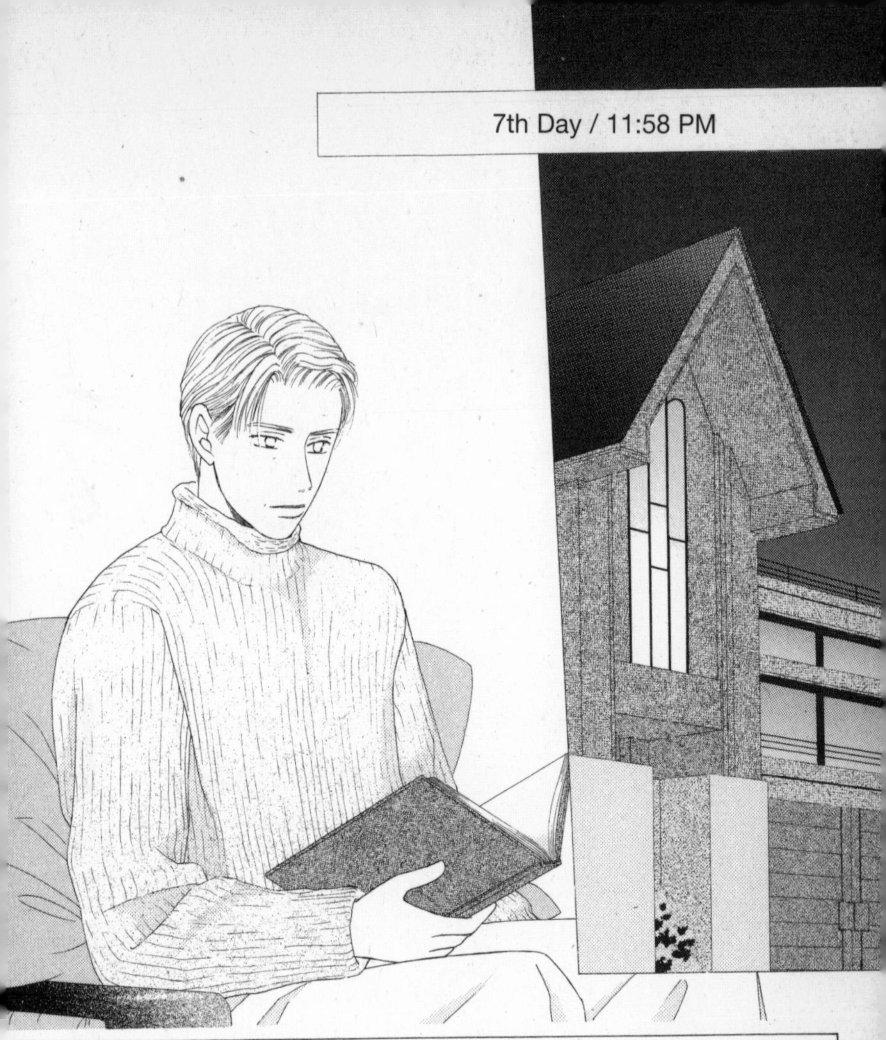
7th Day / 11:58 PM

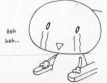

Opera

I'd never seen the real thing even once, but this year I thought I'd give it a try. All alone...

Faust, The Pearl Fishers, and Nibelung's Ring.

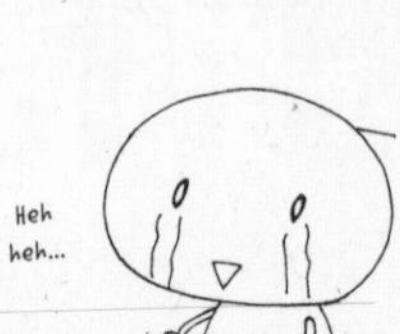
Heh heh...

There are some tickets that cost 40,000 yen! Hyah!

When I go watch kabuki, a lot of other people go with me, which is great. Well, when I'm working, there are a lot of times when I go by myself, too, but...

Opera is so much fun!

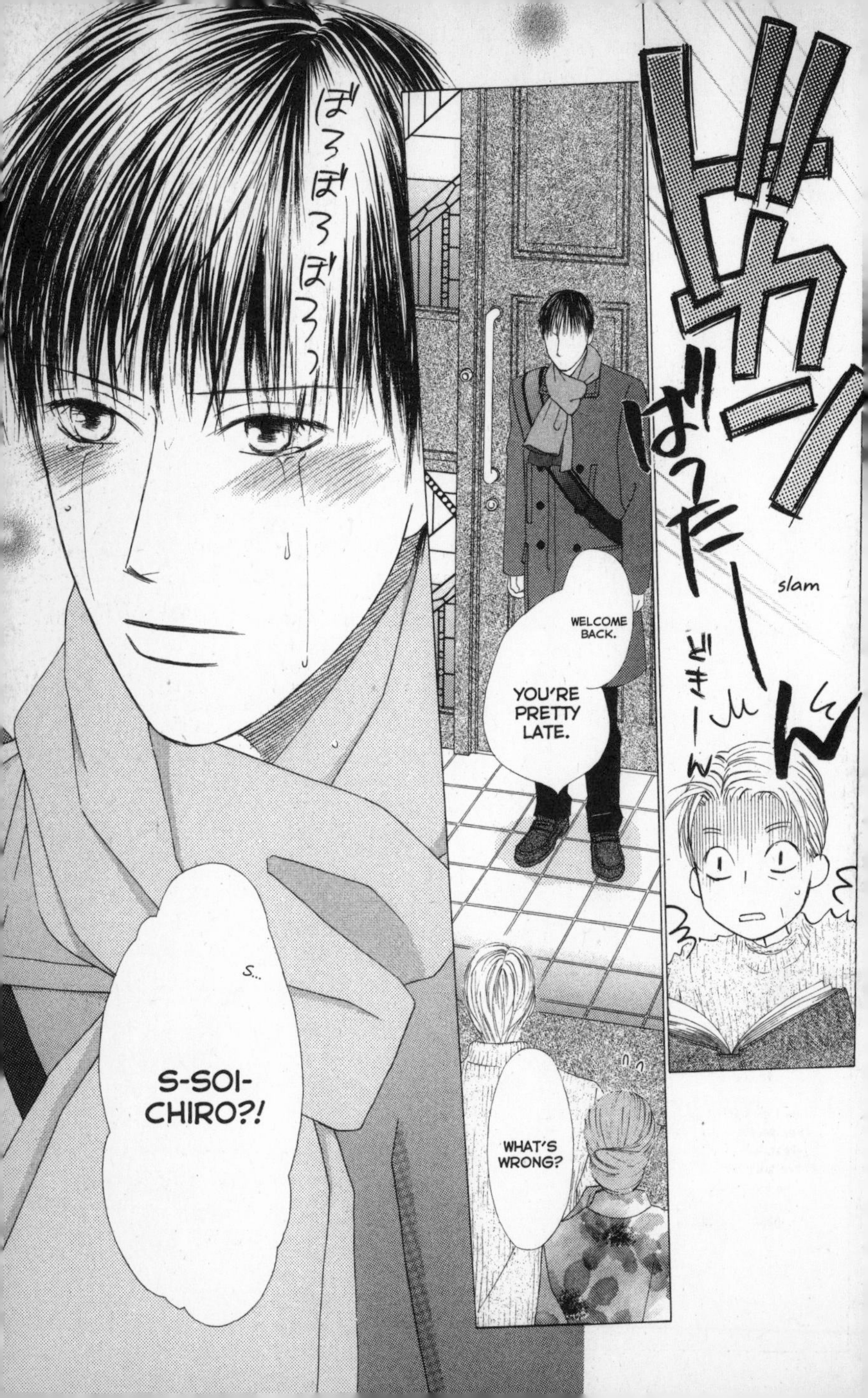
ばったーん
slam
どきーん
WELCOME BACK.
YOU'RE PRETTY LATE.
WHAT'S WRONG?
ぼろぼろぼろっ
S...
S-SOI-CHIRO?!

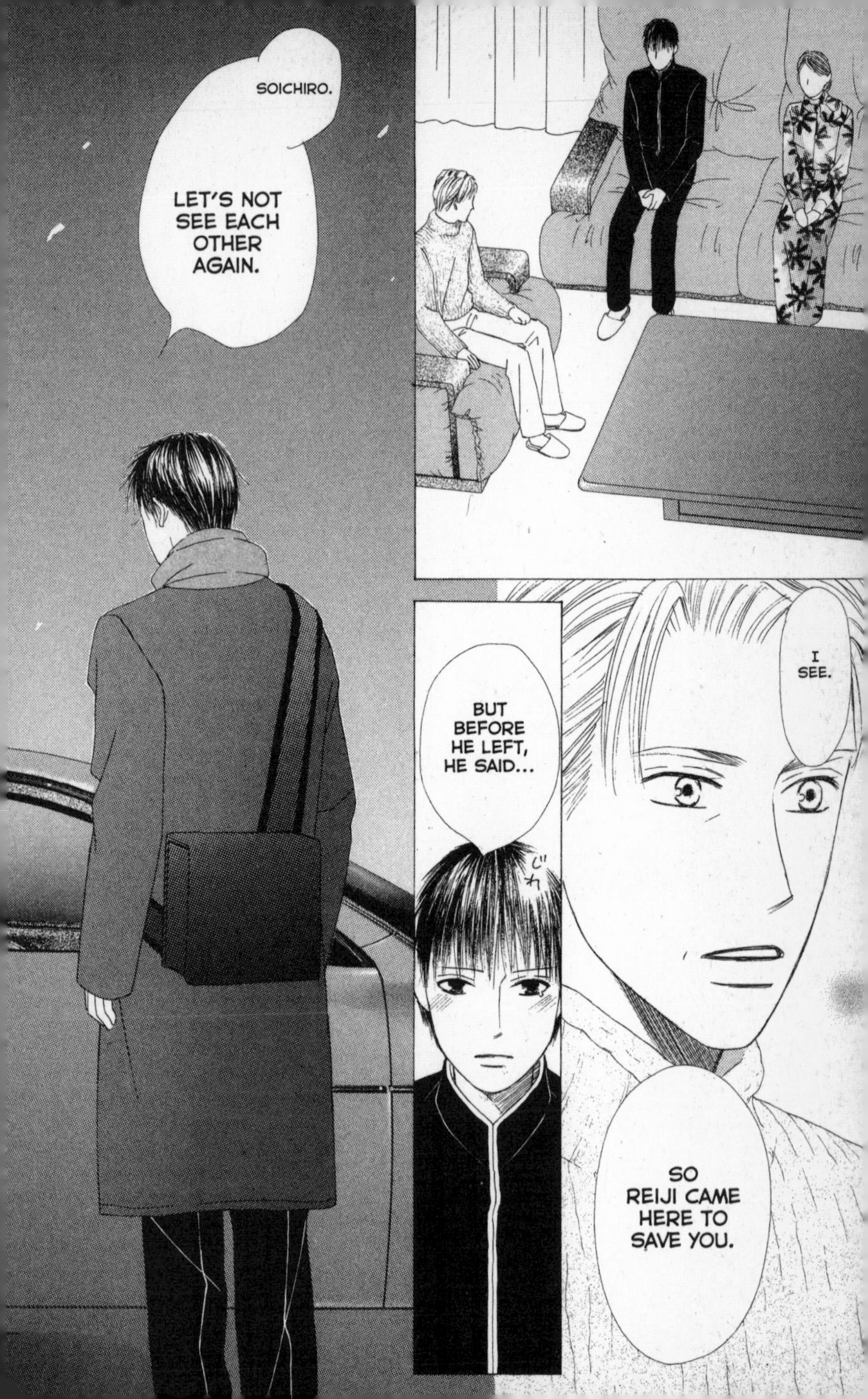
I SEE.
SO REIJI CAME HERE TO SAVE YOU.
じわ
BUT BEFORE HE LEFT, HE SAID...
SOICHIRO.
LET'S NOT SEE EACH OTHER AGAIN.

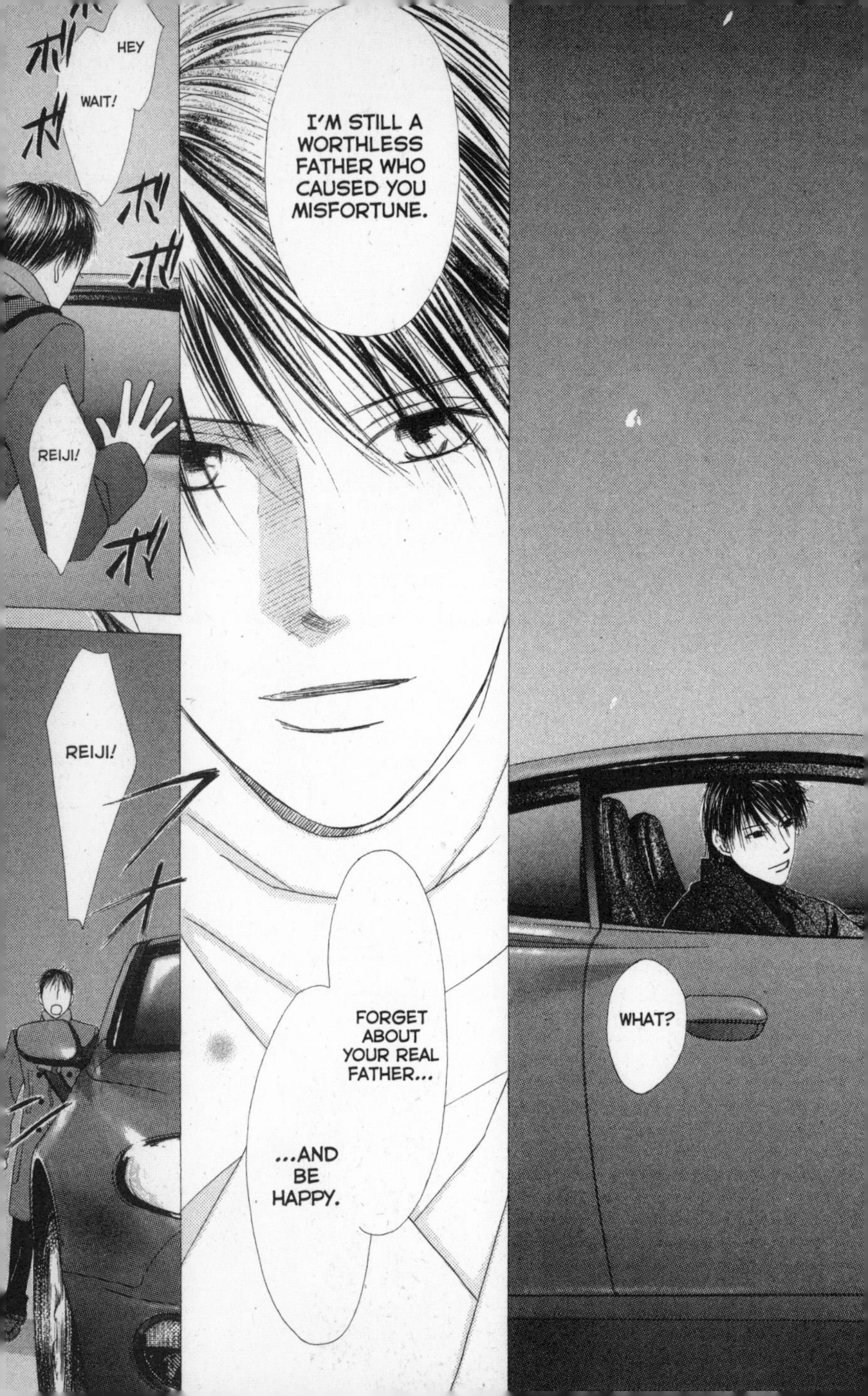

WHAT?
I'M STILL A WORTHLESS FATHER WHO CAUSED YOU MISFORTUNE.
FORGET ABOUT YOUR REAL FATHER...
...AND BE HAPPY.
HEY
WAIT!
REIJI!
REIJI!

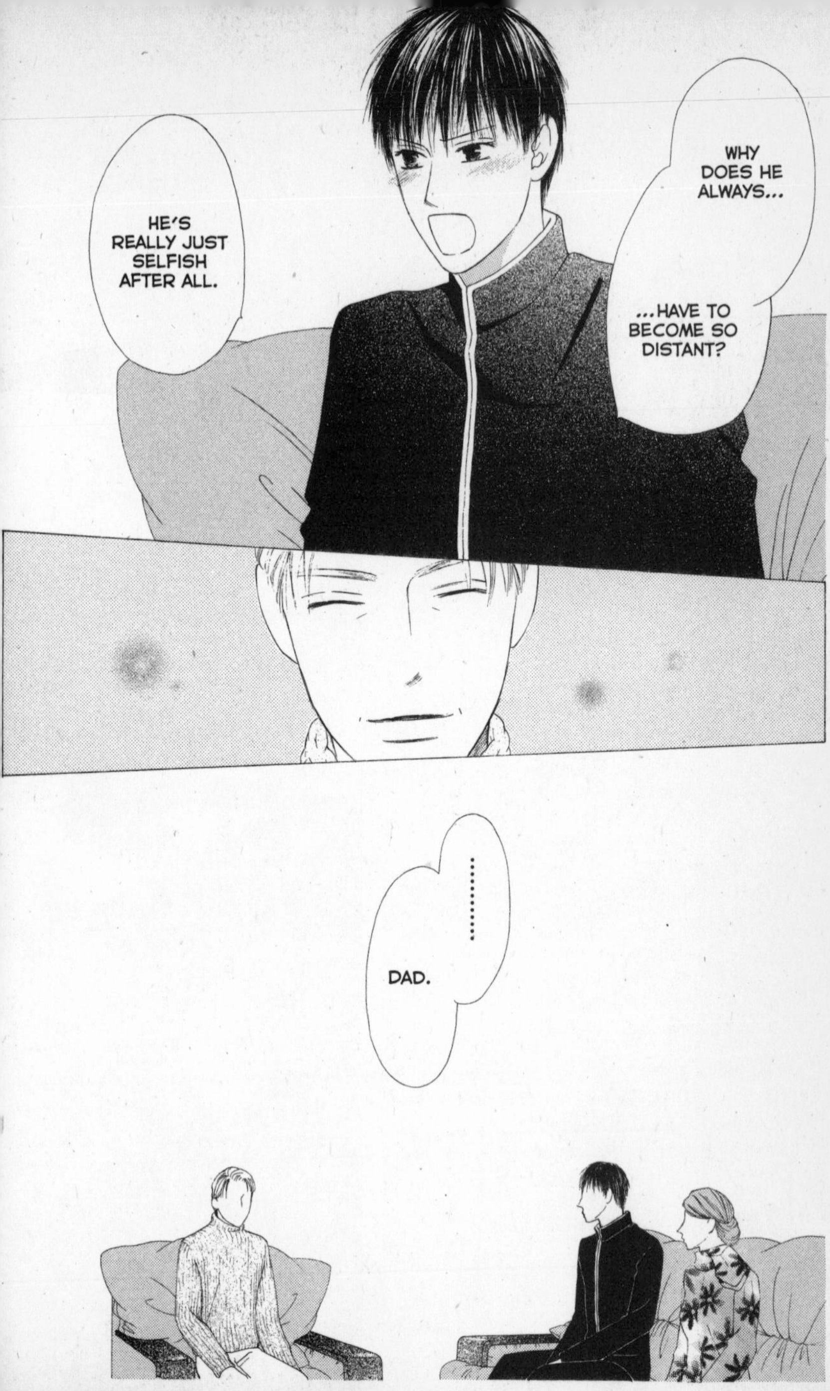
WHY DOES HE ALWAYS...
...HAVE TO BECOME SO DISTANT?
HE'S REALLY JUST SELFISH AFTER ALL.
...... DAD.

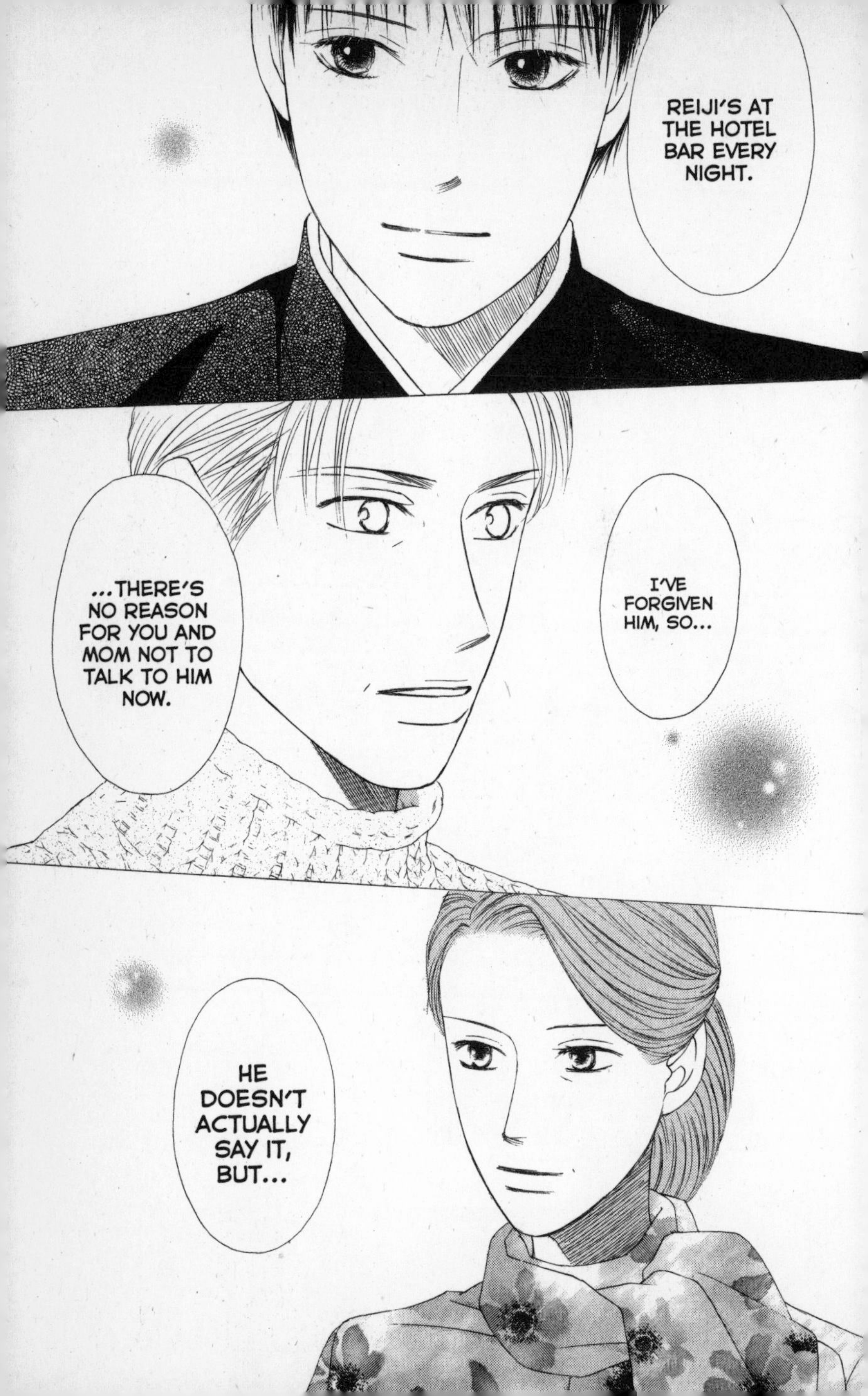
REIJI'S AT THE HOTEL BAR EVERY NIGHT.
I'VE FORGIVEN HIM, SO...
...THERE'S NO REASON FOR YOU AND MOM NOT TO TALK TO HIM NOW.
HE DOESN'T ACTUALLY SAY IT, BUT...

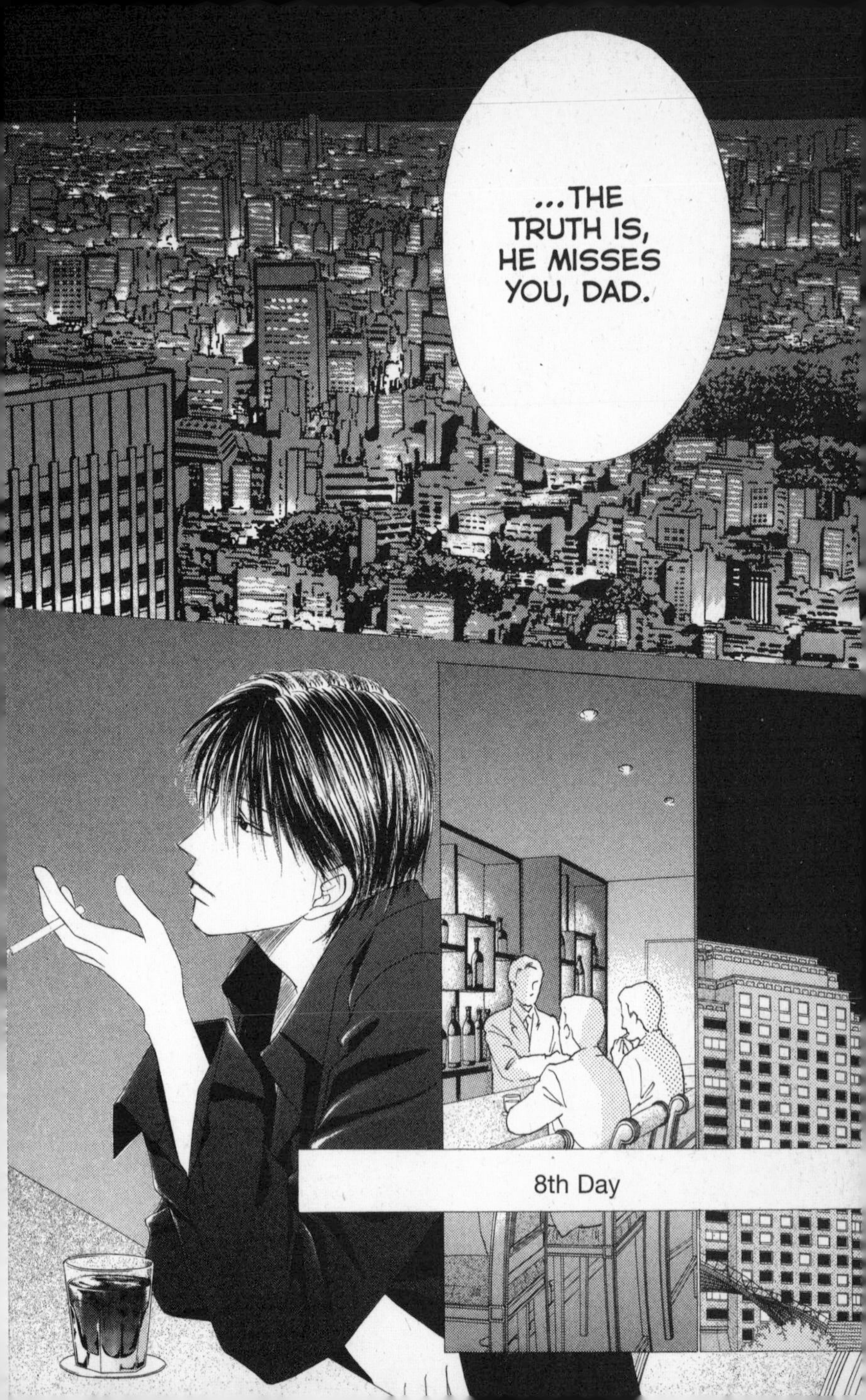
...THE TRUTH IS, HE MISSES YOU, DAD.
8th Day

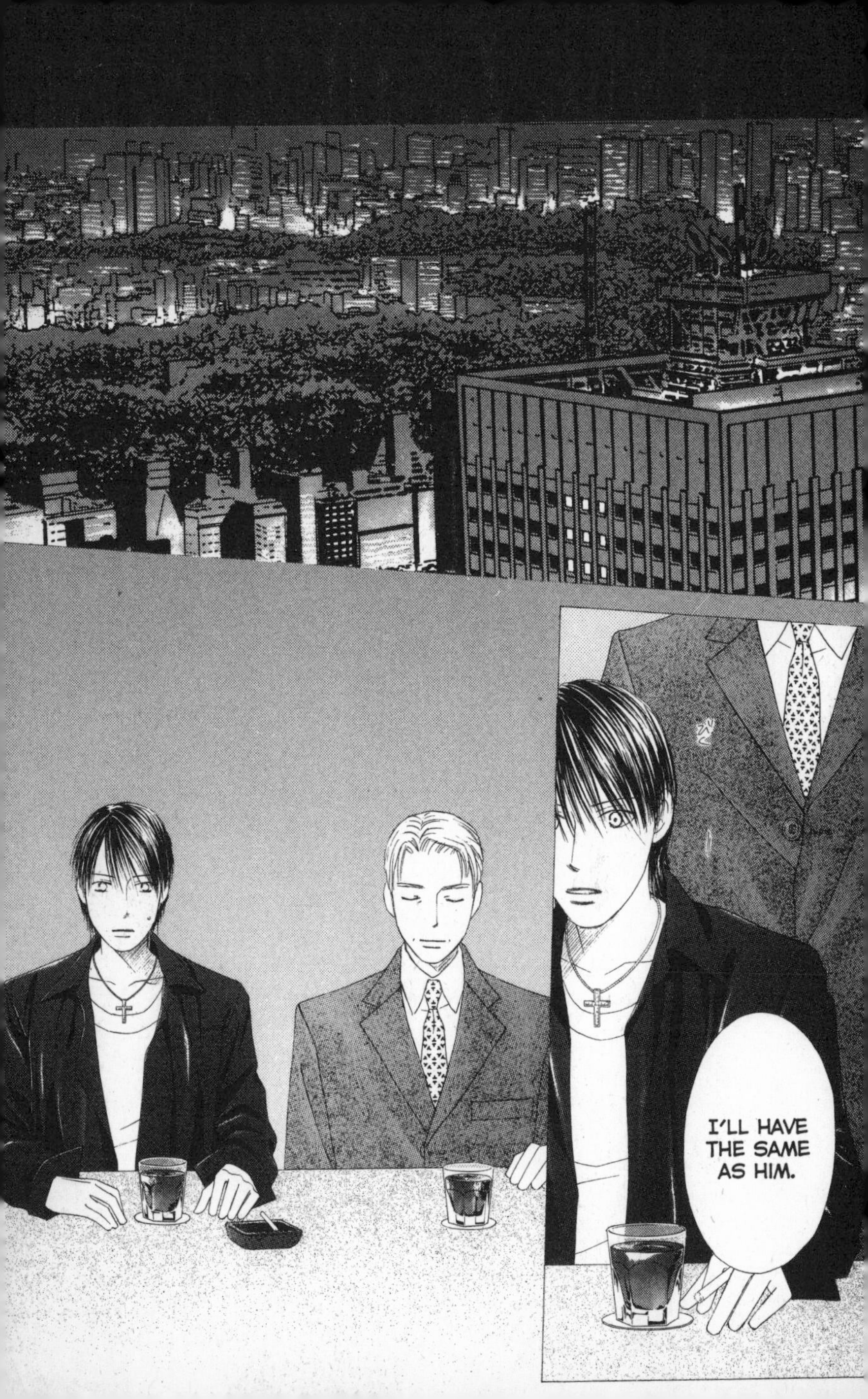
I'LL HAVE THE SAME AS HIM.

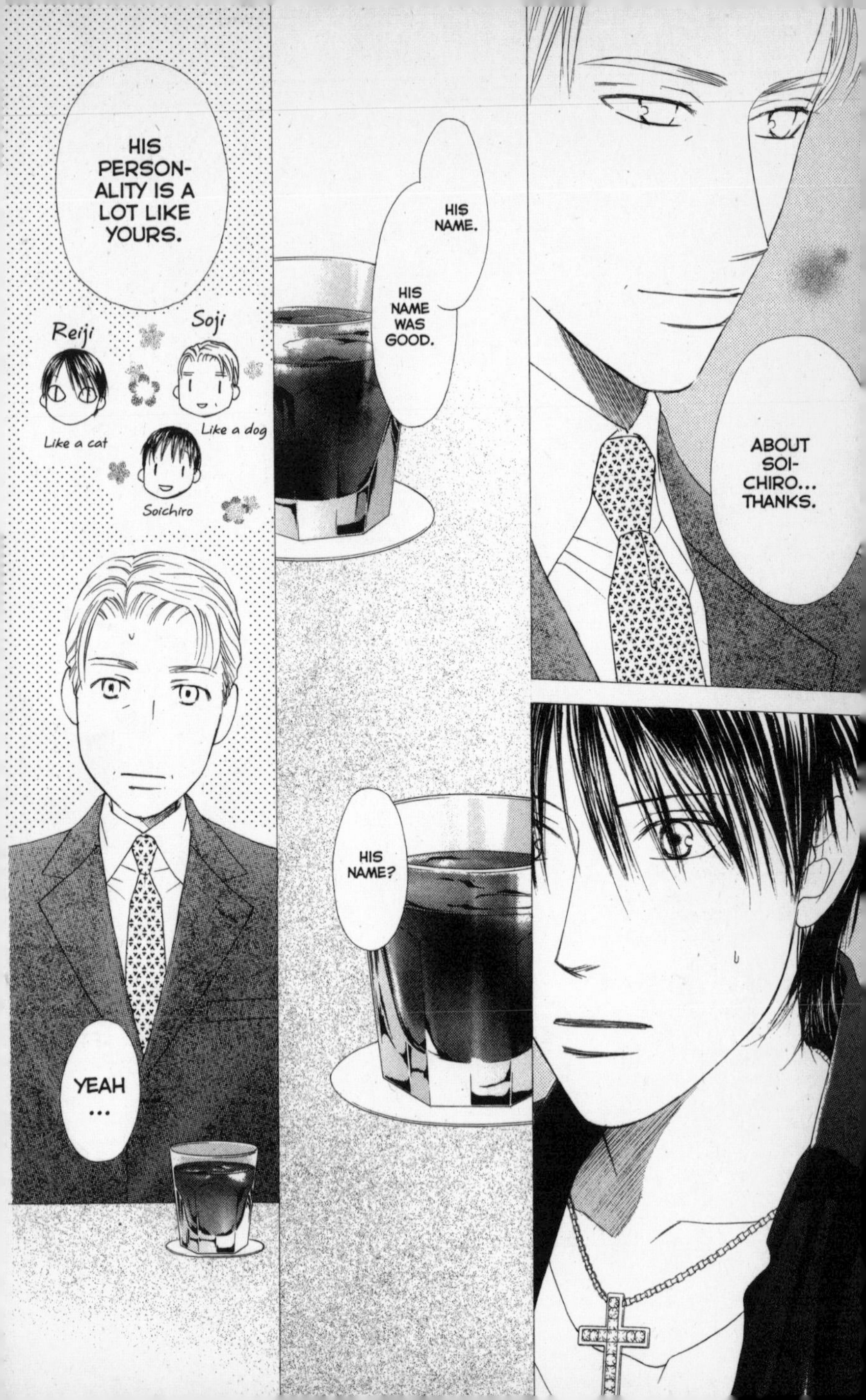
ABOUT SOI-CHIRO... THANKS.
HIS NAME.
HIS NAME WAS GOOD.
HIS NAME?
HIS PERSON-ALITY IS A LOT LIKE YOURS.
Soji
Reiji
Like a dog
Like a cat
Soichiro
YEAH ...

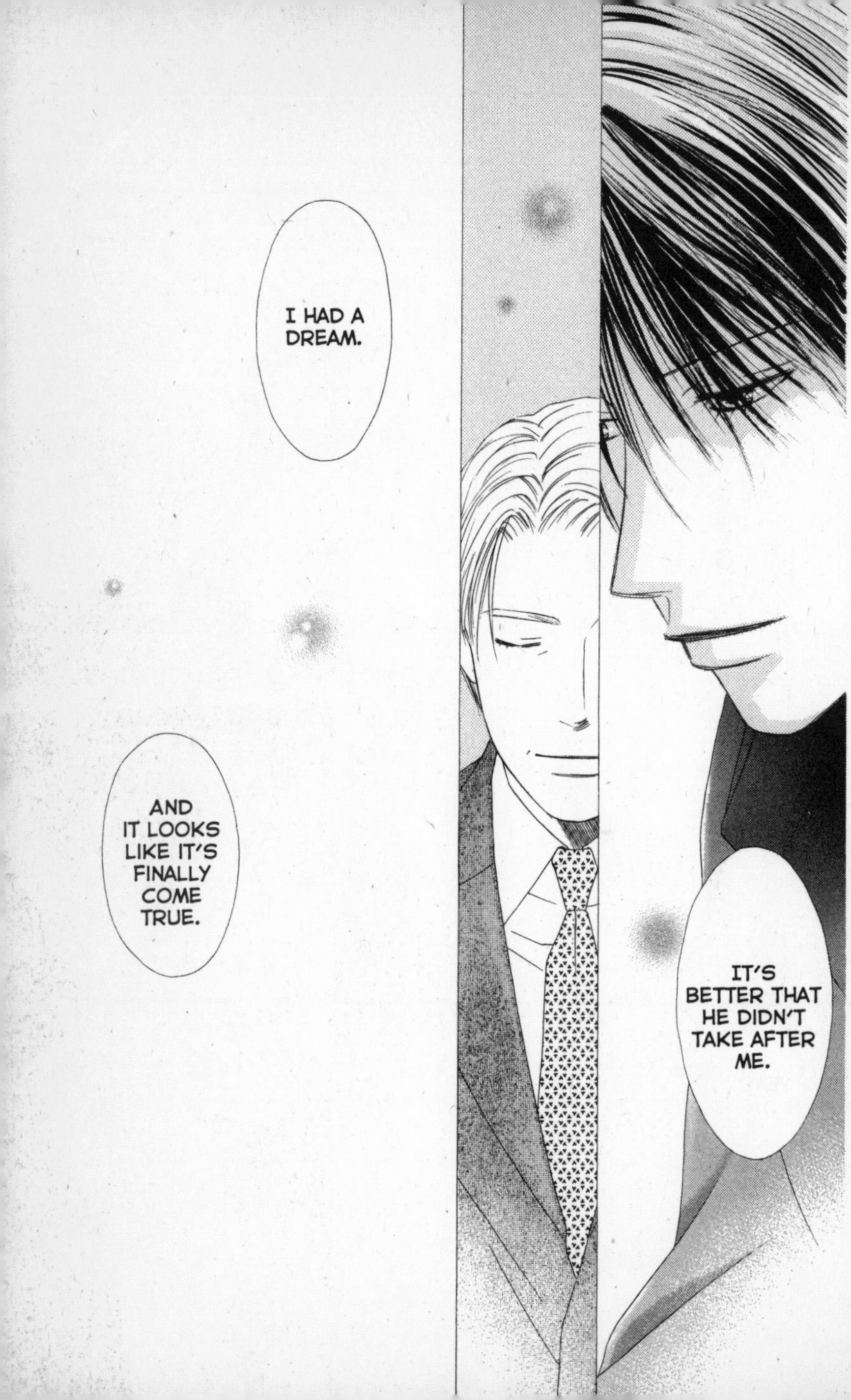
IT'S BETTER THAT HE DIDN'T TAKE AFTER ME.
I HAD A DREAM.
AND IT LOOKS LIKE IT'S FINALLY COME TRUE.

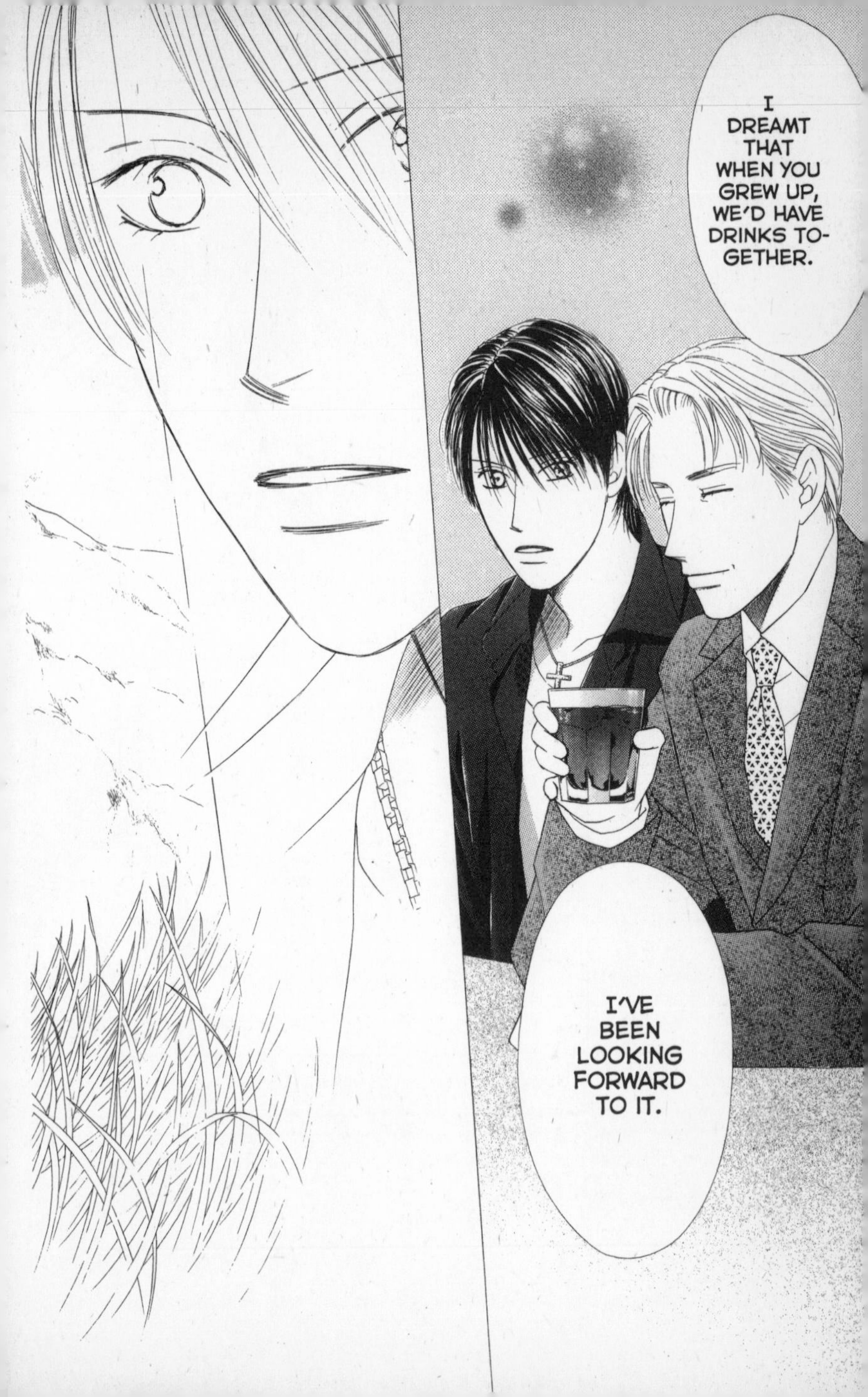
I DREAMT THAT WHEN YOU GREW UP, WE'D HAVE DRINKS TO-GETHER.
I'VE BEEN LOOKING FORWARD TO IT.

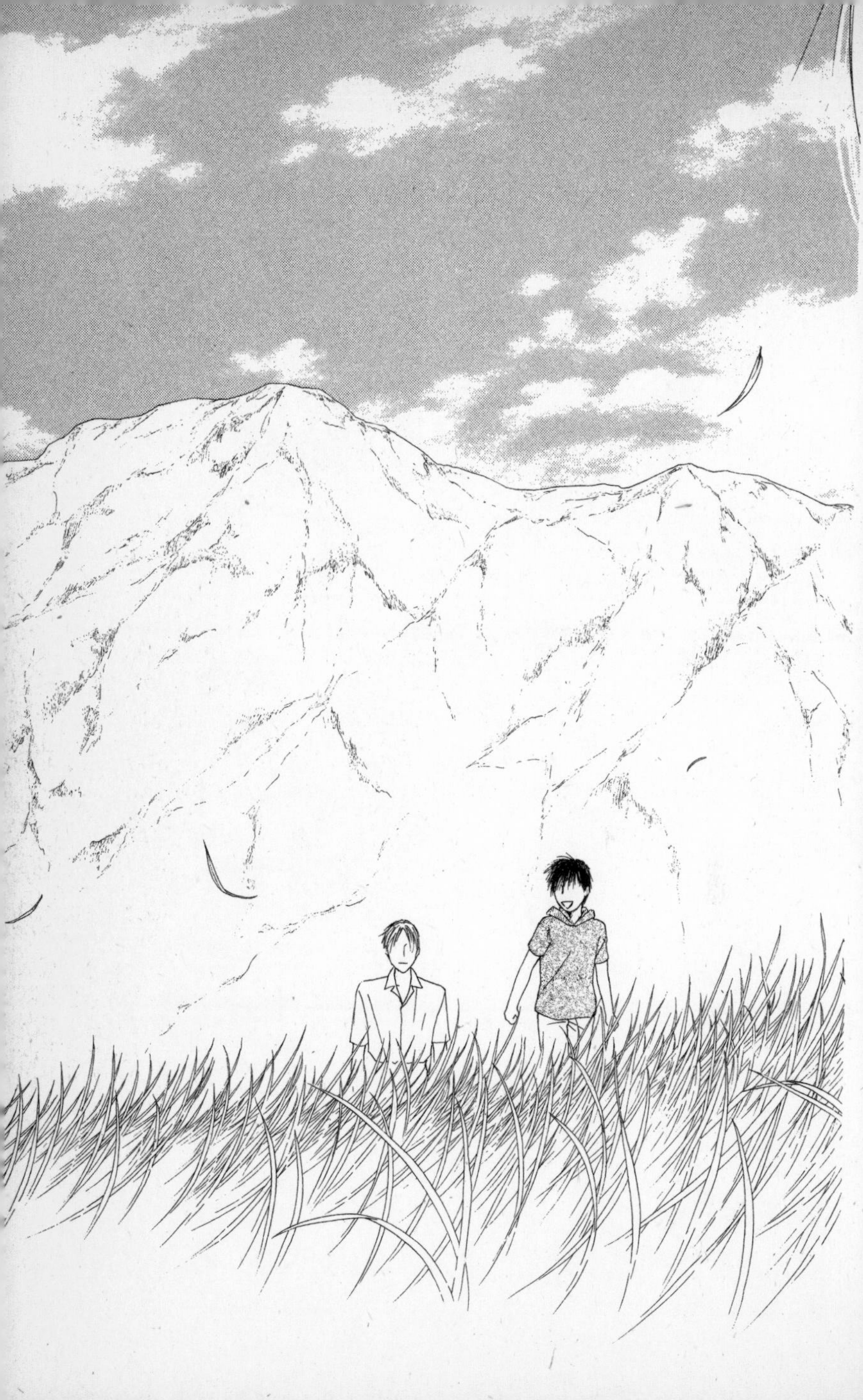

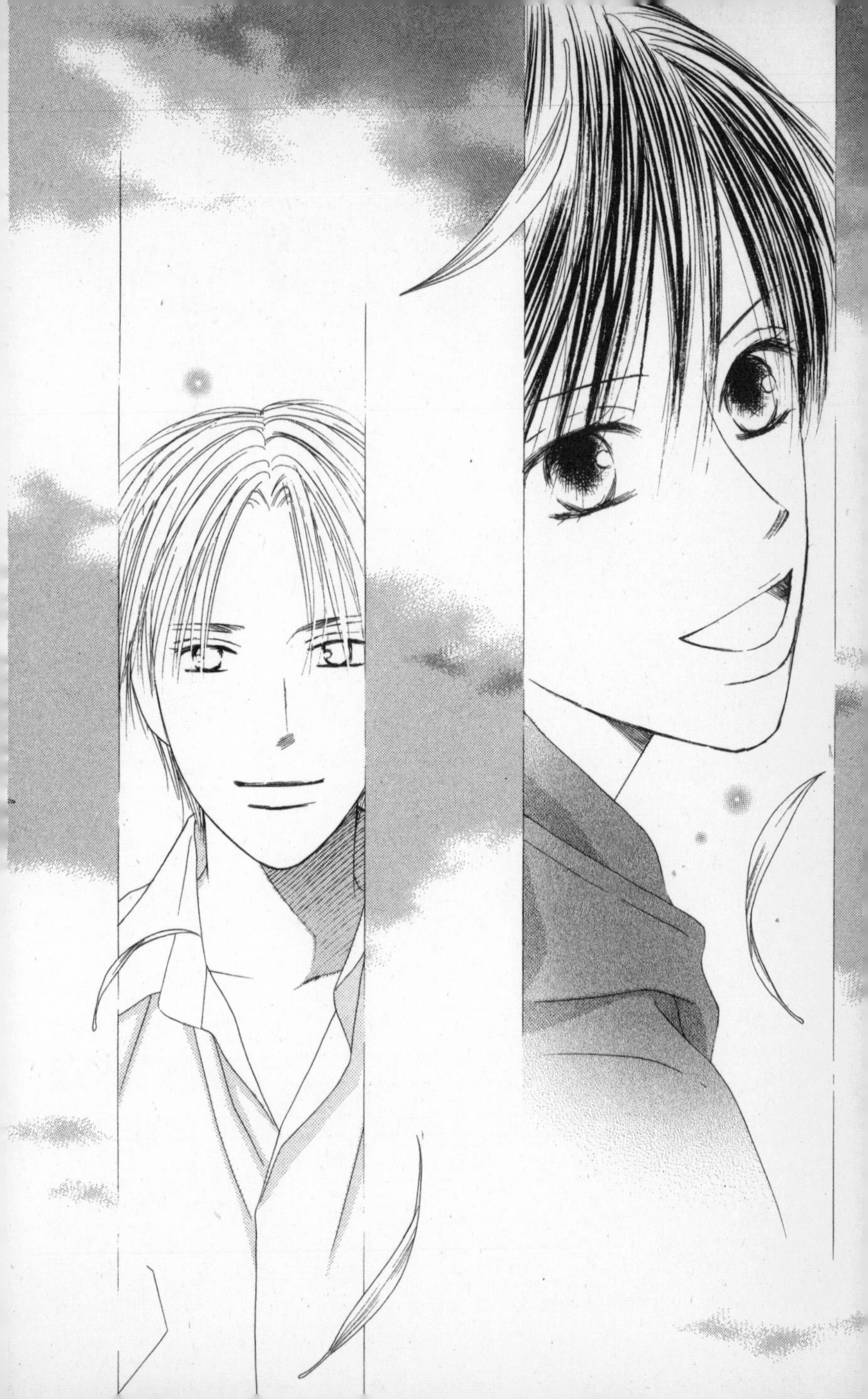

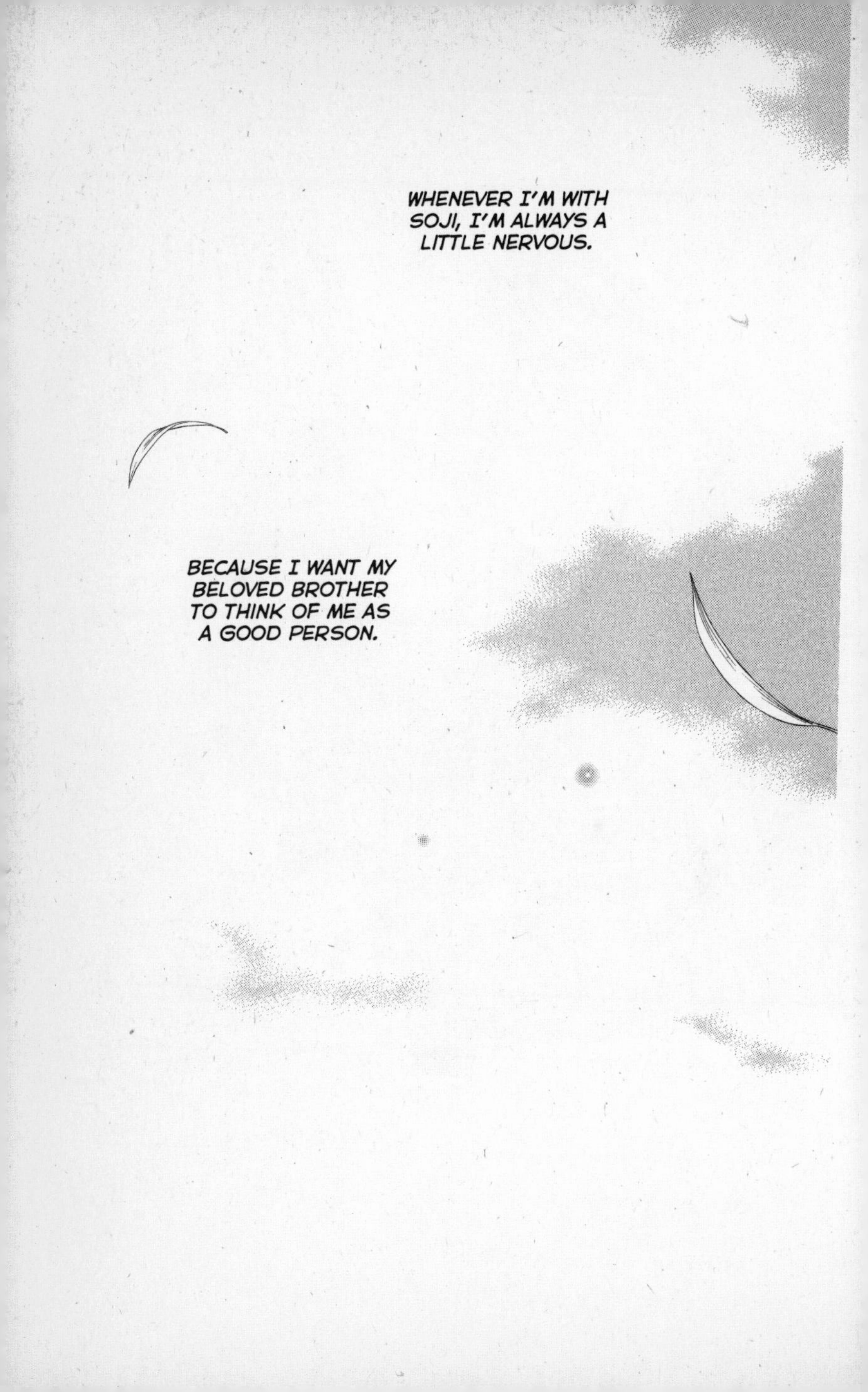
WHENEVER I'M WITH SOJI, I'M ALWAYS A LITTLE NERVOUS.
BECAUSE I WANT MY BELOVED BROTHER TO THINK OF ME AS A GOOD PERSON.

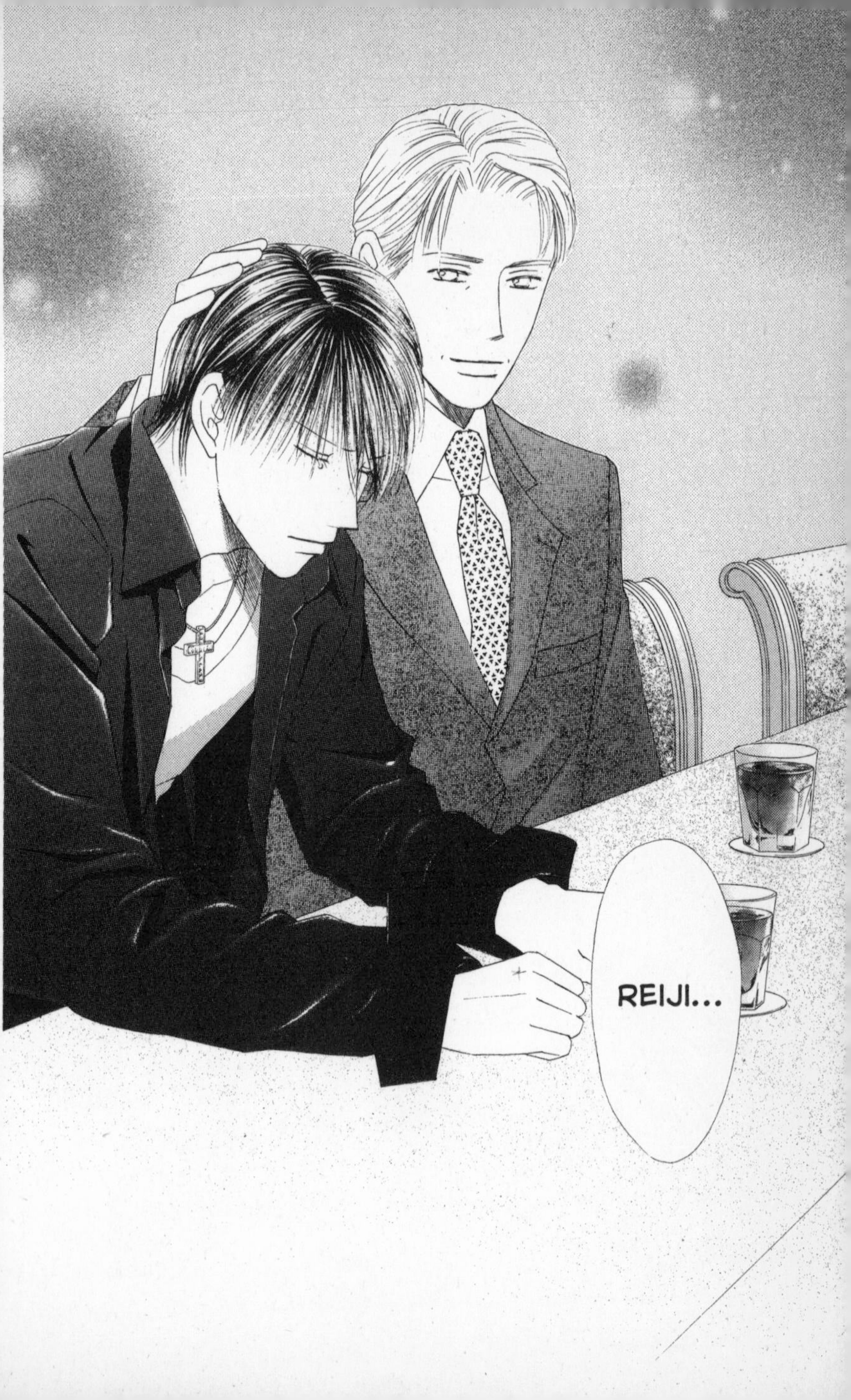
REIJI...

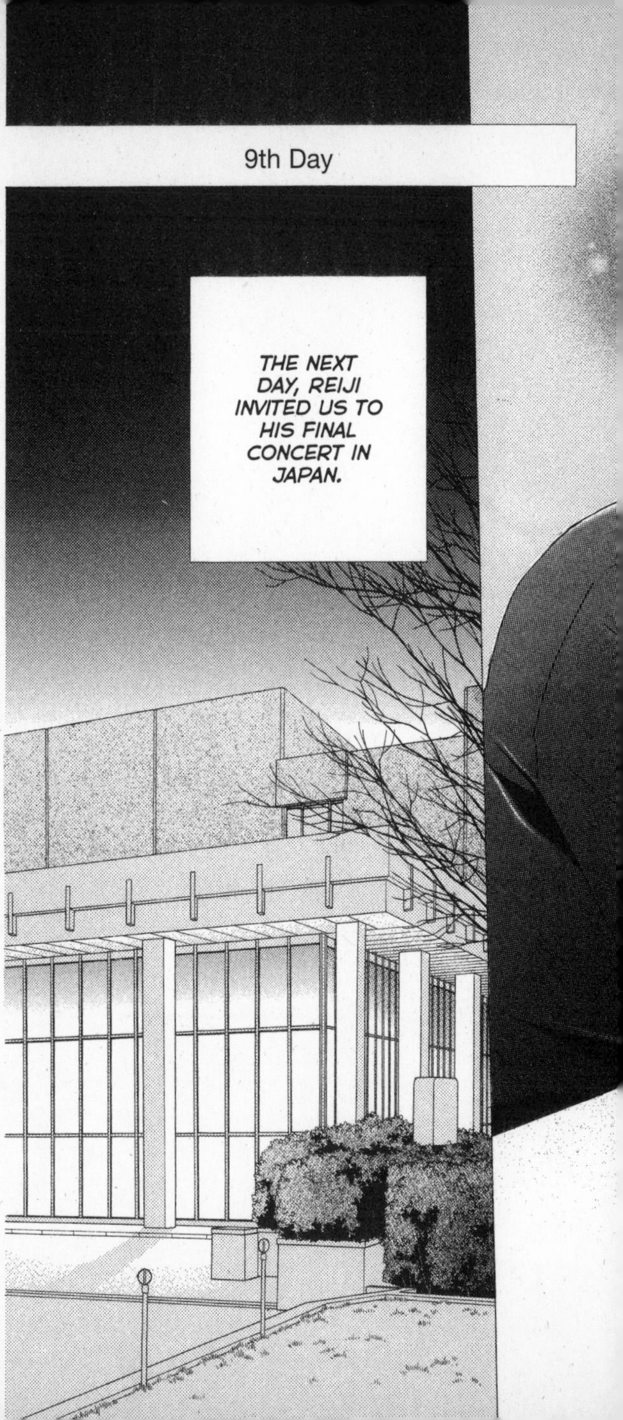
9th Day
THE NEXT DAY, REIJI INVITED US TO HIS FINAL CONCERT IN JAPAN.

2

Jasmine

If I pick the wrong perfume, I get a headache, but I'm not good at choosing. I've always loved the smell of jasmine, so when I went out searching for some, I started to look into all the different kinds.

Oil Collection

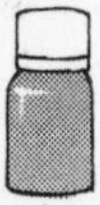

I like Bergamot, too. You can put it on your face or your hands, or even in the bath water.

Soap Collection

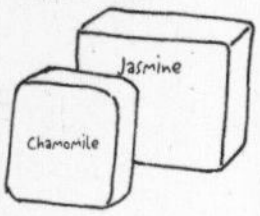
Jasmine
Chamomile

There are all kinds...It's endless! These are made of all natural materials.

Incense Collection

Peony and Rose Incense

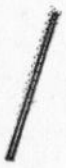

I get the feeling I've heard of this before...I really love it.

Linen Water and Basalt and such...I adore that kind of stuff.

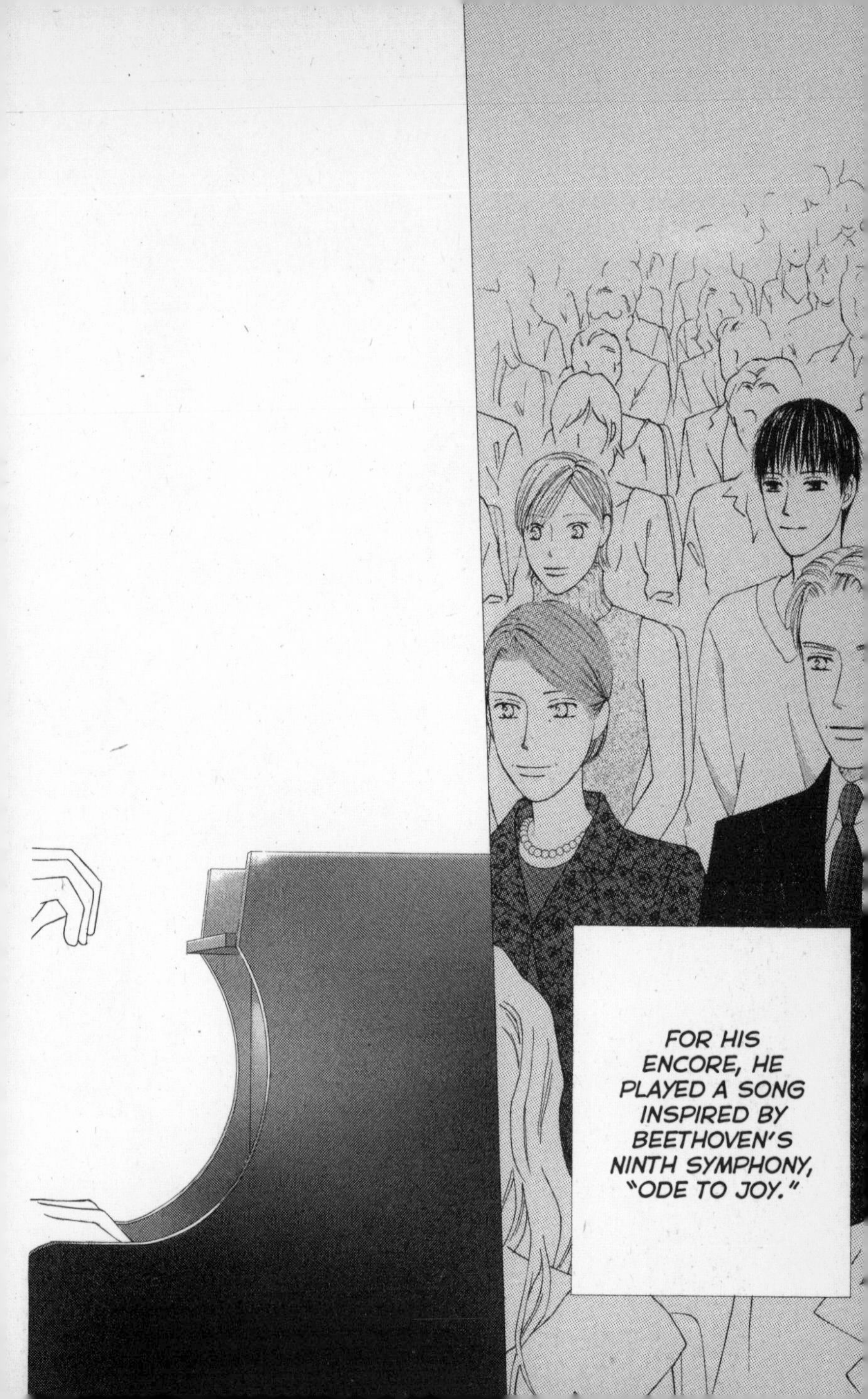
FOR HIS ENCORE, HE PLAYED A SONG INSPIRED BY BEETHOVEN'S NINTH SYMPHONY, "ODE TO JOY."

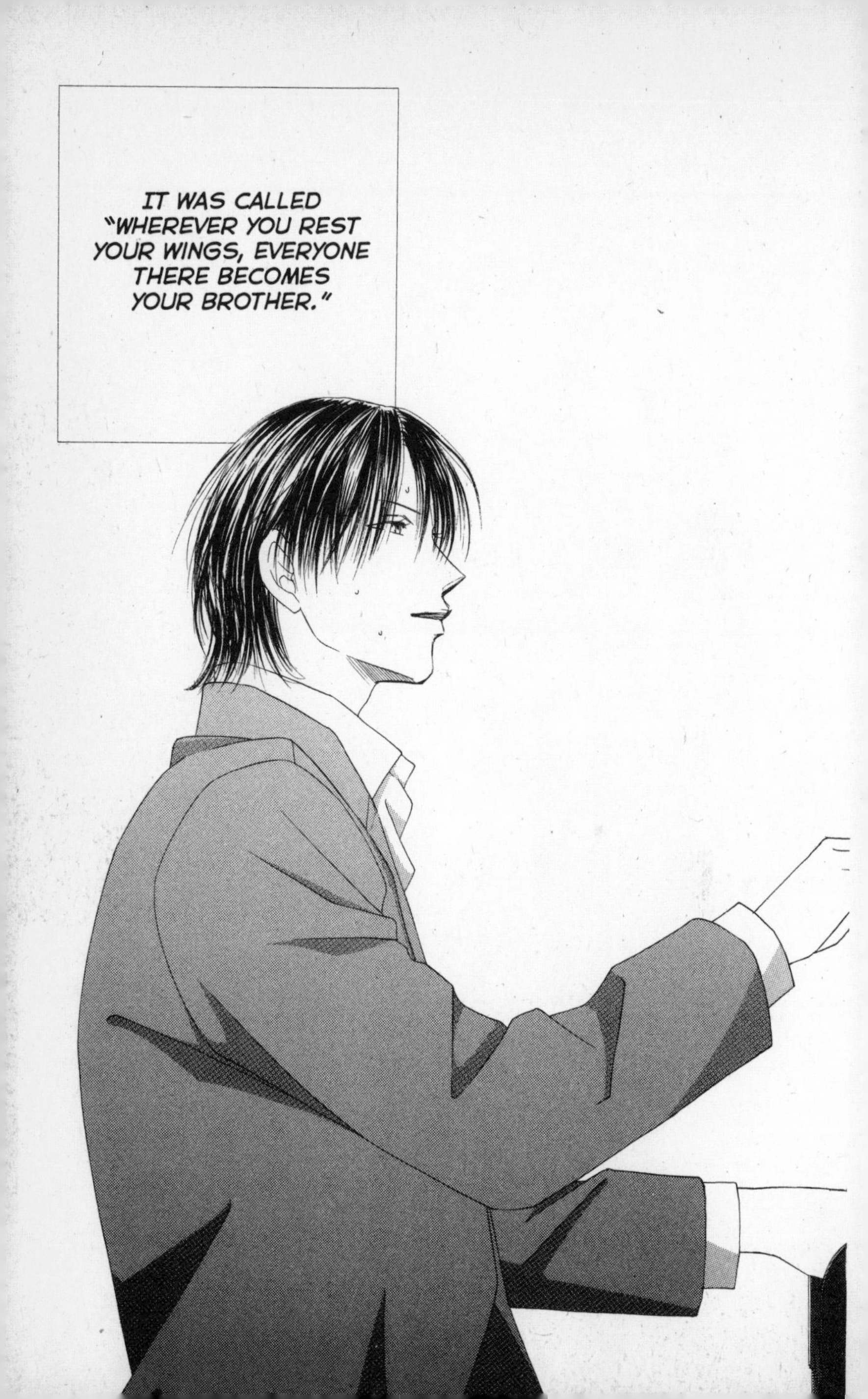
IT WAS CALLED "WHEREVER YOU REST YOUR WINGS, EVERYONE THERE BECOMES YOUR BROTHER."

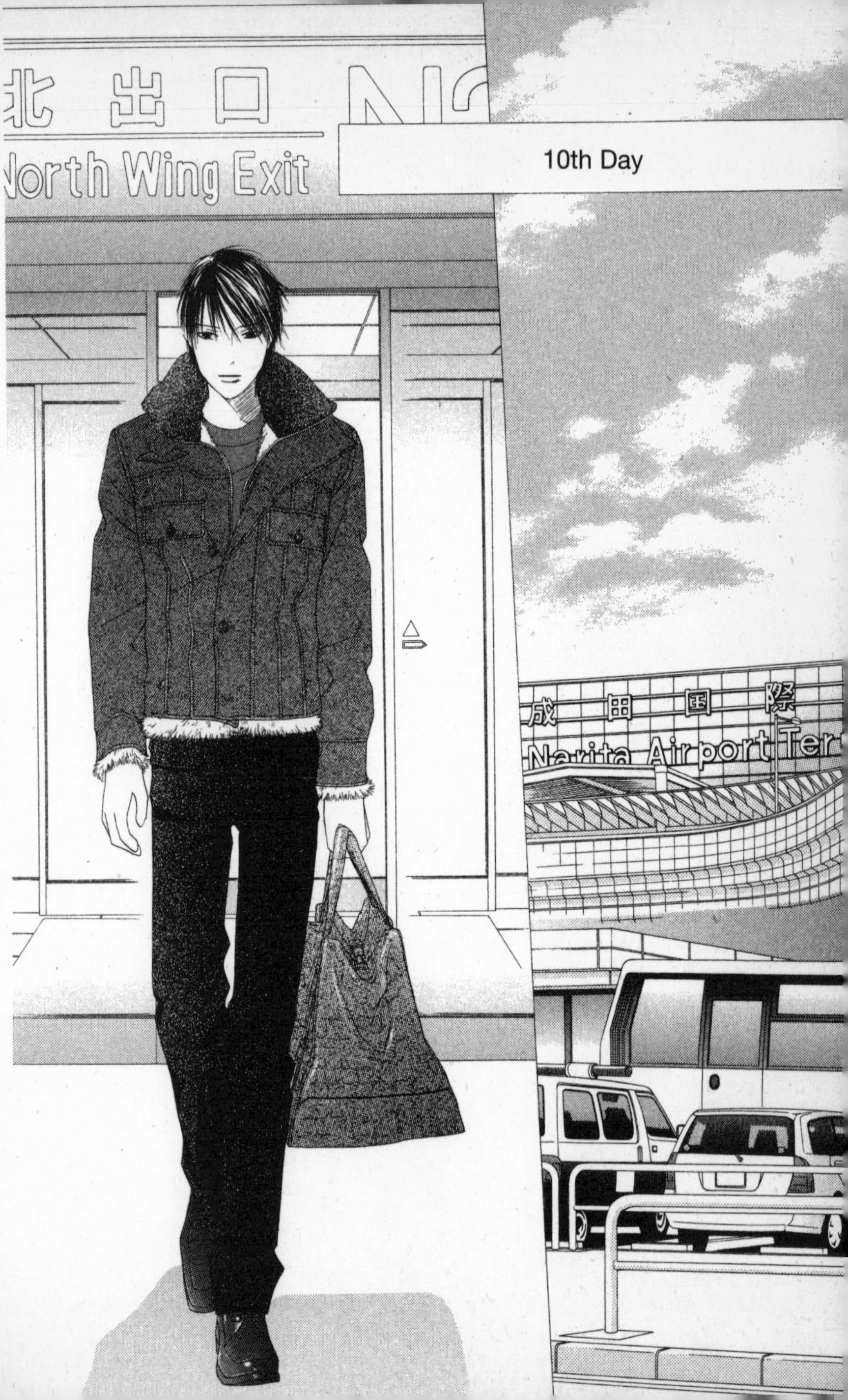
10th Day
成田国際
Narita Airport Ter
北出口
North Wing Exit

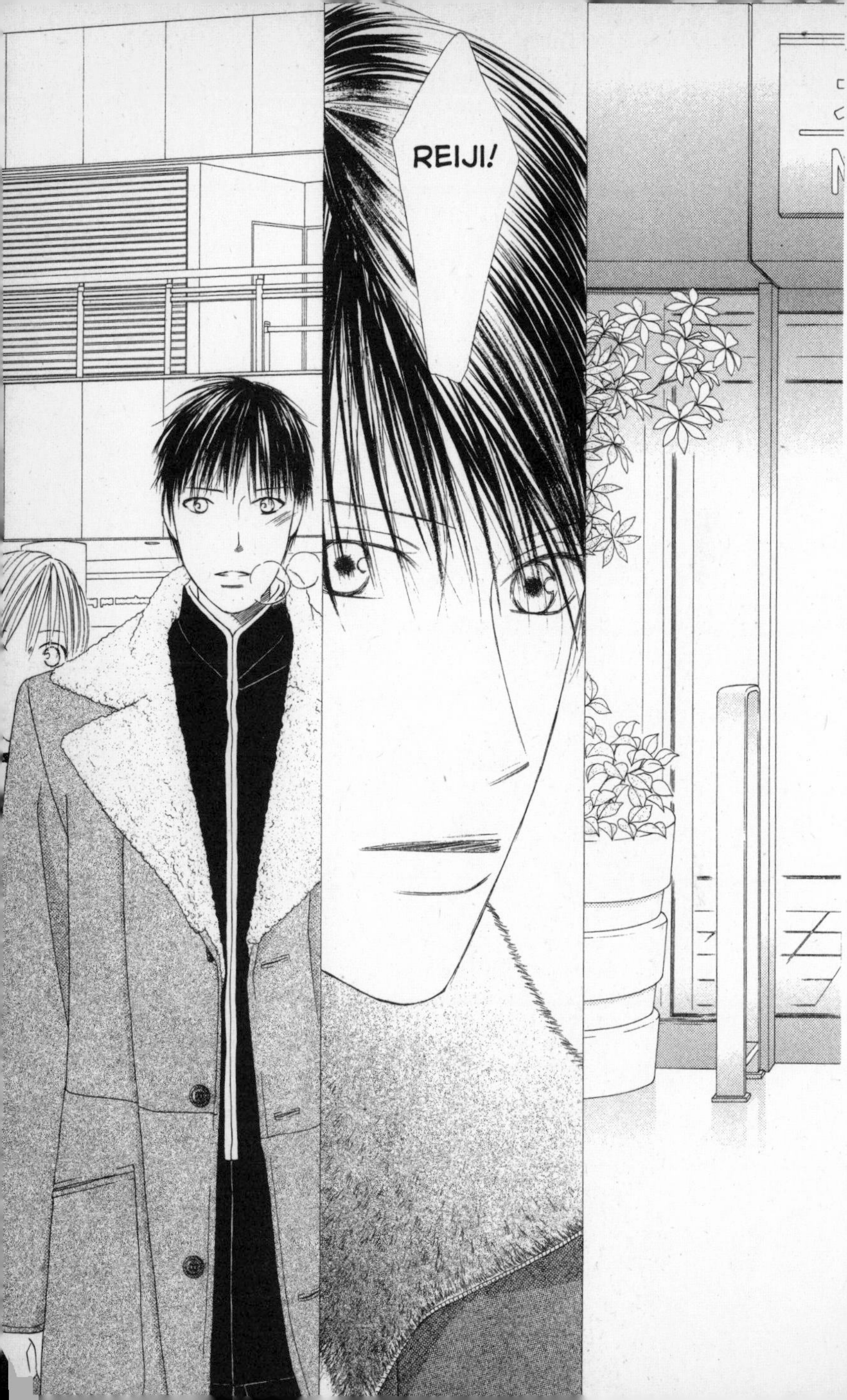
REIJI!

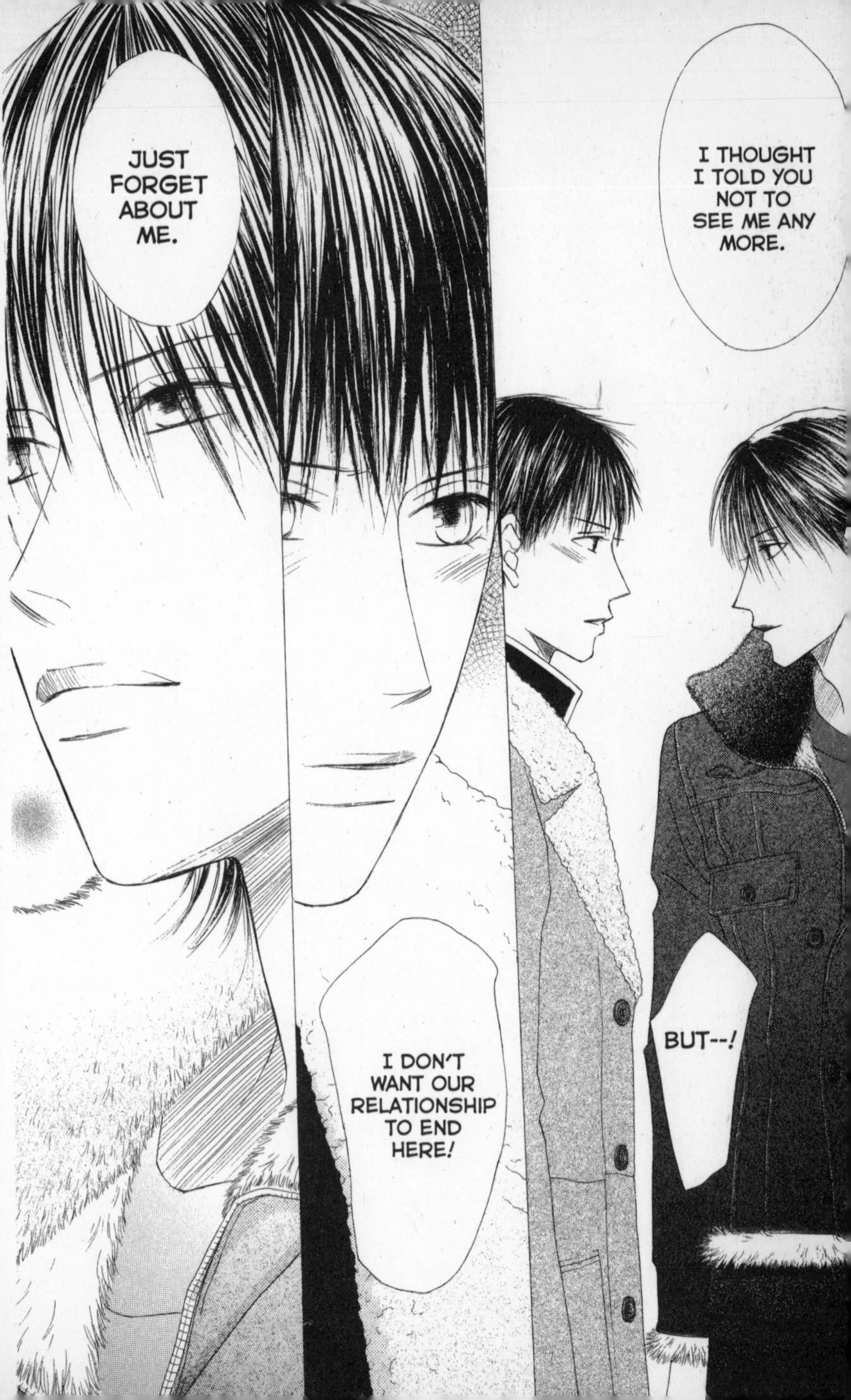
I THOUGHT I TOLD YOU NOT TO SEE ME ANY MORE.
BUT--!
I DON'T WANT OUR RELATIONSHIP TO END HERE!
JUST FORGET ABOUT ME.

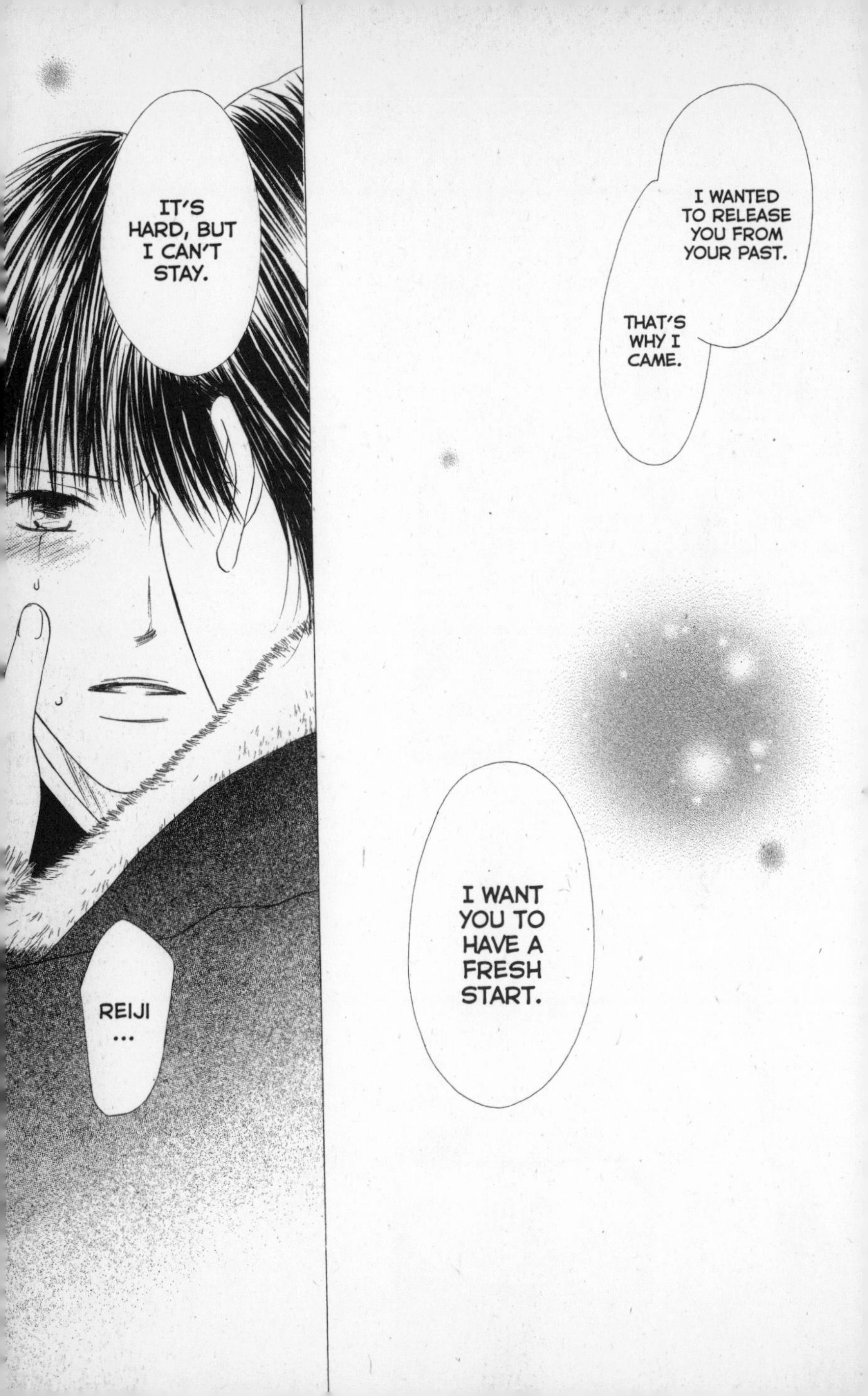
I WANTED TO RELEASE YOU FROM YOUR PAST.
THAT'S WHY I CAME.
I WANT YOU TO HAVE A FRESH START.
IT'S HARD, BUT I CAN'T STAY.
REIJI ...

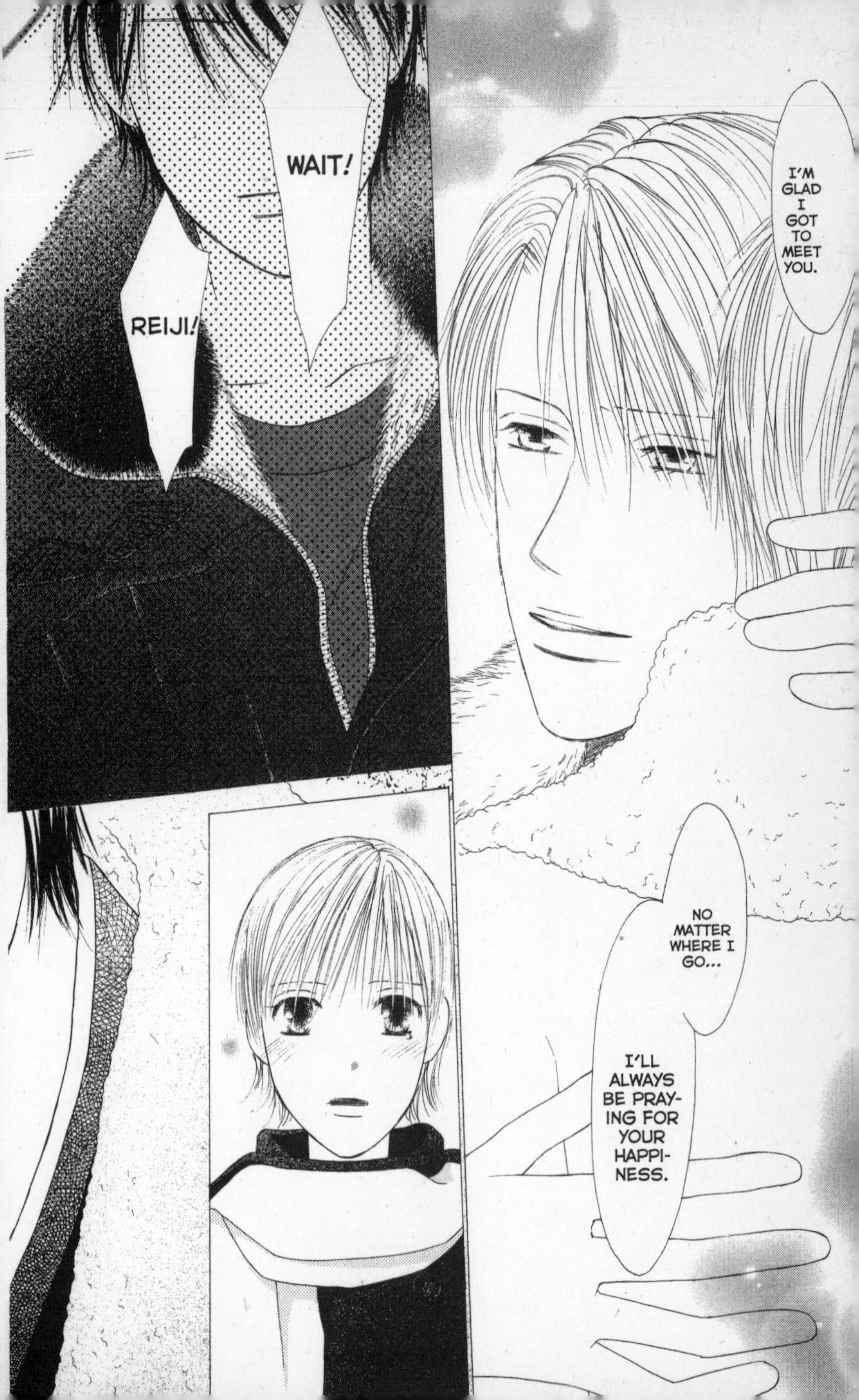
I'M GLAD I GOT TO MEET YOU.
NO MATTER WHERE I GO...
I'LL ALWAYS BE PRAYING FOR YOUR HAPPINESS.
WAIT!
REIJI!

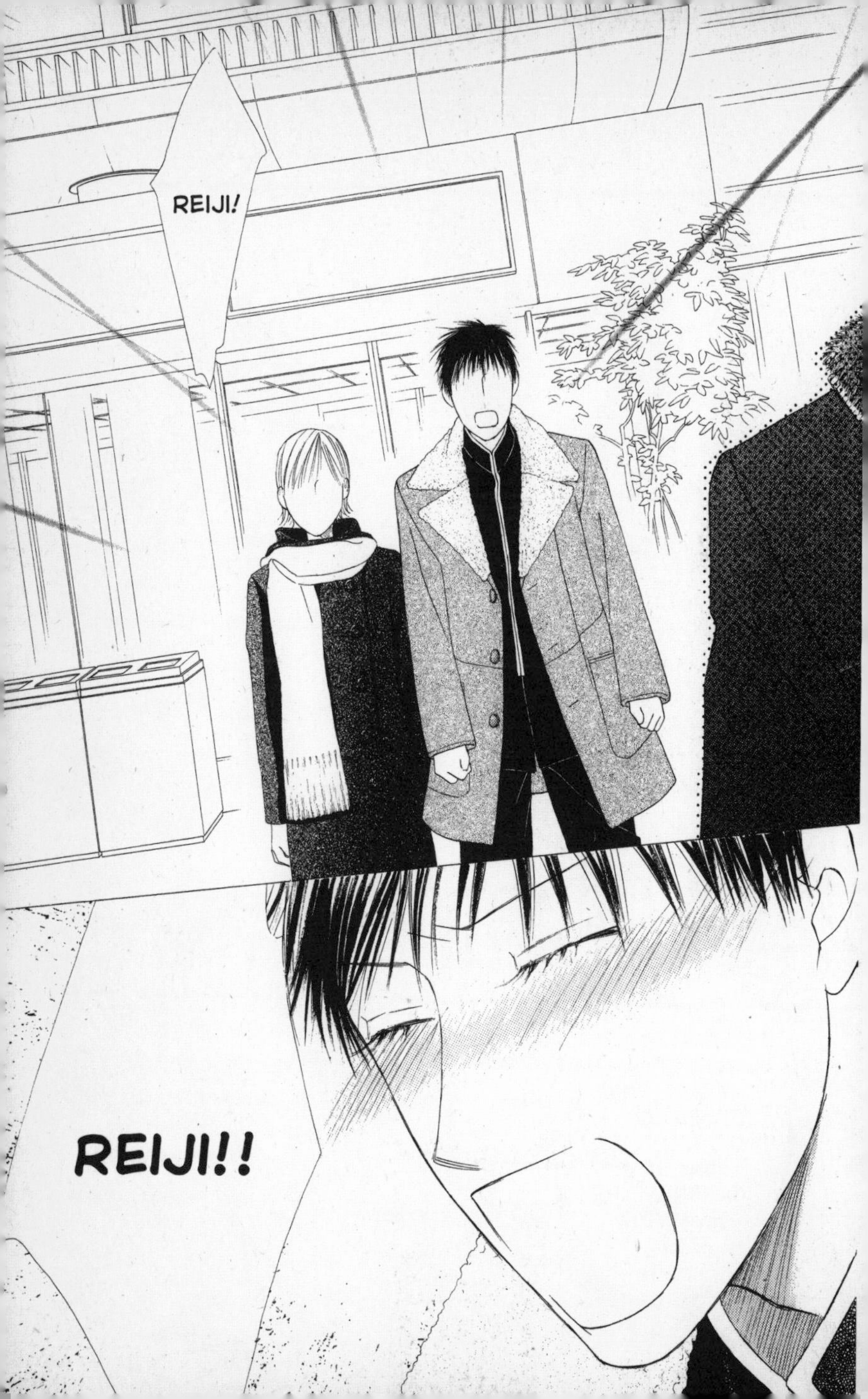
REIJI!
REIJI!!

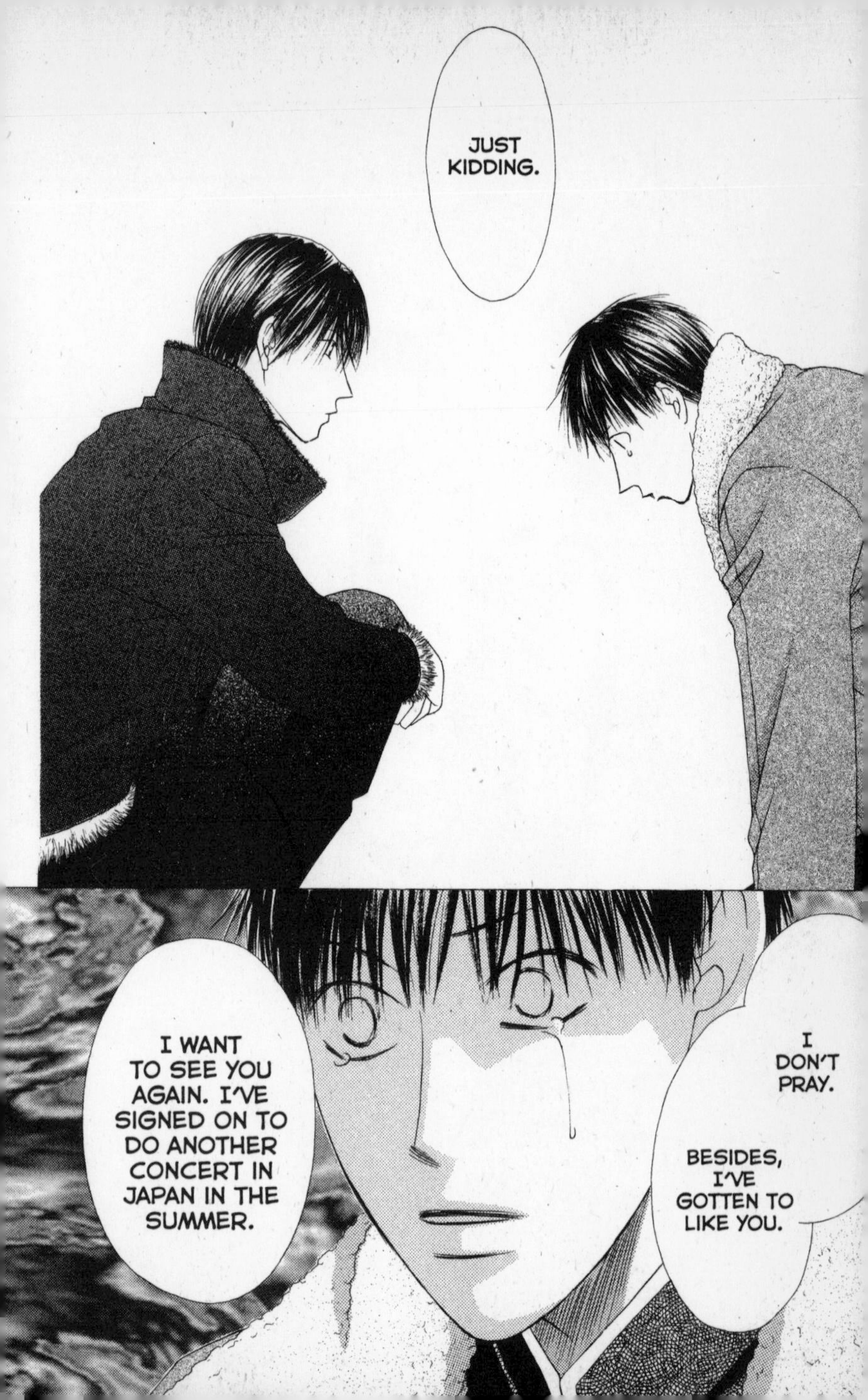
JUST KIDDING.
I DON'T PRAY.
BESIDES, I'VE GOTTEN TO LIKE YOU.
I WANT TO SEE YOU AGAIN. I'VE SIGNED ON TO DO ANOTHER CONCERT IN JAPAN IN THE SUMMER.

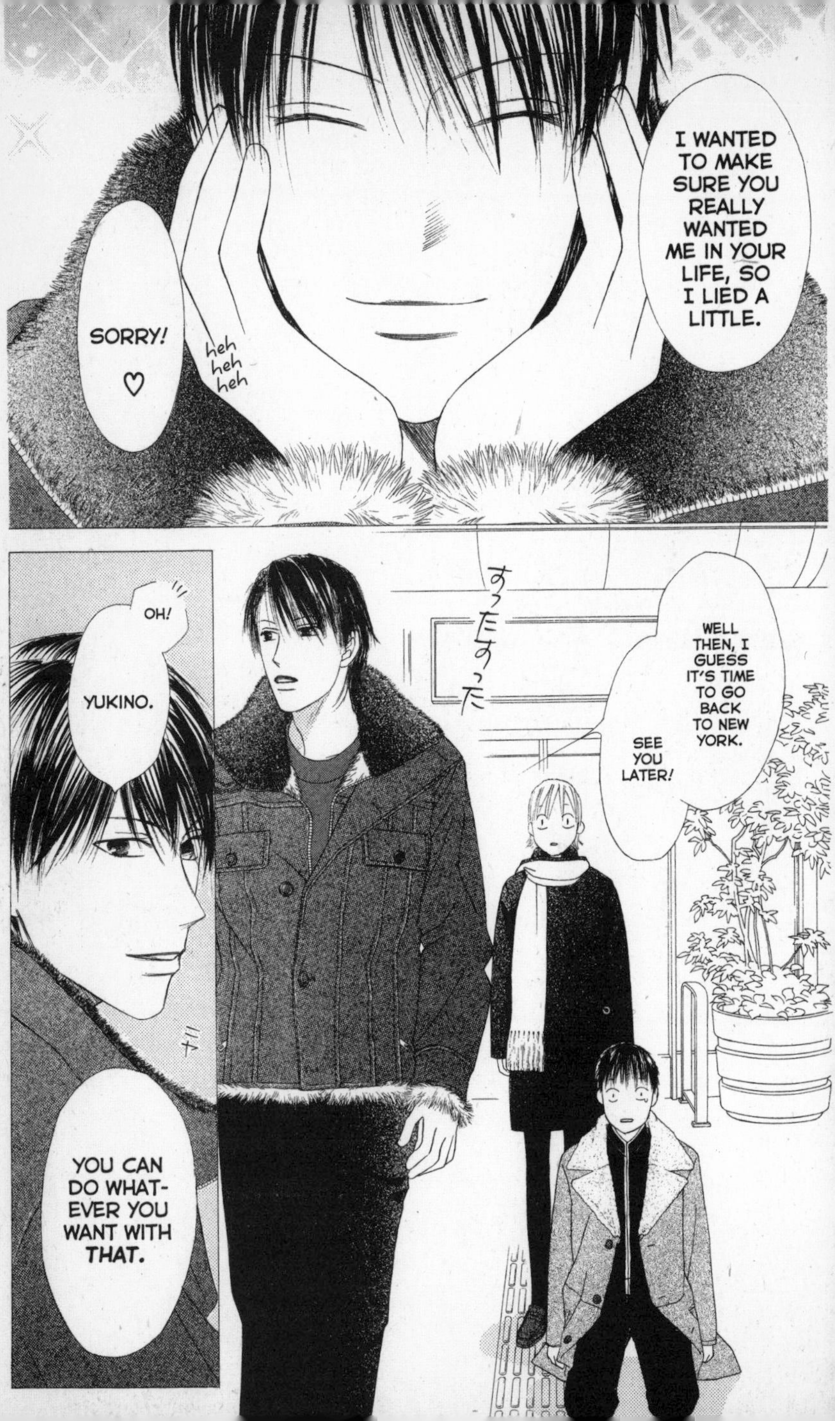

I WANTED TO MAKE SURE YOU REALLY WANTED ME IN YOUR LIFE, SO I LIED A LITTLE.
heh heh heh
SORRY! ♡
WELL THEN, I GUESS IT'S TIME TO GO BACK TO NEW YORK.
SEE YOU LATER!
すったすった
OH!
YUKINO.
ニヤ
YOU CAN DO WHAT-EVER YOU WANT WITH THAT.

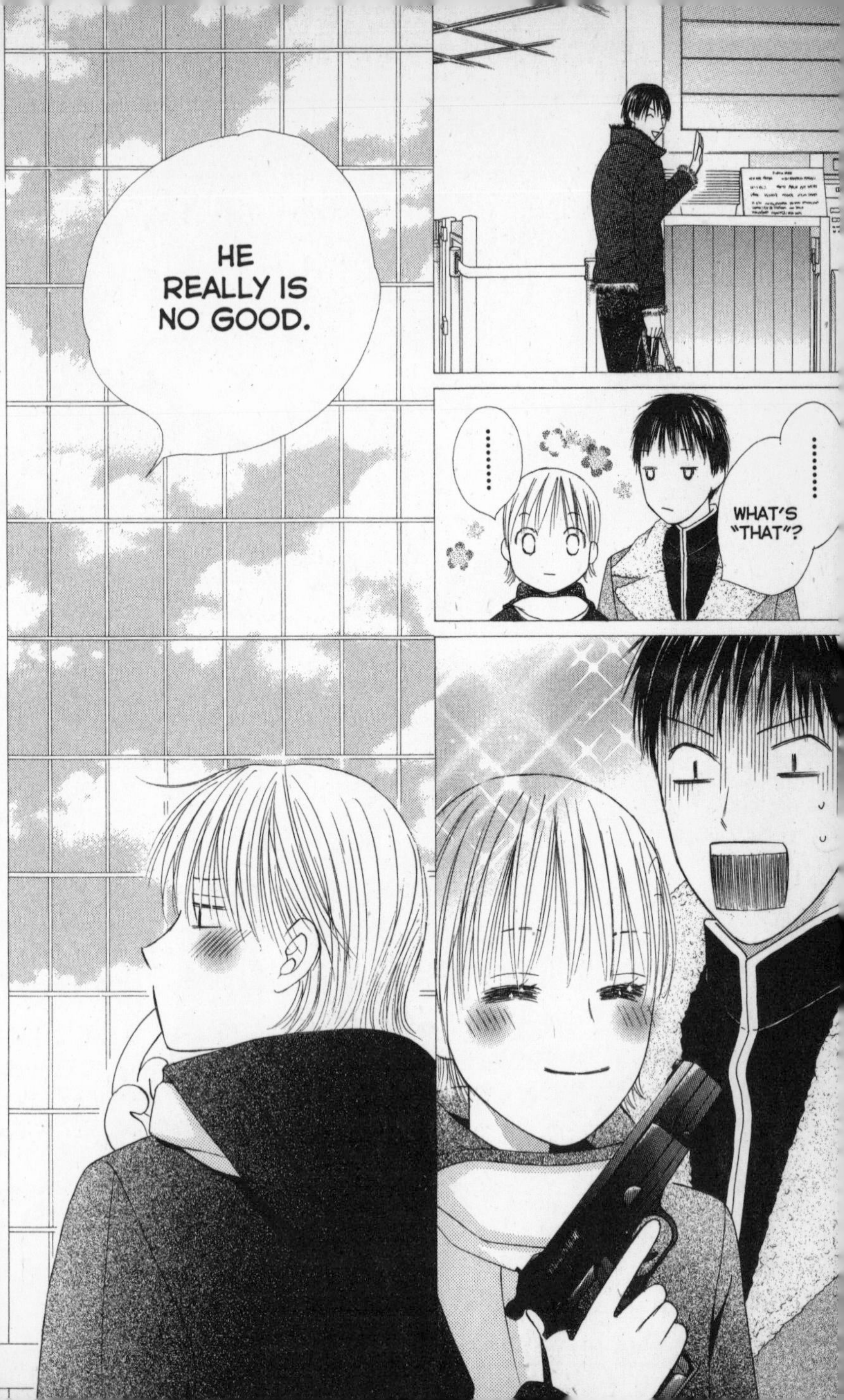
....
WHAT'S "THAT"?
....
HE REALLY IS NO GOOD.

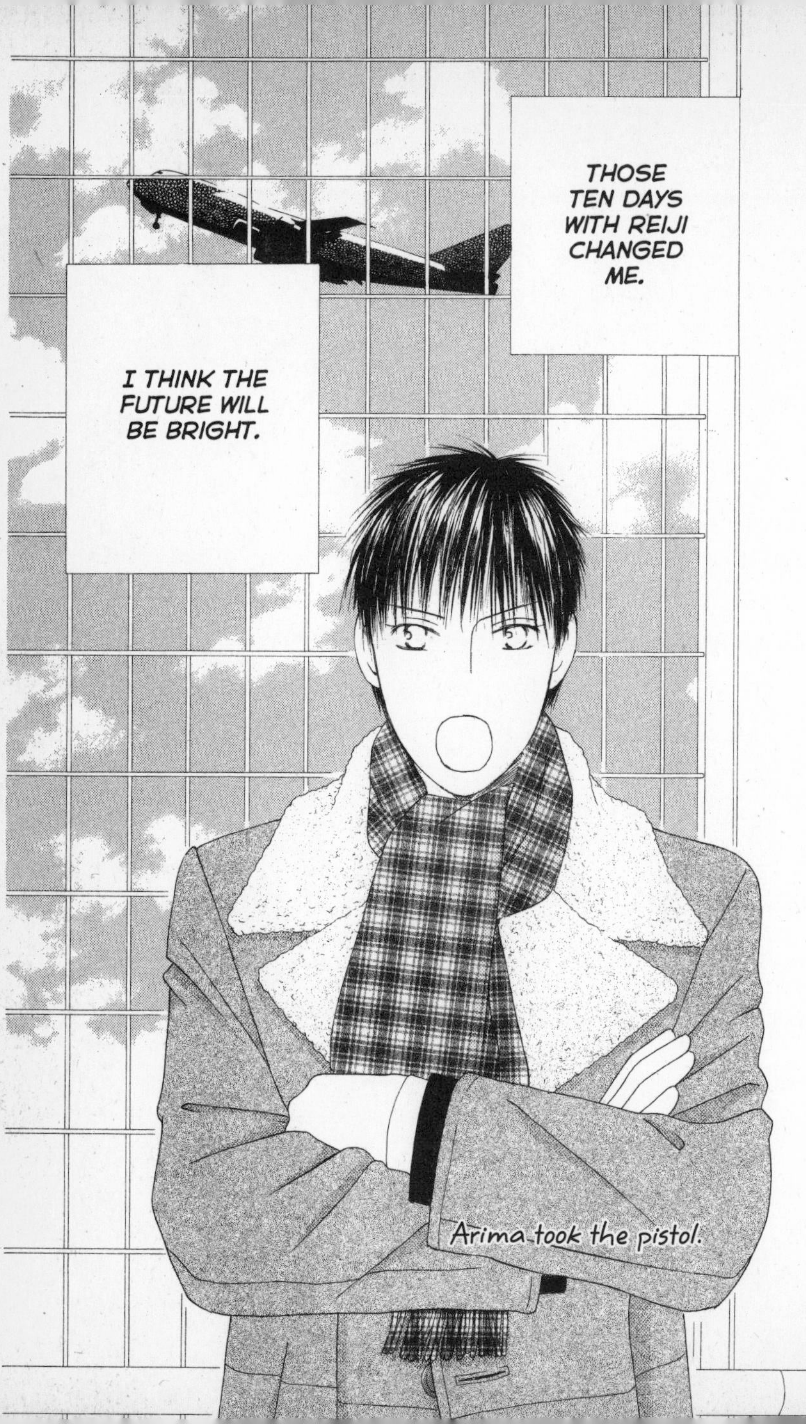
THOSE TEN DAYS WITH REIJI CHANGED ME.
I THINK THE FUTURE WILL BE BRIGHT.
Arima took the pistol.

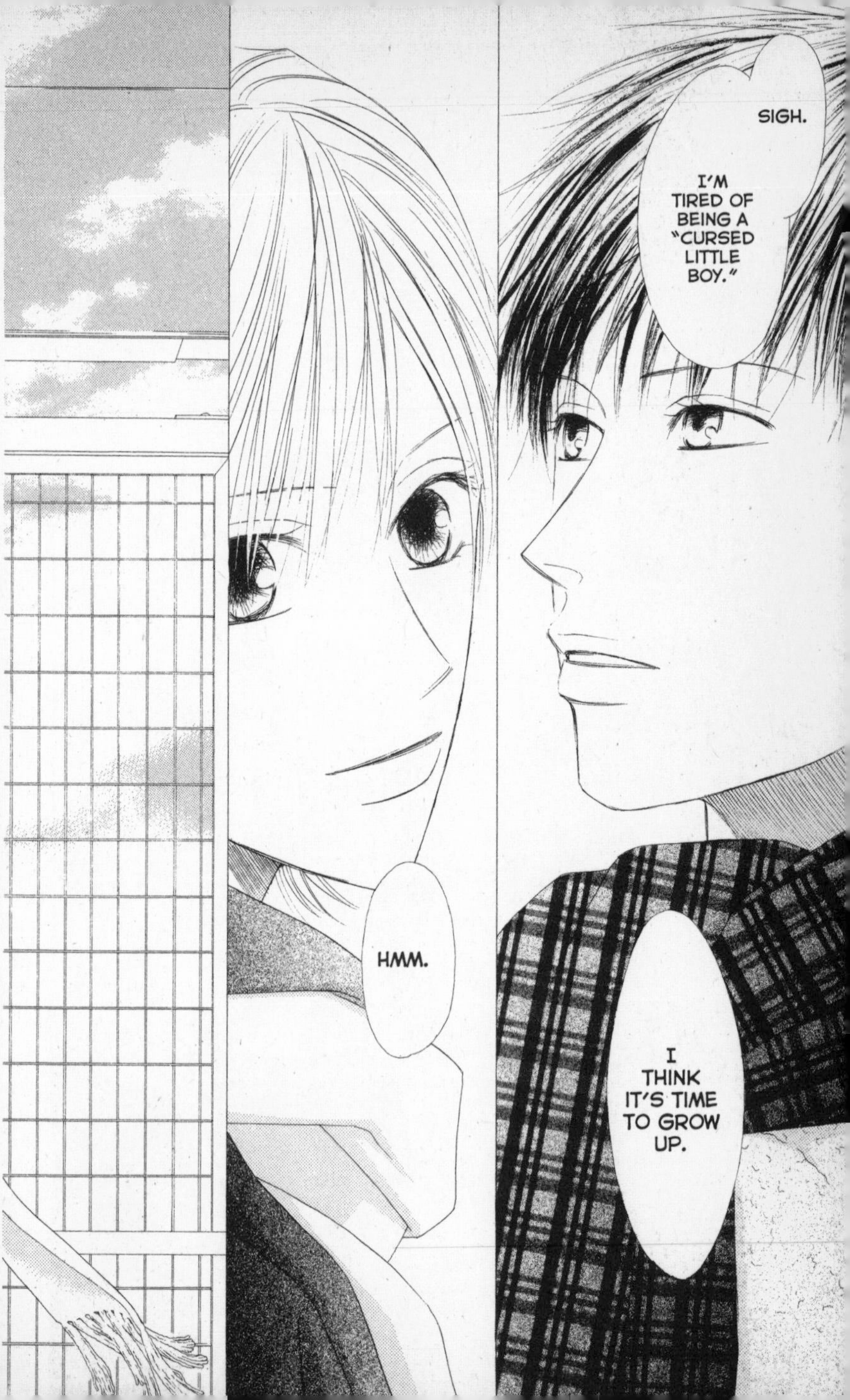
SIGH.
I'M TIRED OF BEING A "CURSED LITTLE BOY."
I THINK IT'S TIME TO GROW UP.
HMM.

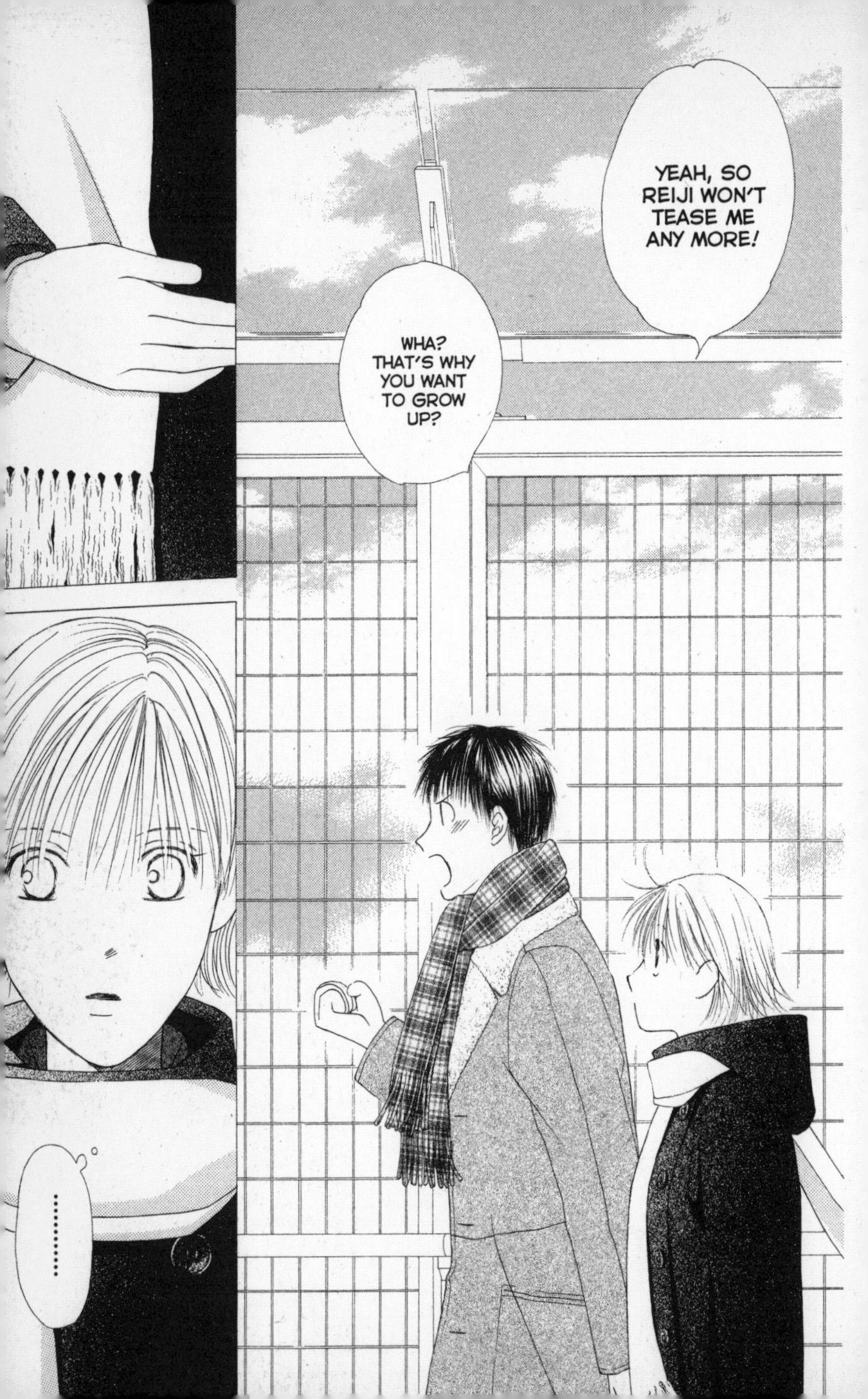
YEAH, SO REIJI WON'T TEASE ME ANY MORE!
WHA? THAT'S WHY YOU WANT TO GROW UP?
....

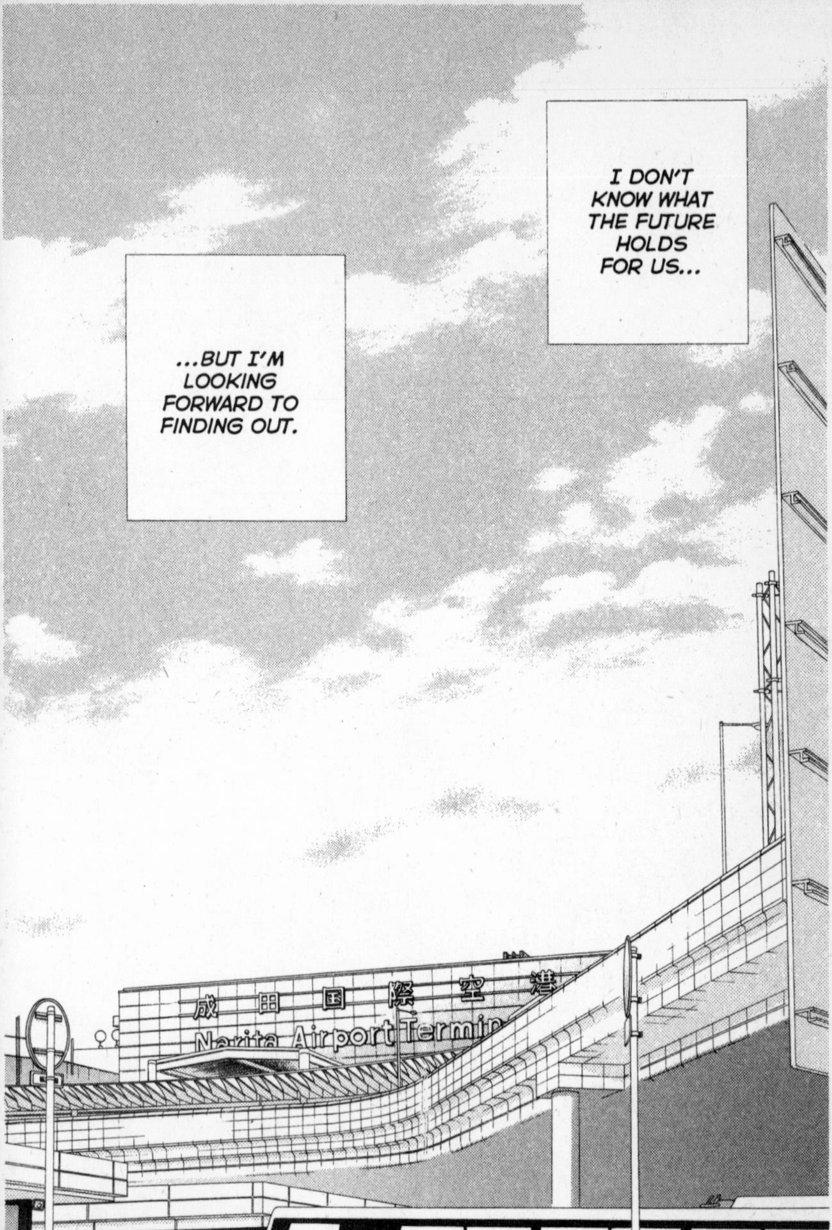
I DON'T KNOW WHAT THE FUTURE HOLDS FOR US...
...BUT I'M LOOKING FORWARD TO FINDING OUT.
成田国際空港
Narita Airport Termin

ACT 95 ★ THE END OF THE JOURNEY / END

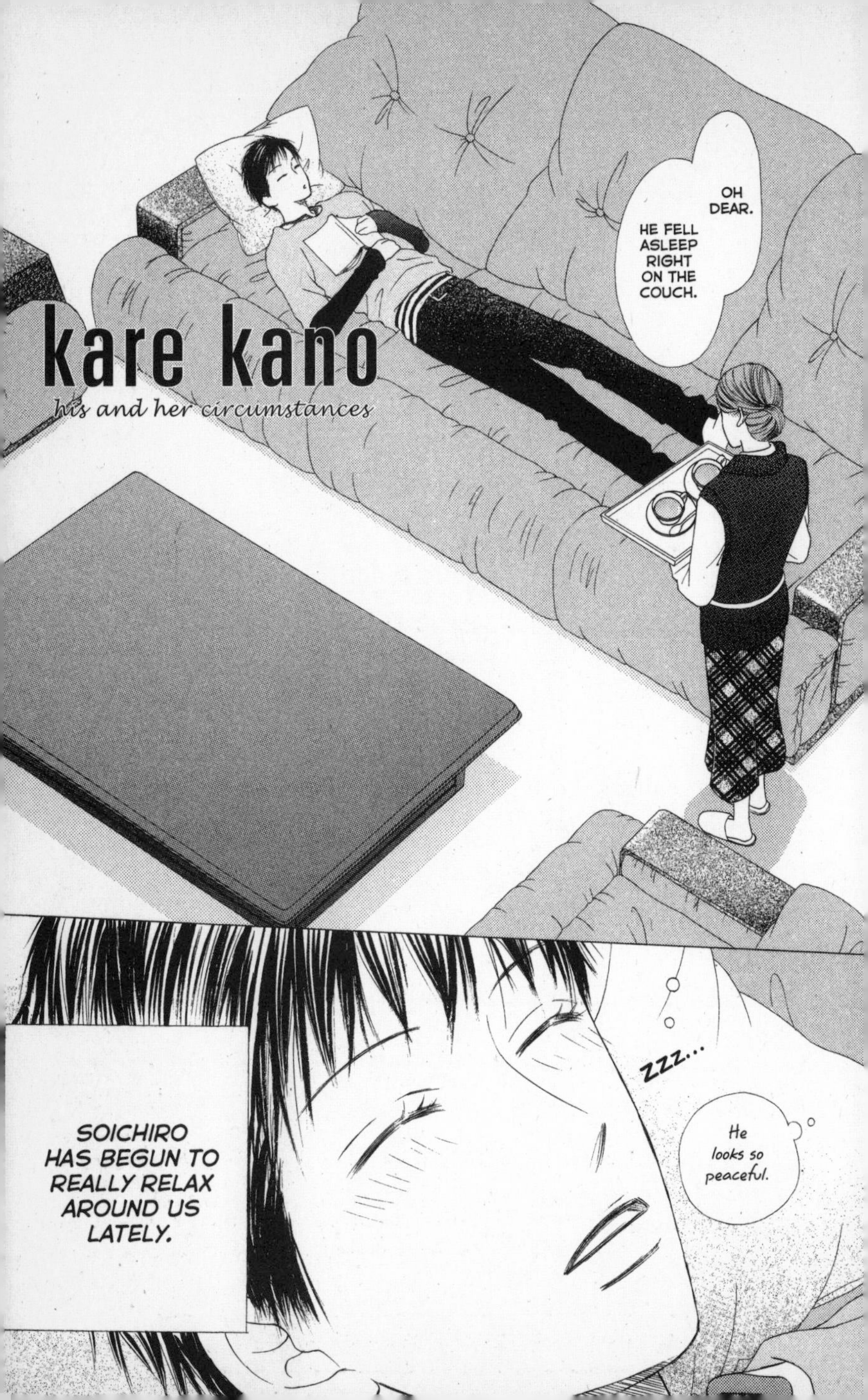
kare kano
his and her circumstances
OH DEAR.
HE FELL ASLEEP RIGHT ON THE COUCH.
ZZZ...
He looks so peaceful.
SOICHIRO HAS BEGUN TO REALLY RELAX AROUND US LATELY.

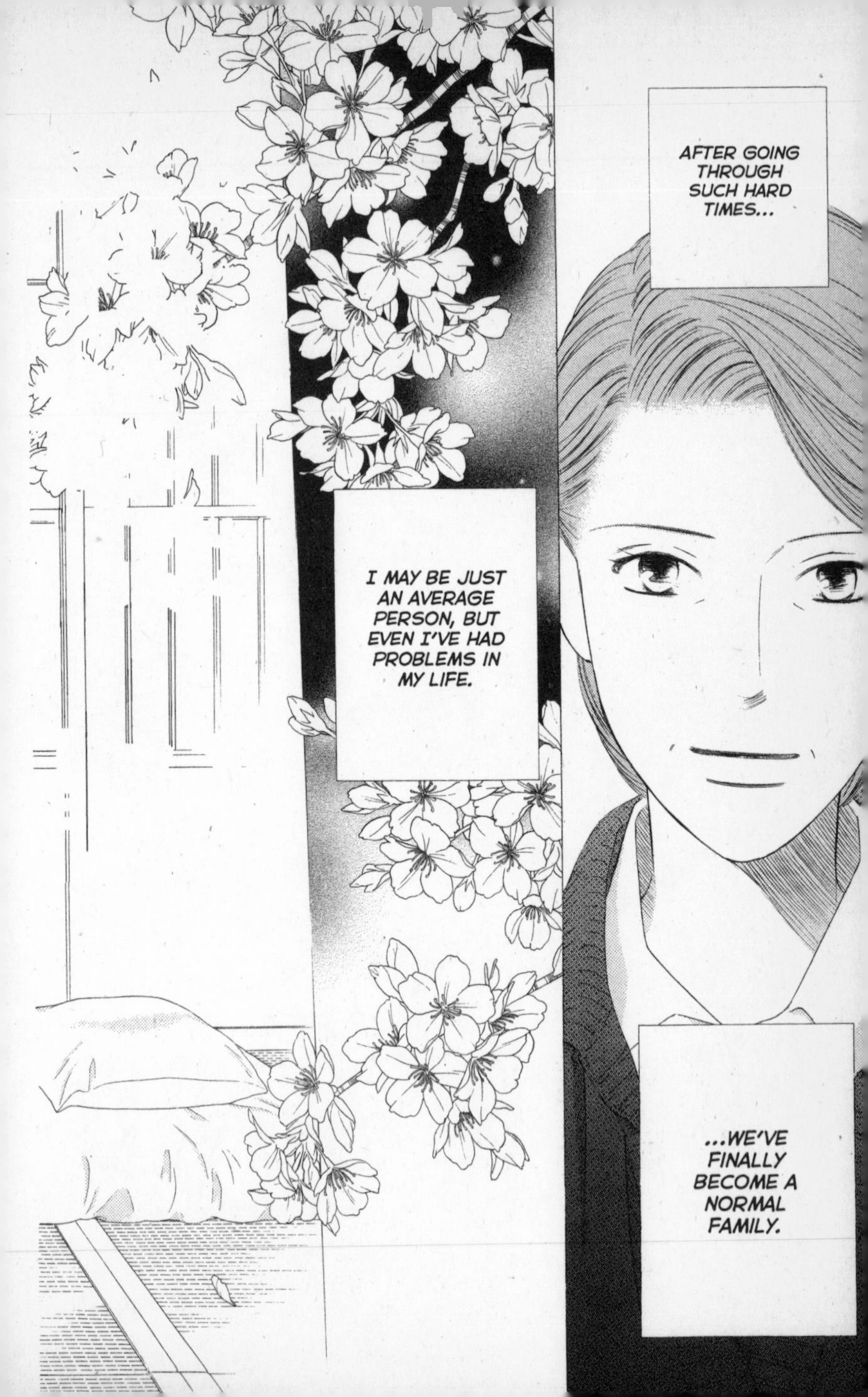
AFTER GOING THROUGH SUCH HARD TIMES...
...WE'VE FINALLY BECOME A NORMAL FAMILY.
I MAY BE JUST AN AVERAGE PERSON, BUT EVEN I'VE HAD PROBLEMS IN MY LIFE.

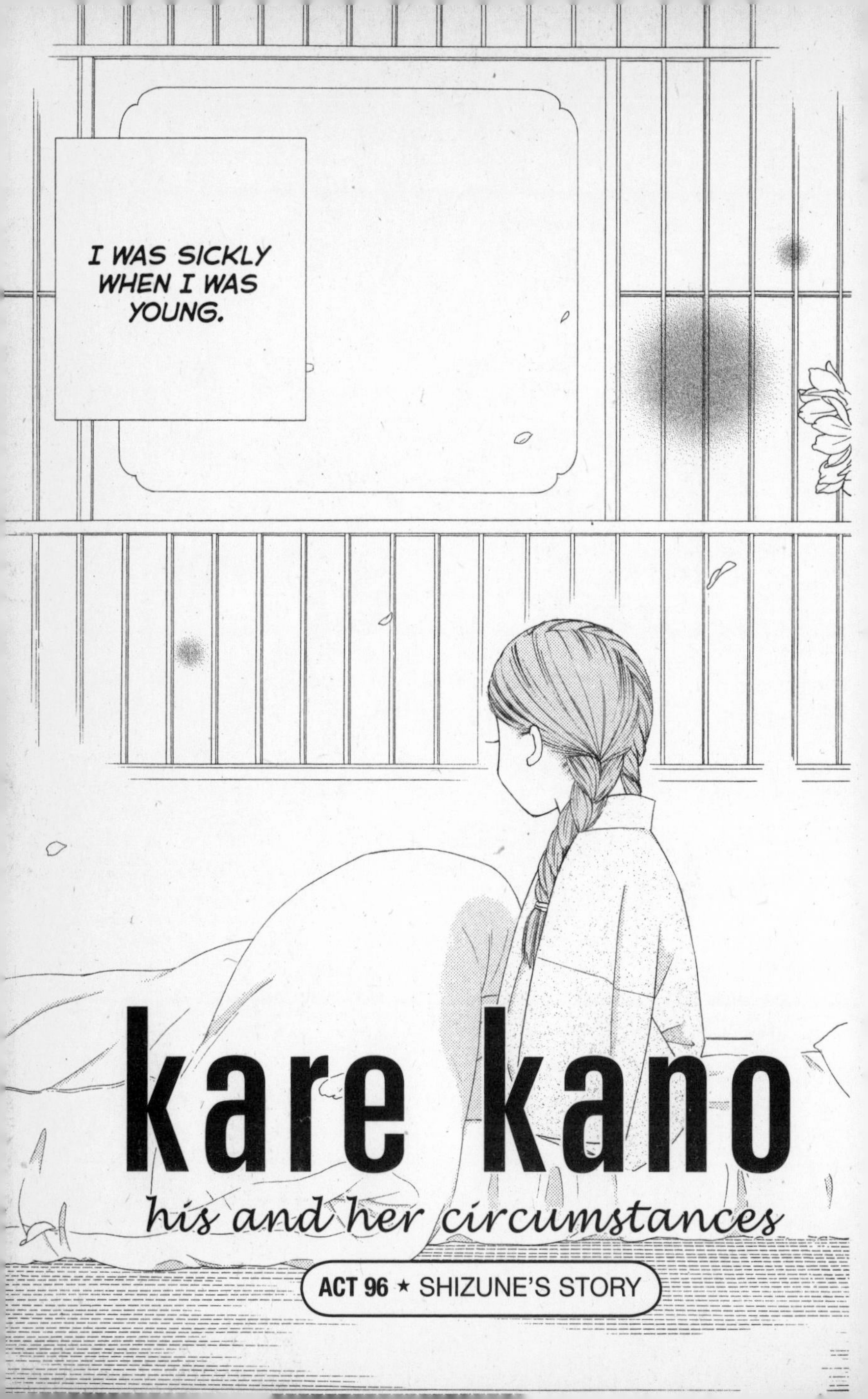
I WAS SICKLY WHEN I WAS YOUNG.
kare kano
his and her circumstances
ACT 96 ★ SHIZUNE'S STORY

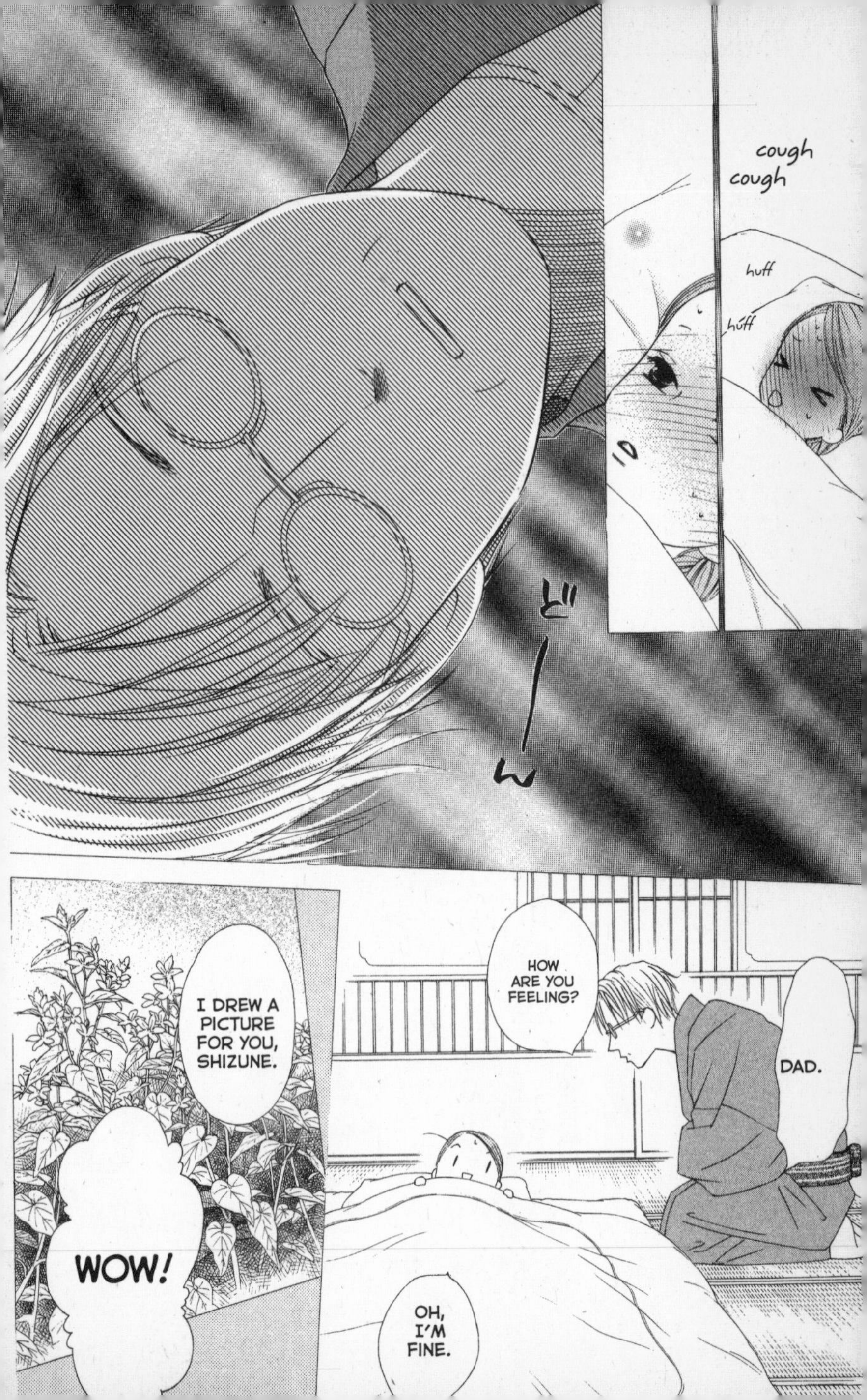
cough
cough
huff
huff
どーん
DAD.
HOW ARE YOU FEELING?
OH, I'M FINE.
I DREW A PICTURE FOR YOU, SHIZUNE.
WOW!

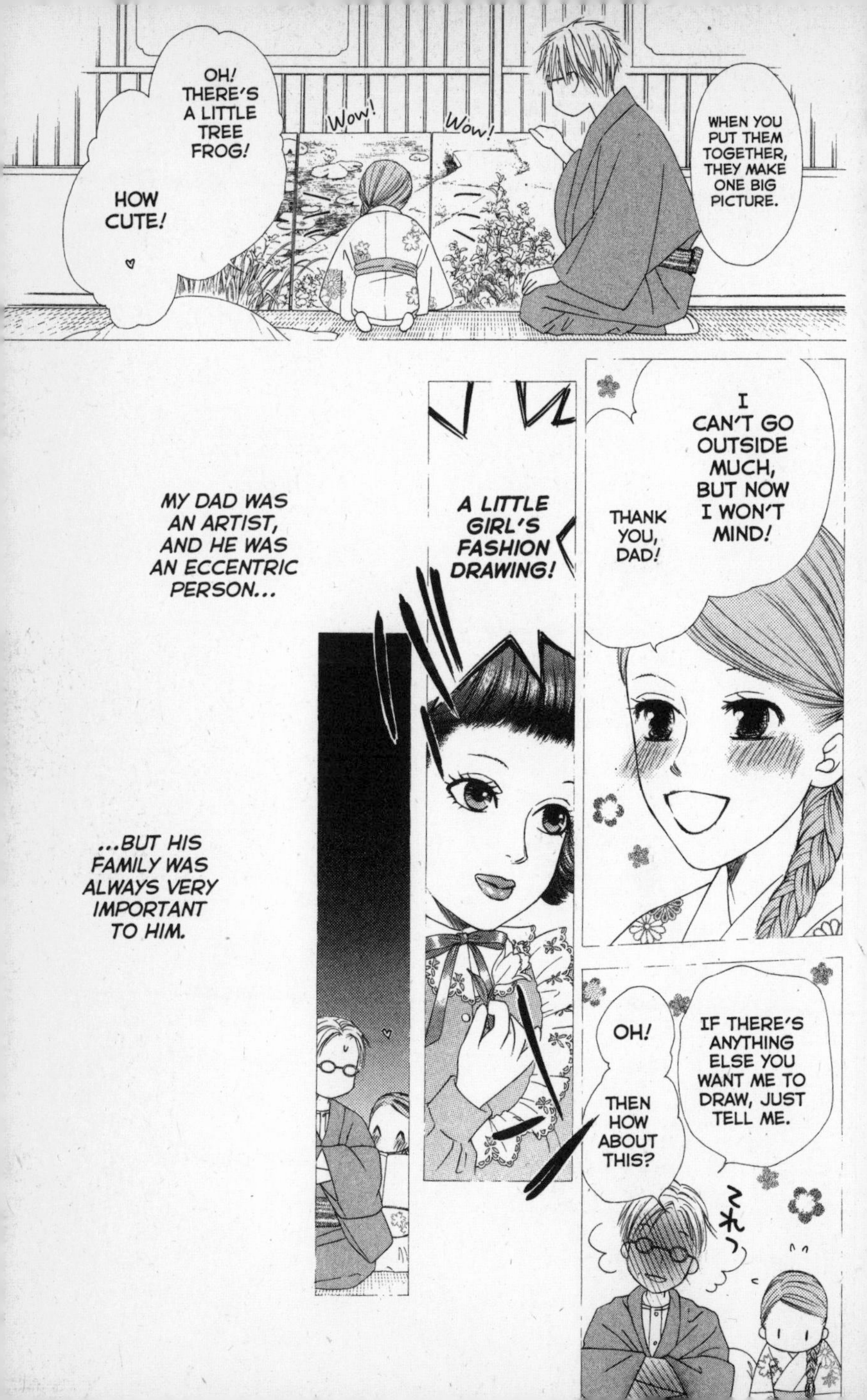
WHEN YOU PUT THEM TOGETHER, THEY MAKE ONE BIG PICTURE.
Wow!
Wow!
OH! THERE'S A LITTLE TREE FROG!
HOW CUTE!
I CAN'T GO OUTSIDE MUCH, BUT NOW I WON'T MIND!
THANK YOU, DAD!
IF THERE'S ANYTHING ELSE YOU WANT ME TO DRAW, JUST TELL ME.
OH!
THEN HOW ABOUT THIS?
これっ
A LITTLE GIRL'S FASHION DRAWING!
MY DAD WAS AN ARTIST, AND HE WAS AN ECCENTRIC PERSON...
...BUT HIS FAMILY WAS ALWAYS VERY IMPORTANT TO HIM.

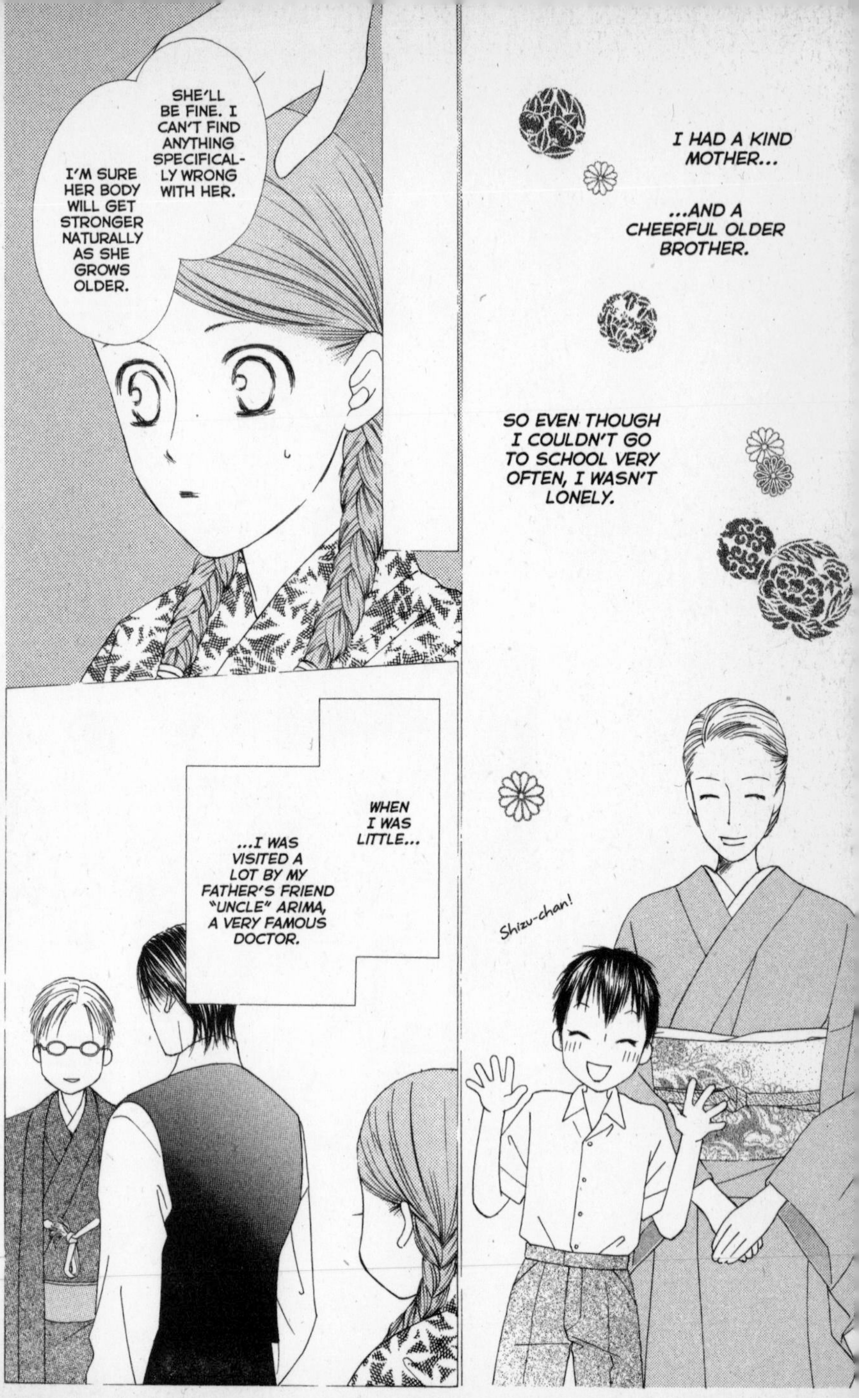
I HAD A KIND MOTHER...
...AND A CHEERFUL OLDER BROTHER.
SO EVEN THOUGH I COULDN'T GO TO SCHOOL VERY OFTEN, I WASN'T LONELY.
Shizu-chan!
SHE'LL BE FINE. I CAN'T FIND ANYTHING SPECIFICAL-LY WRONG WITH HER.
I'M SURE HER BODY WILL GET STRONGER NATURALLY AS SHE GROWS OLDER.
WHEN I WAS LITTLE...
...I WAS VISITED A LOT BY MY FATHER'S FRIEND "UNCLE" ARIMA, A VERY FAMOUS DOCTOR.

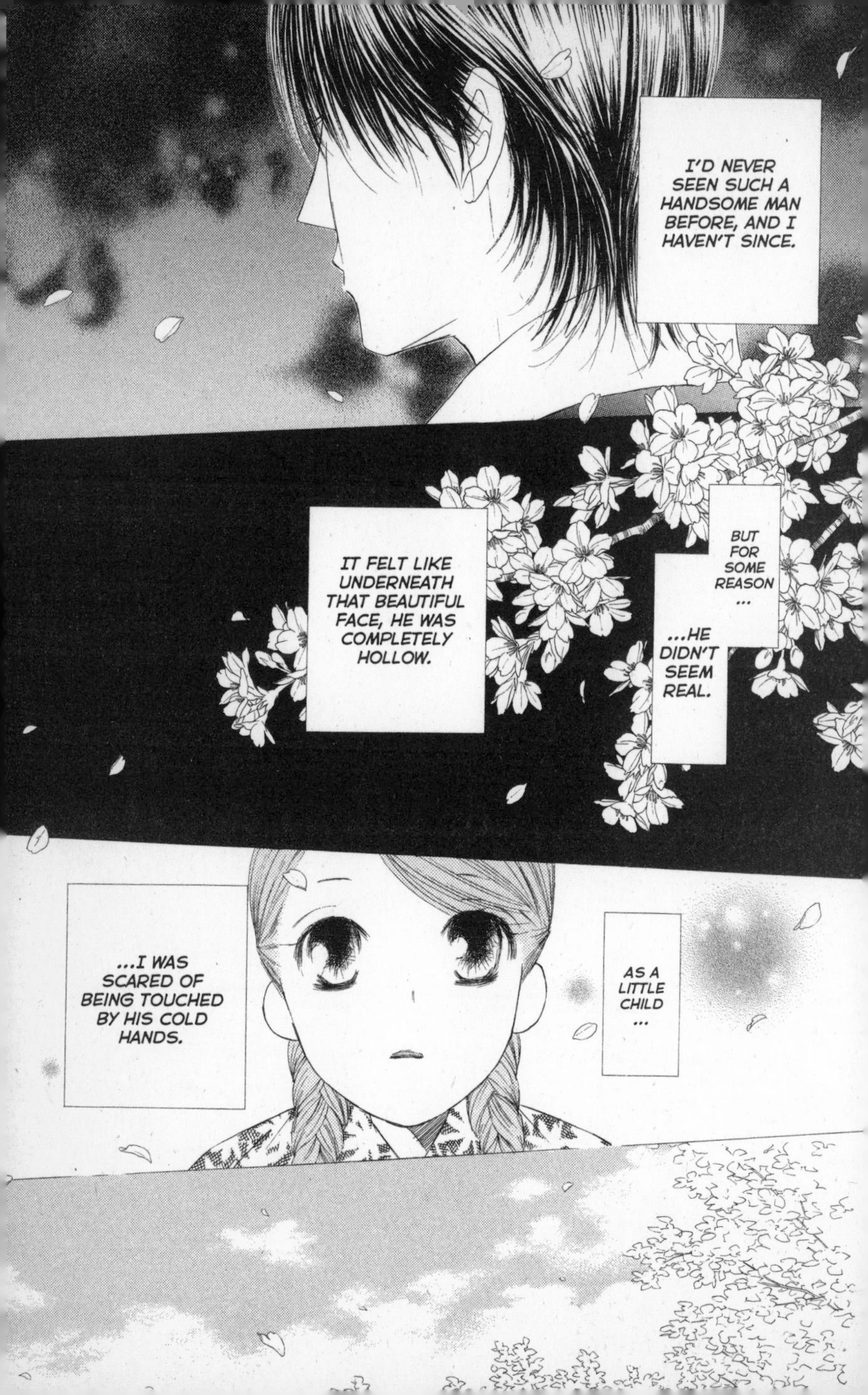
I'D NEVER SEEN SUCH A HANDSOME MAN BEFORE, AND I HAVEN'T SINCE.
BUT FOR SOME REASON ...
...HE DIDN'T SEEM REAL.
IT FELT LIKE UNDERNEATH THAT BEAUTIFUL FACE, HE WAS COMPLETELY HOLLOW.
AS A LITTLE CHILD ...
...I WAS SCARED OF BEING TOUCHED BY HIS COLD HANDS.

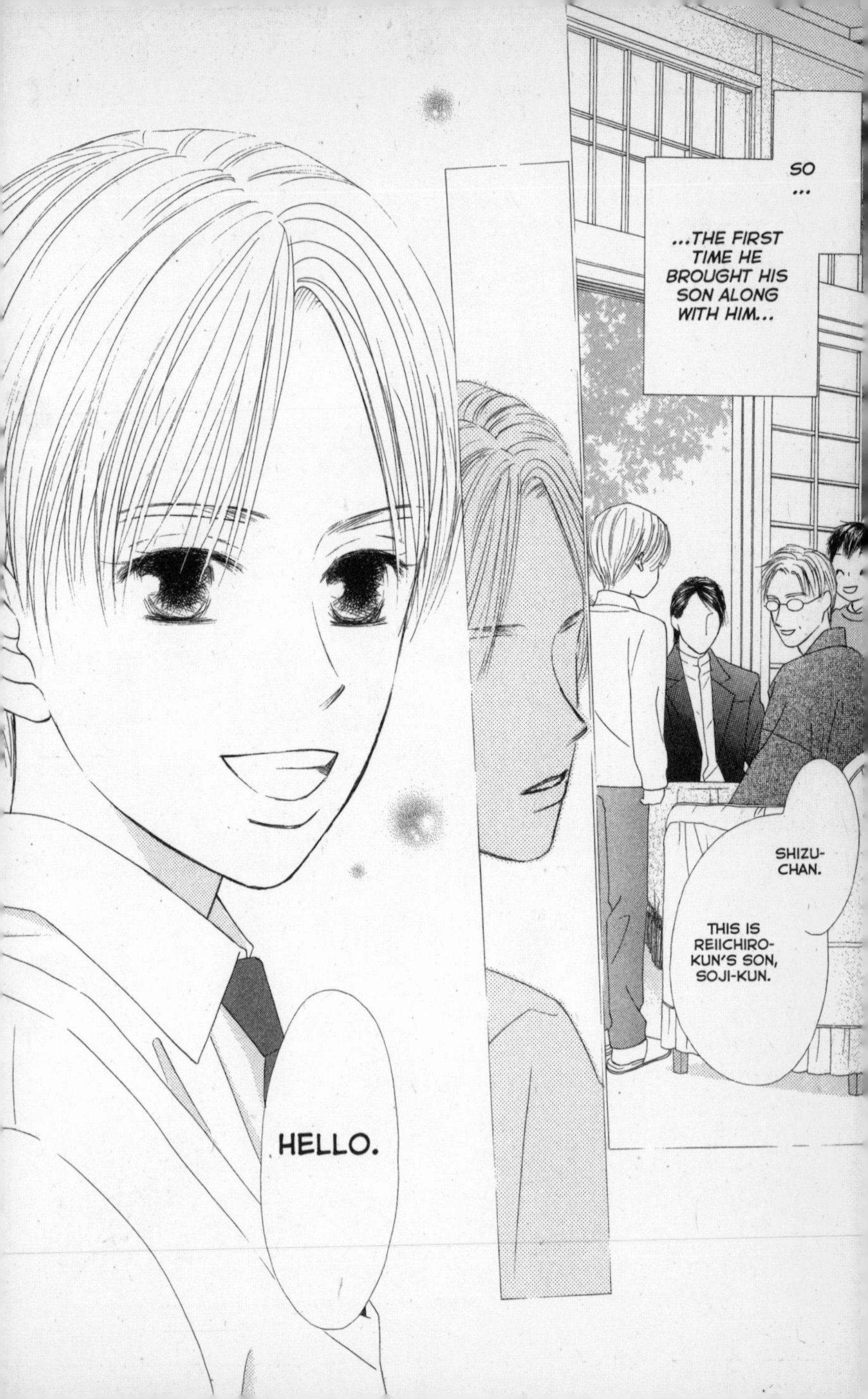
SO ...
...THE FIRST TIME HE BROUGHT HIS SON ALONG WITH HIM...
SHIZU-CHAN.
THIS IS REIICHIRO-KUN'S SON, SOJI-KUN.
HELLO.

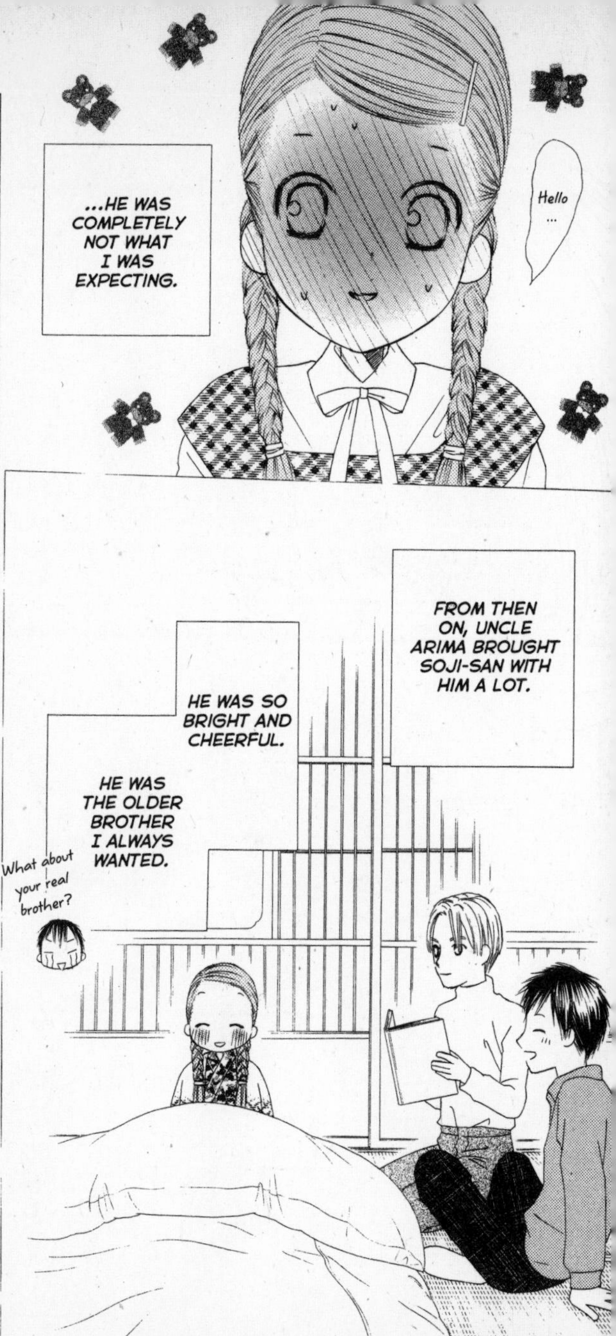
Hello ...
...HE WAS COMPLETELY NOT WHAT I WAS EXPECTING.
FROM THEN ON, UNCLE ARIMA BROUGHT SOJI-SAN WITH HIM A LOT.
HE WAS SO BRIGHT AND CHEERFUL.
HE WAS THE OLDER BROTHER I ALWAYS WANTED.
What about your real brother?

3

米

Rice

All I've been thinking about lately is good rice and miso soup, and I can't stop my quest on the way to Japanese food. I bought books on how to cook rice, and from now on I'm going to boil my rice with nabe. When it turns out well, it turns out REALLY WELL!! Even though it was only regular rice.

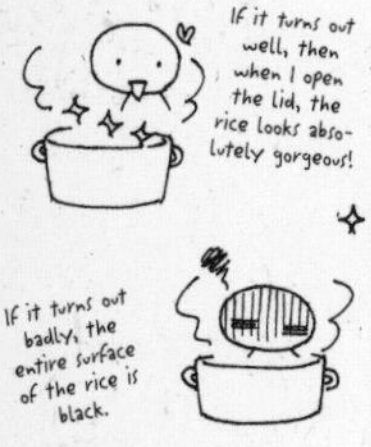
If it turns out well, then when I open the lid, the rice looks absolutely gorgeous!
If it turns out badly, the entire surface of the rice is black.

When I ate Kishimen and Nagoya-cochin in Nagoya, the soup base was so delicious, I started trying to brew it myself. Excuse me, people from Nagoya! Please teach me how you brew your soup base!

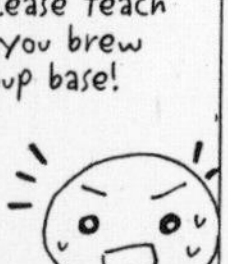

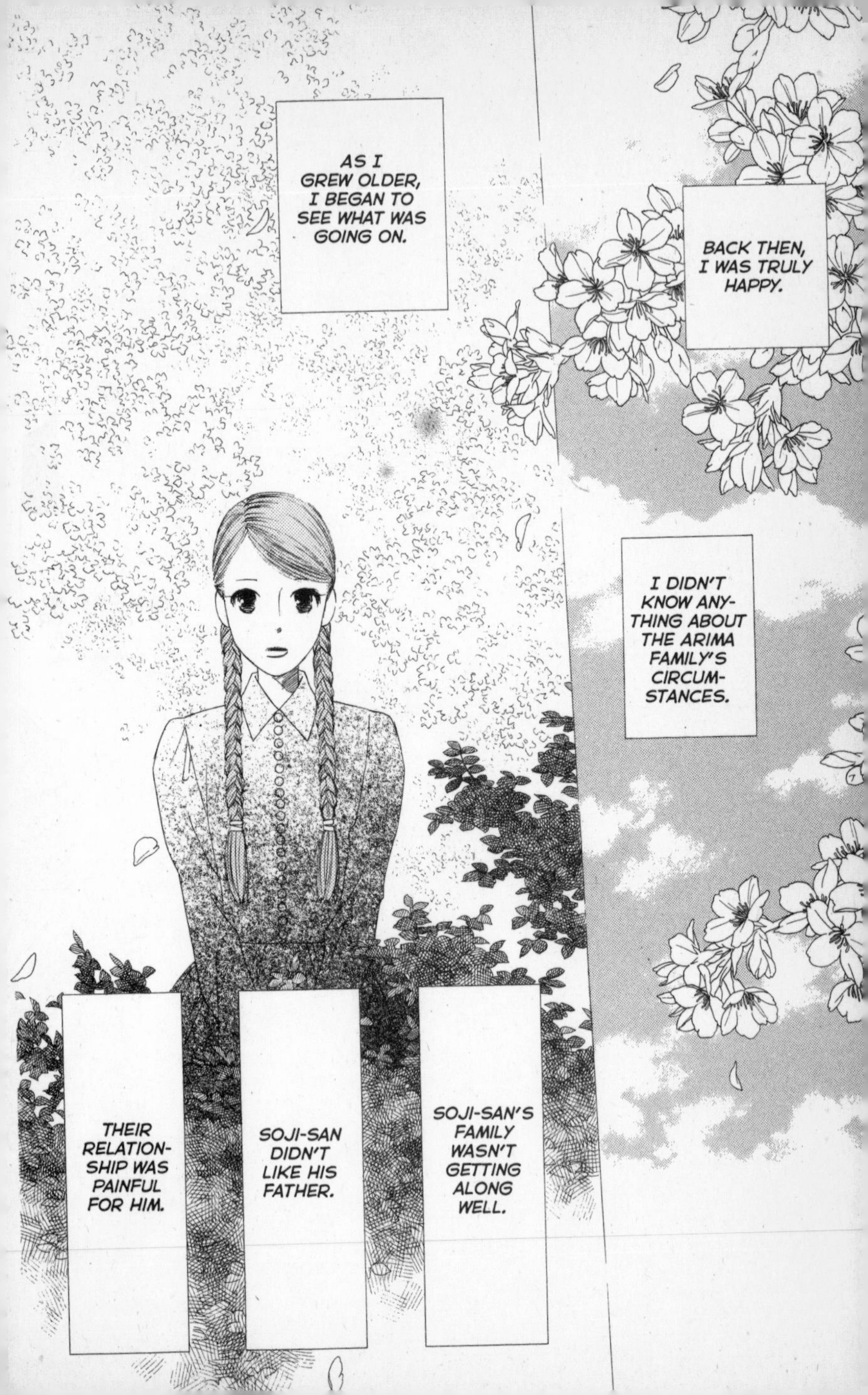
BACK THEN, I WAS TRULY HAPPY.
I DIDN'T KNOW ANY-THING ABOUT THE ARIMA FAMILY'S CIRCUM-STANCES.
AS I GREW OLDER, I BEGAN TO SEE WHAT WAS GOING ON.
SOJI-SAN'S FAMILY WASN'T GETTING ALONG WELL.
SOJI-SAN DIDN'T LIKE HIS FATHER.
THEIR RELATION-SHIP WAS PAINFUL FOR HIM.

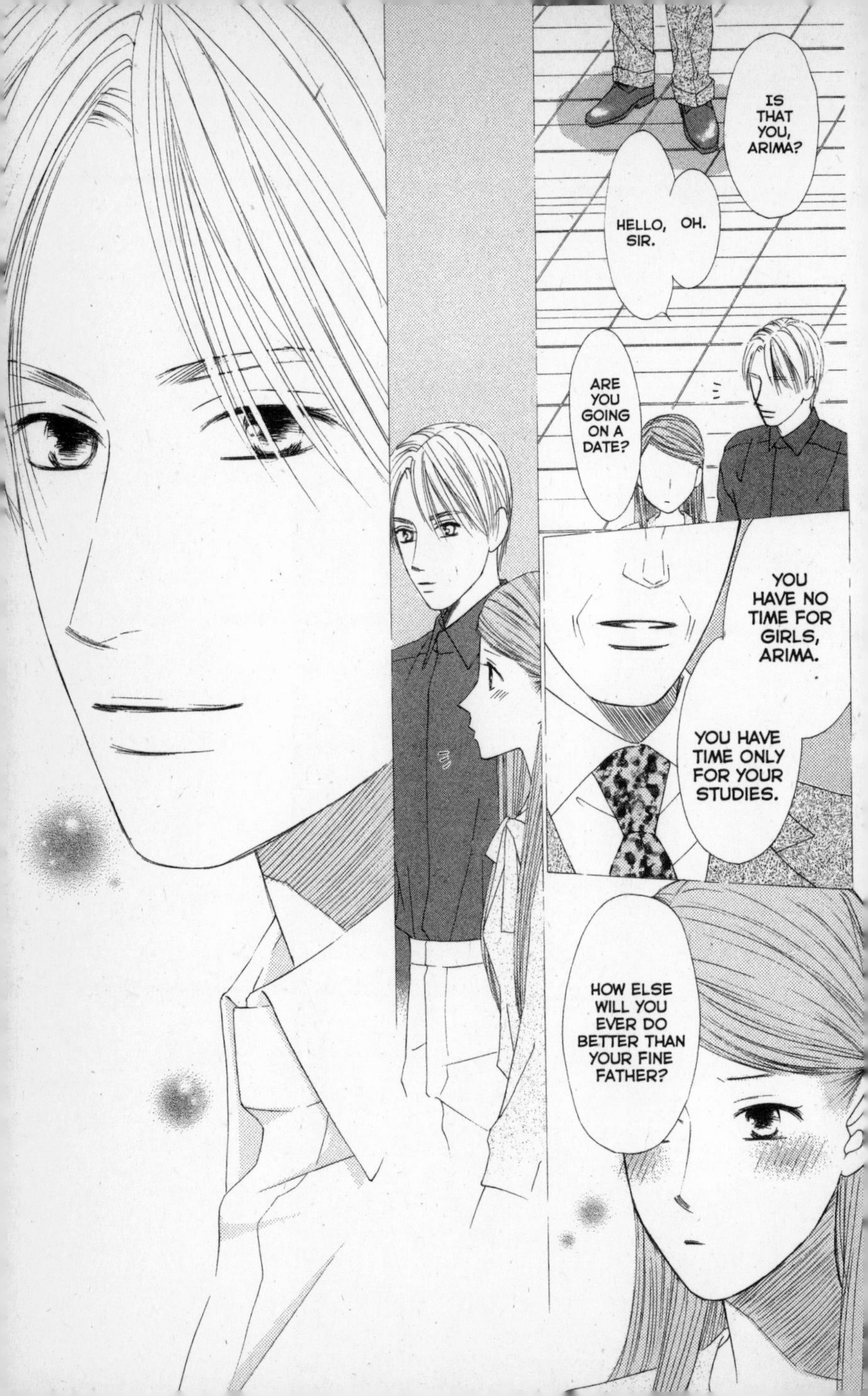
IS THAT YOU, ARIMA?
OH.
HELLO, SIR.
ARE YOU GOING ON A DATE?
YOU HAVE NO TIME FOR GIRLS, ARIMA.
YOU HAVE TIME ONLY FOR YOUR STUDIES.
HOW ELSE WILL YOU EVER DO BETTER THAN YOUR FINE FATHER?

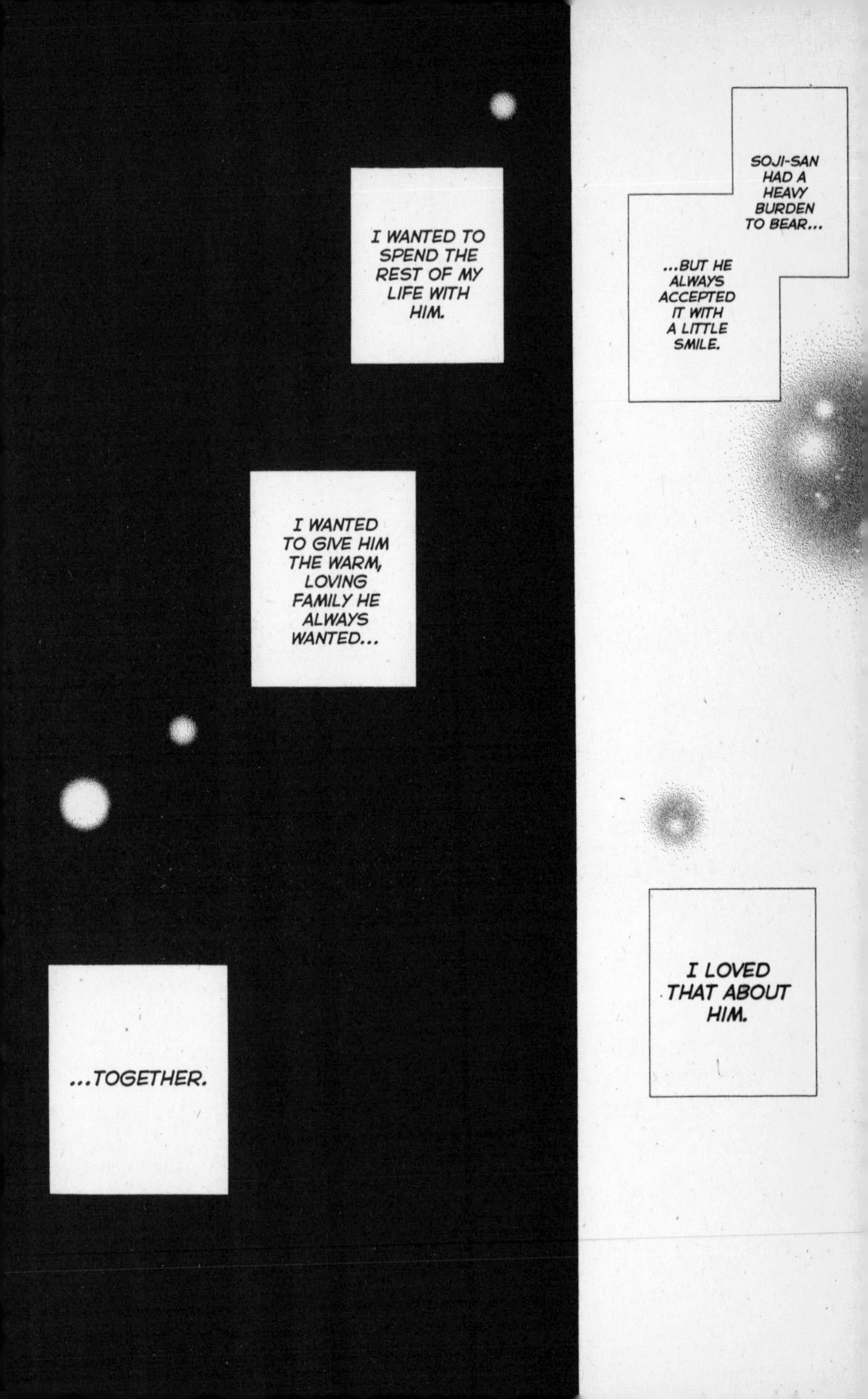
SOJI-SAN HAD A HEAVY BURDEN TO BEAR...
...BUT HE ALWAYS ACCEPTED IT WITH A LITTLE SMILE.
I LOVED THAT ABOUT HIM.
I WANTED TO SPEND THE REST OF MY LIFE WITH HIM.
I WANTED TO GIVE HIM THE WARM, LOVING FAMILY HE ALWAYS WANTED...
...TOGETHER.

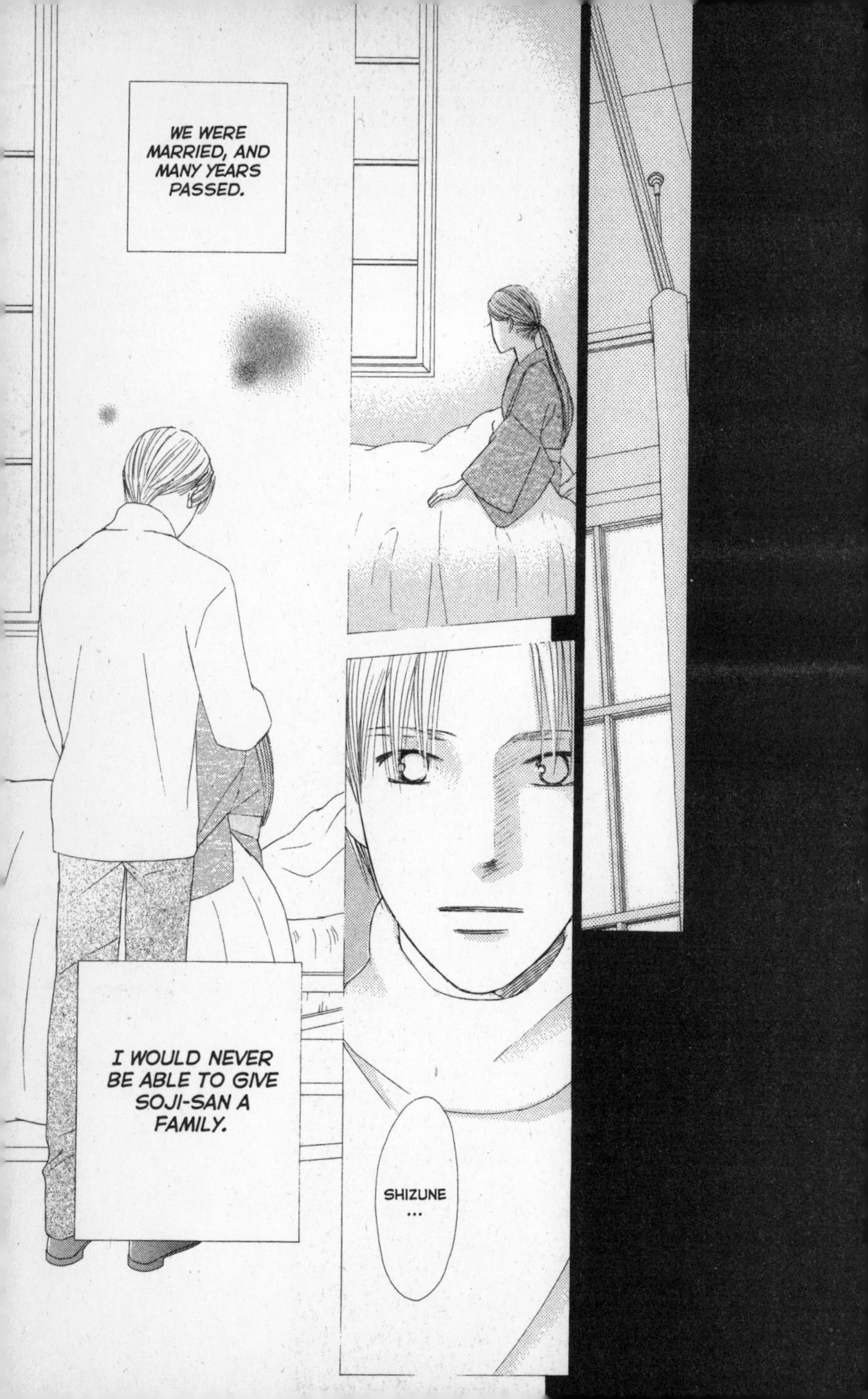
SHIZUNE ...
WE WERE MARRIED, AND MANY YEARS PASSED.
I WOULD NEVER BE ABLE TO GIVE SOJI-SAN A FAMILY.

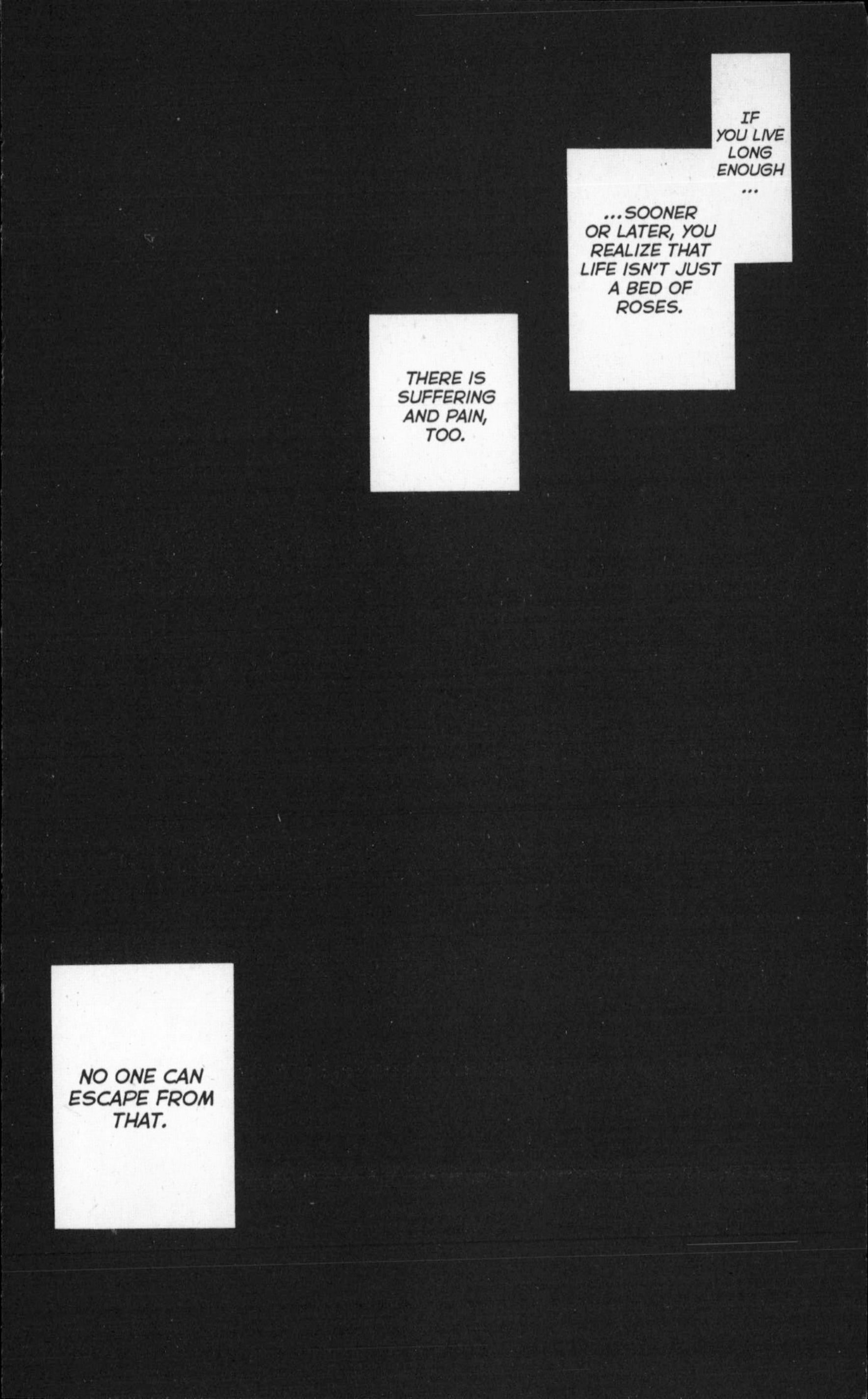

IF YOU LIVE LONG ENOUGH...
...SOONER OR LATER, YOU REALIZE THAT LIFE ISN'T JUST A BED OF ROSES.
THERE IS SUFFERING AND PAIN, TOO.
NO ONE CAN ESCAPE FROM THAT.

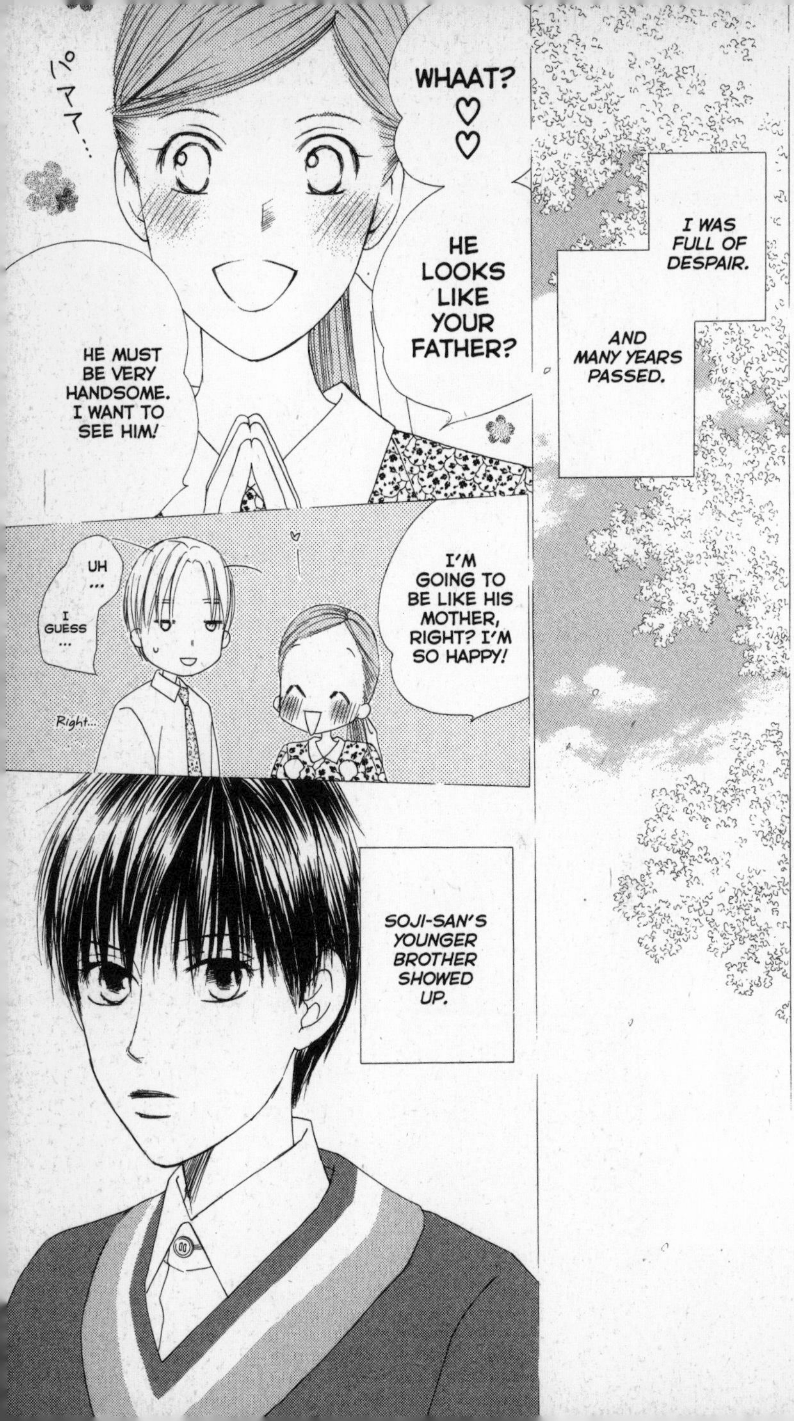

I WAS FULL OF DESPAIR.
AND MANY YEARS PASSED.
WHAAT? ♡ ♡
HE LOOKS LIKE YOUR FATHER?
HE MUST BE VERY HANDSOME. I WANT TO SEE HIM!
パァァ…
I'M GOING TO BE LIKE HIS MOTHER, RIGHT? I'M SO HAPPY!
UH ... I GUESS ...
Right...
SOJI-SAN'S YOUNGER BROTHER SHOWED UP.

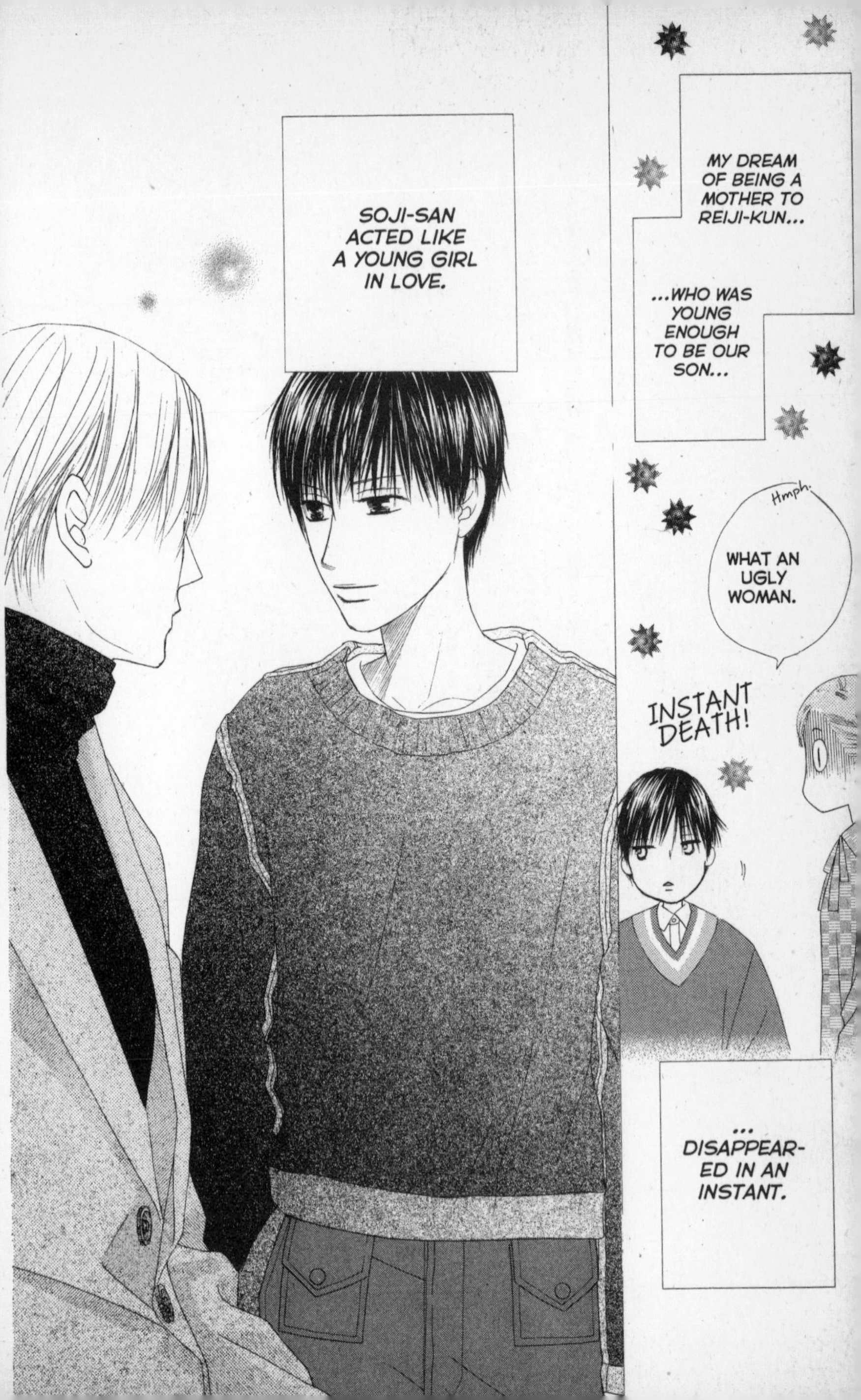
MY DREAM OF BEING A MOTHER TO REIJI-KUN...
...WHO WAS YOUNG ENOUGH TO BE OUR SON...
Hmph.
WHAT AN UGLY WOMAN.
INSTANT DEATH!
...DISAPPEARED IN AN INSTANT.
SOJI-SAN ACTED LIKE A YOUNG GIRL IN LOVE.

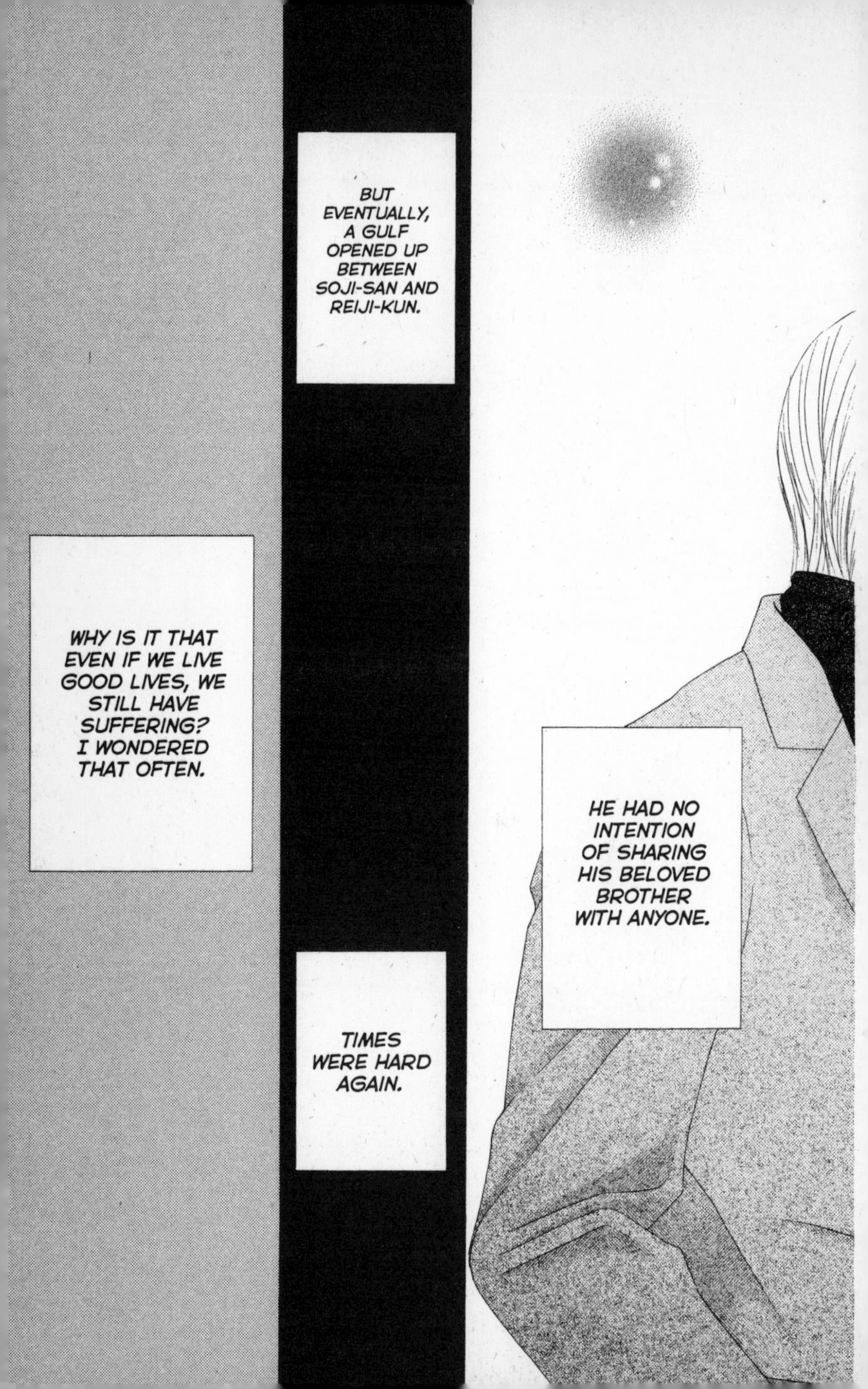
HE HAD NO INTENTION OF SHARING HIS BELOVED BROTHER WITH ANYONE.
BUT EVENTUALLY, A GULF OPENED UP BETWEEN SOJI-SAN AND REIJI-KUN.
TIMES WERE HARD AGAIN.
WHY IS IT THAT EVEN IF WE LIVE GOOD LIVES, WE STILL HAVE SUFFERING? I WONDERED THAT OFTEN.

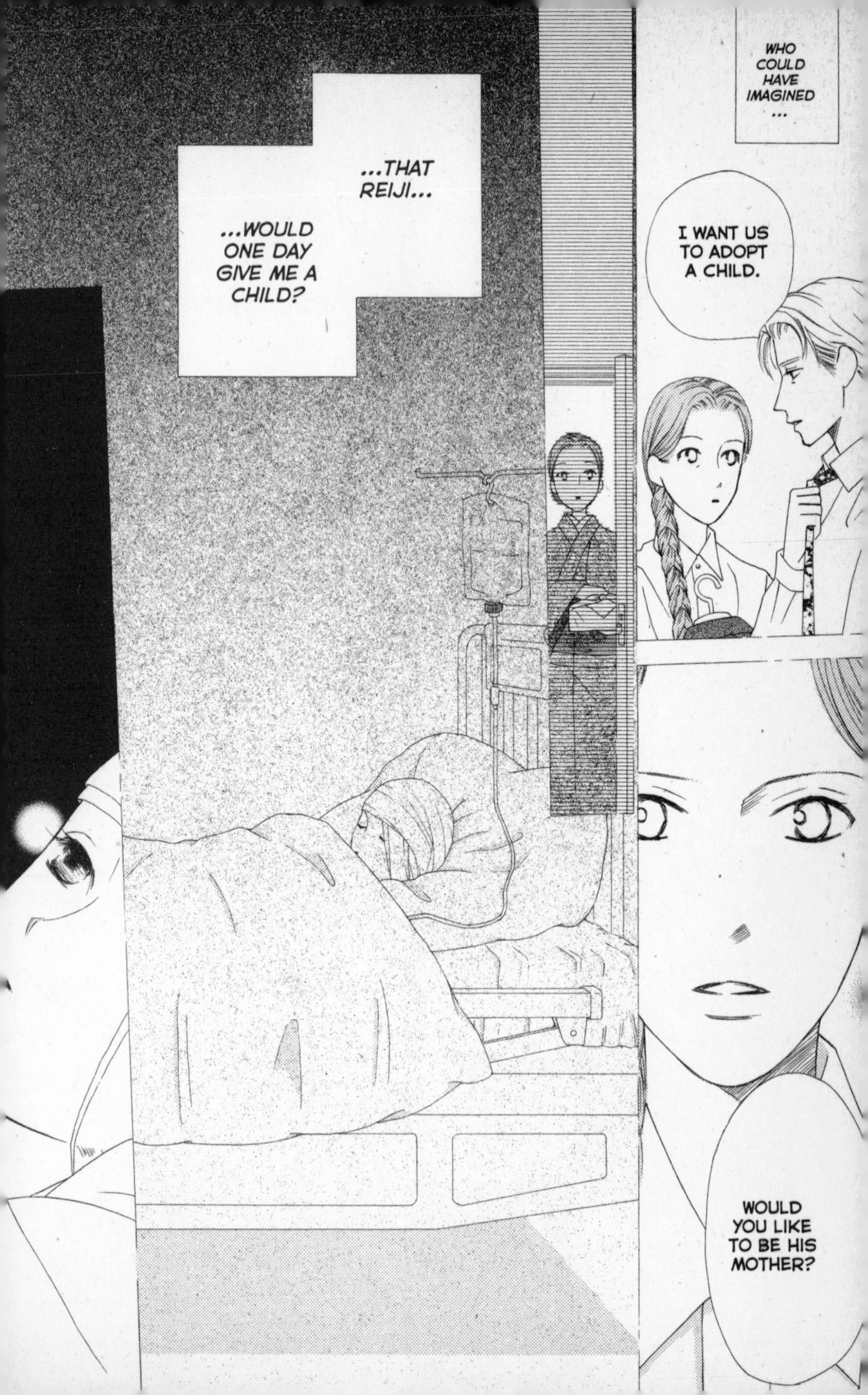
WHO COULD HAVE IMAGINED ...
I WANT US TO ADOPT A CHILD.
WOULD YOU LIKE TO BE HIS MOTHER?
...THAT REIJI...
...WOULD ONE DAY GIVE ME A CHILD?

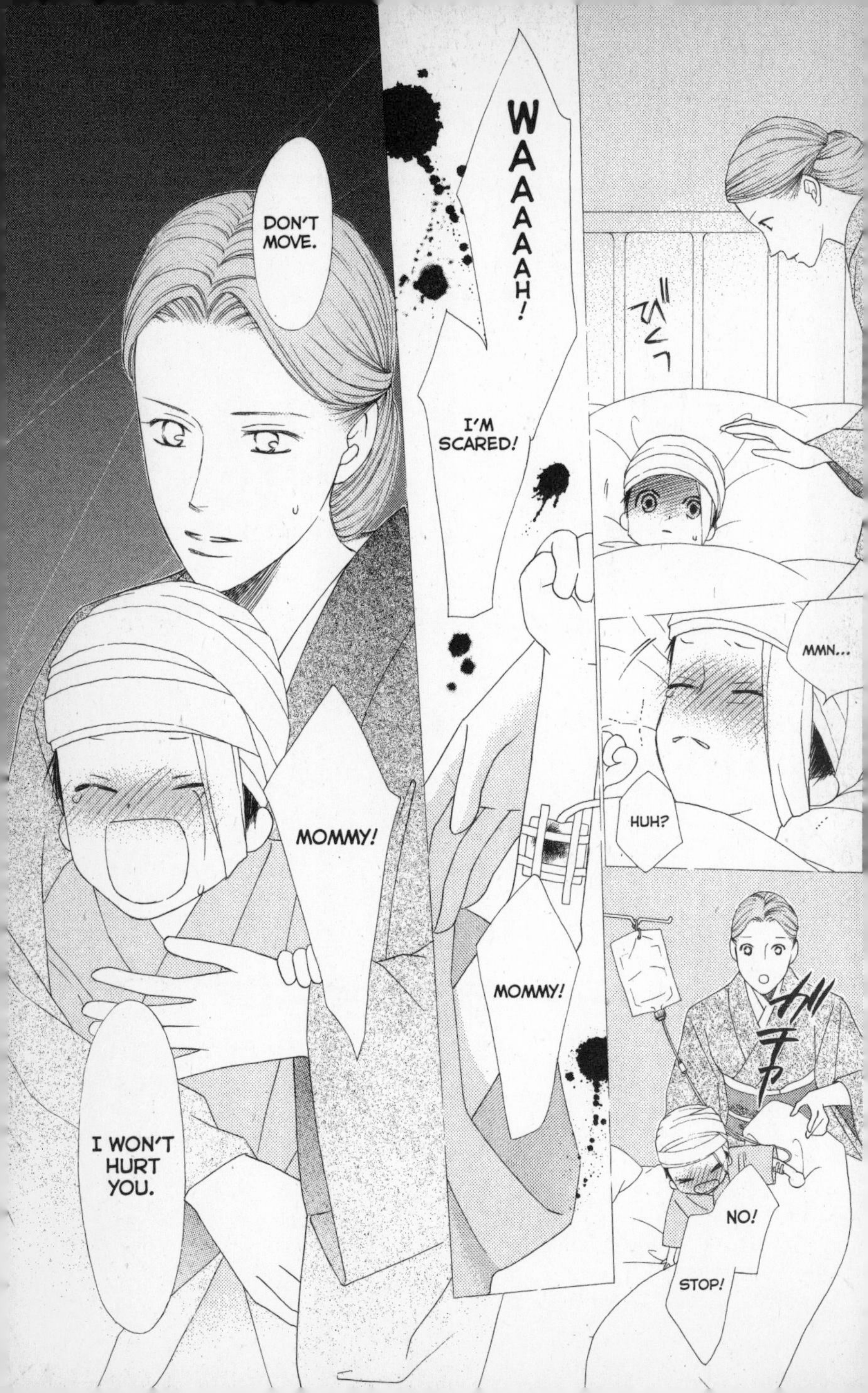

びくっ
MMN...
HUH?
ガチャ
NO!
STOP!
WAAAAAAH!
I'M SCARED!
MOMMY!
DON'T MOVE.
MOMMY!
I WON'T HURT YOU.

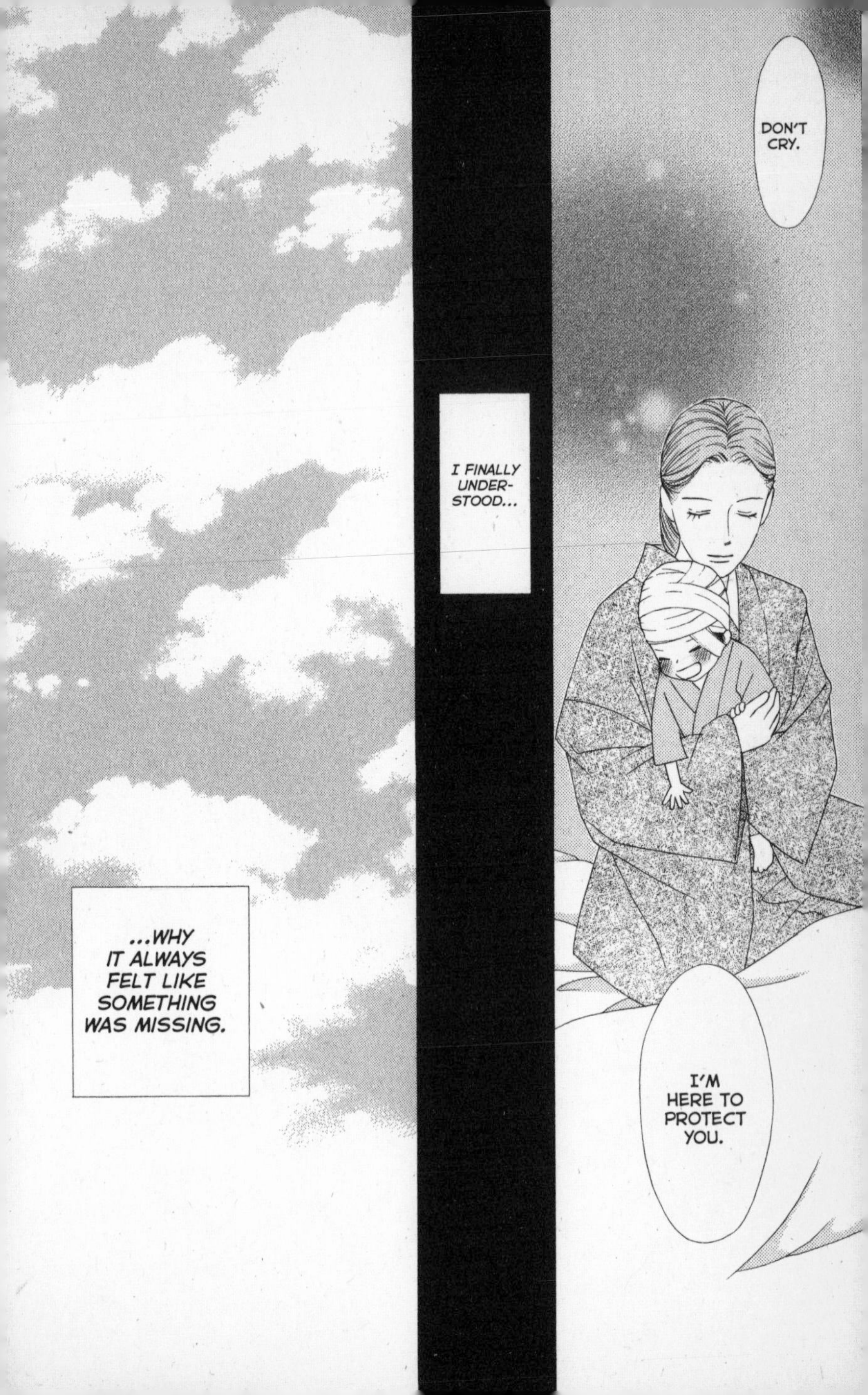
DON'T CRY.
I'M HERE TO PROTECT YOU.
I FINALLY UNDER-STOOD...
...WHY IT ALWAYS FELT LIKE SOMETHING WAS MISSING.

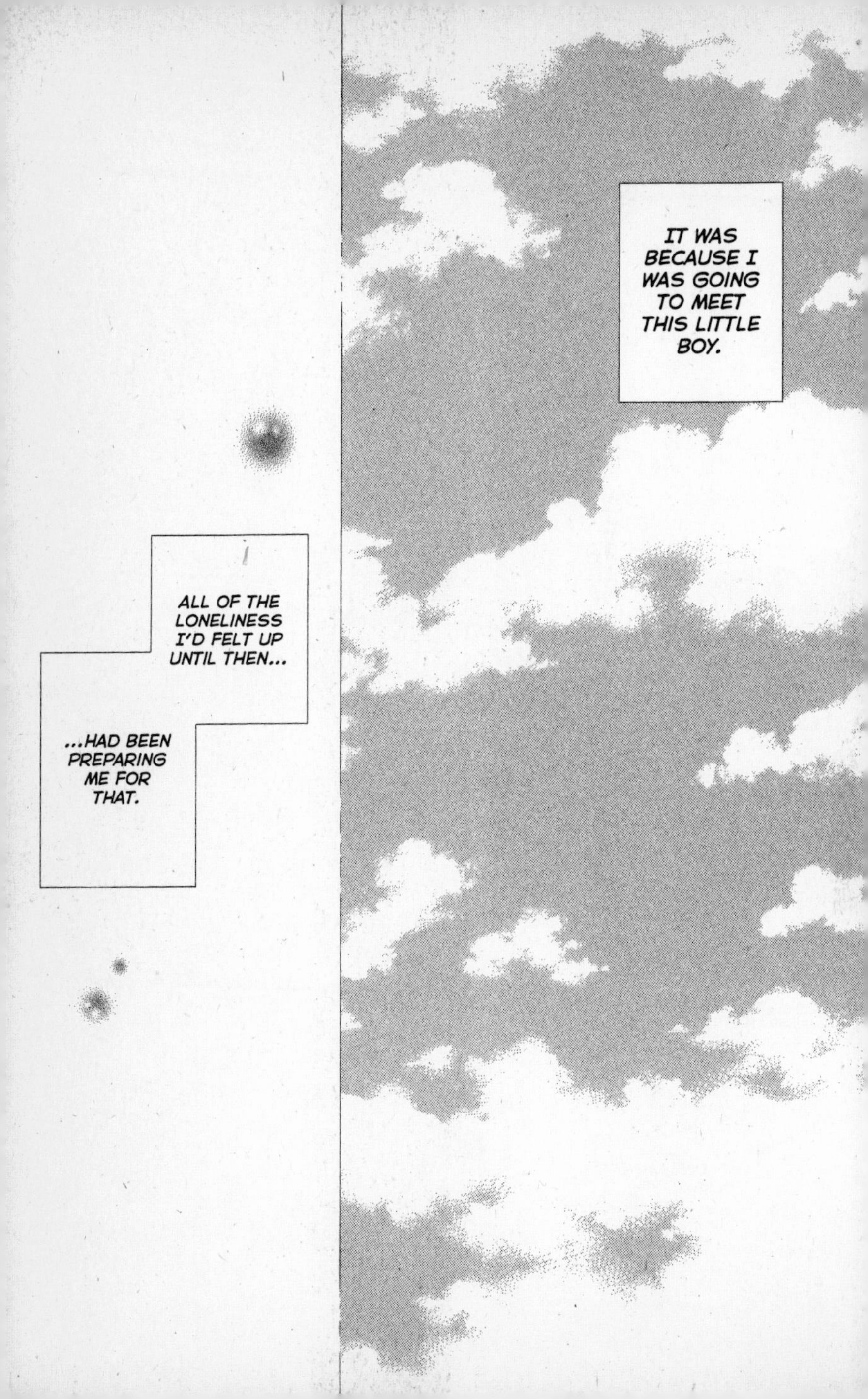
IT WAS BECAUSE I WAS GOING TO MEET THIS LITTLE BOY.
ALL OF THE LONELINESS I'D FELT UP UNTIL THEN...
...HAD BEEN PREPARING ME FOR THAT.

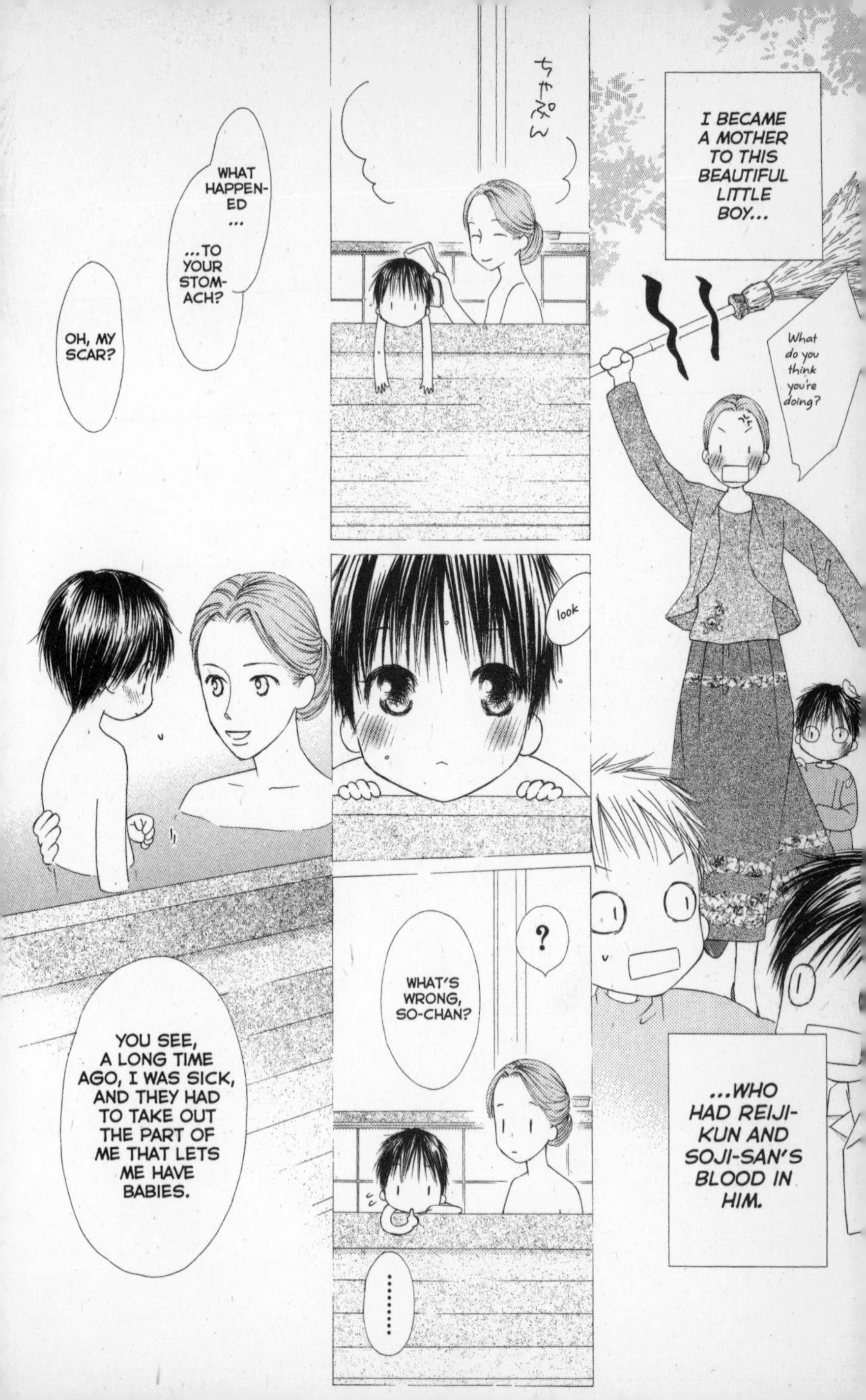

I BECAME A MOTHER TO THIS BEAUTIFUL LITTLE BOY...
What do you think you're doing?
...WHO HAD REIJI-KUN AND SOJI-SAN'S BLOOD IN HIM.
ちゃぷん
look
?
WHAT'S WRONG, SO-CHAN?
......
WHAT HAPPEN-ED ...
...TO YOUR STOM-ACH?
OH, MY SCAR?
YOU SEE, A LONG TIME AGO, I WAS SICK, AND THEY HAD TO TAKE OUT THE PART OF ME THAT LETS ME HAVE BABIES.

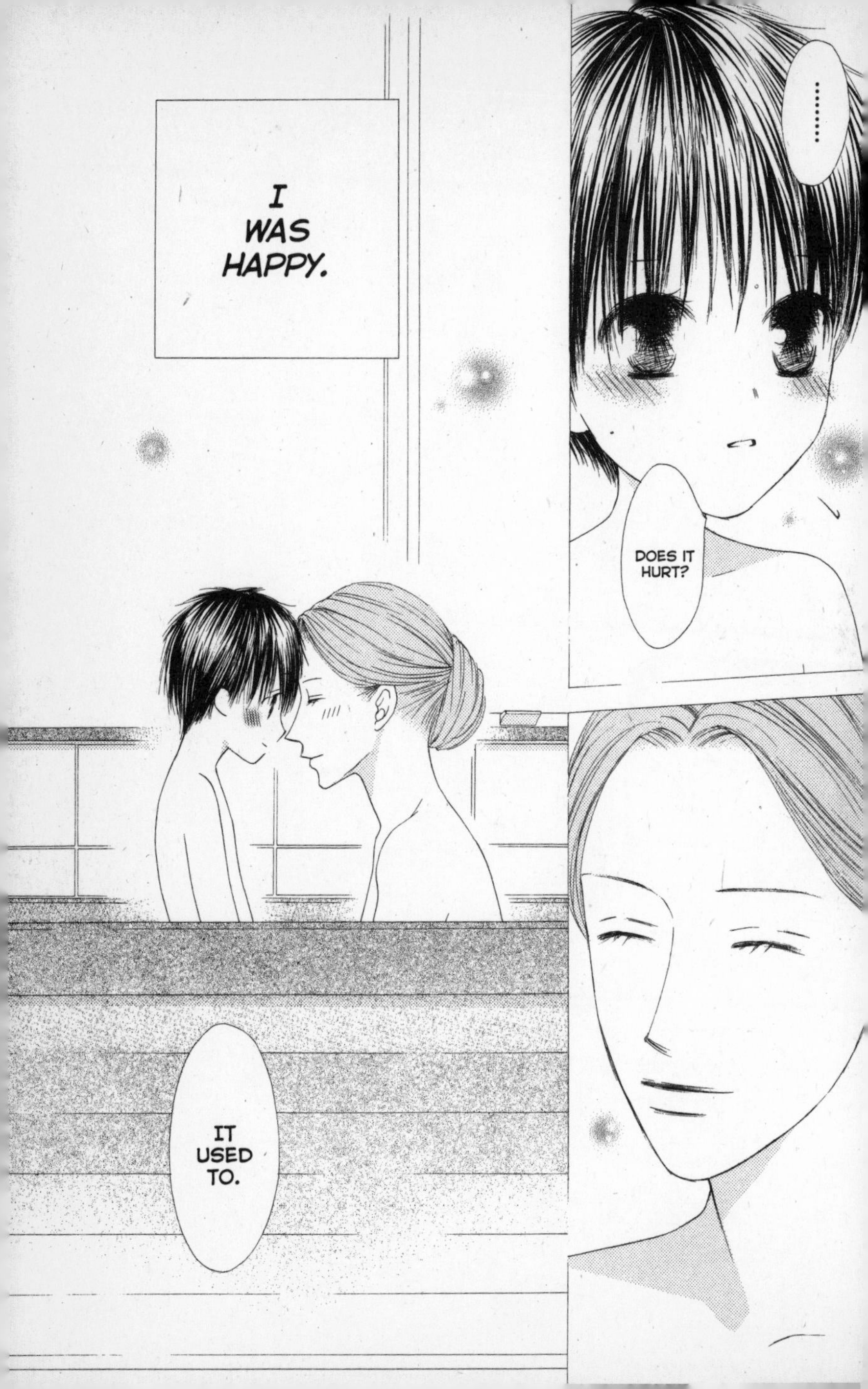
......
DOES IT HURT?
I WAS HAPPY.
IT USED TO.

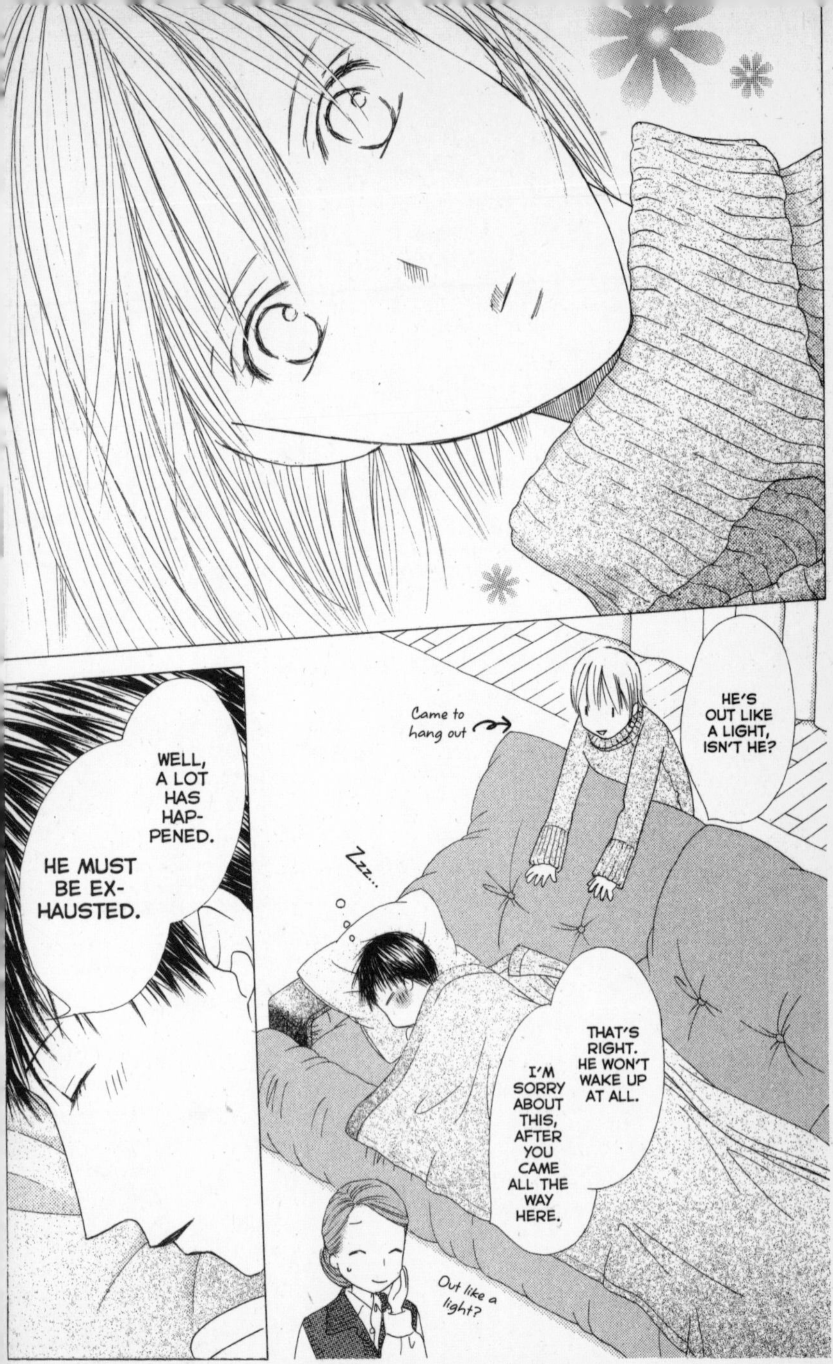
HE'S OUT LIKE A LIGHT, ISN'T HE?
Came to hang out
Zzz...
THAT'S RIGHT. HE WON'T WAKE UP AT ALL.
I'M SORRY ABOUT THIS, AFTER YOU CAME ALL THE WAY HERE.
Out like a light?
WELL, A LOT HAS HAP-PENED.
HE MUST BE EX-HAUSTED.

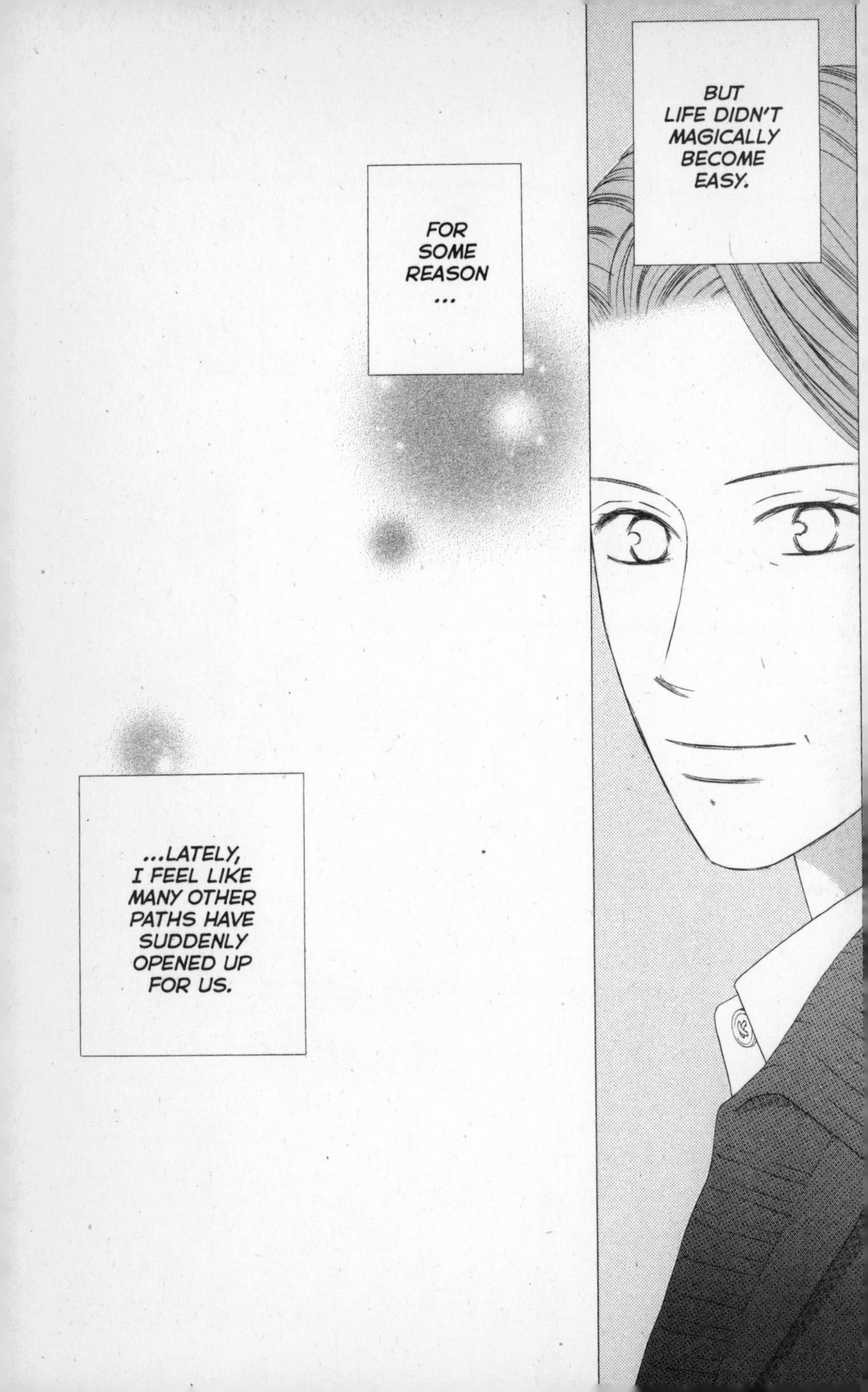
BUT LIFE DIDN'T MAGICALLY BECOME EASY.
FOR SOME REASON ...
...LATELY, I FEEL LIKE MANY OTHER PATHS HAVE SUDDENLY OPENED UP FOR US.

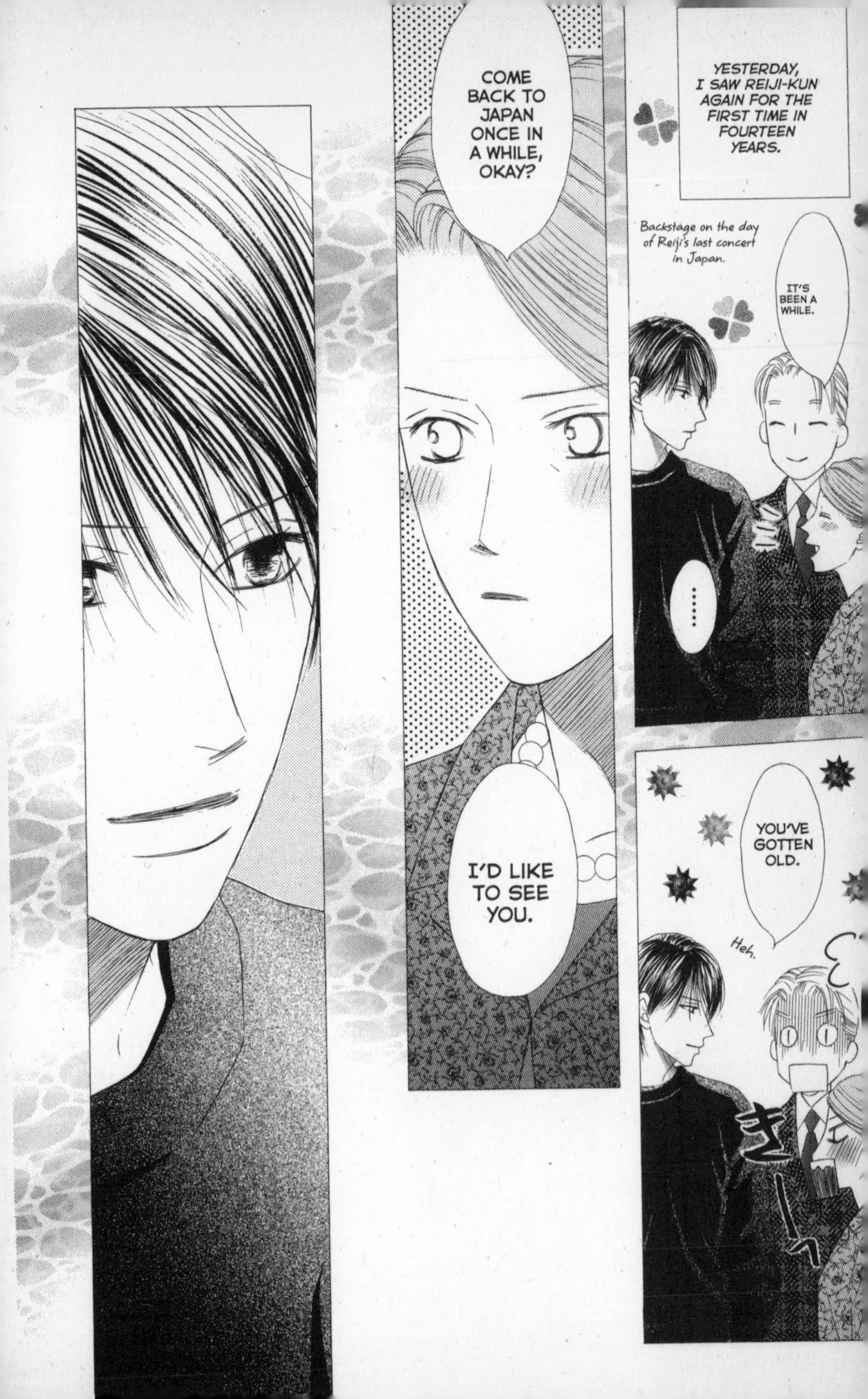
YESTERDAY, I SAW REIJI-KUN AGAIN FOR THE FIRST TIME IN FOURTEEN YEARS.
Backstage on the day of Reiji's last concert in Japan.
IT'S BEEN A WHILE.
......
YOU'VE GOTTEN OLD.
Heh.
COME BACK TO JAPAN ONCE IN A WHILE, OKAY?
I'D LIKE TO SEE YOU.

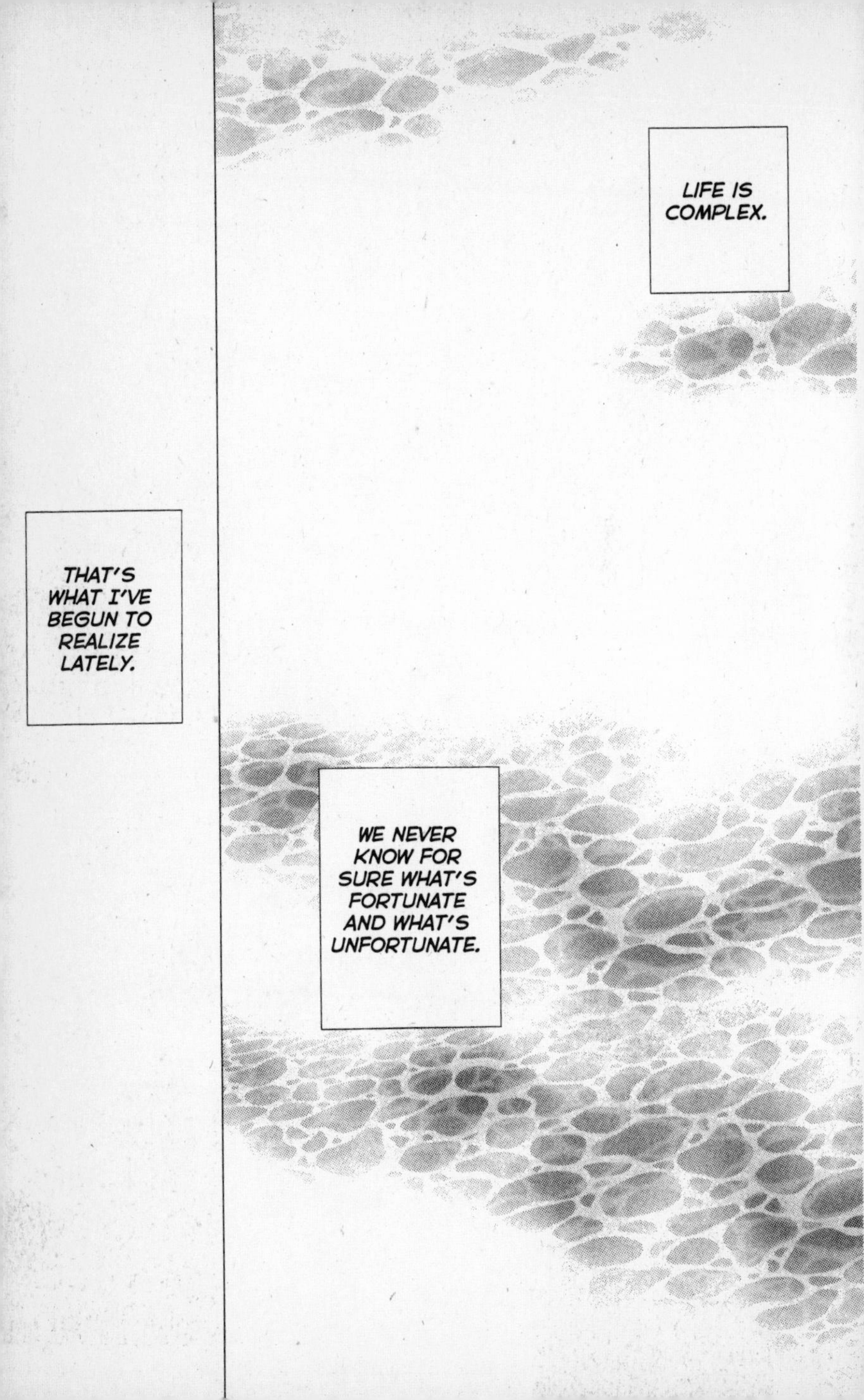
LIFE IS COMPLEX.
WE NEVER KNOW FOR SURE WHAT'S FORTUNATE AND WHAT'S UNFORTUNATE.
THAT'S WHAT I'VE BEGUN TO REALIZE LATELY.

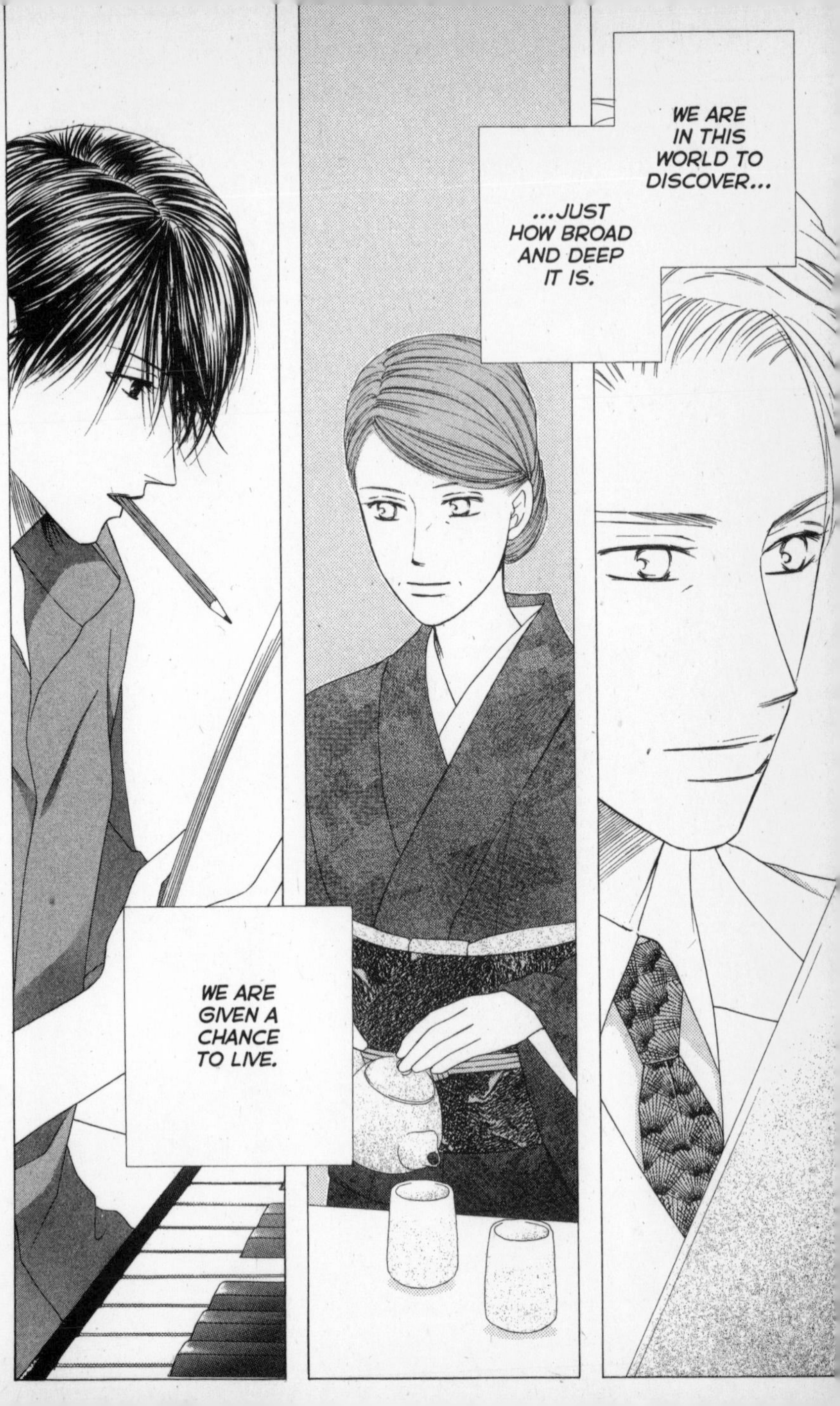
WE ARE IN THIS WORLD TO DISCOVER...
...JUST HOW BROAD AND DEEP IT IS.
WE ARE GIVEN A CHANCE TO LIVE.

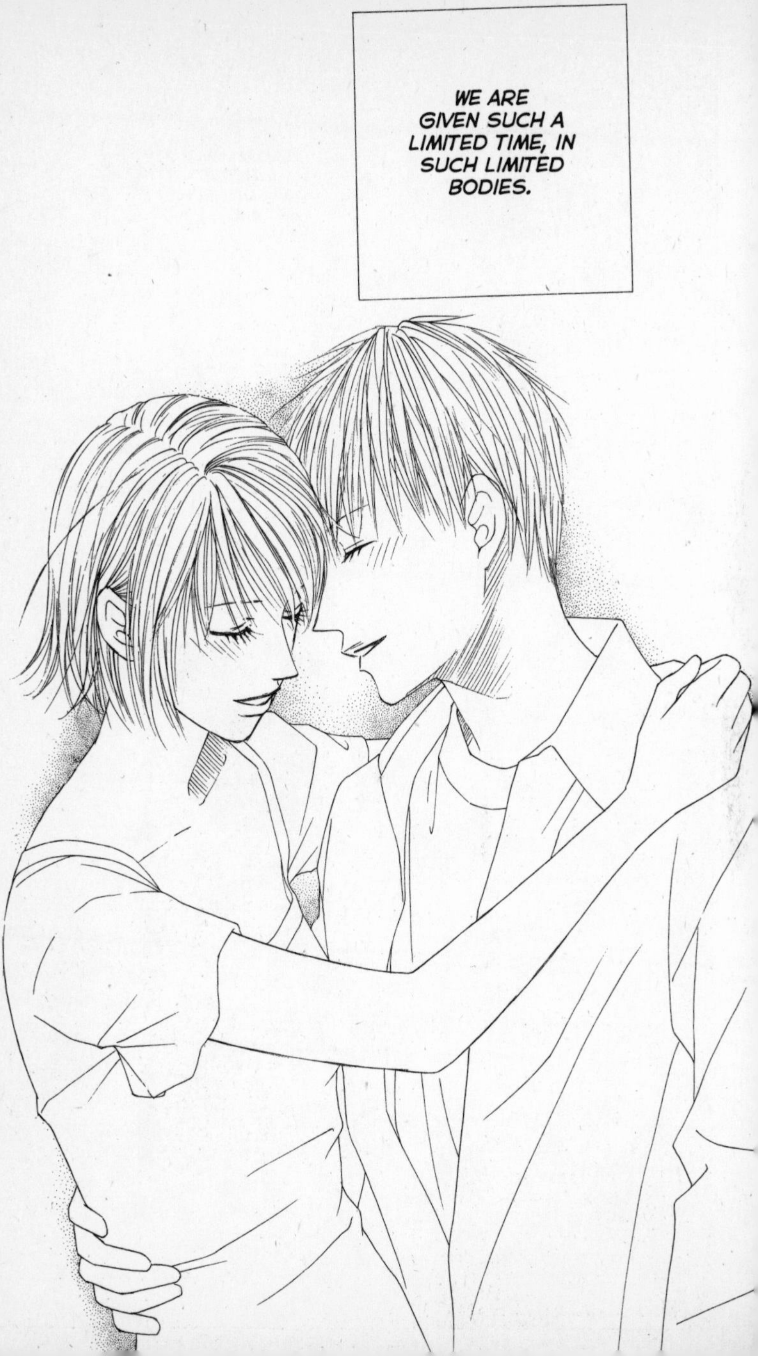
WE ARE GIVEN SUCH A LIMITED TIME, IN SUCH LIMITED BODIES.

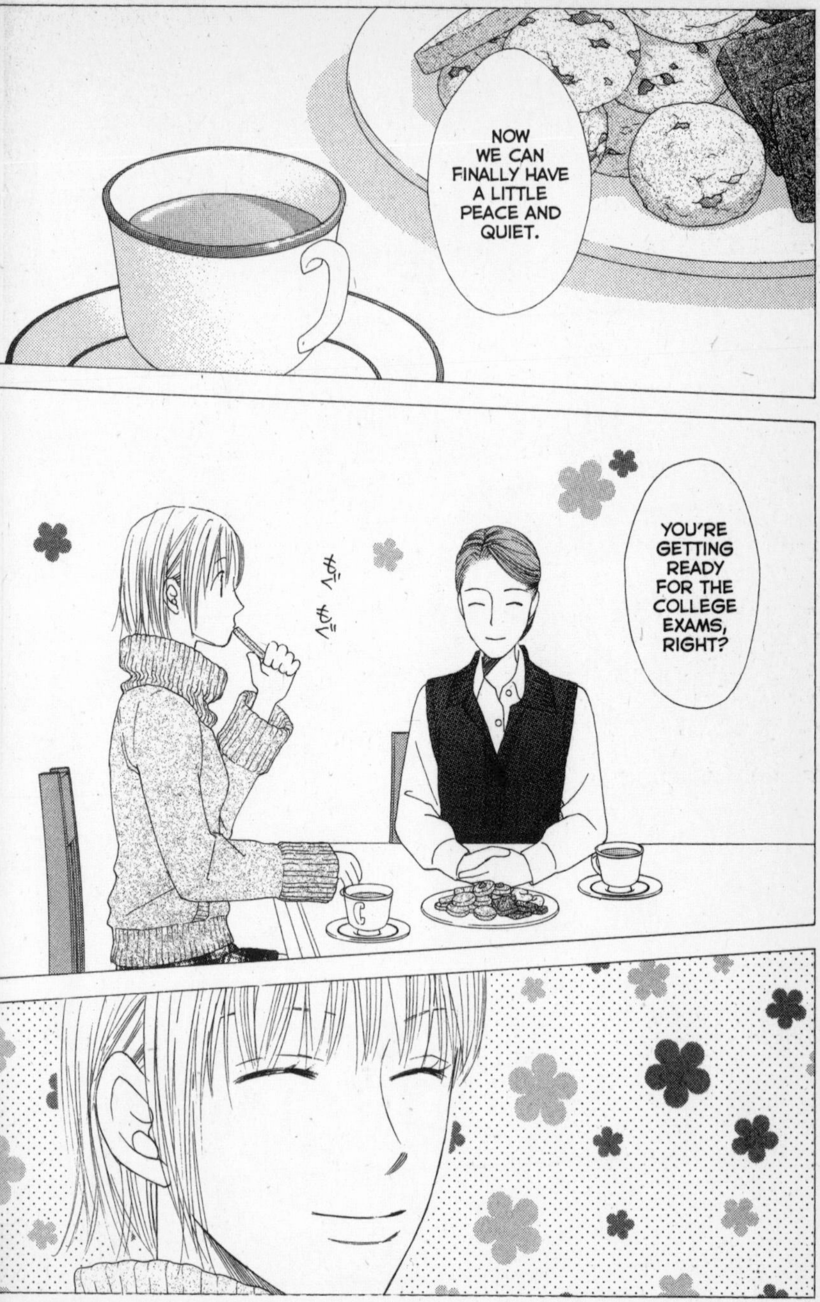
NOW WE CAN FINALLY HAVE A LITTLE PEACE AND QUIET.
YOU'RE GETTING READY FOR THE COLLEGE EXAMS, RIGHT?
もぐ もぐ

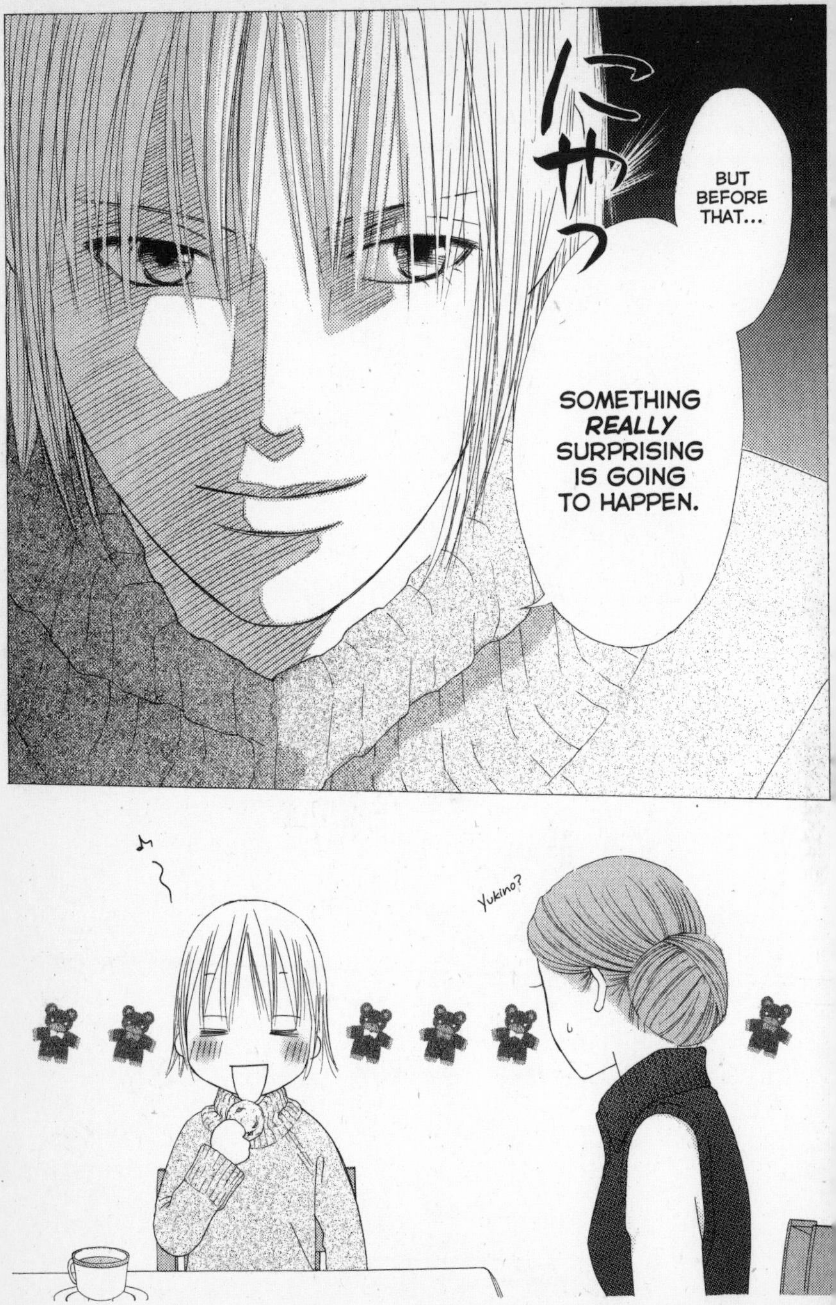
にやっ
BUT BEFORE THAT...
SOMETHING *REALLY* SURPRISING IS GOING TO HAPPEN.
Yukino?

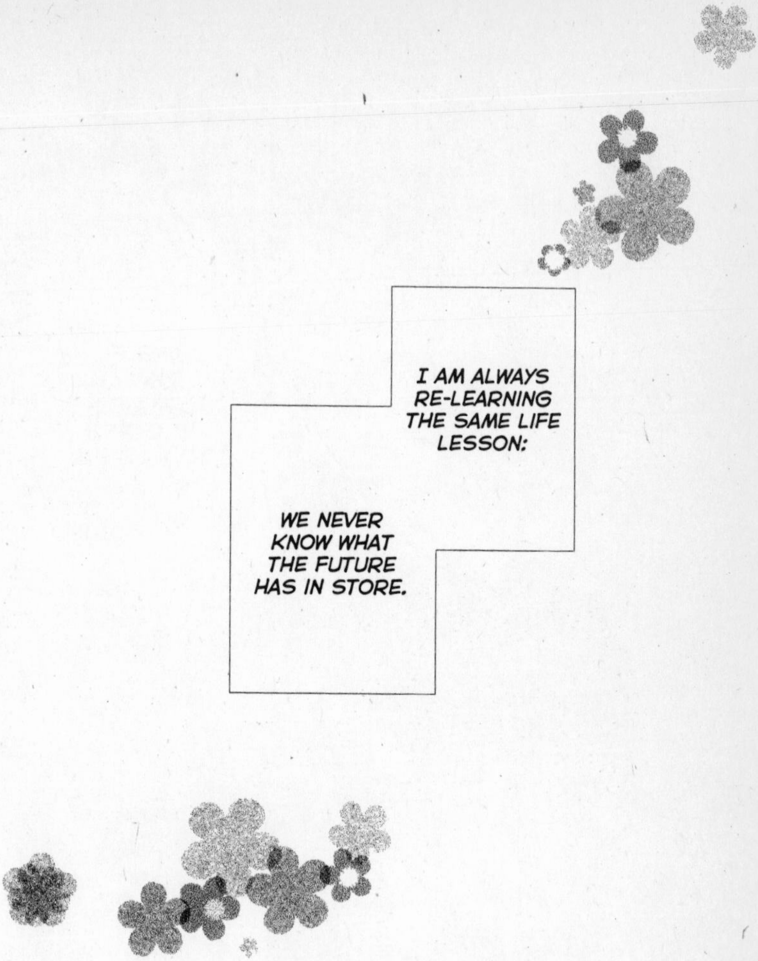
I AM ALWAYS RE-LEARNING THE SAME LIFE LESSON:
WE NEVER KNOW WHAT THE FUTURE HAS IN STORE.

ACT 96 ★ SHIZUNE'S STORY / END

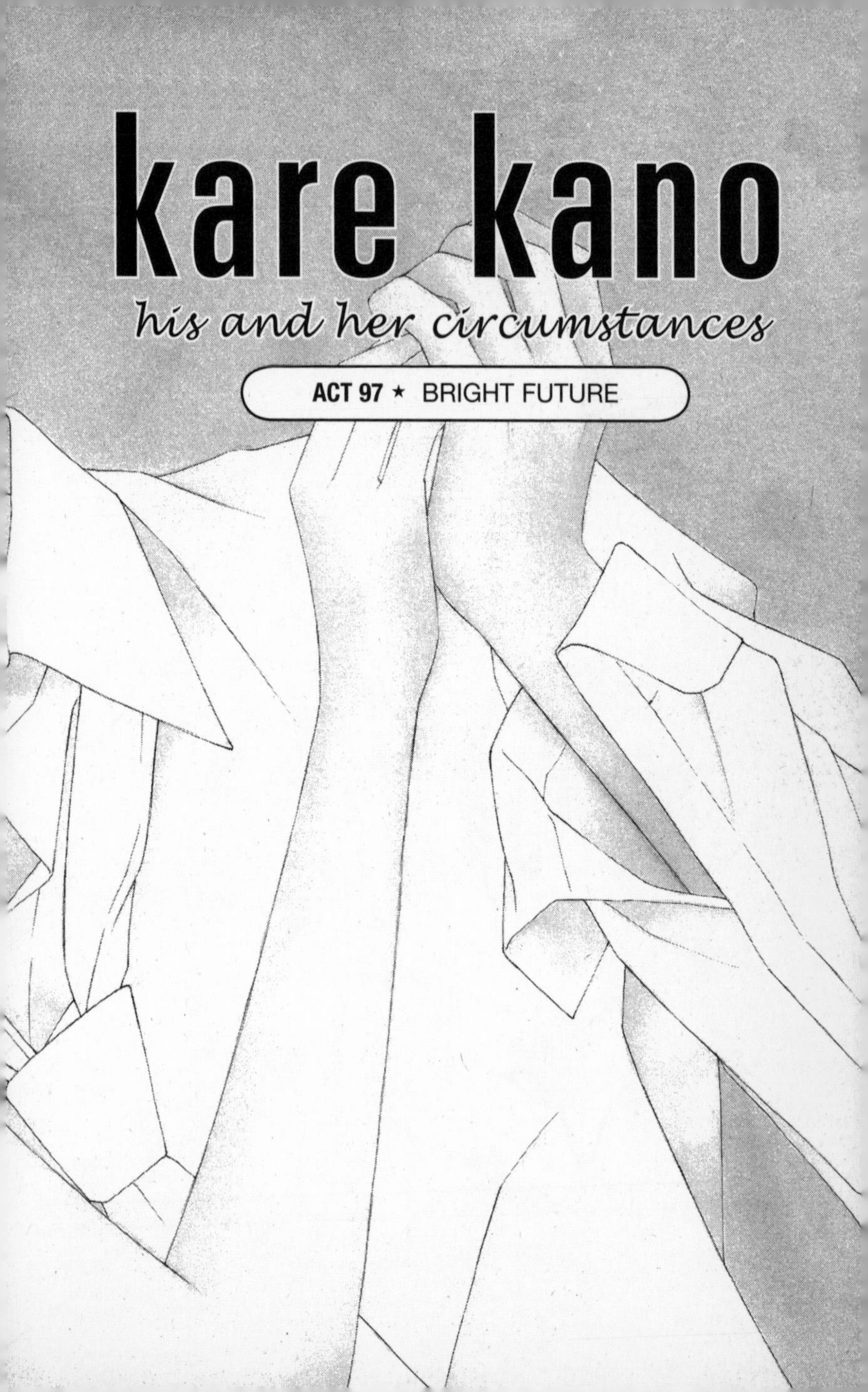
kare kano
his and her circumstances
ACT 97 ★ BRIGHT FUTURE

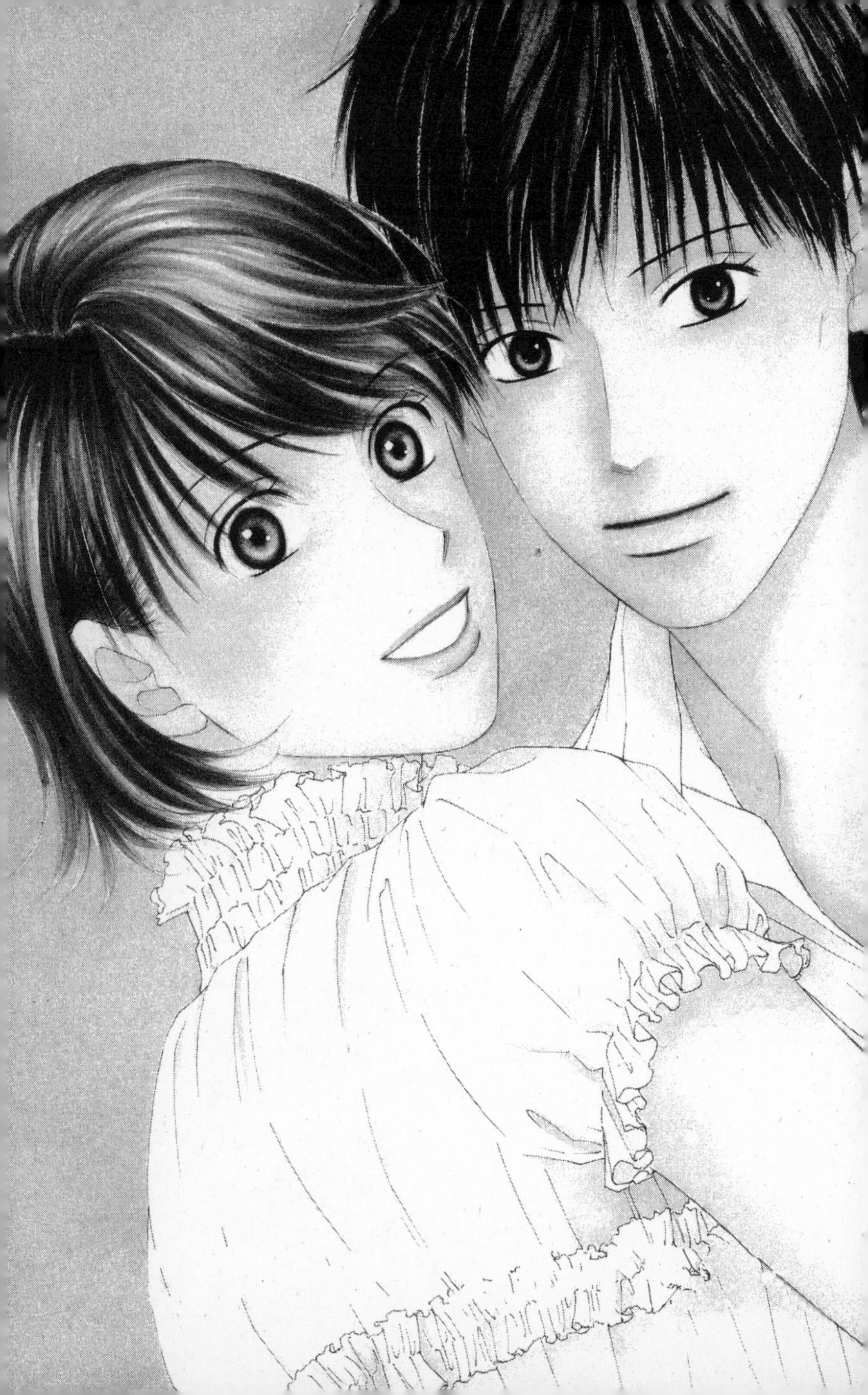

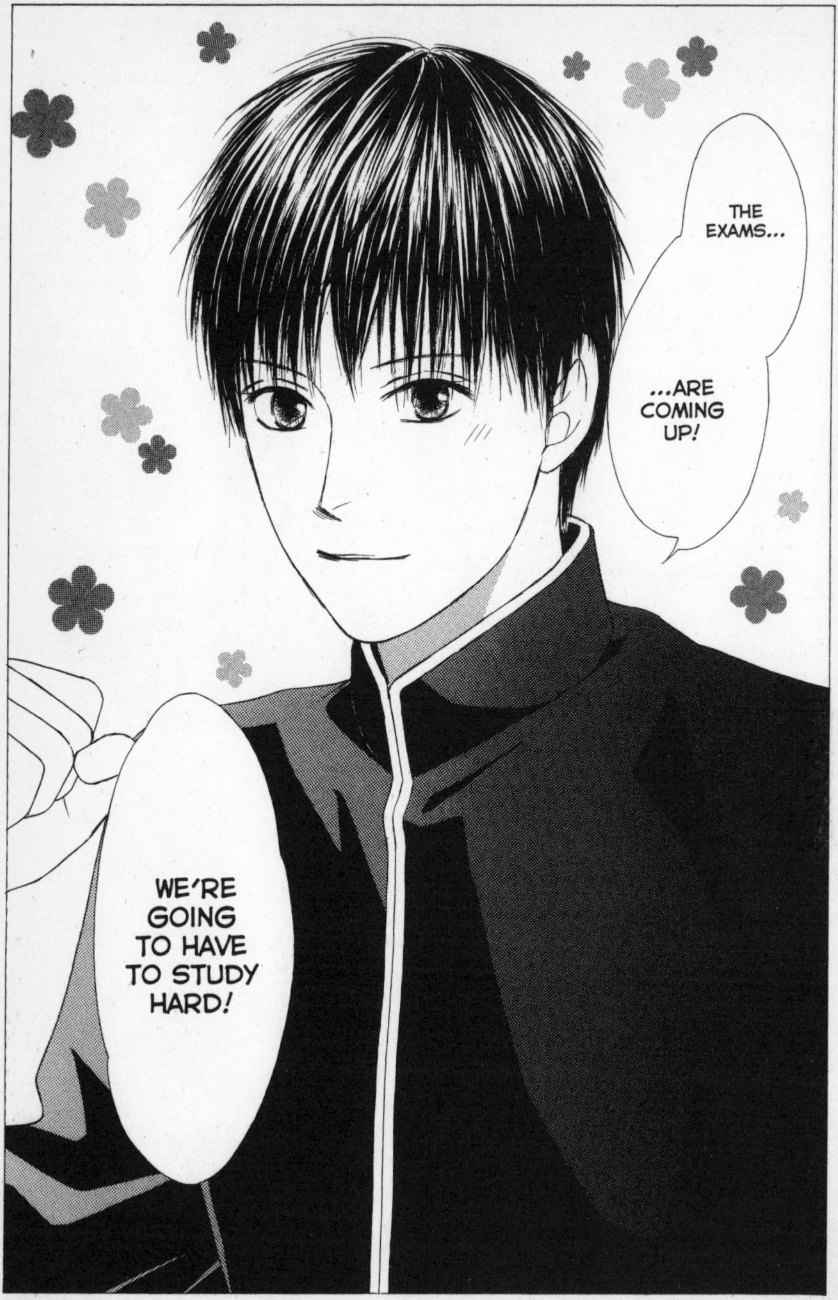
THE EXAMS...
...ARE COMING UP!
WE'RE GOING TO HAVE TO STUDY HARD!

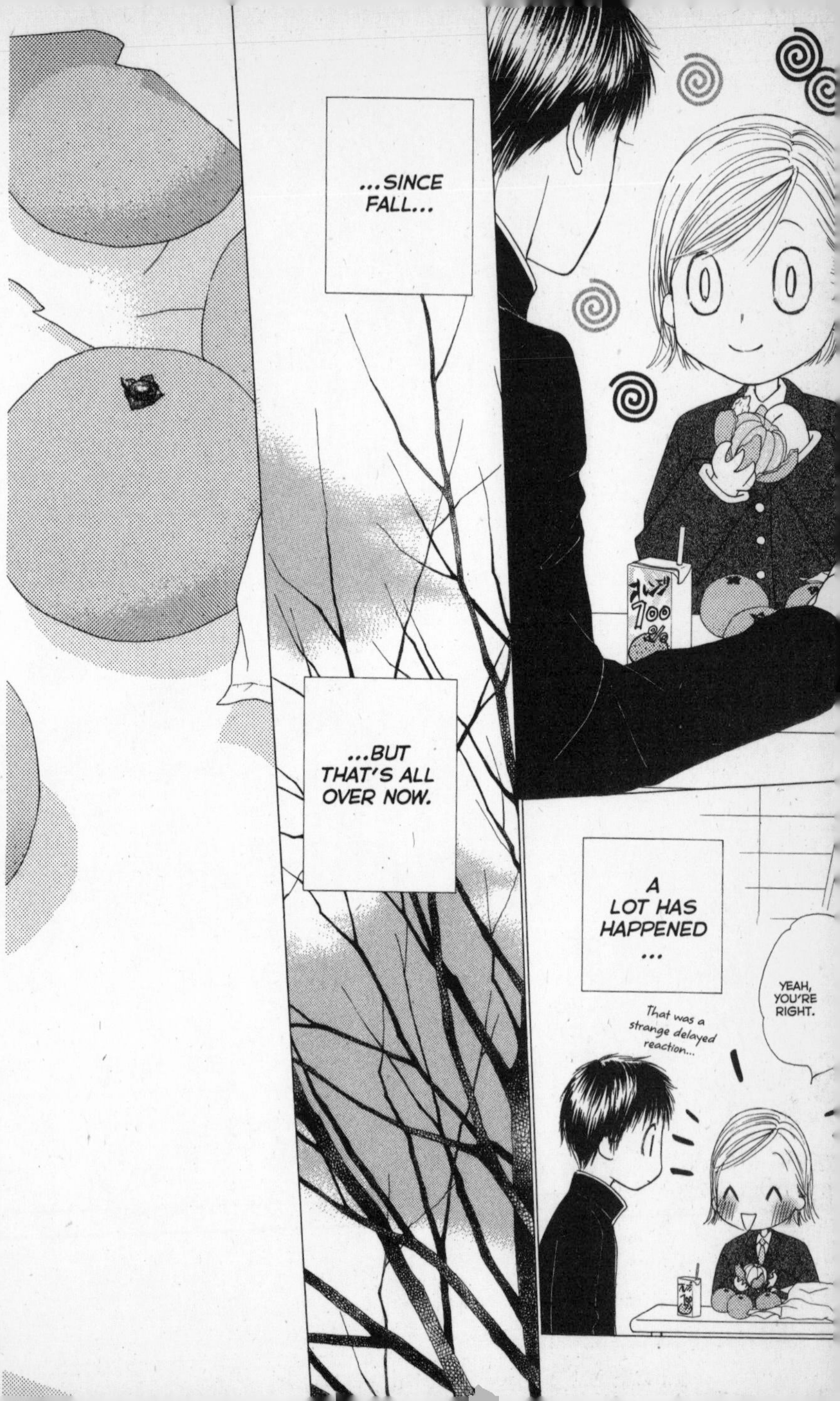
A LOT HAS HAPPENED ...
YEAH, YOU'RE RIGHT.
That was a strange delayed reaction...
...SINCE FALL...
...BUT THAT'S ALL OVER NOW.

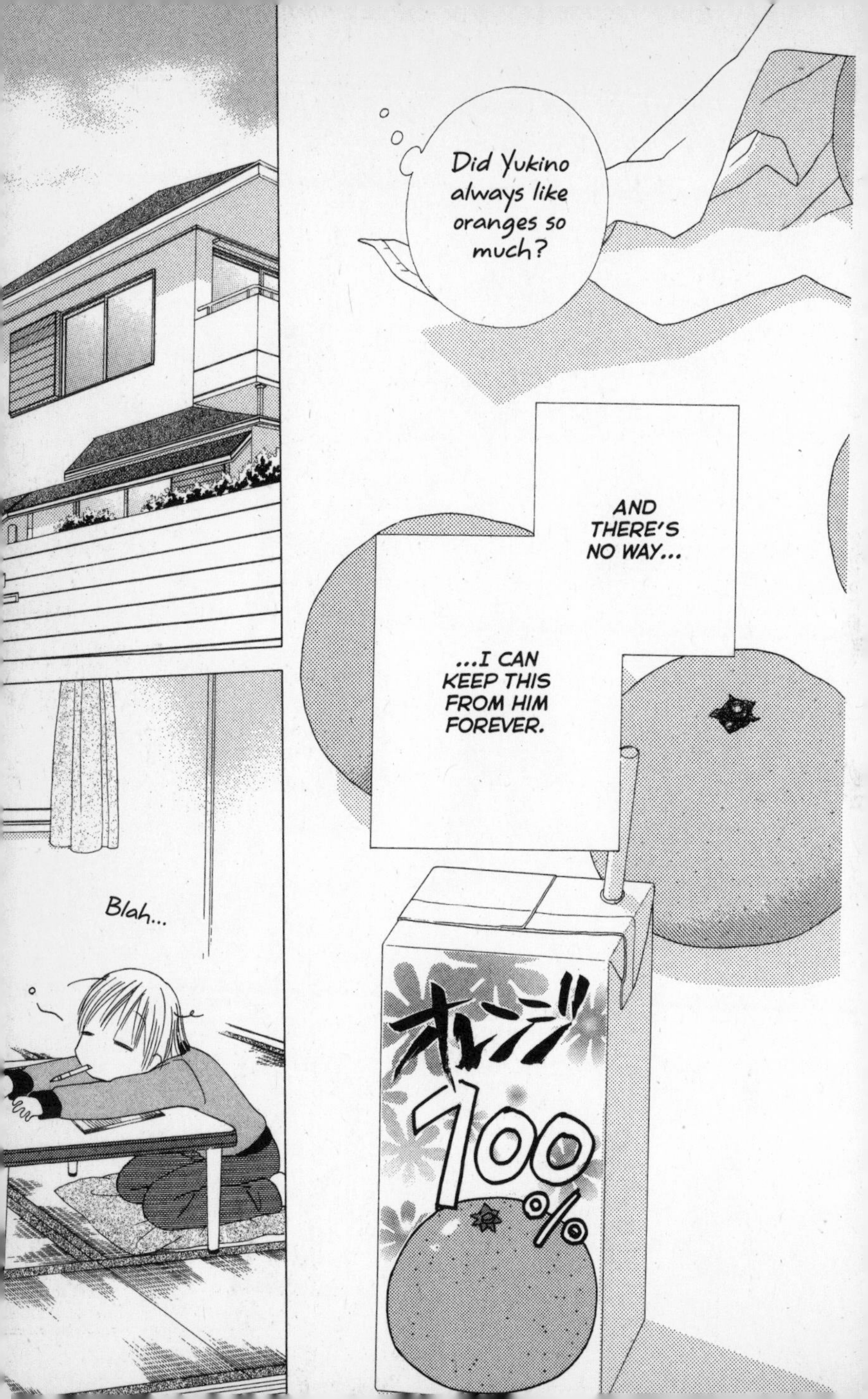
Did Yukino always like oranges so much?
AND THERE'S NO WAY...
...I CAN KEEP THIS FROM HIM FOREVER.
オレンジ
100%
Blah...

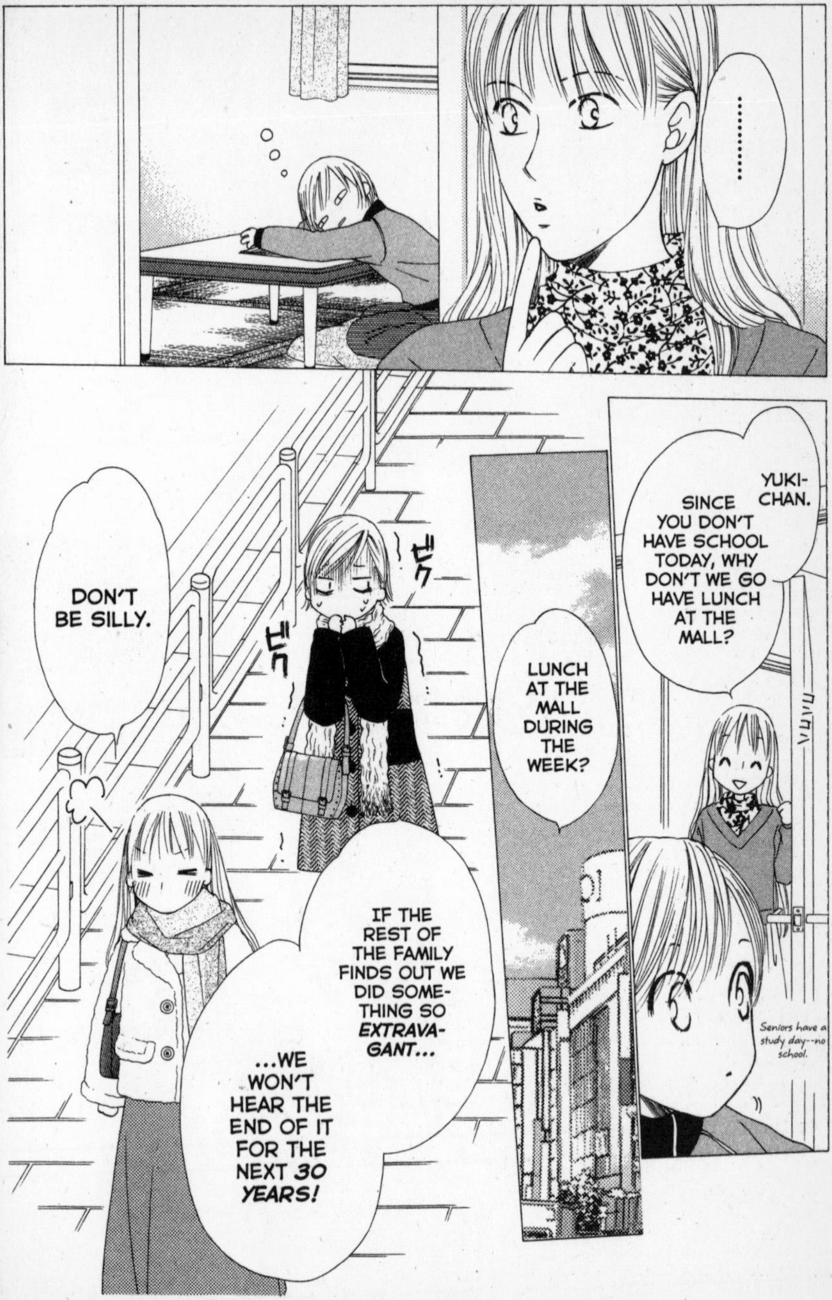
......
YUKI-CHAN.
SINCE YOU DON'T HAVE SCHOOL TODAY, WHY DON'T WE GO HAVE LUNCH AT THE MALL?
Seniors have a study day--no school.
LUNCH AT THE MALL DURING THE WEEK?
DON'T BE SILLY.
ビク
ビク
IF THE REST OF THE FAMILY FINDS OUT WE DID SOME-THING SO *EXTRAVA-GANT...*
...WE WON'T HEAR THE END OF IT FOR THE NEXT *30 YEARS!*

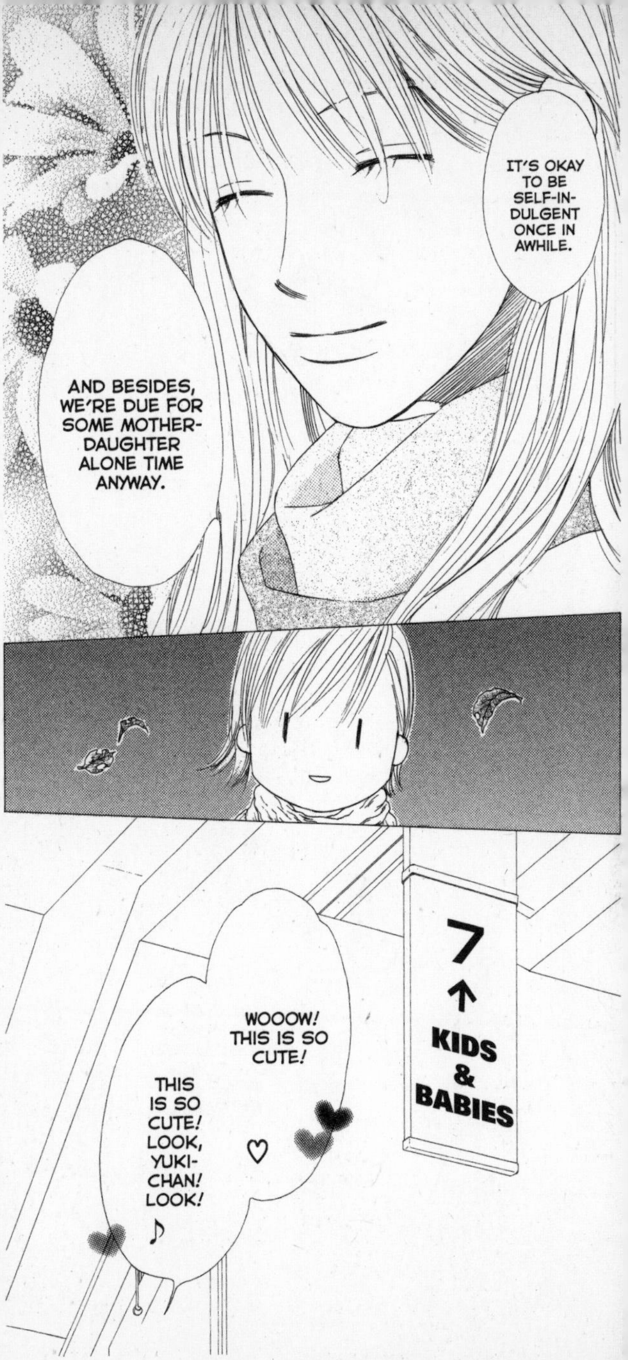
IT'S OKAY TO BE SELF-INDULGENT ONCE IN AWHILE.
AND BESIDES, WE'RE DUE FOR SOME MOTHER-DAUGHTER ALONE TIME ANYWAY.
7 ↑ KIDS & BABIES
WOOOW! THIS IS SO CUTE!
THIS IS SO CUTE! LOOK, YUKI-CHAN! LOOK! ♪

4

Cleaning

I've been reading some books on different cleaning techniques. They've opened my eyes to the theory of cleaning.

For example, it's better to clean a little bit at a time.

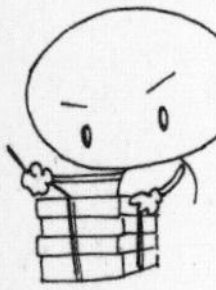

I clean when I take a break from work. (For about ten minutes at a time.)

How to maintain leather bags and leather shoes, how to clean windows and sliding panels, how to wax furniture, how to pick the right detergent, and on and on! I want to learn all of these basic things... really well.

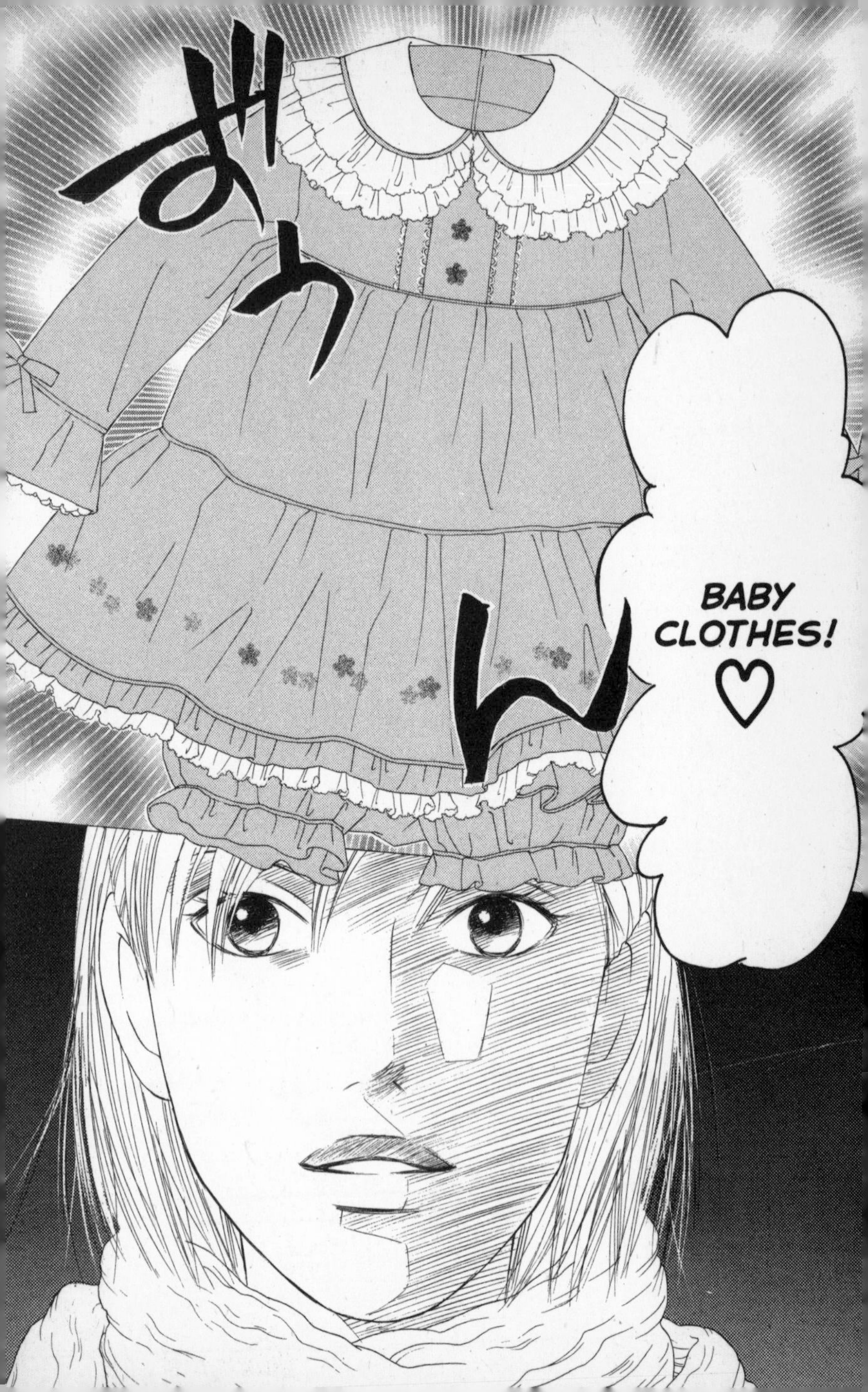
BABY CLOTHES! ♡
ずぅん

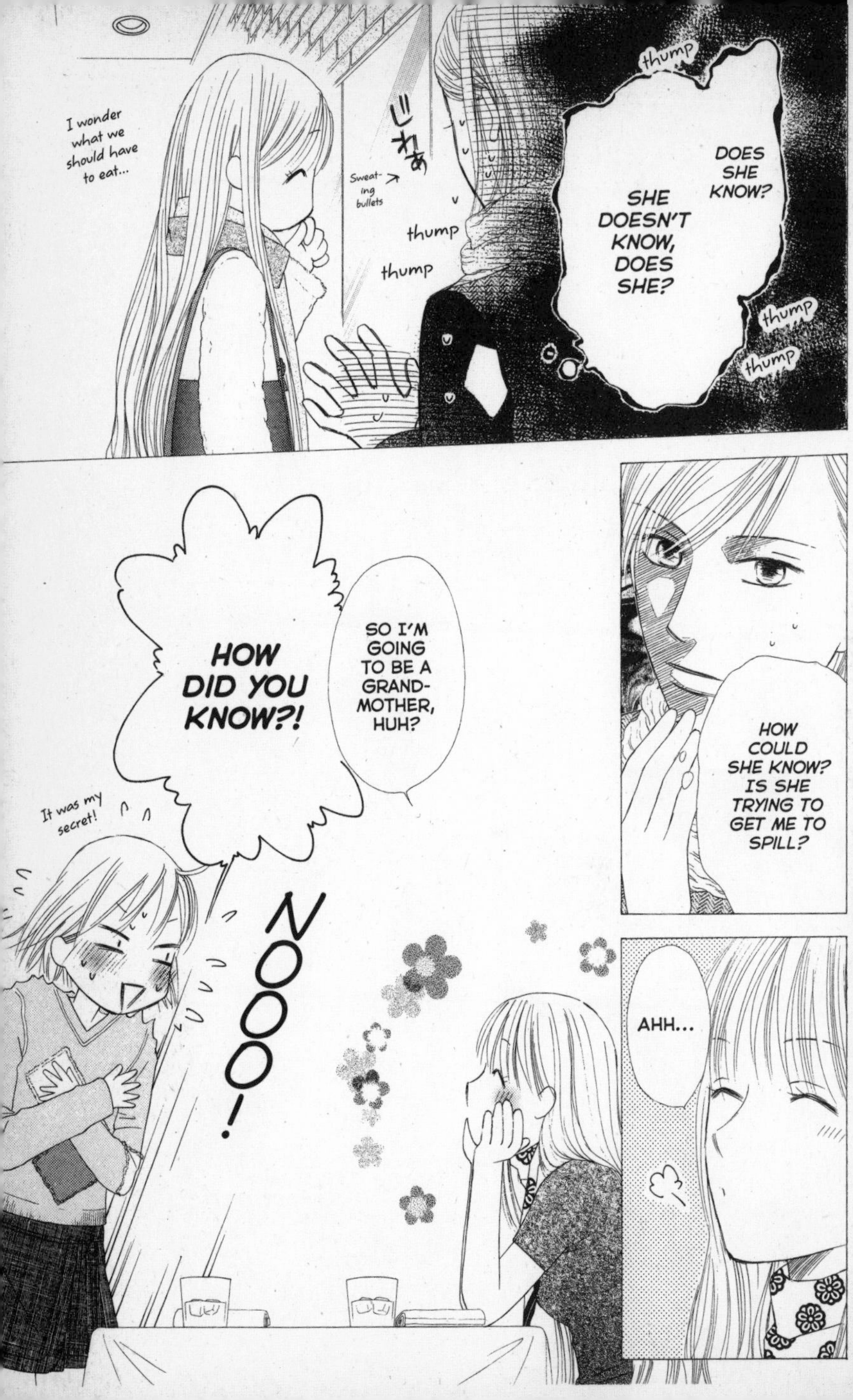
thump
DOES SHE KNOW?
SHE DOESN'T KNOW, DOES SHE?
thump
thump
じわあ
Sweat-ing bullets
thump
thump
I wonder what we should have to eat...
HOW COULD SHE KNOW? IS SHE TRYING TO GET ME TO SPILL?
AHH...
SO I'M GOING TO BE A GRAND-MOTHER, HUH?
HOW DID YOU KNOW?!
It was my secret!
NOOOO!

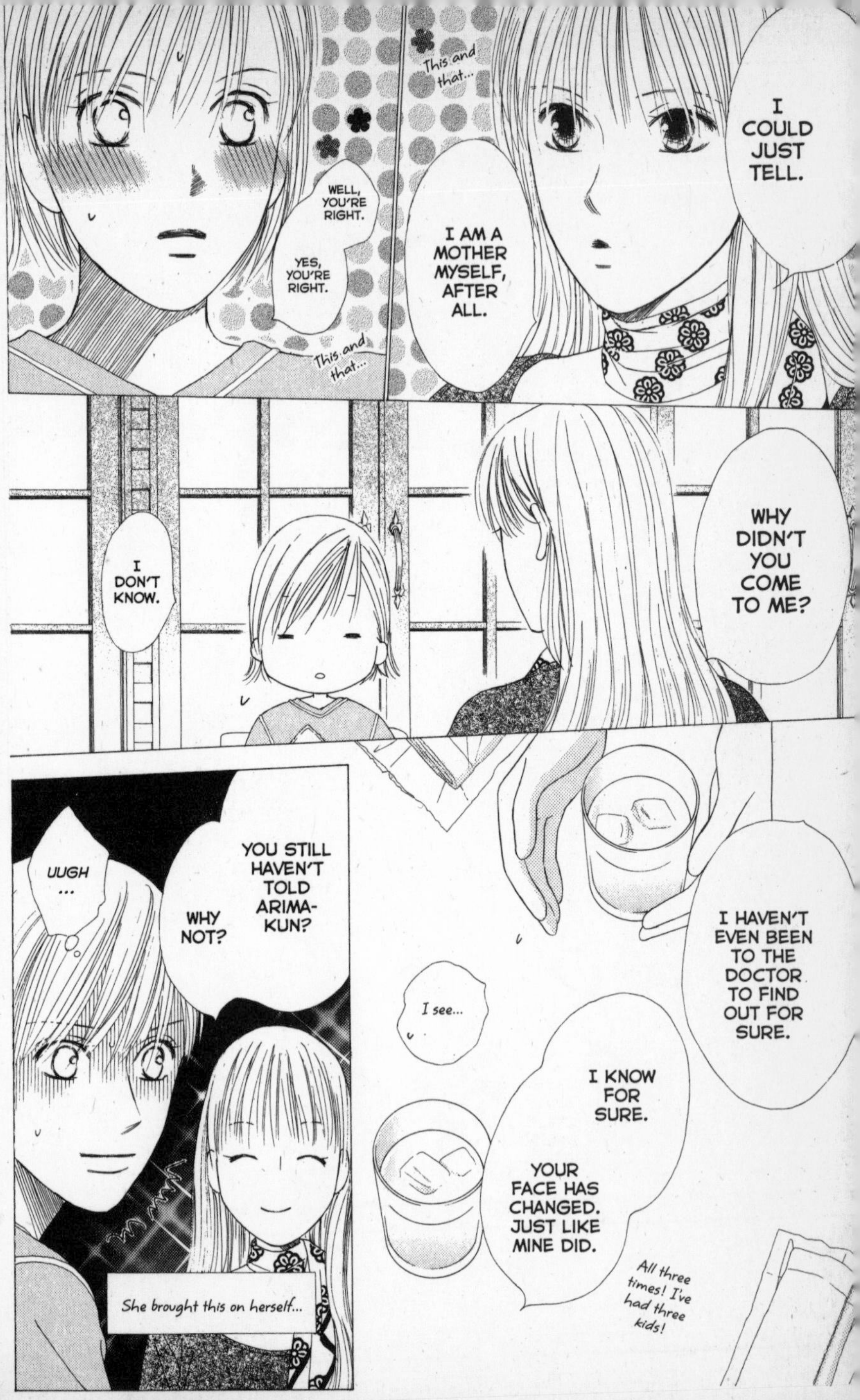
I COULD JUST TELL.
I AM A MOTHER MYSELF, AFTER ALL.
This and that...
WELL, YOU'RE RIGHT.
YES, YOU'RE RIGHT.
This and that...
WHY DIDN'T YOU COME TO ME?
I DON'T KNOW.
I HAVEN'T EVEN BEEN TO THE DOCTOR TO FIND OUT FOR SURE.
I see...
I KNOW FOR SURE.
YOUR FACE HAS CHANGED. JUST LIKE MINE DID.
All three times! I've had three kids!
YOU STILL HAVEN'T TOLD ARIMA-KUN?
WHY NOT?
UUGH...
She brought this on herself...

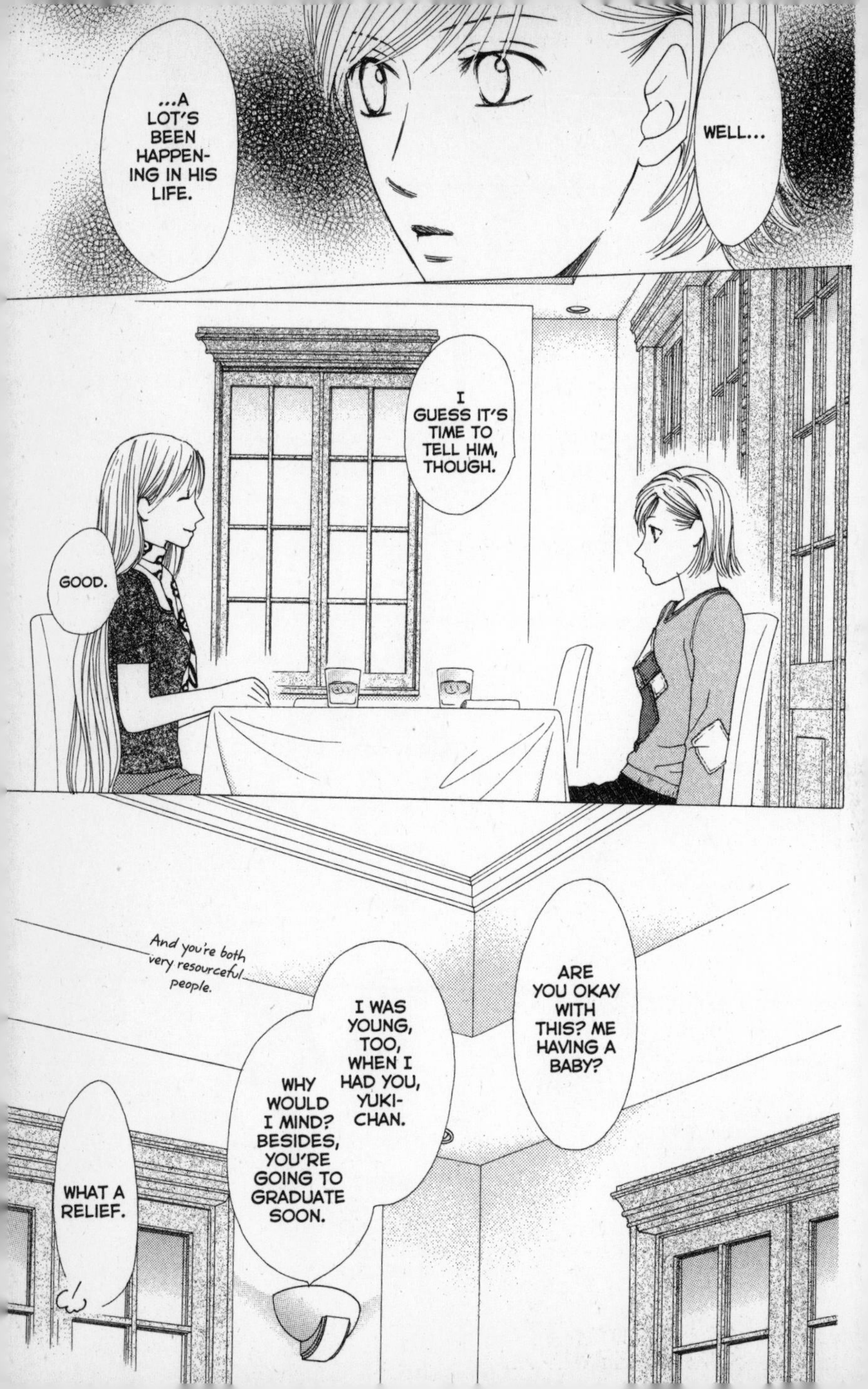
WELL...
...A LOT'S BEEN HAPPENING IN HIS LIFE.
I GUESS IT'S TIME TO TELL HIM, THOUGH.
GOOD.
ARE YOU OKAY WITH THIS? ME HAVING A BABY?
I WAS YOUNG, TOO, WHEN I HAD YOU, YUKI-CHAN.
WHY WOULD I MIND? BESIDES, YOU'RE GOING TO GRADUATE SOON.
And you're both very resourceful people.
WHAT A RELIEF.

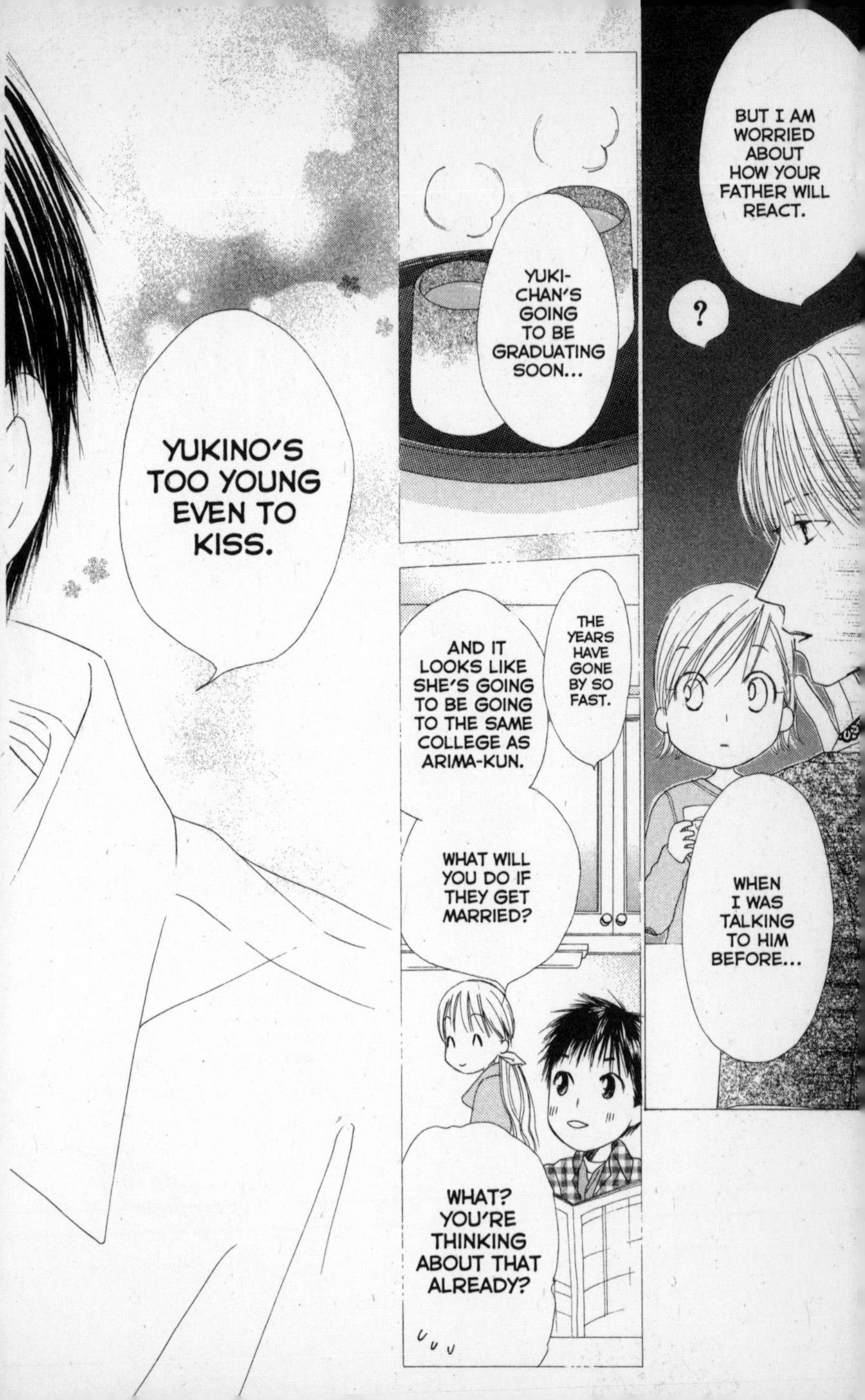
BUT I AM WORRIED ABOUT HOW YOUR FATHER WILL REACT.
?
WHEN I WAS TALKING TO HIM BEFORE...
YUKI-CHAN'S GOING TO BE GRADUATING SOON...
THE YEARS HAVE GONE BY SO FAST.
AND IT LOOKS LIKE SHE'S GOING TO BE GOING TO THE SAME COLLEGE AS ARIMA-KUN.
WHAT WILL YOU DO IF THEY GET MARRIED?
WHAT? YOU'RE THINKING ABOUT THAT ALREADY?
YUKINO'S TOO YOUNG EVEN TO KISS.

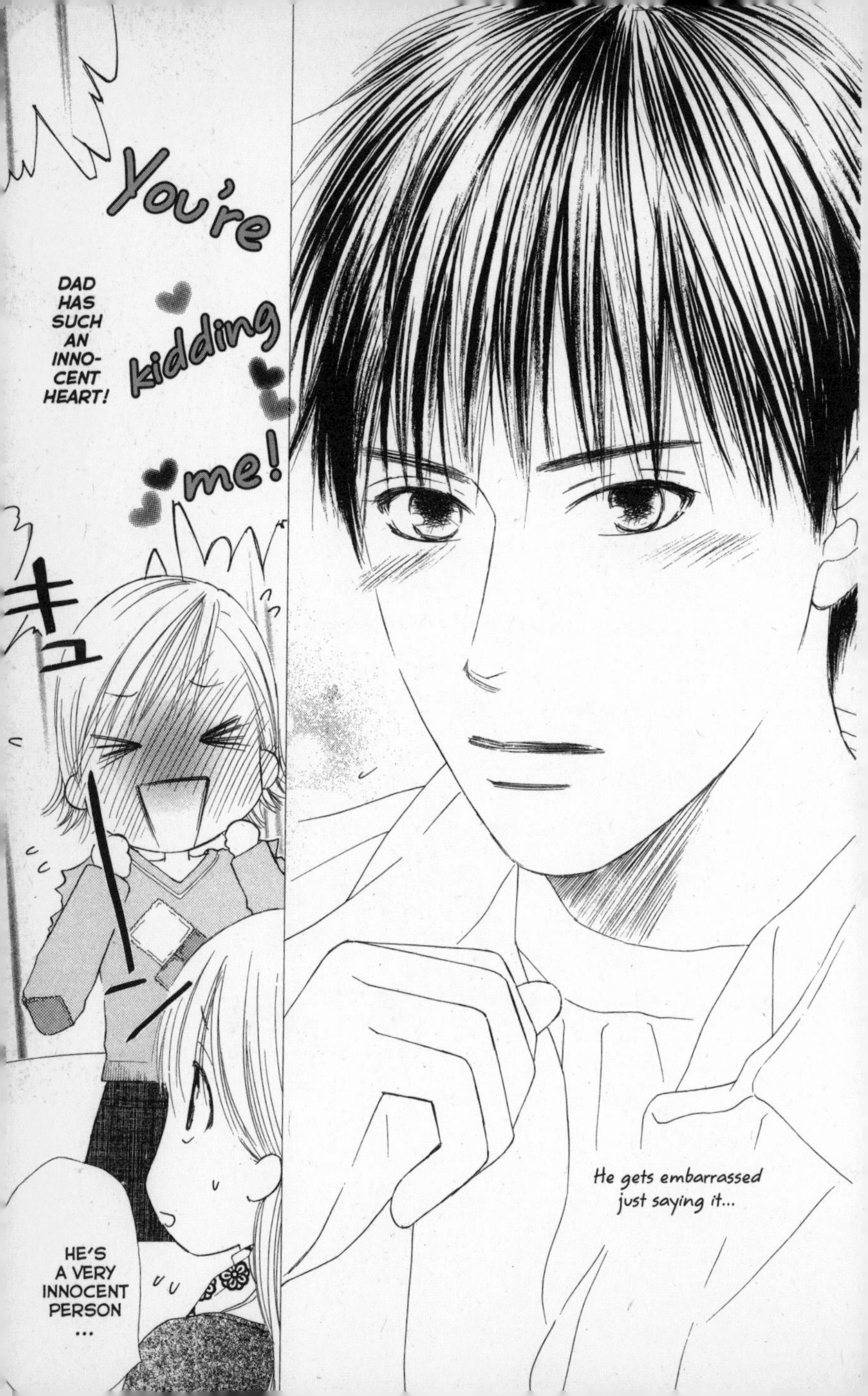
He gets embarrassed just saying it...
You're kidding me!
DAD HAS SUCH AN INNO-CENT HEART!
キュー
HE'S A VERY INNOCENT PERSON ...

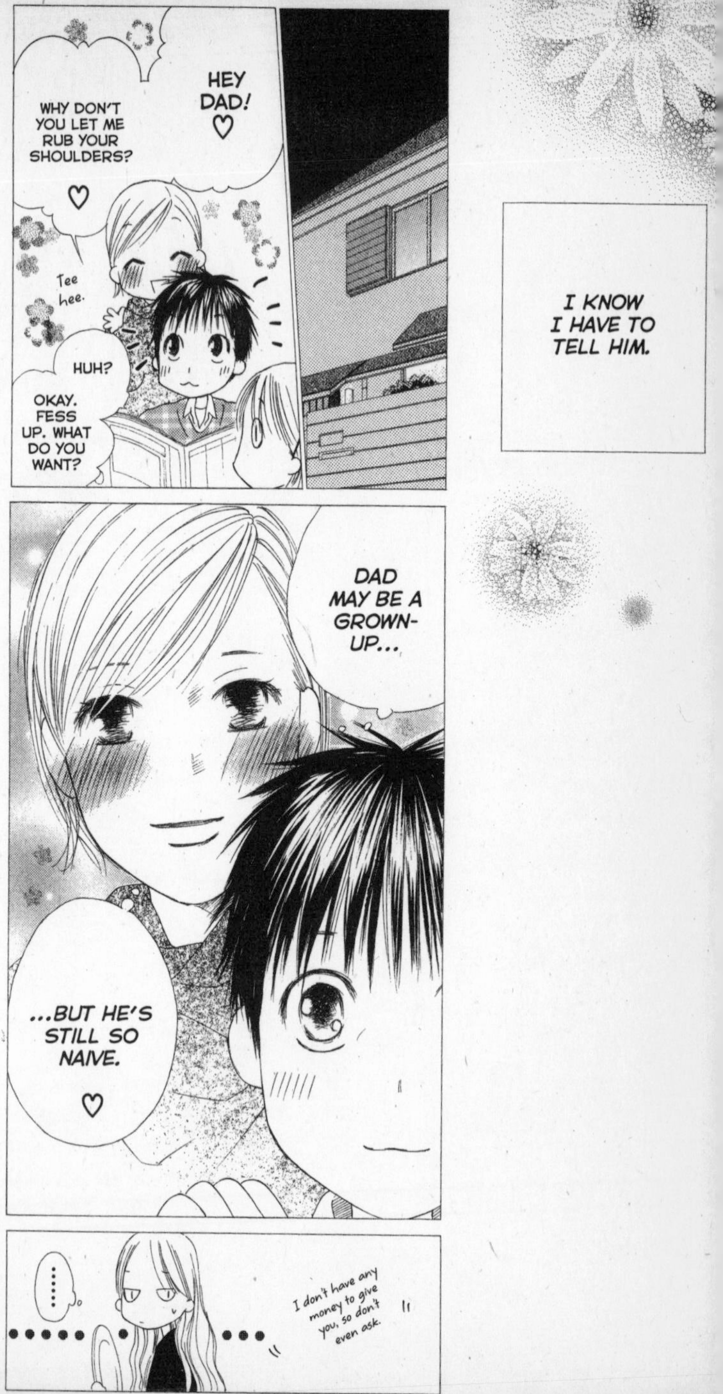
I KNOW I HAVE TO TELL HIM.
HEY DAD! ♡
WHY DON'T YOU LET ME RUB YOUR SHOULDERS? ♡
Tee hee.
HUH?
OKAY. FESS UP. WHAT DO YOU WANT?
DAD MAY BE A GROWN-UP...
...BUT HE'S STILL SO NAIVE. ♡
I don't have any money to give you, so don't even ask.
......

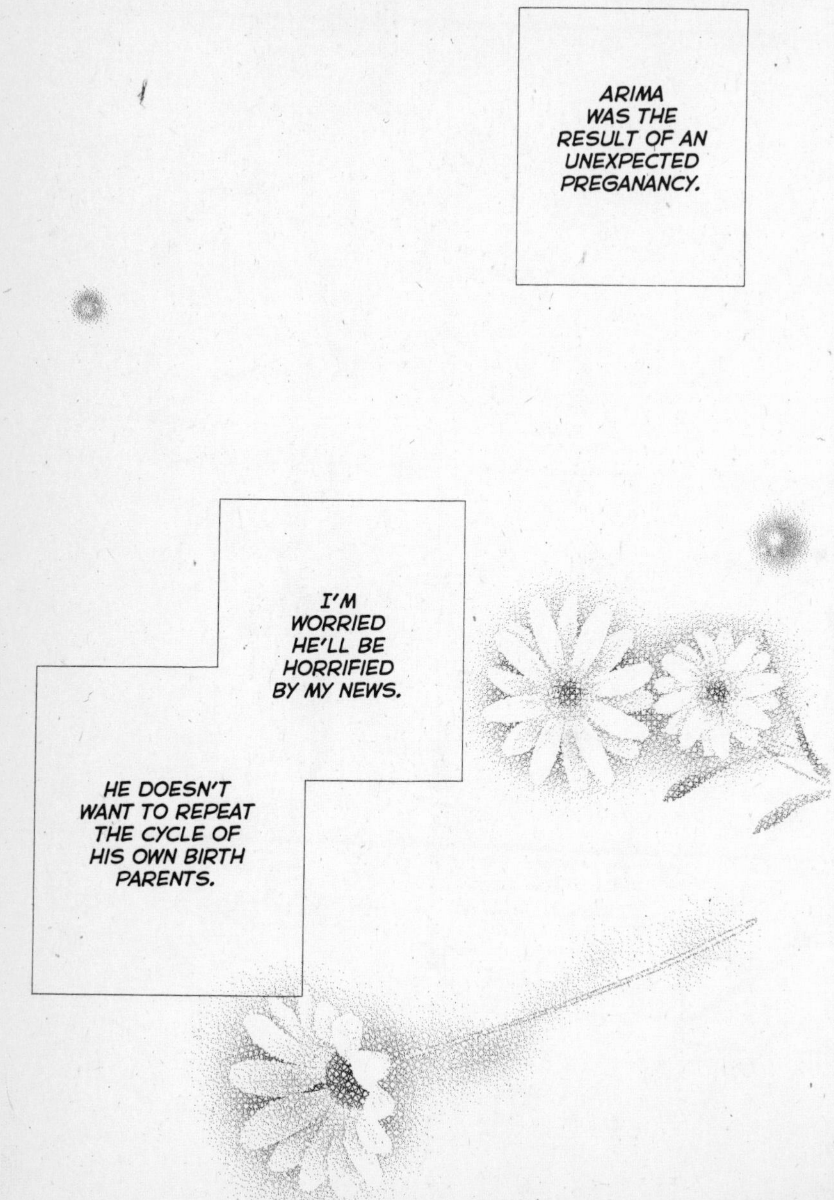
ARIMA WAS THE RESULT OF AN UNEXPECTED PREGANANCY.
I'M WORRIED HE'LL BE HORRIFIED BY MY NEWS.
HE DOESN'T WANT TO REPEAT THE CYCLE OF HIS OWN BIRTH PARENTS.

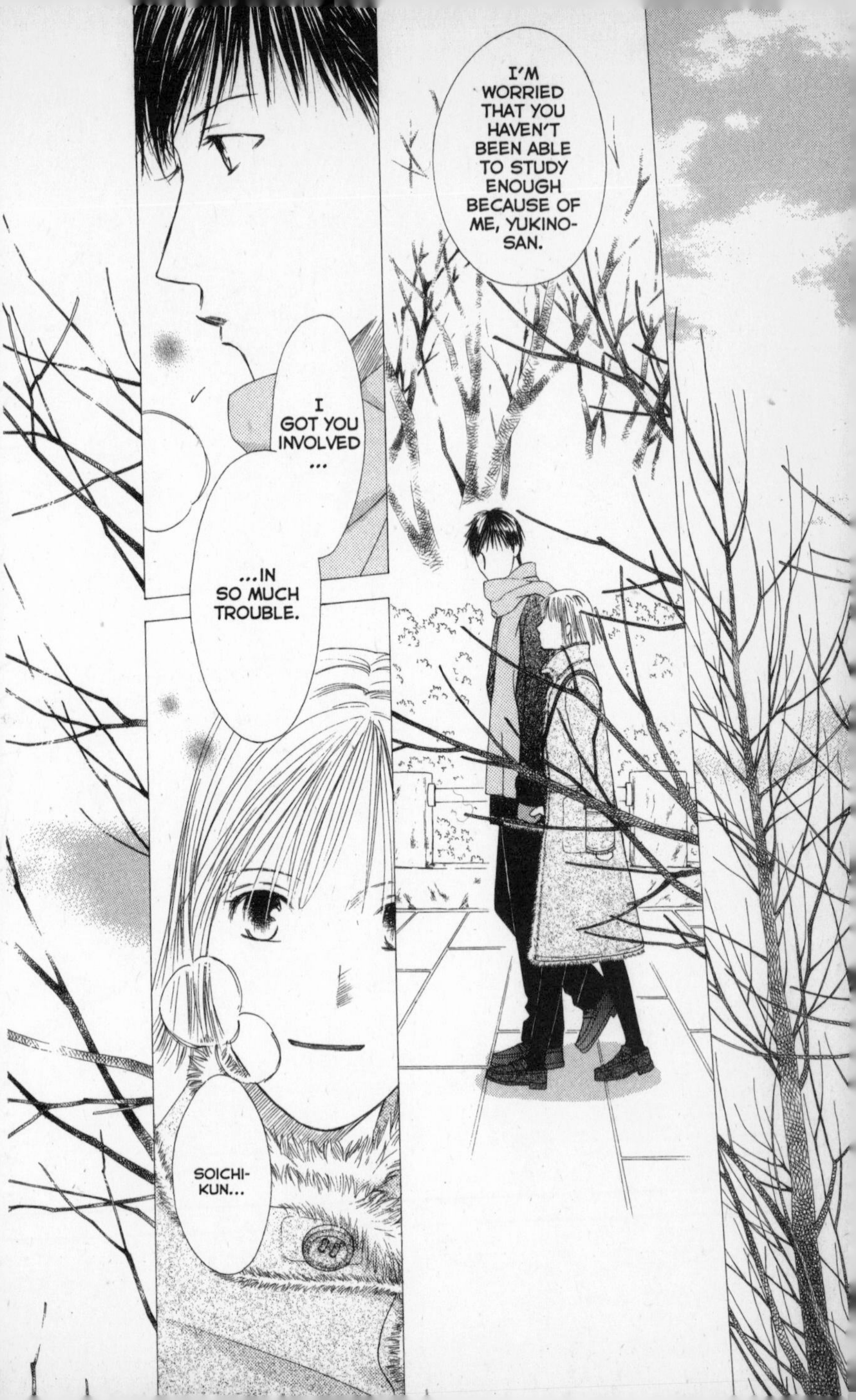
I'M WORRIED THAT YOU HAVEN'T BEEN ABLE TO STUDY ENOUGH BECAUSE OF ME, YUKINO-SAN.
I GOT YOU INVOLVED ...
...IN SO MUCH TROUBLE.
SOICHI-KUN...

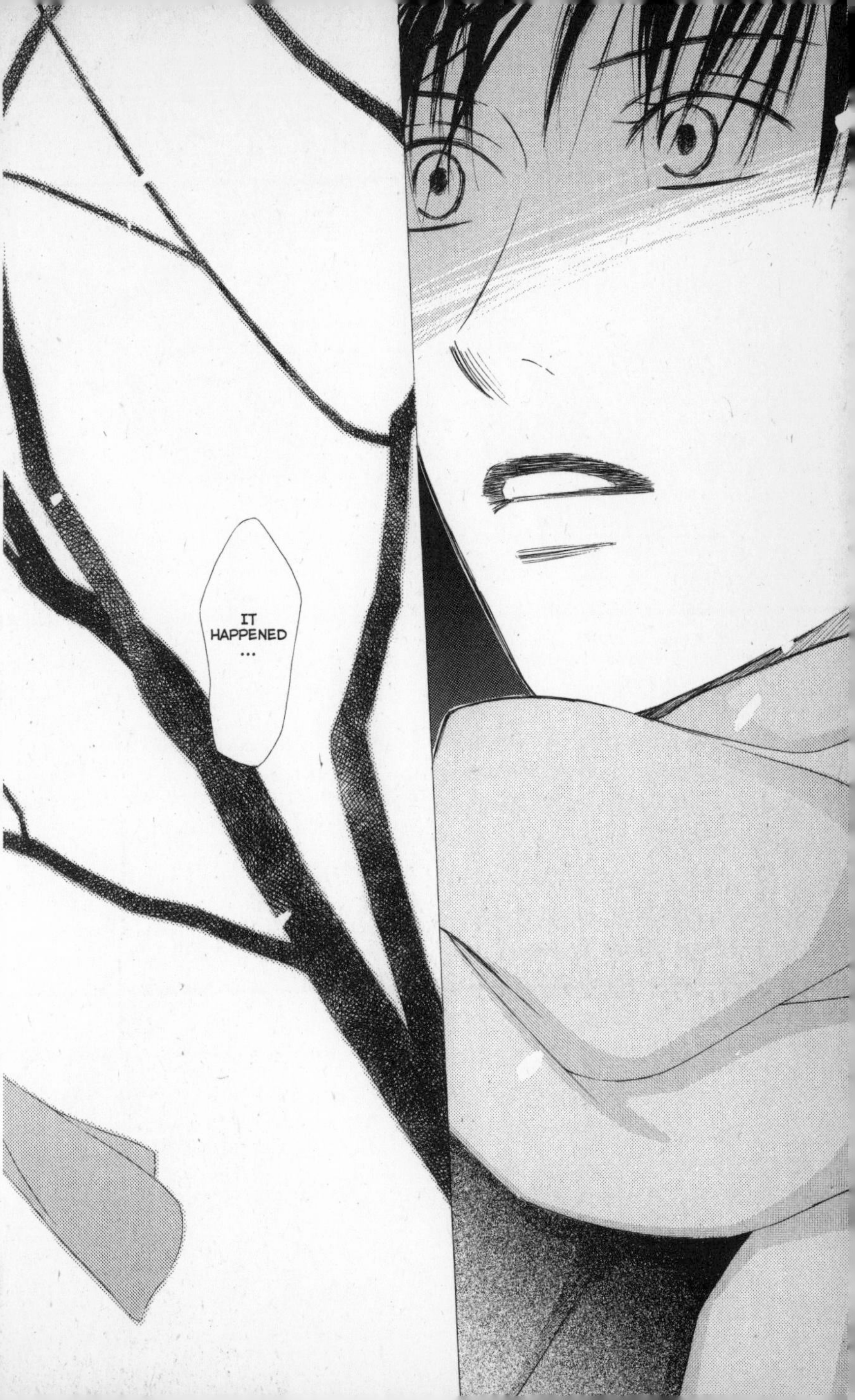
IT HAPPENED ...

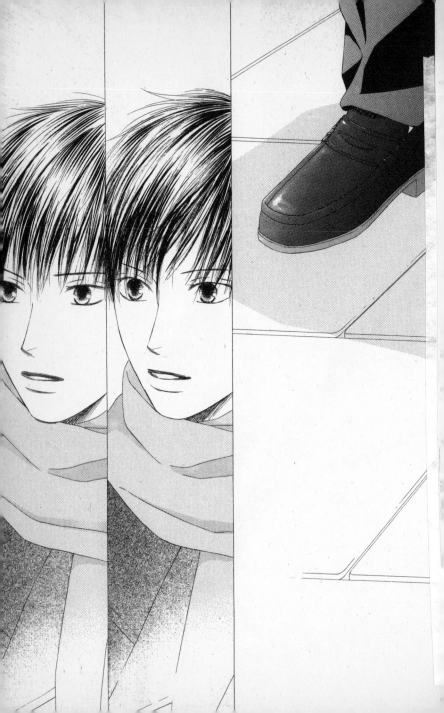

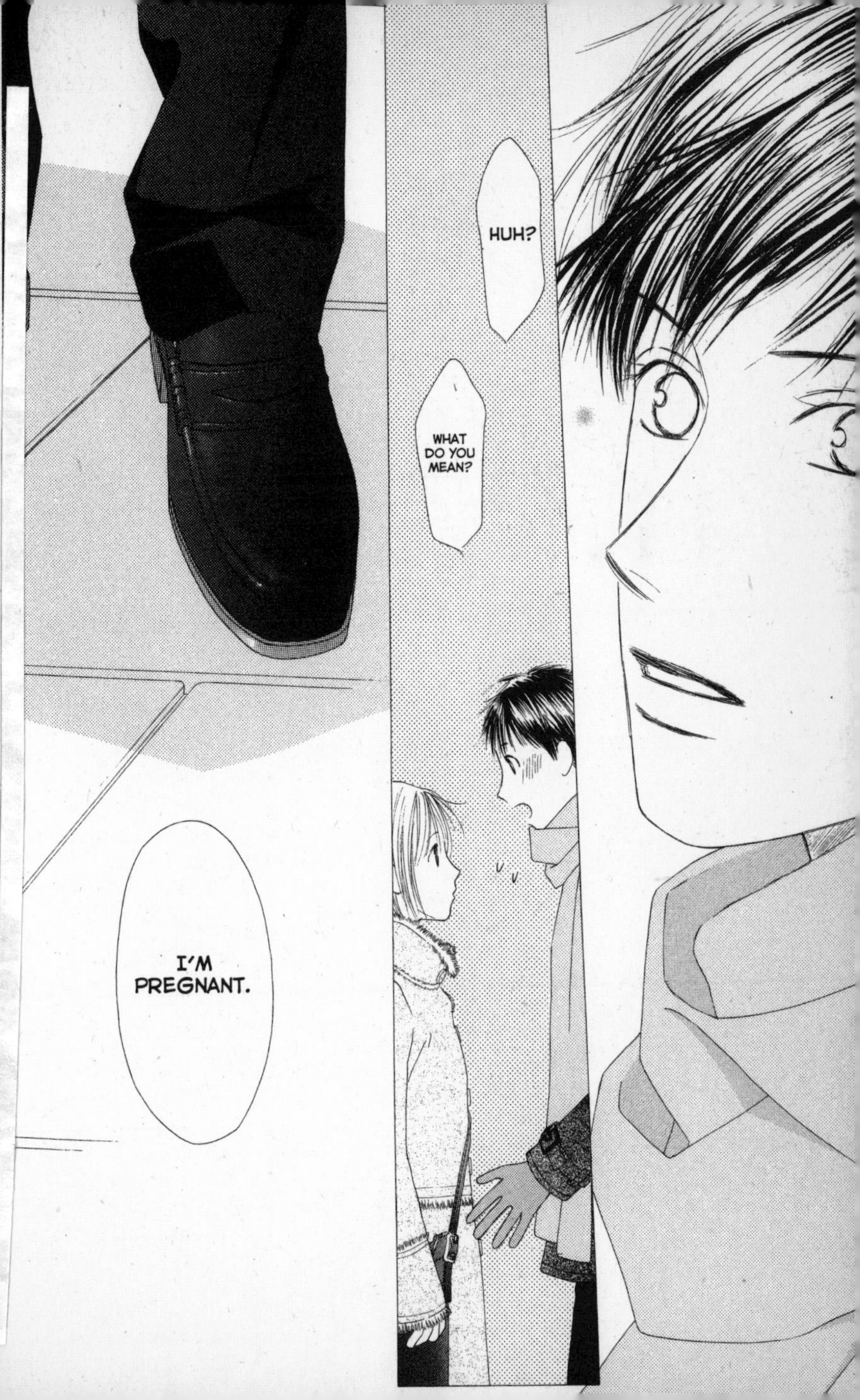
HUH?
WHAT DO YOU MEAN?
I'M PREGNANT.

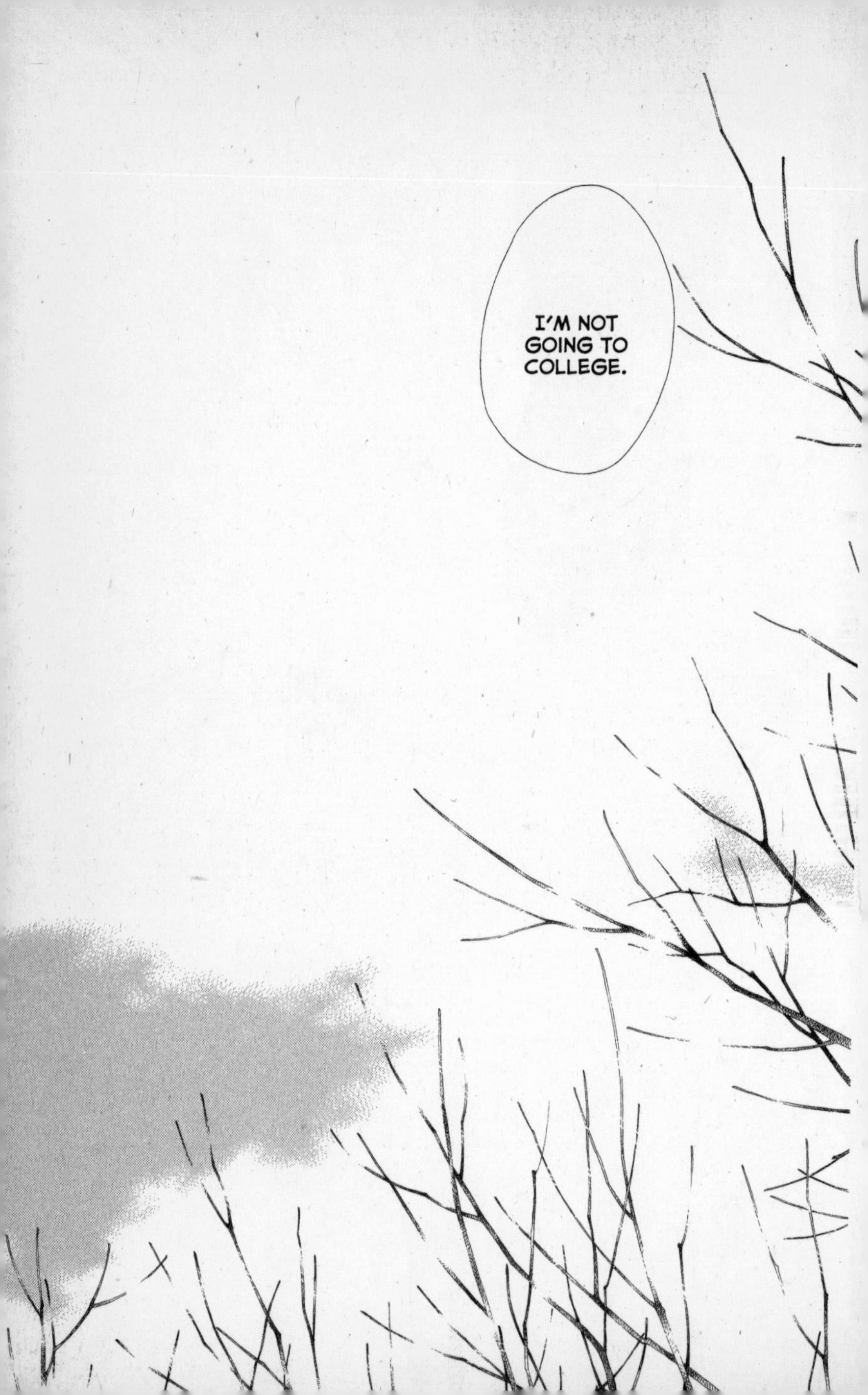
I'M NOT GOING TO COLLEGE.

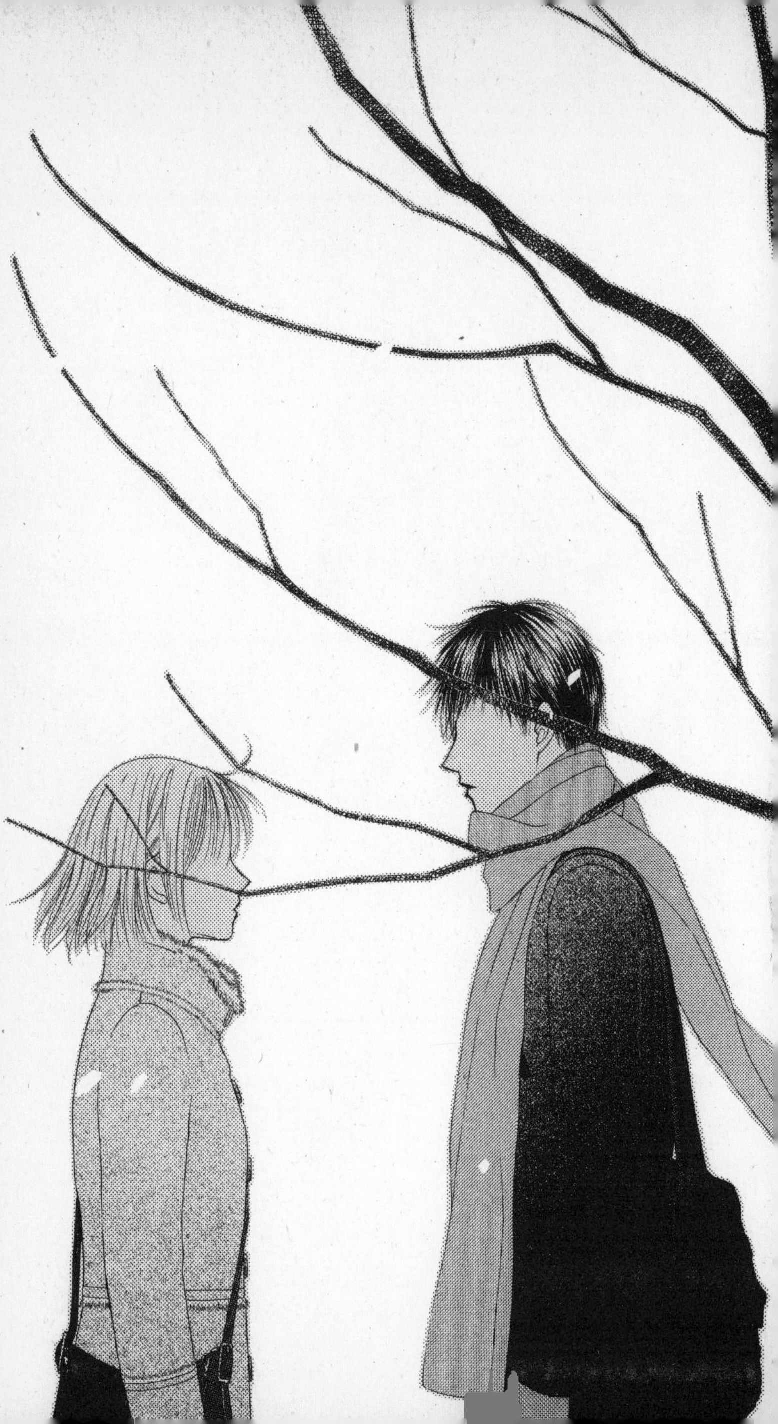

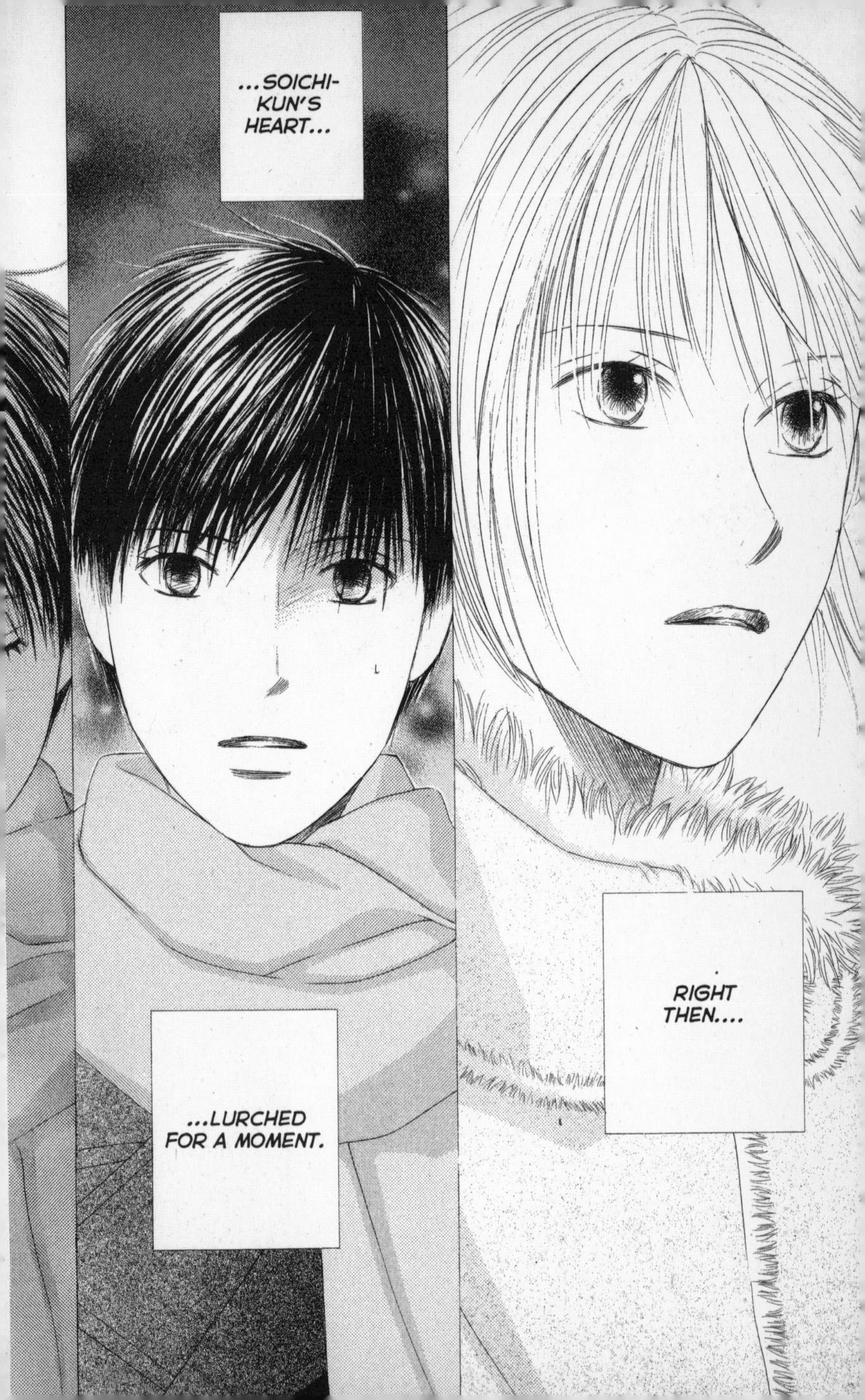
RIGHT THEN....
...SOICHI-KUN'S HEART...
...LURCHED FOR A MOMENT.

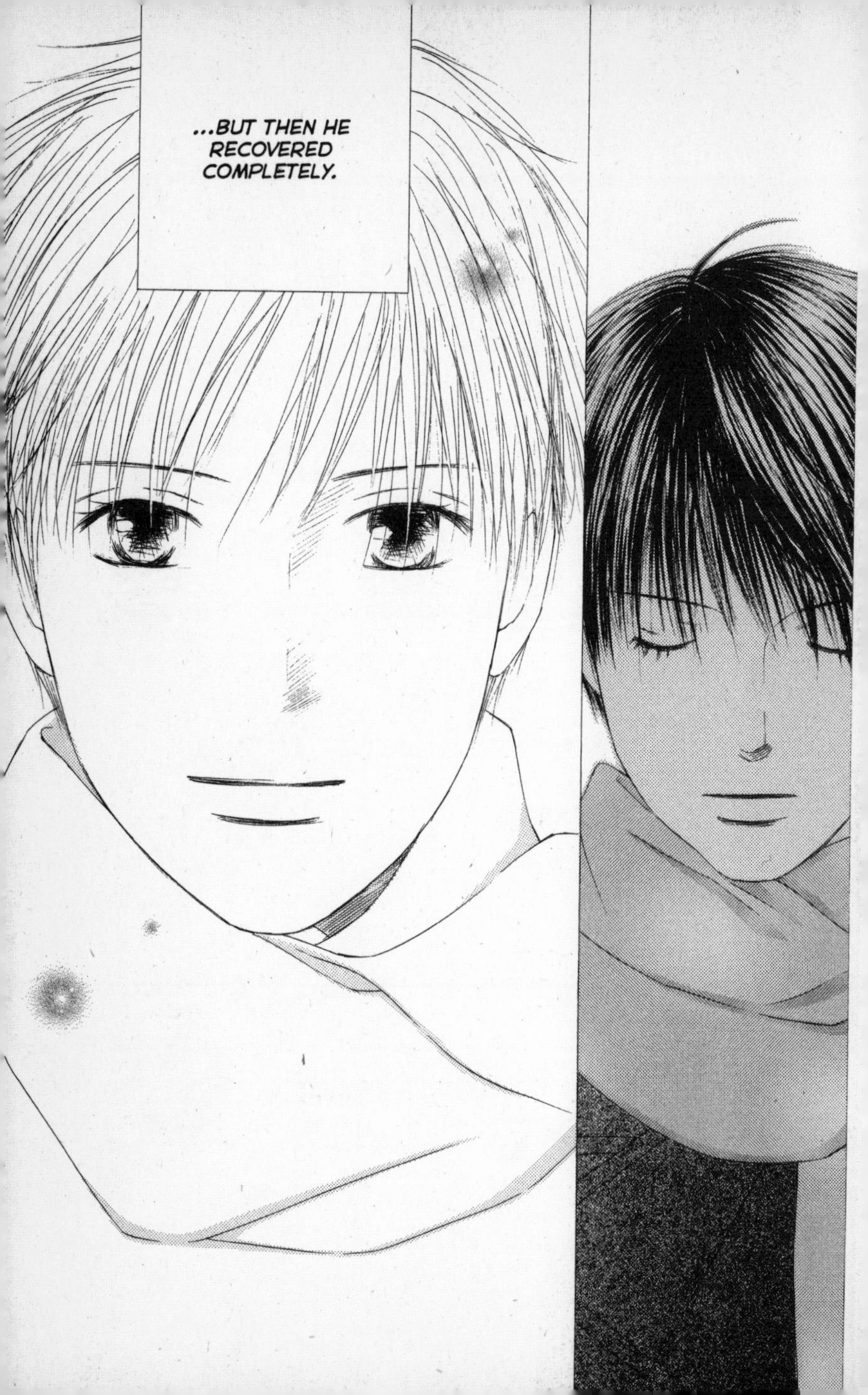
...BUT THEN HE RECOVERED COMPLETELY.

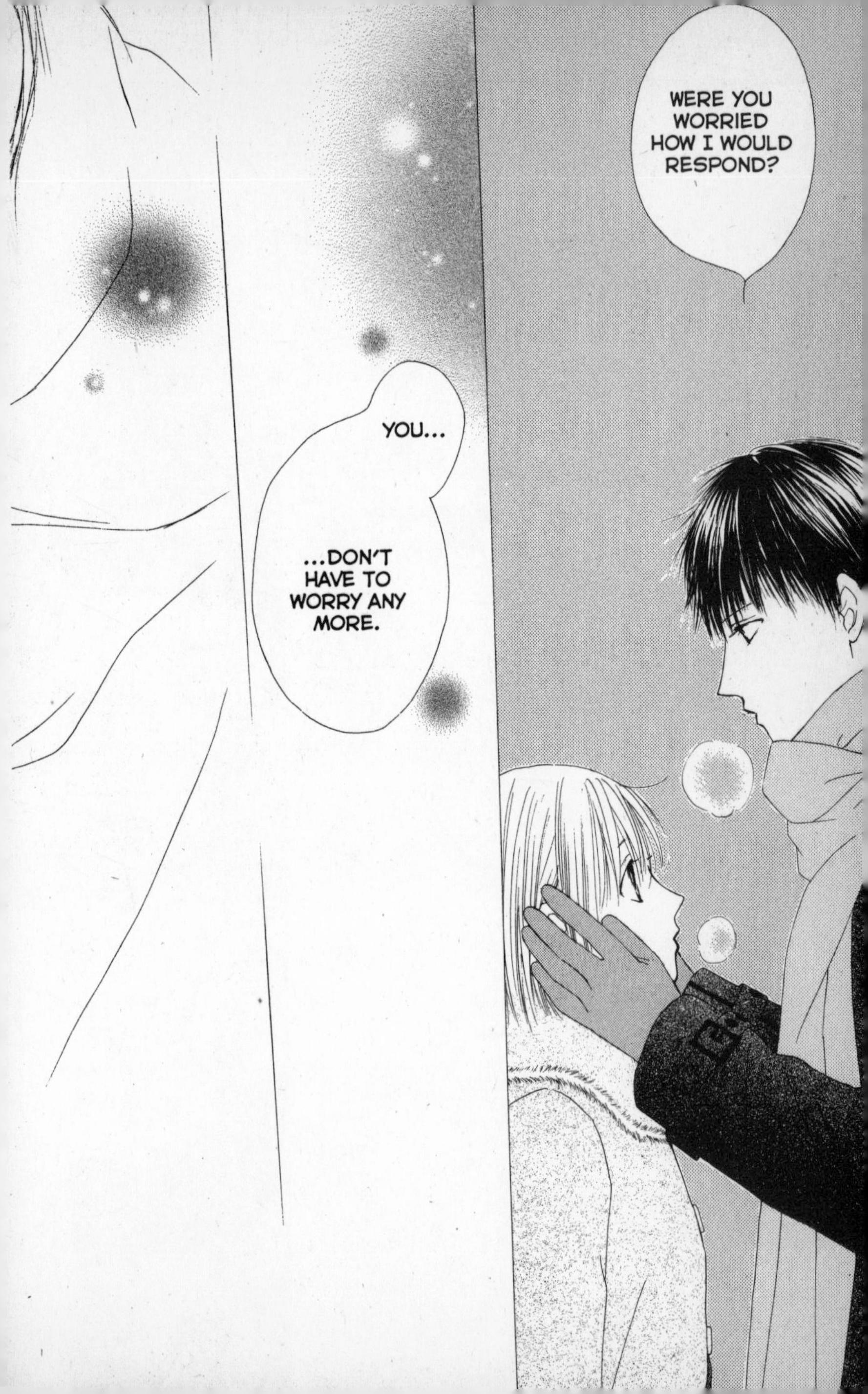
WERE YOU WORRIED HOW I WOULD RESPOND?
YOU...
...DON'T HAVE TO WORRY ANY MORE.

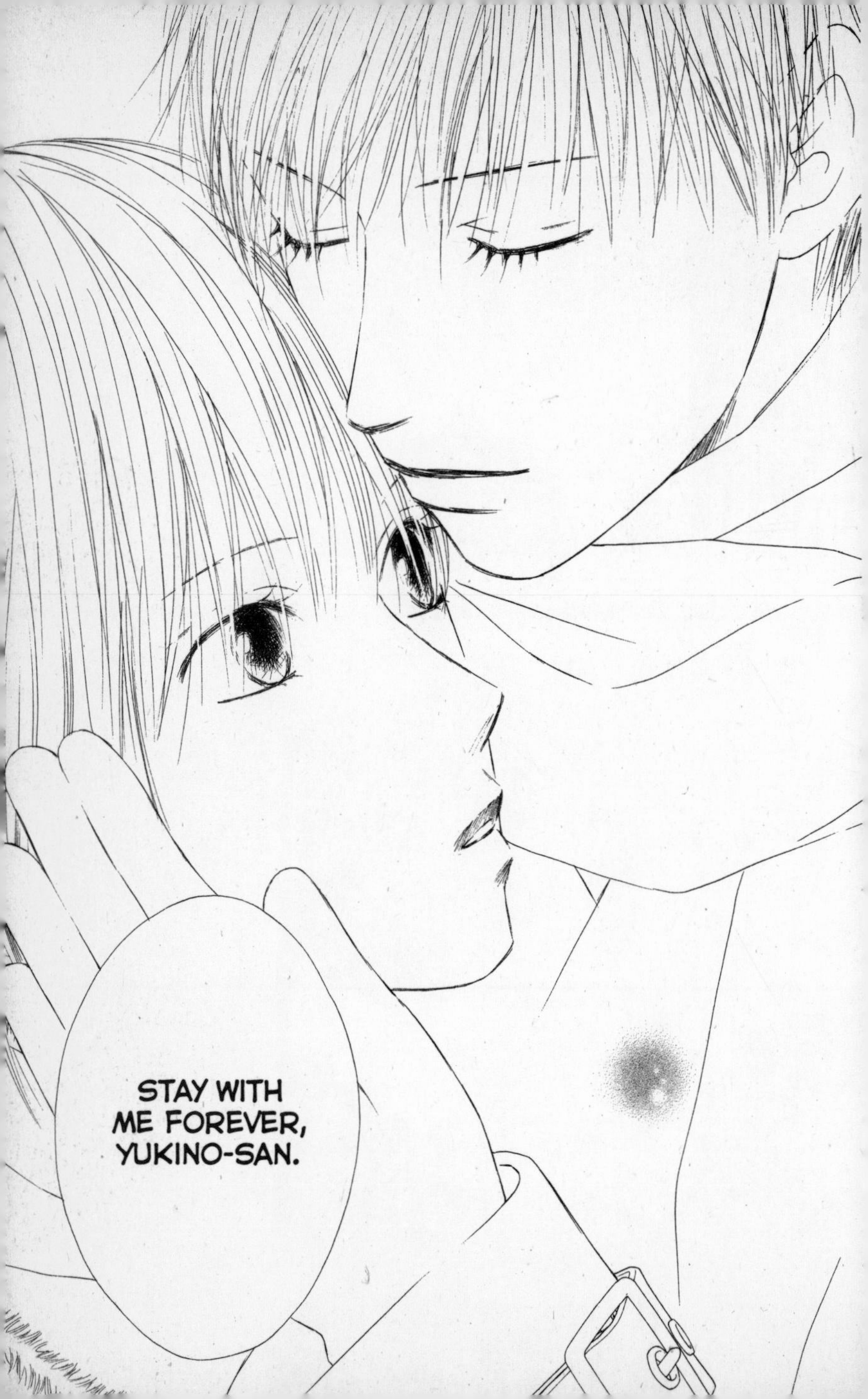
STAY WITH ME FOREVER, YUKINO-SAN.

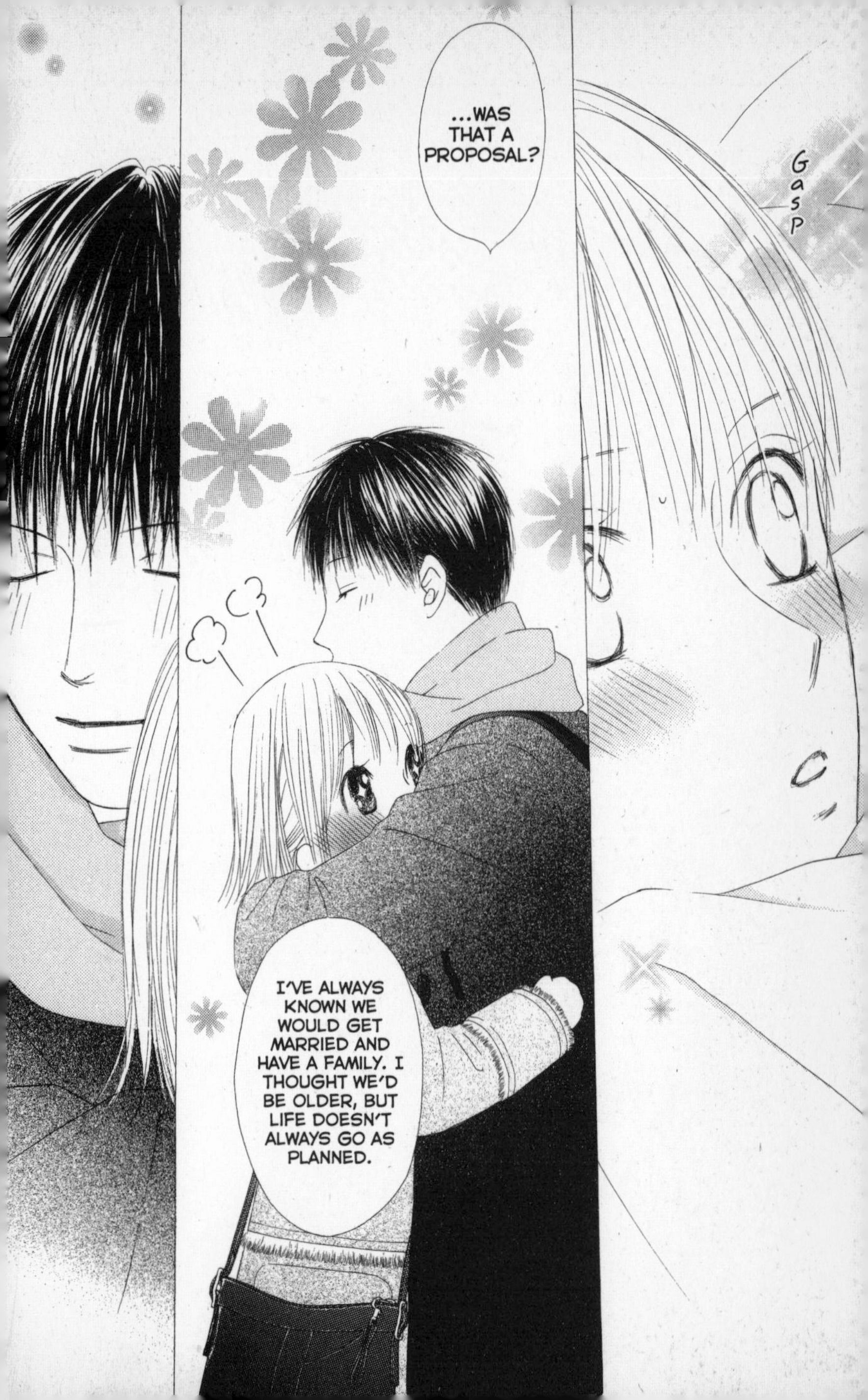
Gasp
...WAS THAT A PROPOSAL?
I'VE ALWAYS KNOWN WE WOULD GET MARRIED AND HAVE A FAMILY. I THOUGHT WE'D BE OLDER, BUT LIFE DOESN'T ALWAYS GO AS PLANNED.

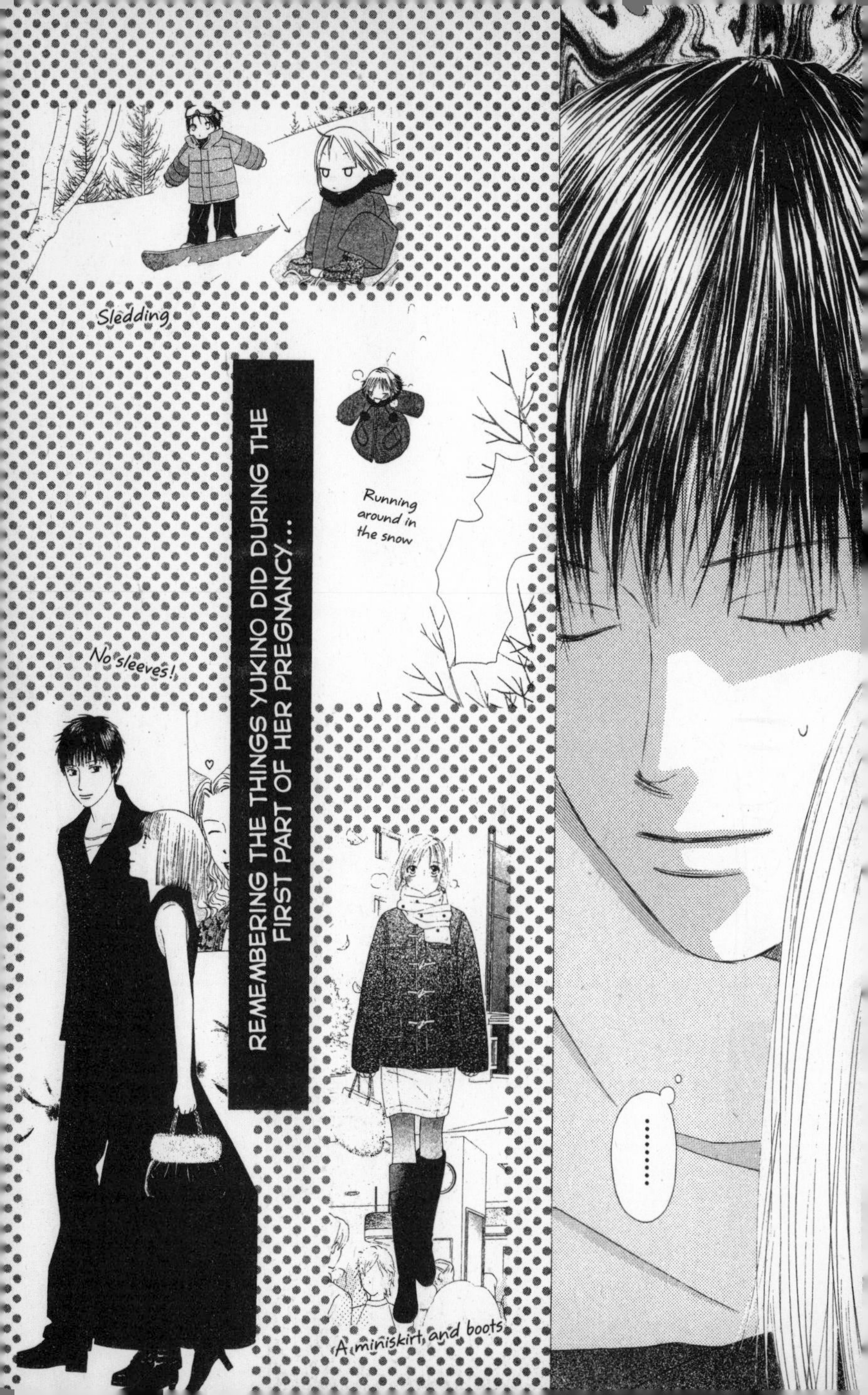
......
REMEMBERING THE THINGS YUKINO DID DURING THE FIRST PART OF HER PREGNANCY...
Sledding
Running around in the snow
A miniskirt and boots
No sleeves!

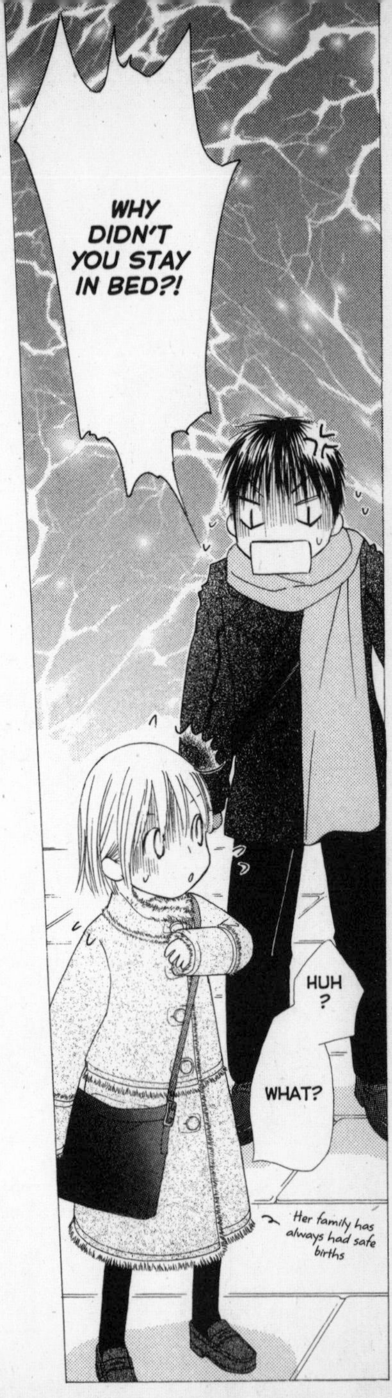
WHY DIDN'T YOU STAY IN BED?!
HUH?
WHAT?
Her family has always had safe births
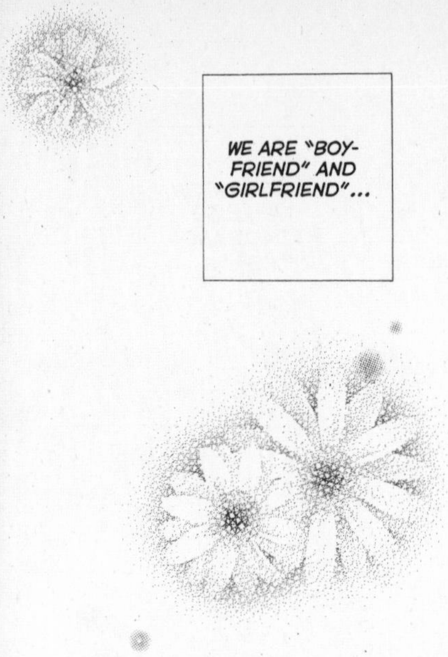
WE ARE "BOY-FRIEND" AND "GIRLFRIEND"...

...BUT SOON WE'LL BE "DAD" AND "MOM"...

...AS WELL AS "HUSBAND" AND "WIFE."

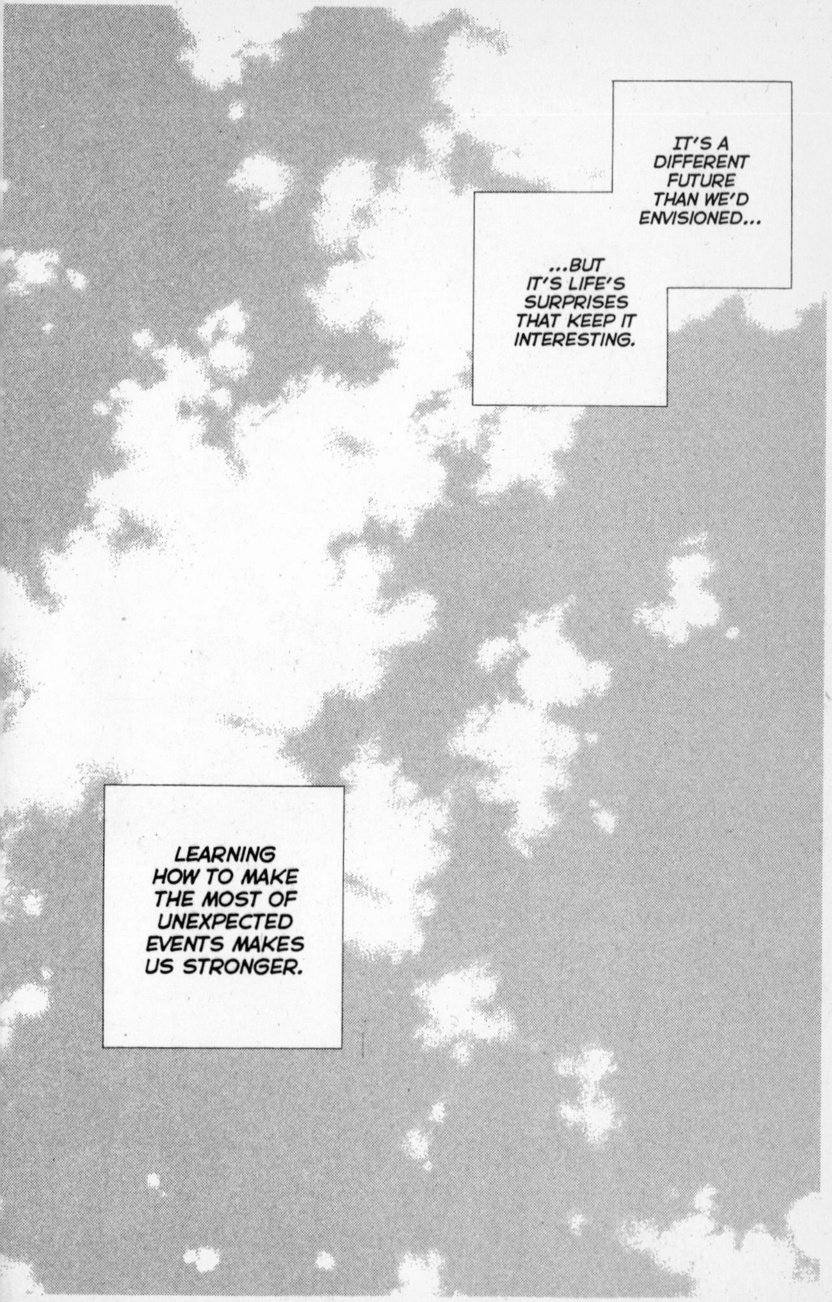
IT'S A DIFFERENT FUTURE THAN WE'D ENVISIONED...
...BUT IT'S LIFE'S SURPRISES THAT KEEP IT INTERESTING.
LEARNING HOW TO MAKE THE MOST OF UNEXPECTED EVENTS MAKES US STRONGER.

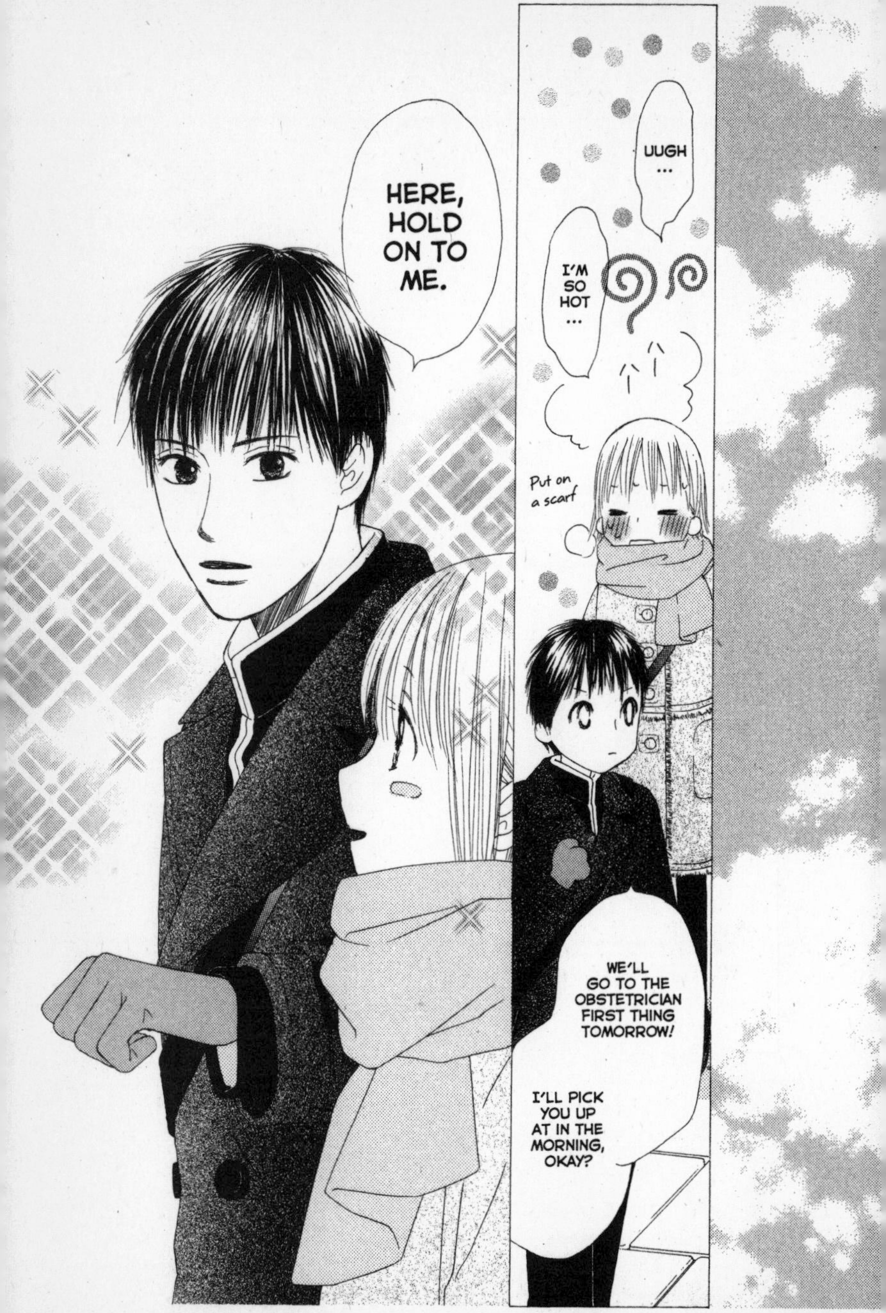
UUGH ...
I'M SO HOT ...
Put on a scarf
WE'LL GO TO THE OBSTETRICIAN FIRST THING TOMORROW!
I'LL PICK YOU UP AT IN THE MORNING, OKAY?
HERE, HOLD ON TO ME.

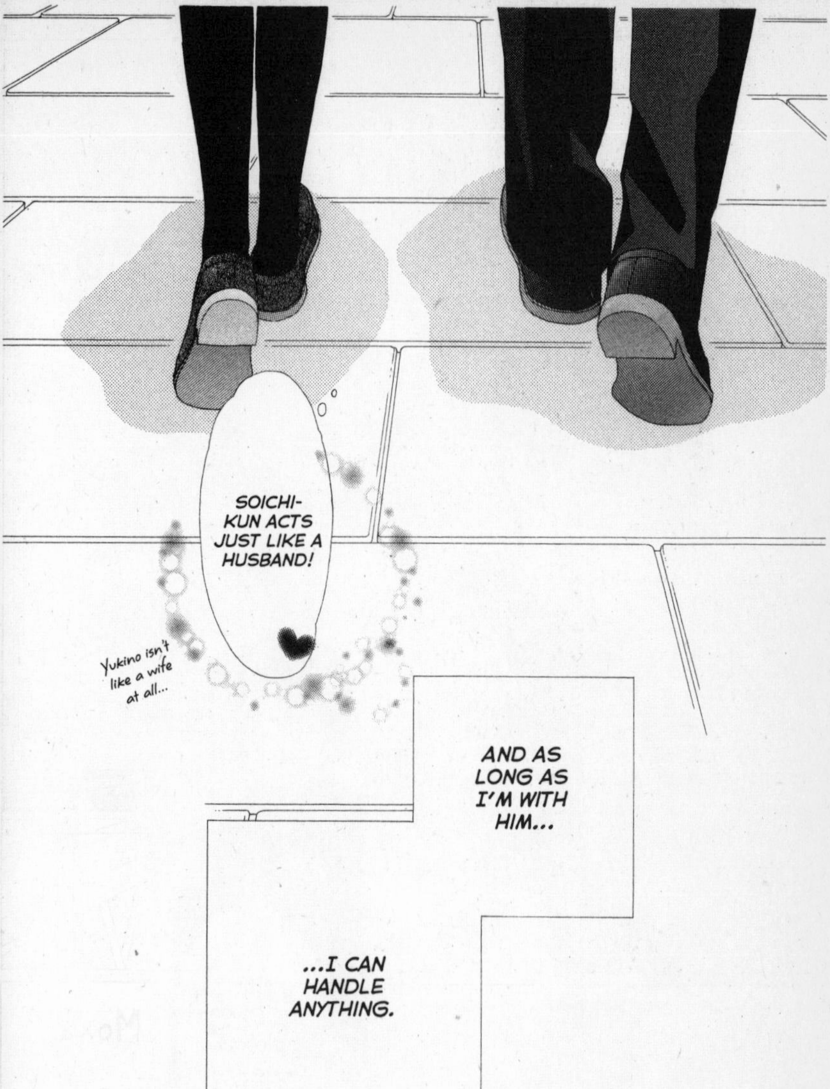
SOICHI-KUN ACTS JUST LIKE A HUSBAND!
Yukino isn't like a wife at all...
AND AS LONG AS I'M WITH HIM...
...I CAN HANDLE ANYTHING.

ACT 97 ★ BRIGHT FUTURE / END

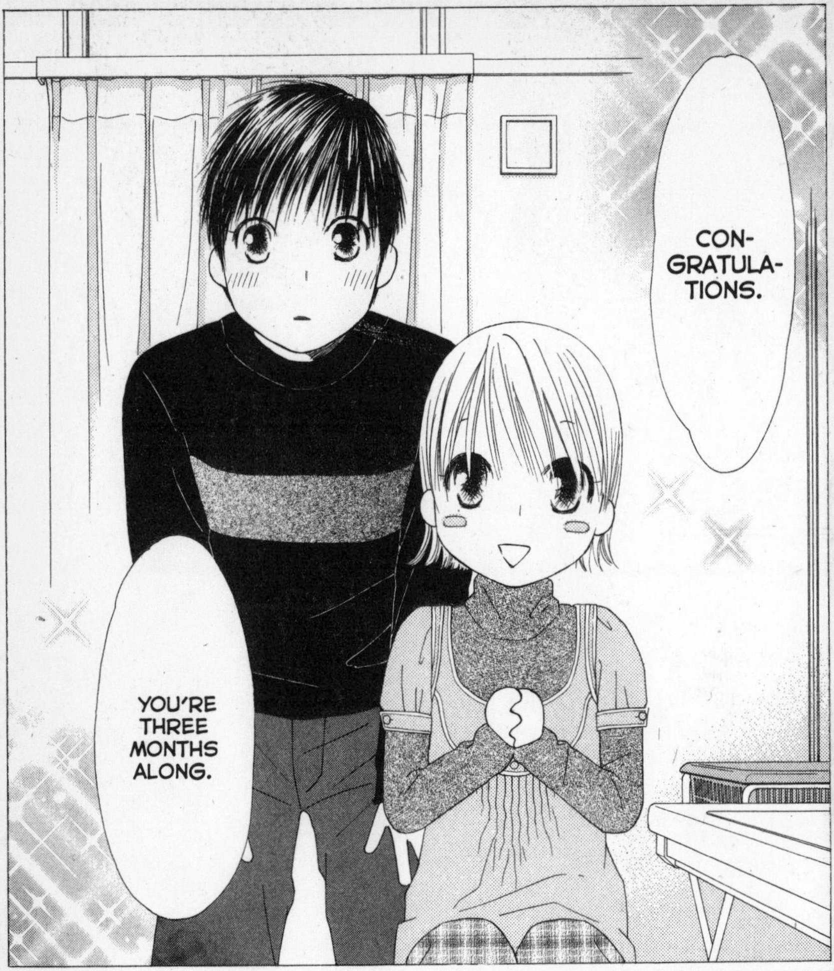
CON-GRATULA-TIONS.
YOU'RE THREE MONTHS ALONG.
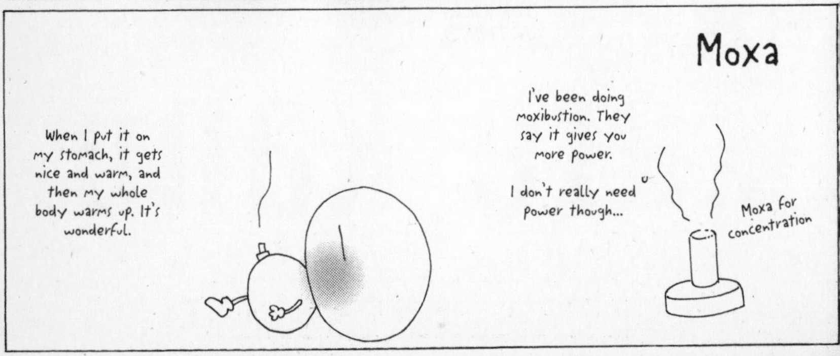
Moxa
I've been doing moxibustion. They say it gives you more power.
I don't really need power though...
Moxa for concentration
When I put it on my stomach, it gets nice and warm, and then my whole body warms up. It's wonderful.

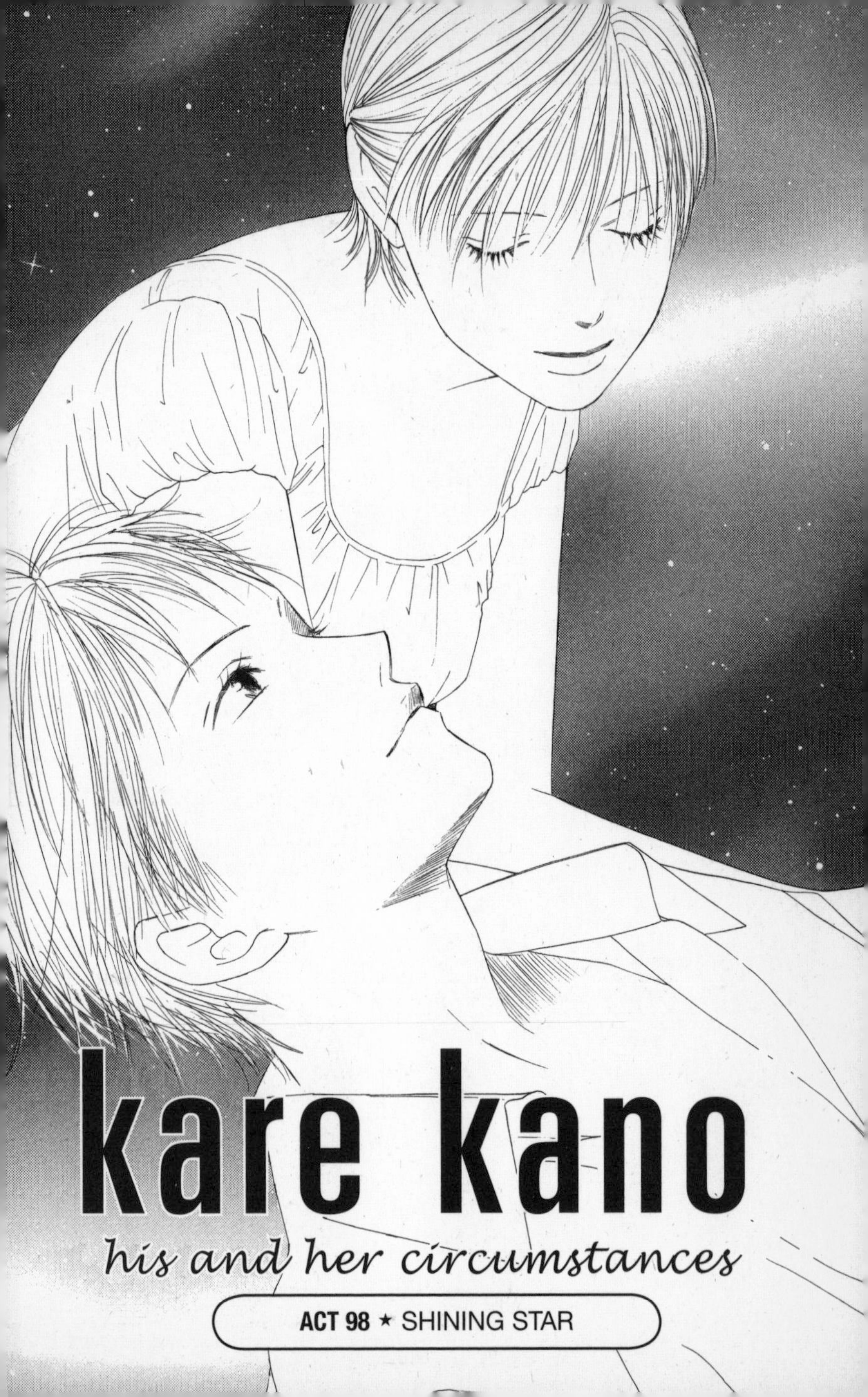
kare kano
his and her circumstances
ACT 98 ★ SHINING STAR

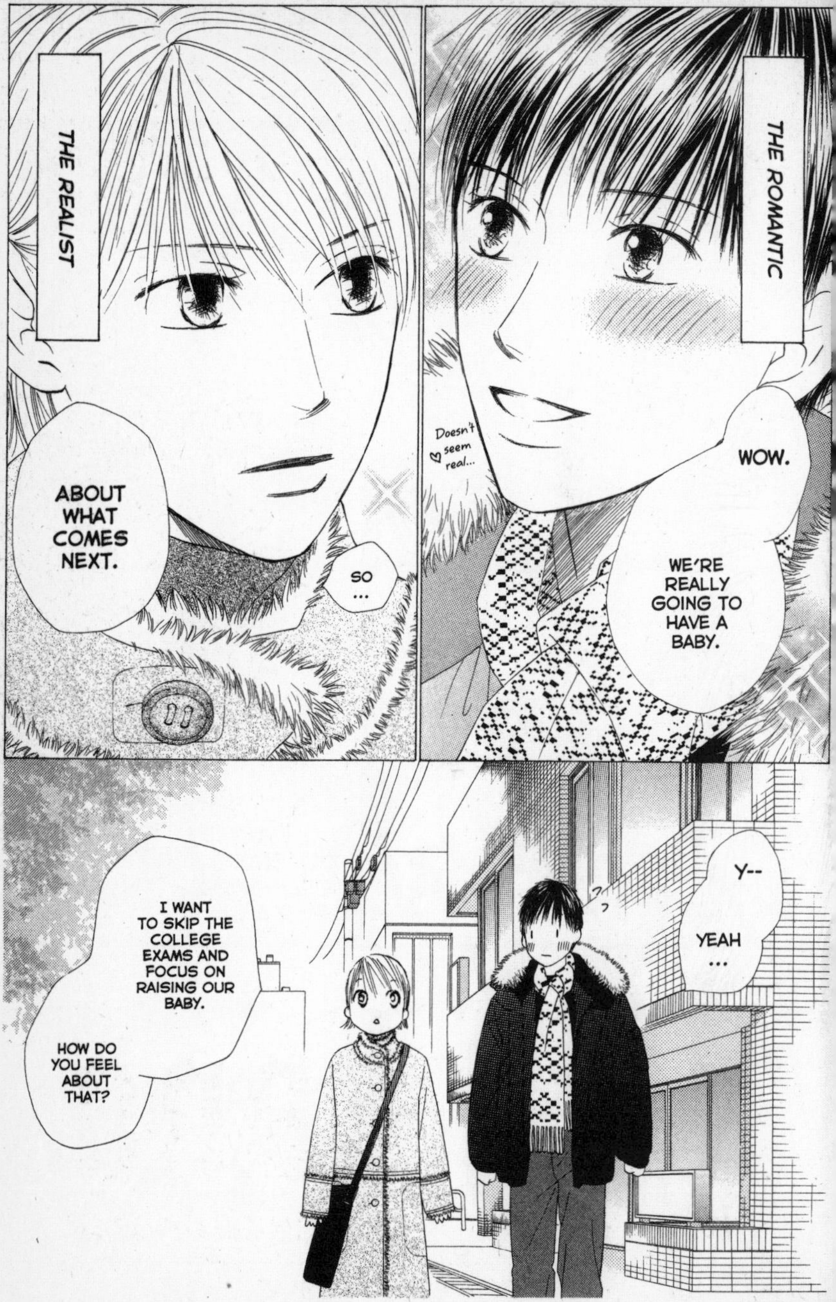
THE ROMANTIC
WOW.
WE'RE REALLY GOING TO HAVE A BABY.
Doesn't seem real...
THE REALIST
SO ...
ABOUT WHAT COMES NEXT.
Y--
YEAH ...
I WANT TO SKIP THE COLLEGE EXAMS AND FOCUS ON RAISING OUR BABY.
HOW DO YOU FEEL ABOUT THAT?

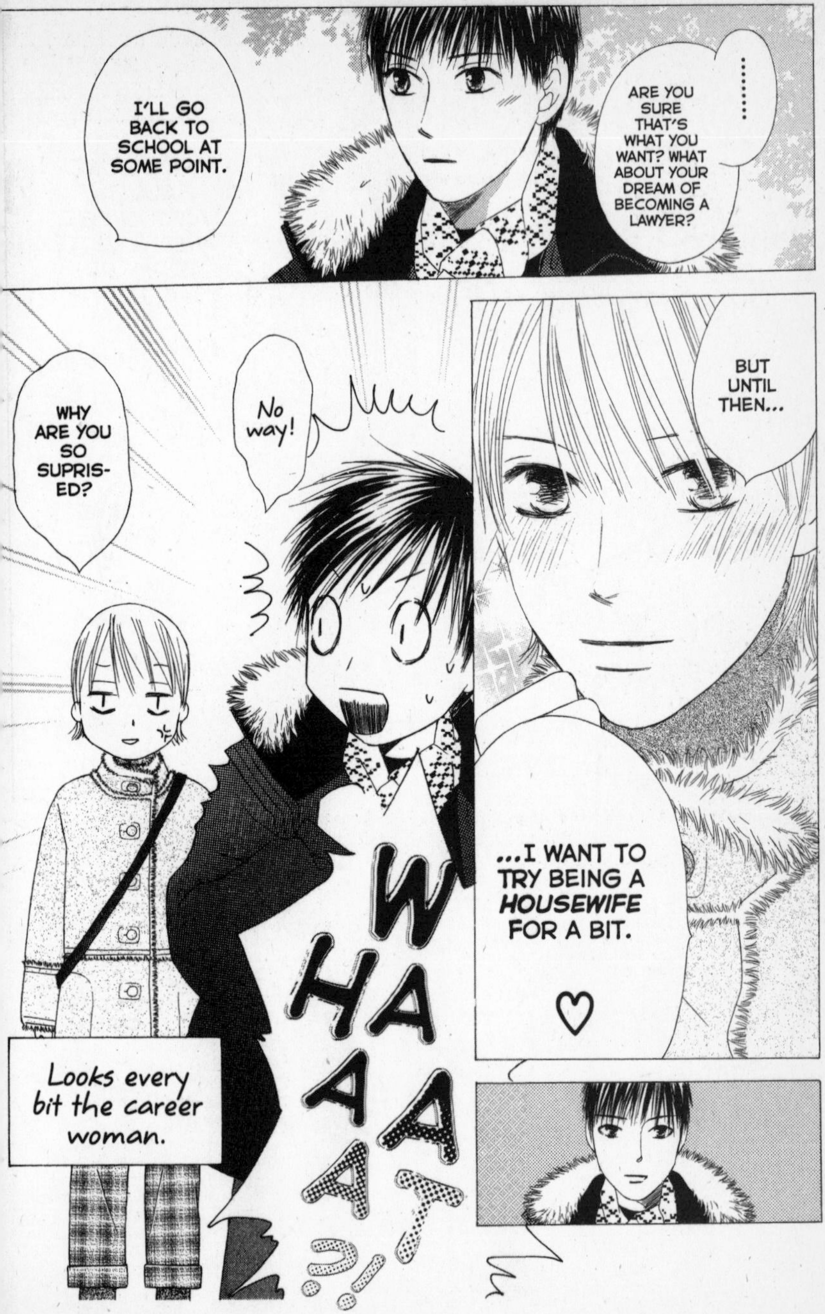
......
ARE YOU SURE THAT'S WHAT YOU WANT? WHAT ABOUT YOUR DREAM OF BECOMING A LAWYER?
I'LL GO BACK TO SCHOOL AT SOME POINT.
BUT UNTIL THEN...
...I WANT TO TRY BEING A *HOUSEWIFE* FOR A BIT. ♡
WHAAAAT?!
No way!
WHY ARE YOU SO SUPRIS-ED?
Looks every bit the career woman.

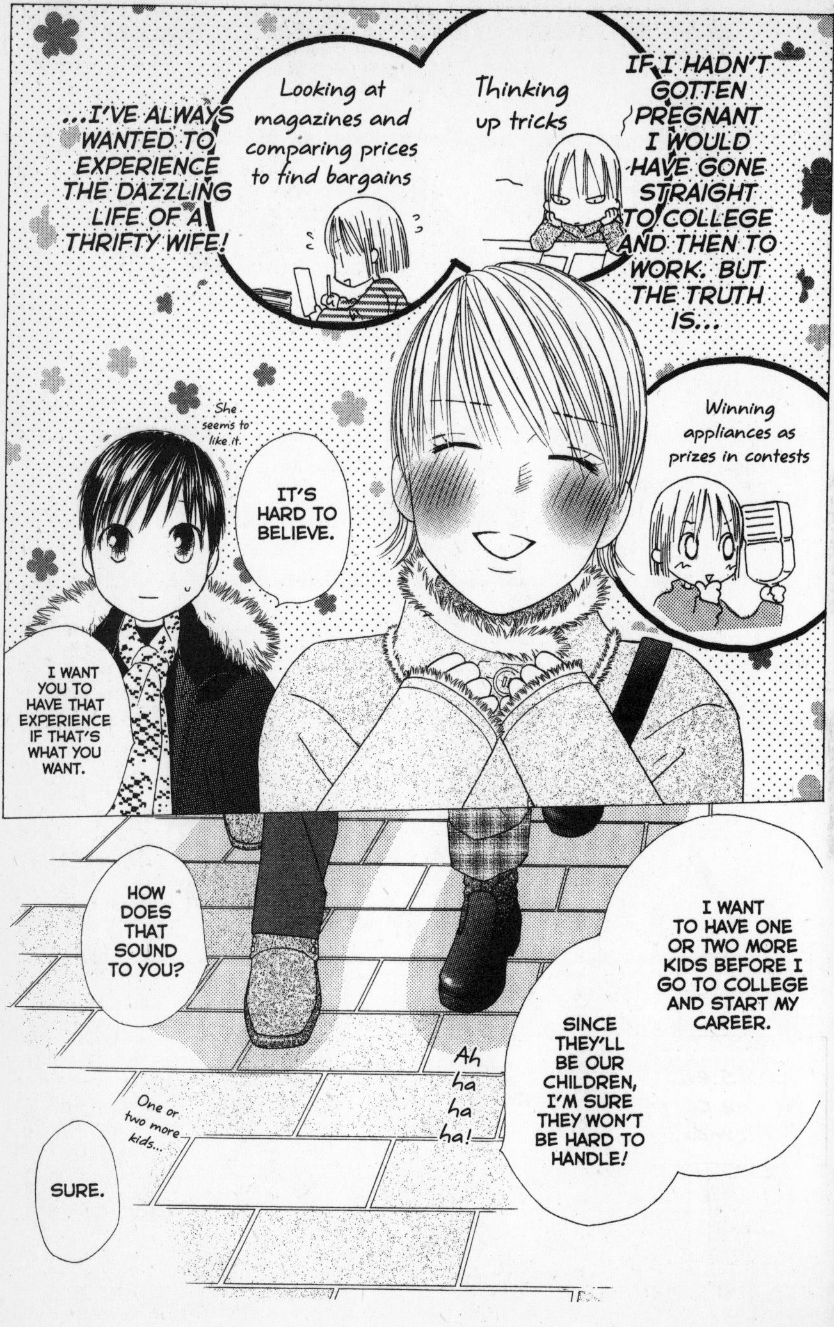
IF I HADN'T GOTTEN PREGNANT I WOULD HAVE GONE STRAIGHT TO COLLEGE AND THEN TO WORK. BUT THE TRUTH IS...
...I'VE ALWAYS WANTED TO EXPERIENCE THE DAZZLING LIFE OF A THRIFTY WIFE!
Thinking up tricks
Looking at magazines and comparing prices to find bargains
Winning appliances as prizes in contests
IT'S HARD TO BELIEVE.
She seems to like it.
I WANT YOU TO HAVE THAT EXPERIENCE IF THAT'S WHAT YOU WANT.
I WANT TO HAVE ONE OR TWO MORE KIDS BEFORE I GO TO COLLEGE AND START MY CAREER.
HOW DOES THAT SOUND TO YOU?
SINCE THEY'LL BE OUR CHILDREN, I'M SURE THEY WON'T BE HARD TO HANDLE!
Ah ha ha ha!
One or two more kids...
SURE.

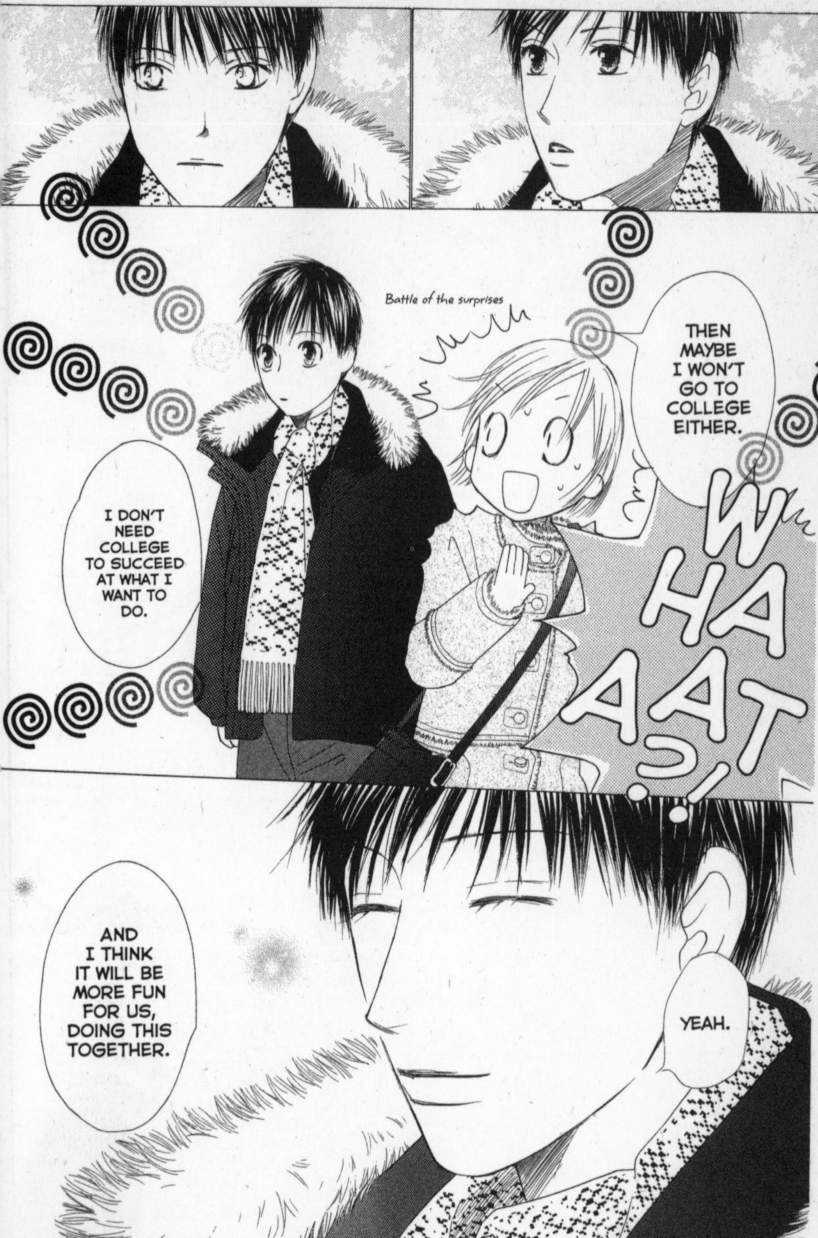
THEN MAYBE I WON'T GO TO COLLEGE EITHER.
WHAAAT?!
Battle of the surprises
I DON'T NEED COLLEGE TO SUCCEED AT WHAT I WANT TO DO.
AND I THINK IT WILL BE MORE FUN FOR US, DOING THIS TOGETHER.
YEAH.

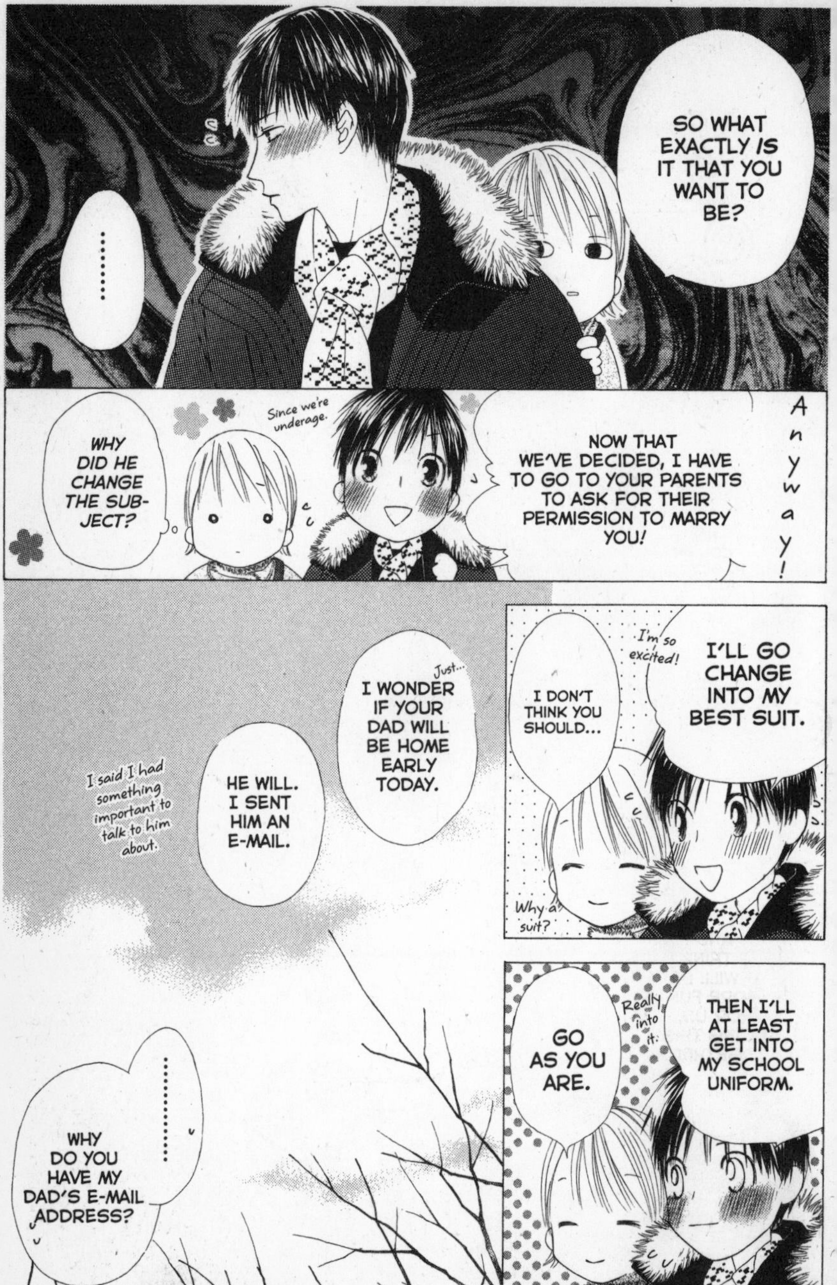
SO WHAT EXACTLY IS IT THAT YOU WANT TO BE?
....
Anyway!
NOW THAT WE'VE DECIDED, I HAVE TO GO TO YOUR PARENTS TO ASK FOR THEIR PERMISSION TO MARRY YOU!
Since we're underage.
WHY DID HE CHANGE THE SUBJECT?
I'LL GO CHANGE INTO MY BEST SUIT.
I'm so excited!
I DON'T THINK YOU SHOULD...
Why a suit?
THEN I'LL AT LEAST GET INTO MY SCHOOL UNIFORM.
Really into it.
GO AS YOU ARE.
Just...
I WONDER IF YOUR DAD WILL BE HOME EARLY TODAY.
HE WILL. I SENT HIM AN E-MAIL.
I said I had something important to talk to him about.
....
WHY DO YOU HAVE MY DAD'S E-MAIL ADDRESS?

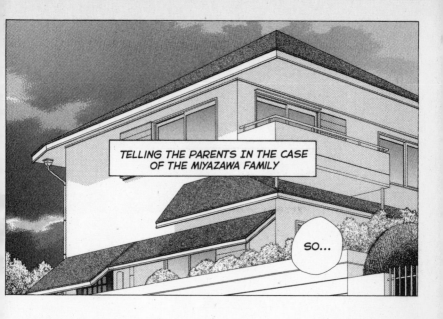

TELLING THE PARENTS IN THE CASE OF THE MIYAZAWA FAMILY

SO...

...WHAT WAS IT THAT YOU WANTED TO TALK ABOUT?

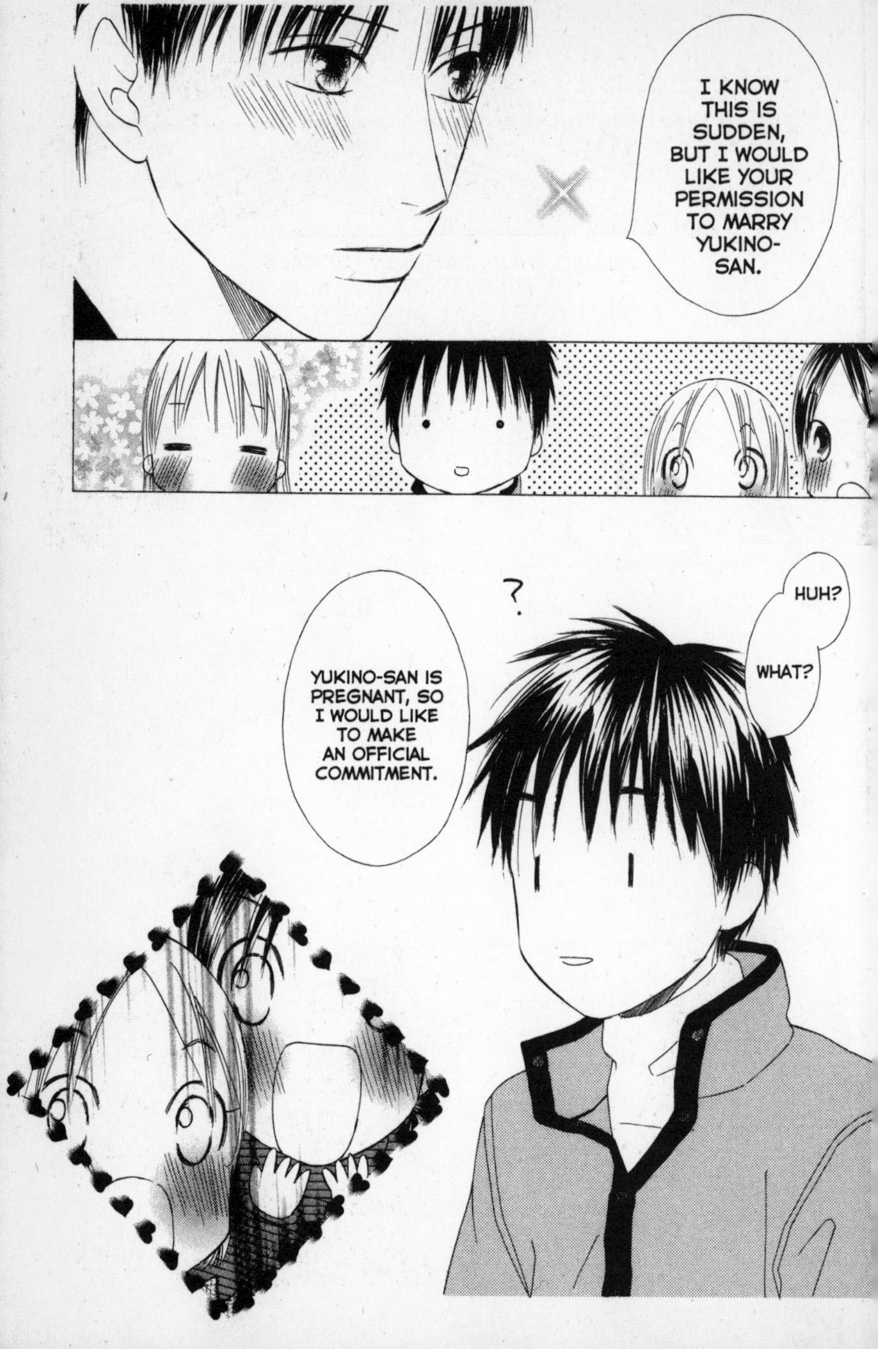
I KNOW THIS IS SUDDEN, BUT I WOULD LIKE YOUR PERMISSION TO MARRY YUKINO-SAN.
HUH?
WHAT?
YUKINO-SAN IS PREGNANT, SO I WOULD LIKE TO MAKE AN OFFICIAL COMMITMENT.
?

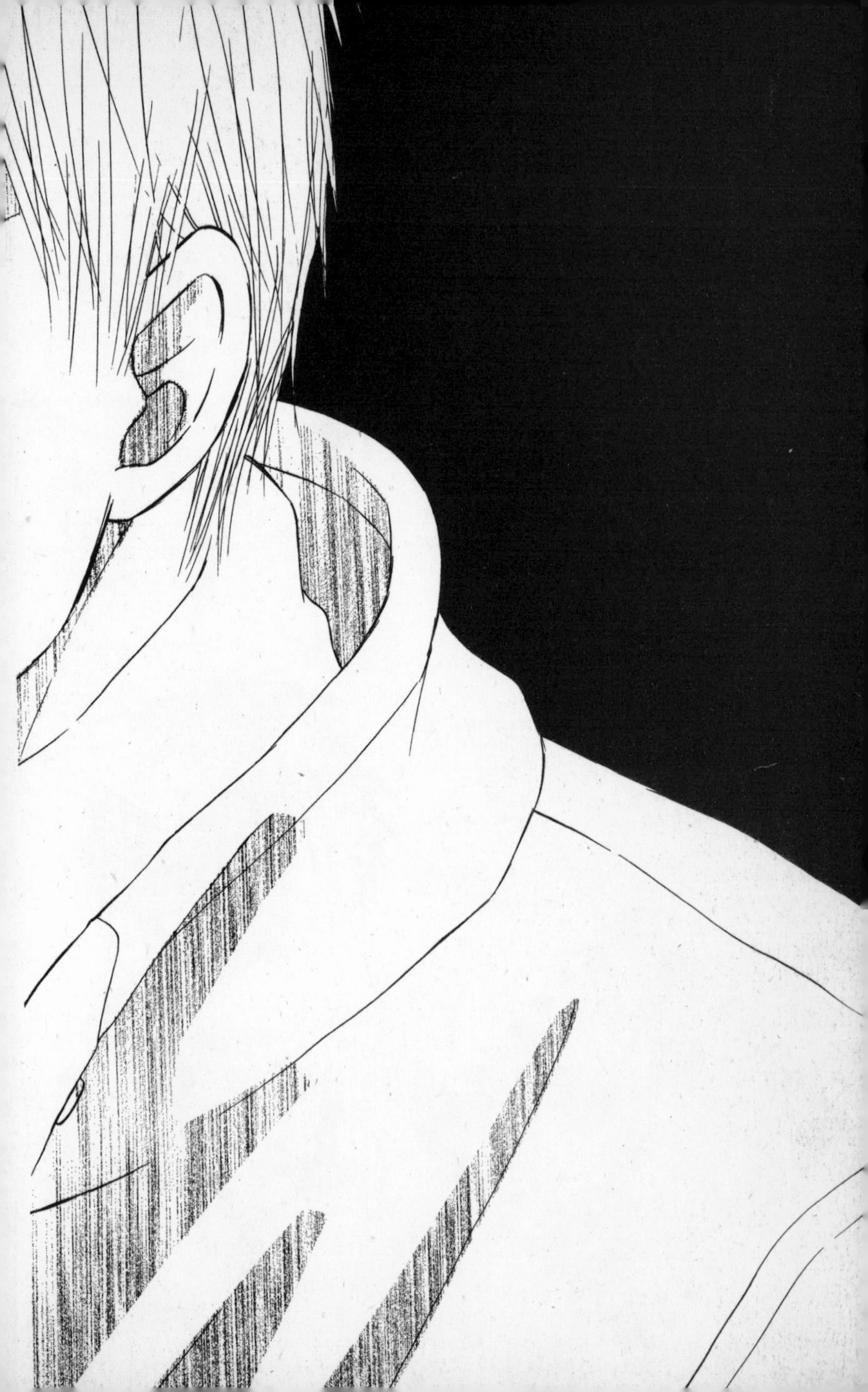

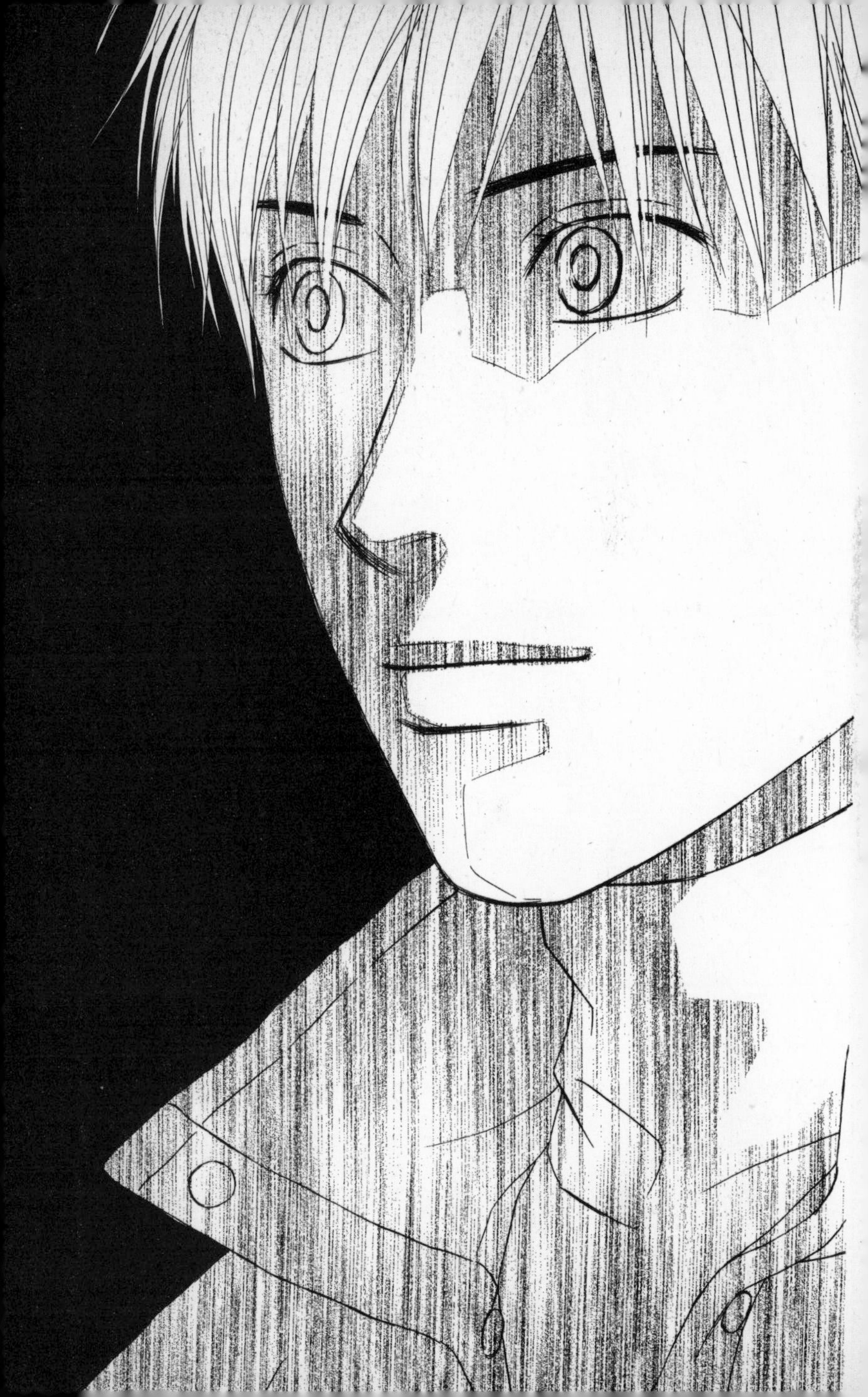

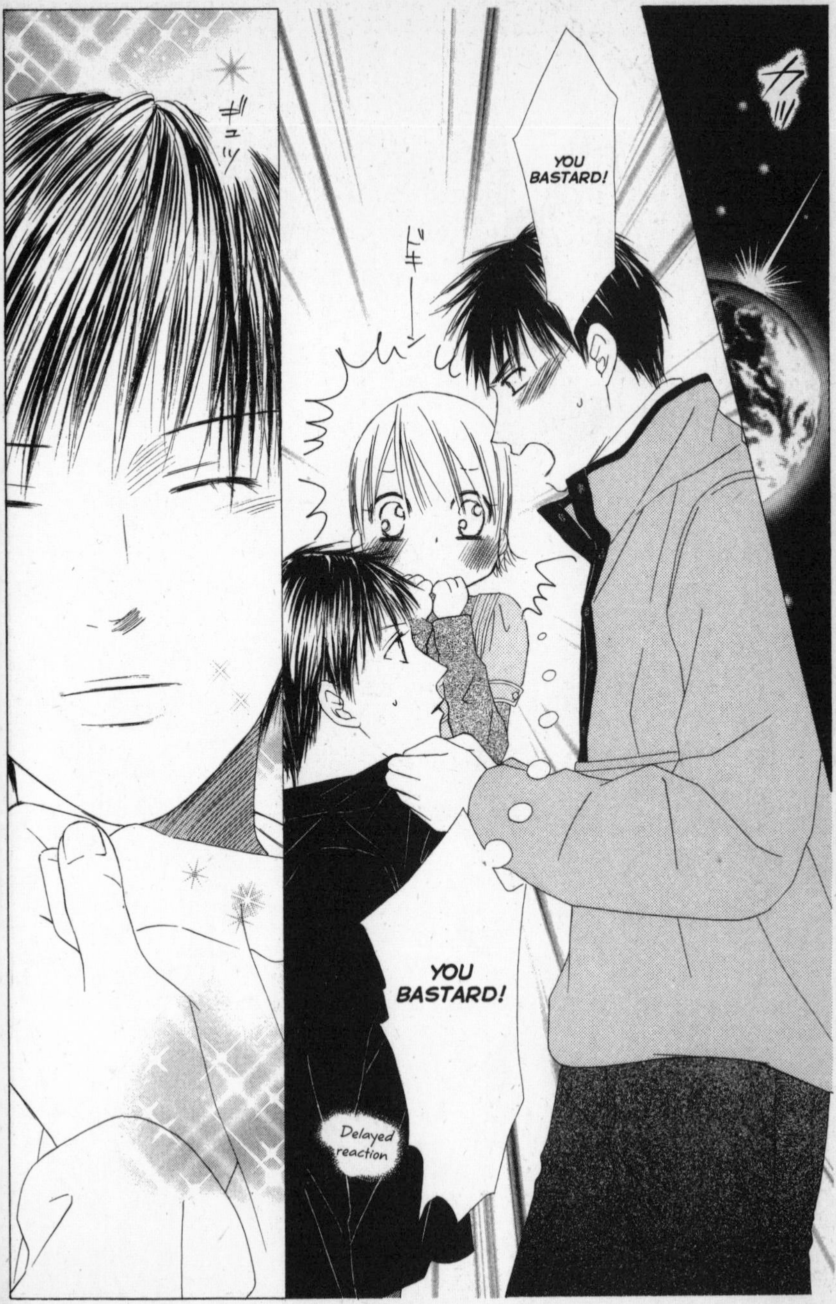
YOU BASTARD!
ドキー
YOU BASTARD!
Delayed reaction
ギュッ

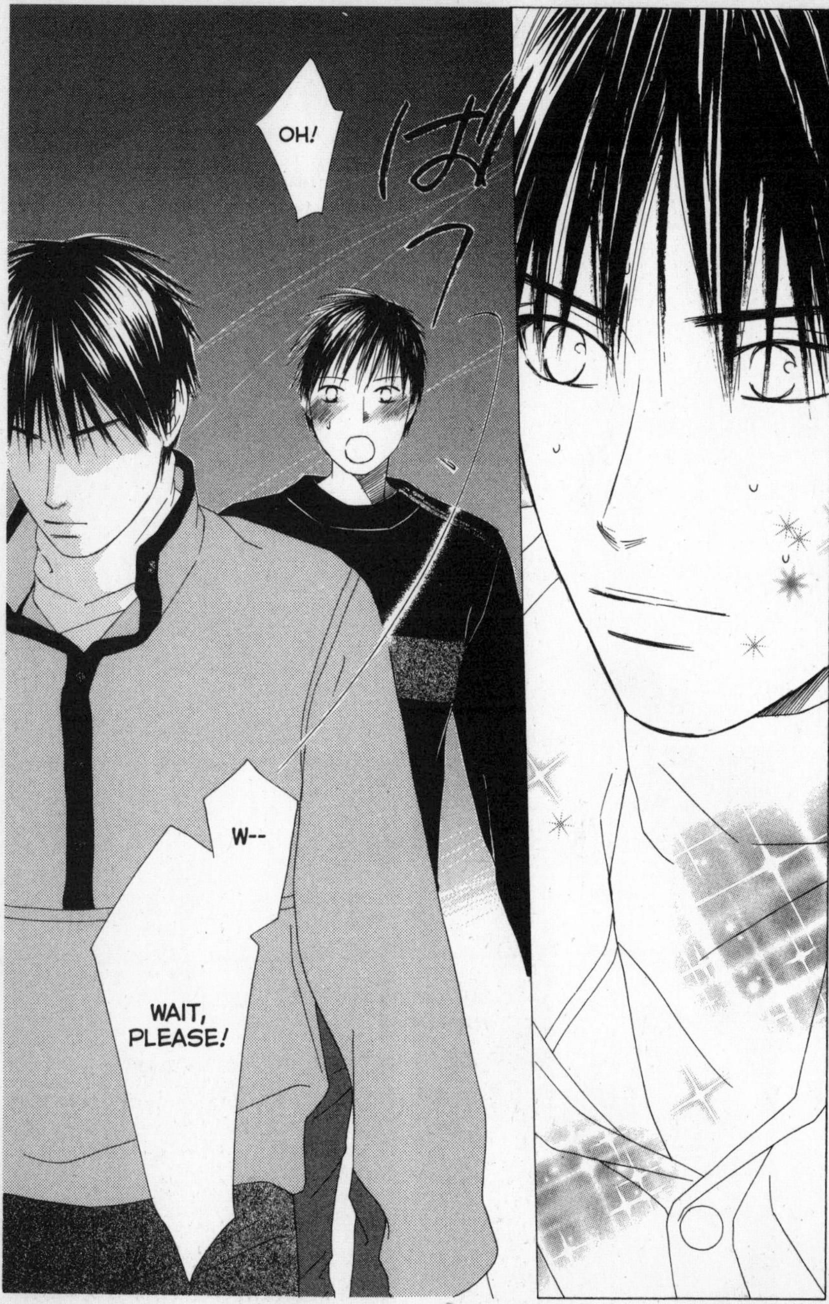
OH!
はっ
W--
WAIT, PLEASE!

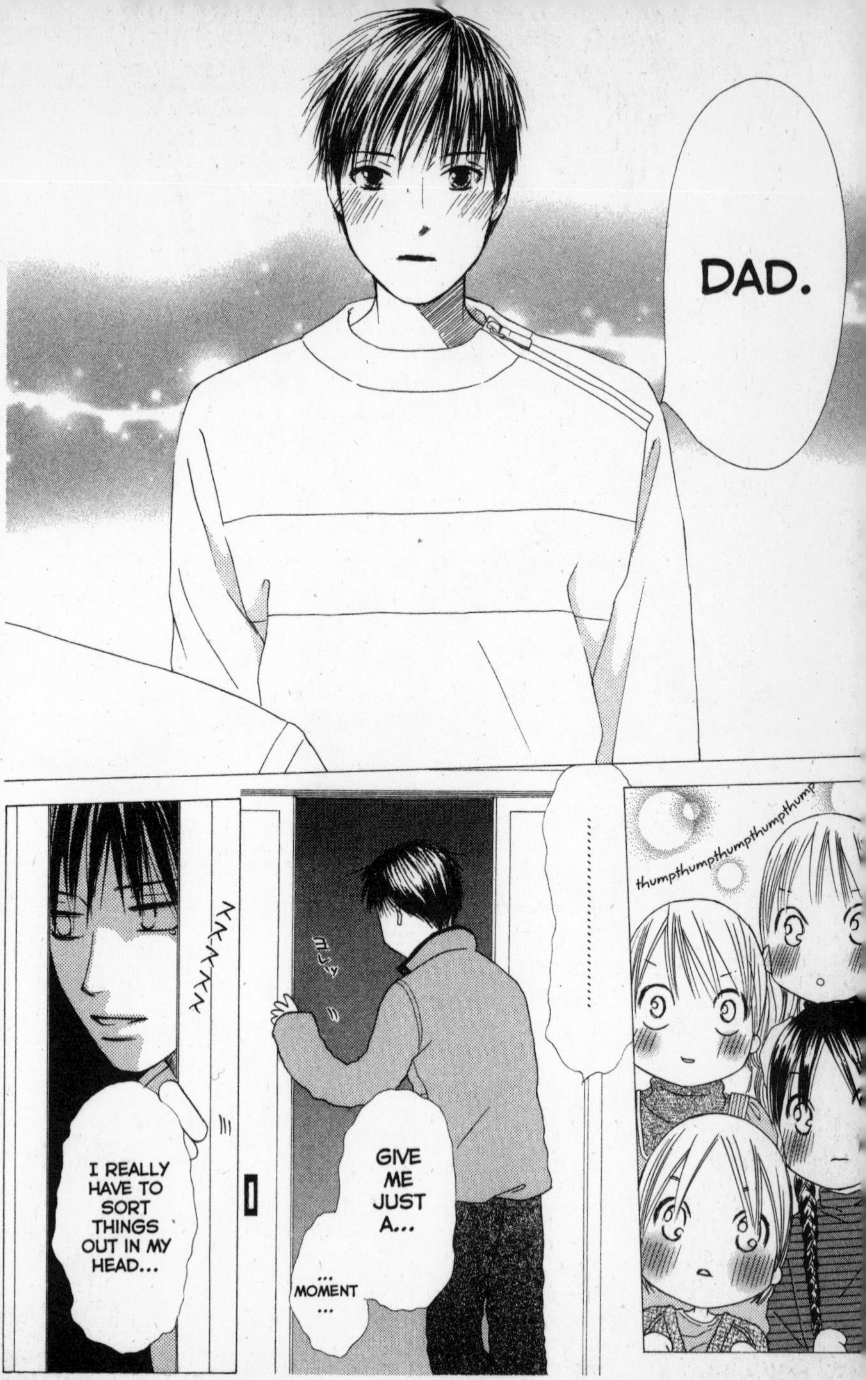
DAD.
thumpthumpthumpthumpthump
....
GIVE ME JUST A...
...MOMENT...
I REALLY HAVE TO SORT THINGS OUT IN MY HEAD...

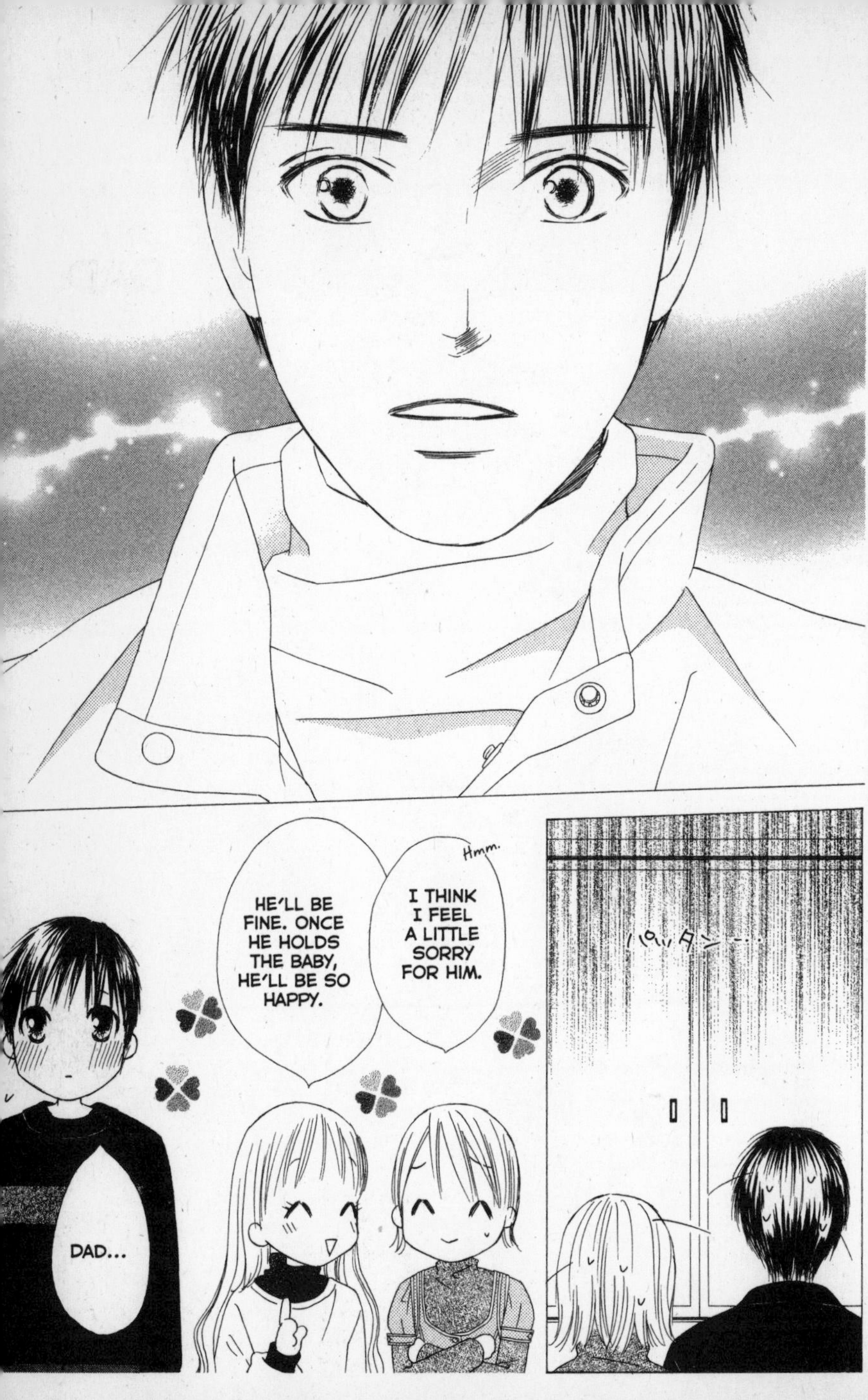
パッタン…
Hmm.
I THINK I FEEL A LITTLE SORRY FOR HIM.
HE'LL BE FINE. ONCE HE HOLDS THE BABY, HE'LL BE SO HAPPY.
DAD...

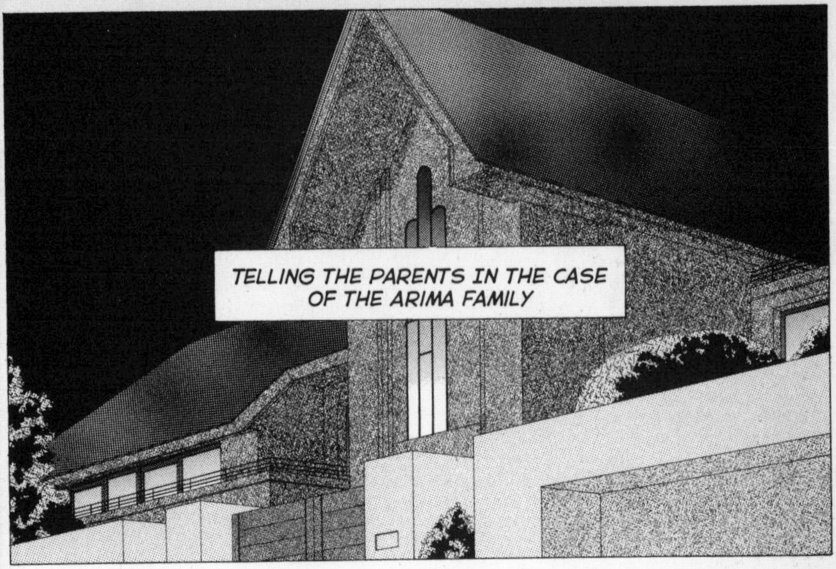
TELLING THE PARENTS IN THE CASE OF THE ARIMA FAMILY

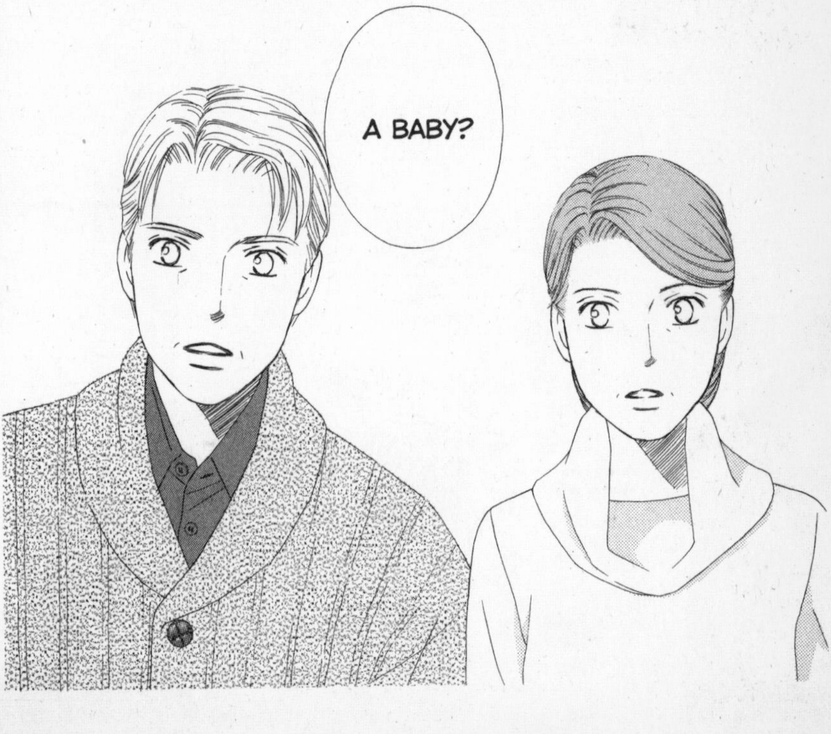
A BABY?

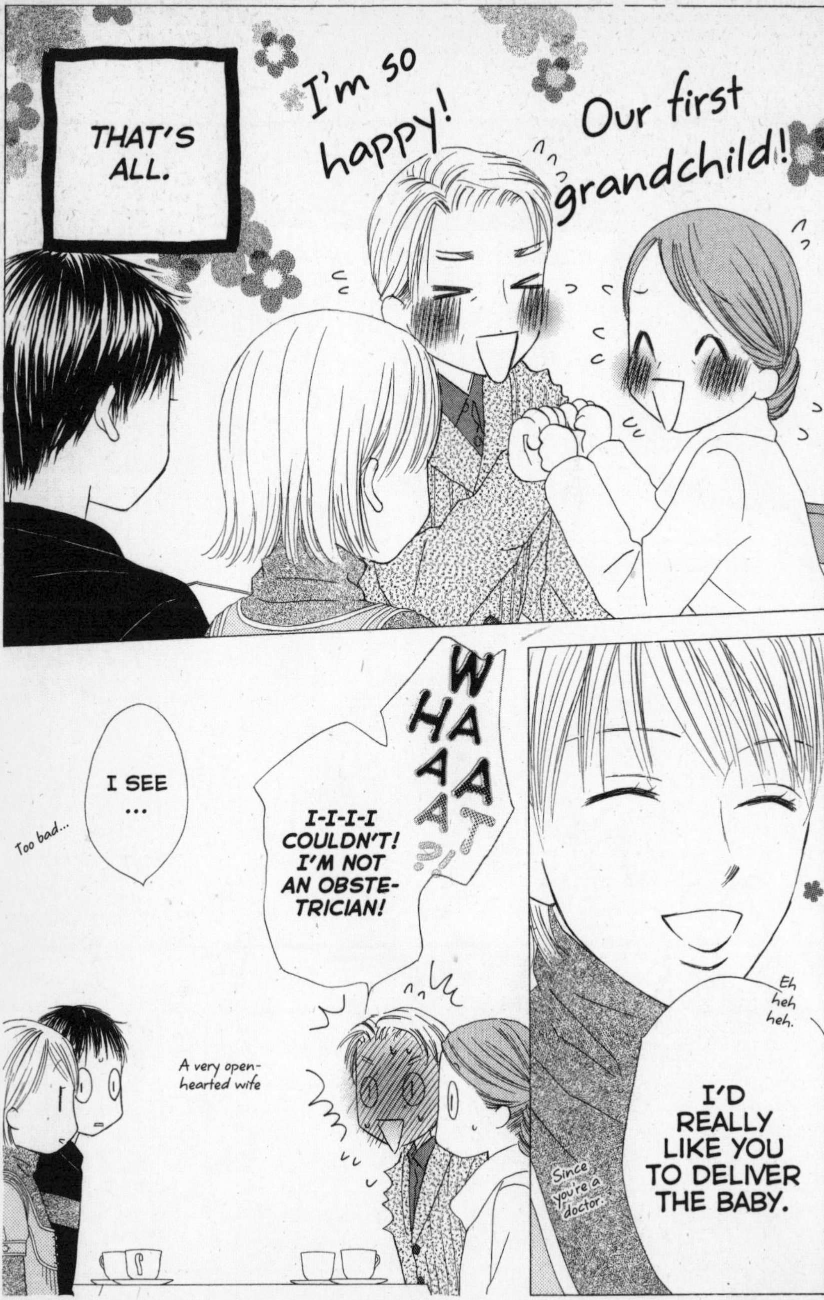
Our first grandchild!
I'm so happy!
THAT'S ALL.
I'D REALLY LIKE YOU TO DELIVER THE BABY.
Eh heh heh.
Since you're a doctor.
WHAAAT?!
I-I-I-I COULDN'T! I'M NOT AN OBSTE-TRICIAN!
I SEE...
Too bad...
A very open-hearted wife

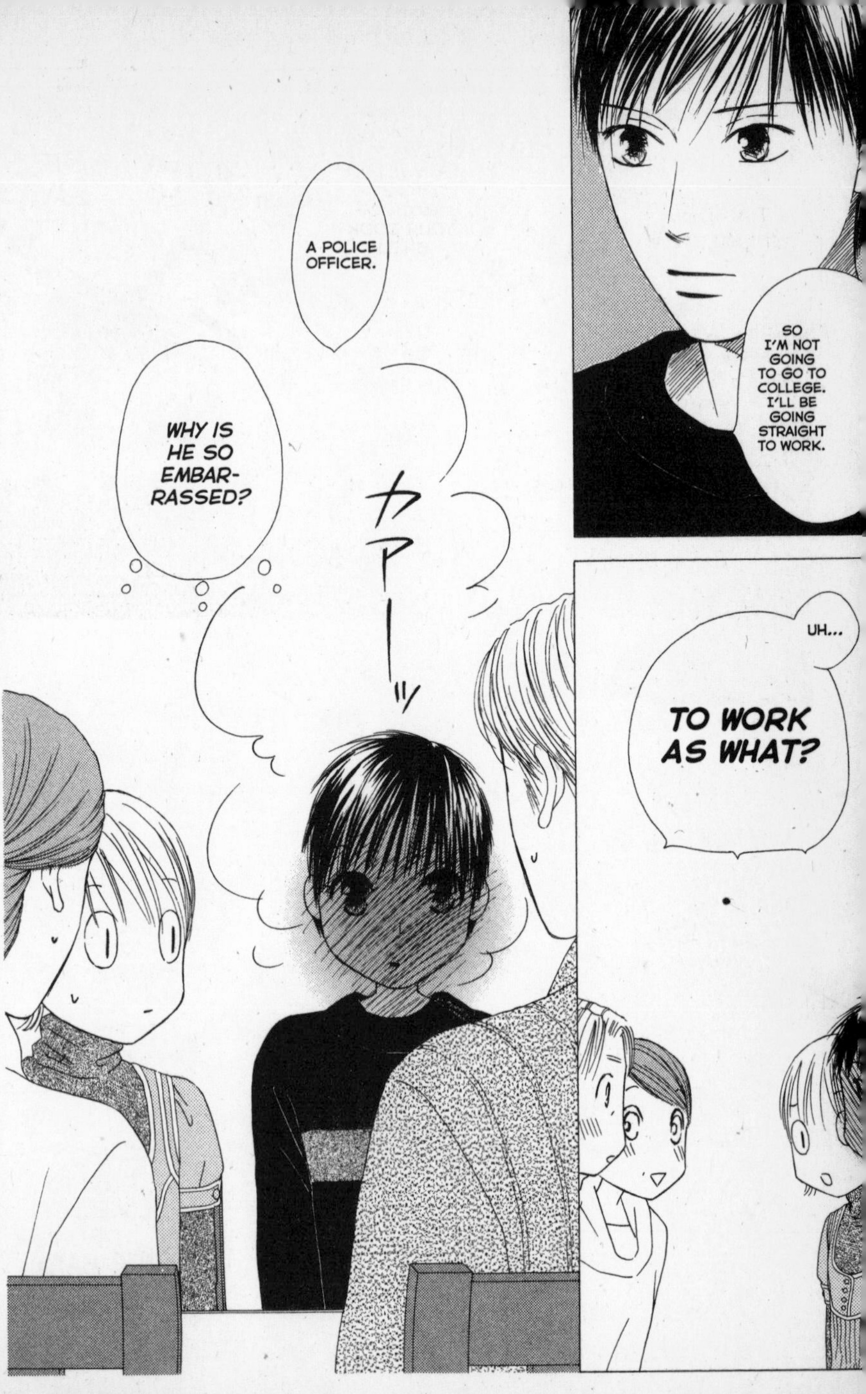
SO I'M NOT GOING TO GO TO COLLEGE. I'LL BE GOING STRAIGHT TO WORK.
UH...
TO WORK AS WHAT?
A POLICE OFFICER.
カァーッ
WHY IS HE SO EMBAR-RASSED?

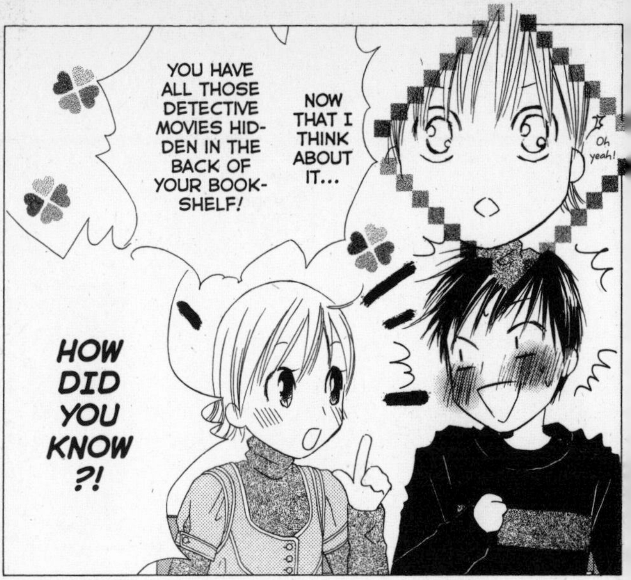
NOW THAT I THINK ABOUT IT...
YOU HAVE ALL THOSE DETECTIVE MOVIES HIDDEN IN THE BACK OF YOUR BOOKSHELF!
Oh yeah!
HOW DID YOU KNOW ?!

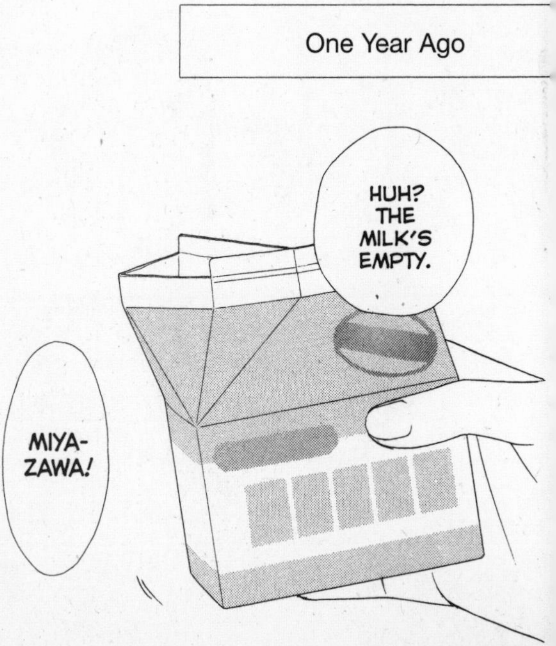
One Year Ago
HUH? THE MILK'S EMPTY.
MIYAZAWA!

5

This is my last chat space.

In this volume, Reiji-san goes back to New York, and with that, that difficult development in the story ended as well. It's like a load has been lifted off of my back.

This entire series will come to an end in the next volume. I'm going to enjoy writing the rest of the story as much as I can.

I'd be very happy if you would read the last volume as well.

see ya! (-.-)

Send letters to:
T 101-0063
Tokyo-to, Chiyoda-ku,
Kanda Awaji-cho 2-2-2
Hakusensha
Monthly Lala Editing
Department

S. Taneoka
N. Shimizu
R. Ogawa
Y. Etou
R. Takahashi
The therapists at the massage parlor
and K.U

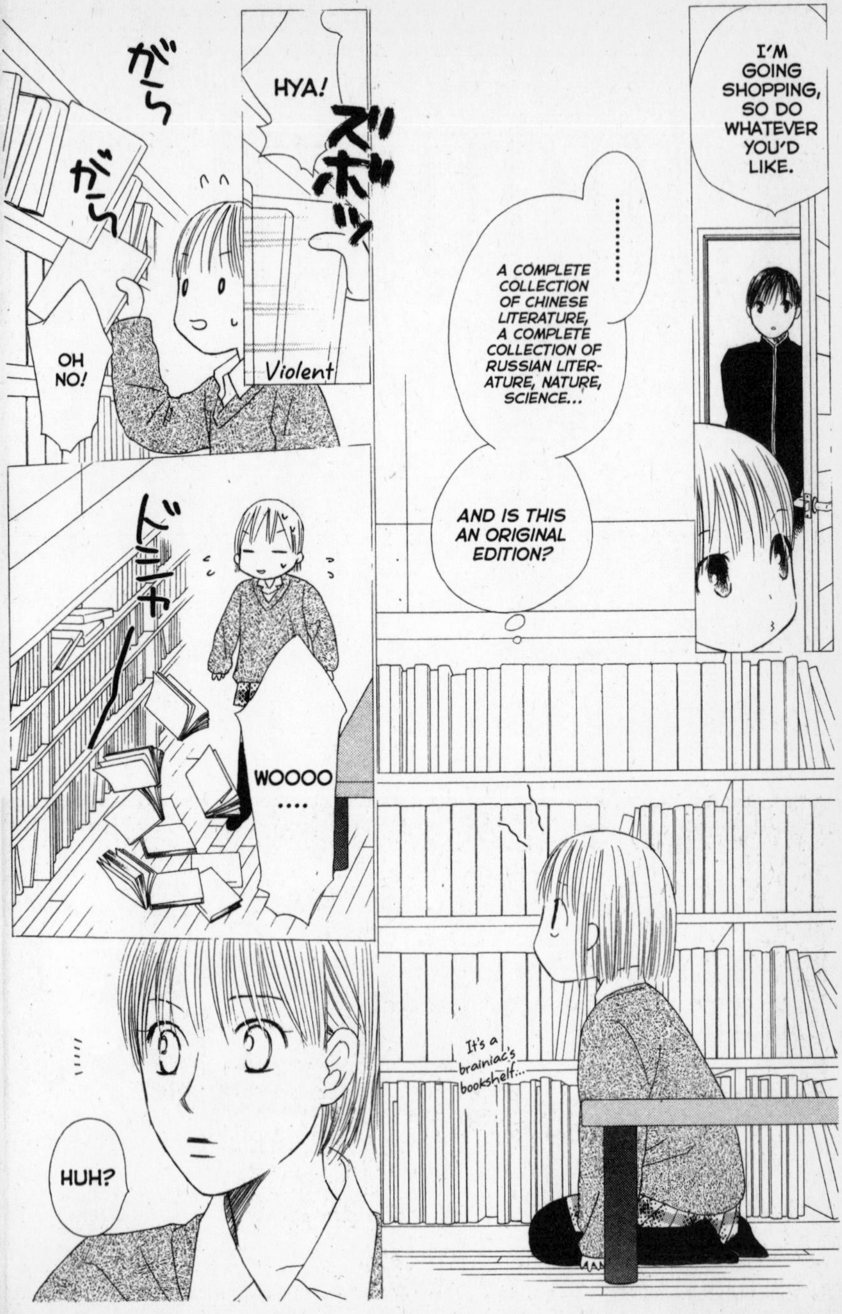

I'M GOING SHOPPING, SO DO WHATEVER YOU'D LIKE.
......
A COMPLETE COLLECTION OF CHINESE LITERATURE, A COMPLETE COLLECTION OF RUSSIAN LITERATURE, NATURE, SCIENCE...
AND IS THIS AN ORIGINAL EDITION?
It's a brainiac's bookshelf...
HYA!
ズボッ
Violent
がら
がら
OH NO!
ドシャーー
WOOOO ....
...
HUH?

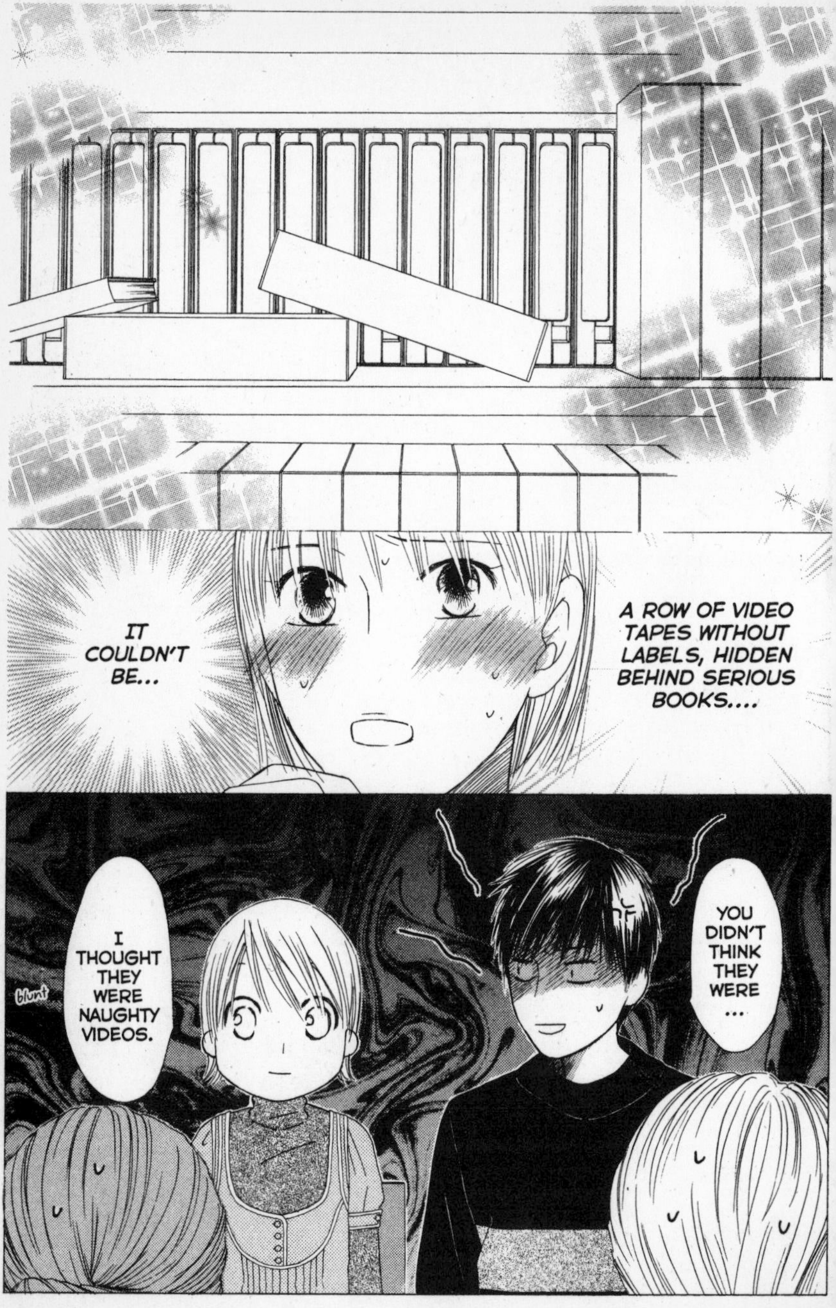
A ROW OF VIDEO TAPES WITHOUT LABELS, HIDDEN BEHIND SERIOUS BOOKS....
IT COULDN'T BE...
YOU DIDN'T THINK THEY WERE ...
I THOUGHT THEY WERE NAUGHTY VIDEOS.
blunt

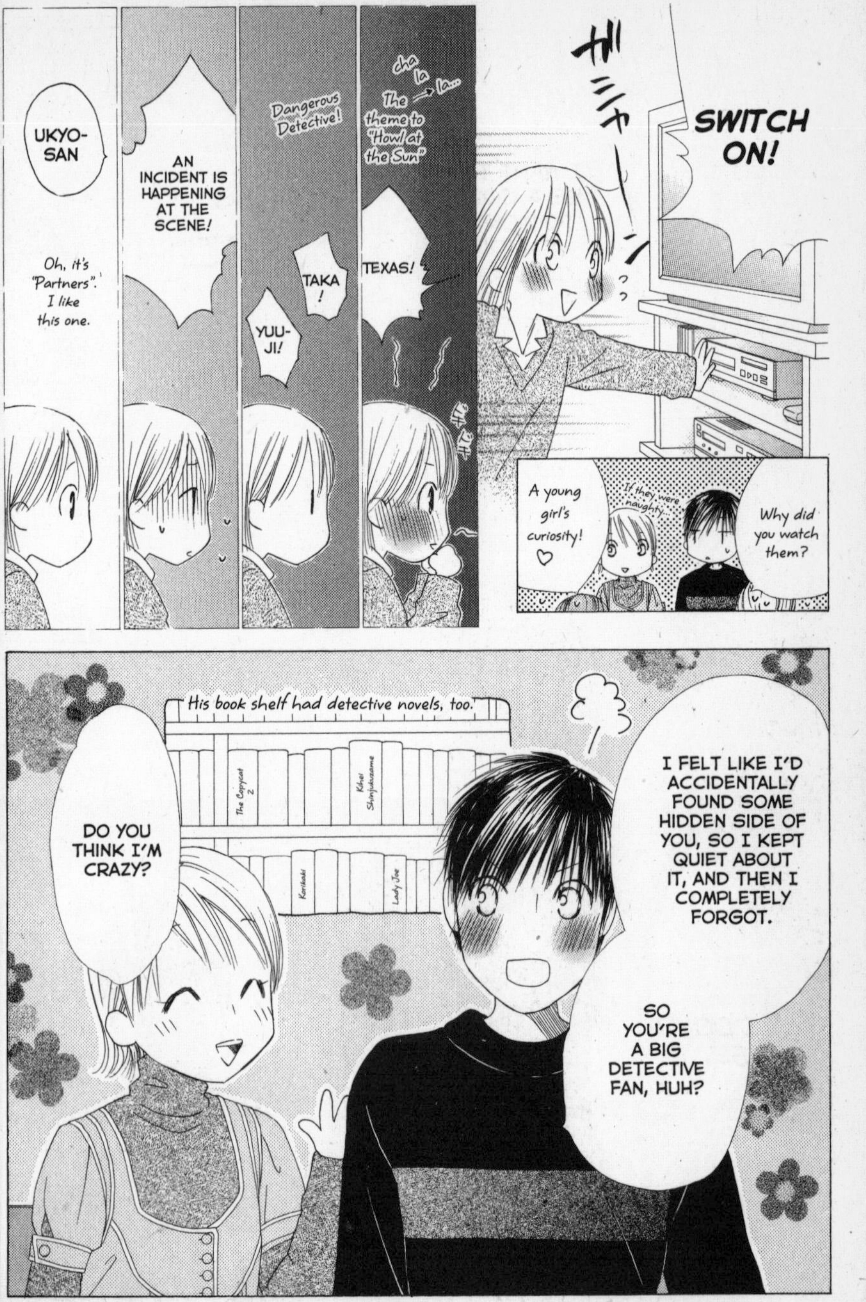

ガシャーン
SWITCH ON!
Why did you watch them?
If they were naughty...
A young girl's curiosity! ♡
cha la The → la... theme to "Howl at the Sun"
TEXAS!
Dangerous Detective!
TAKA!
YUU-JI!
AN INCIDENT IS HAPPENING AT THE SCENE!
UKYO-SAN
Oh, it's "Partners". I like this one.
I FELT LIKE I'D ACCIDENTALLY FOUND SOME HIDDEN SIDE OF YOU, SO I KEPT QUIET ABOUT IT, AND THEN I COMPLETELY FORGOT.
SO YOU'RE A BIG DETECTIVE FAN, HUH?
His book shelf had detective novels, too.
The Copycat 2
Kihei Shinjukuzame
Lady Joe
DO YOU THINK I'M CRAZY?

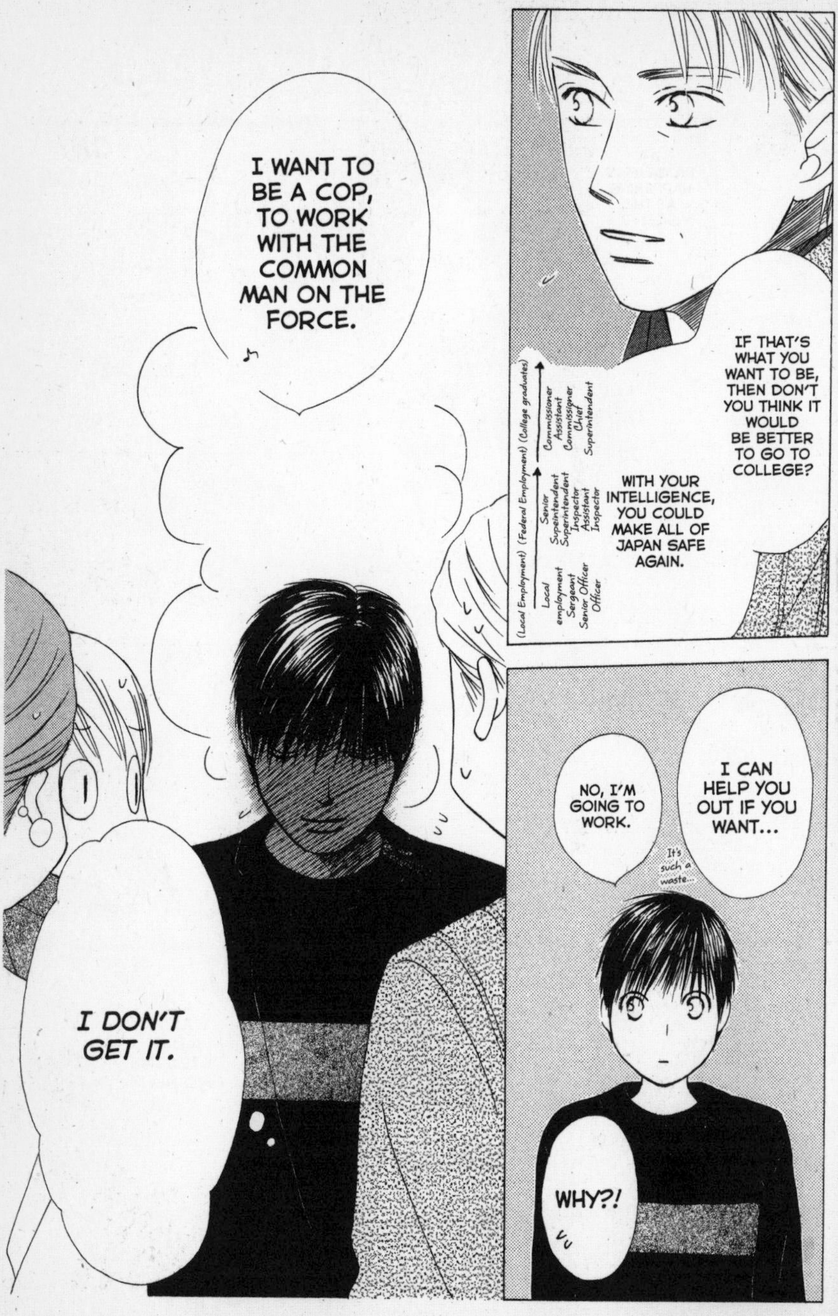
IF THAT'S WHAT YOU WANT TO BE, THEN DON'T YOU THINK IT WOULD BE BETTER TO GO TO COLLEGE?
WITH YOUR INTELLIGENCE, YOU COULD MAKE ALL OF JAPAN SAFE AGAIN.
(Local Employment) Local employment Sergeant Senior Officer Officer
(Federal Employment) Senior Superintendent Superintendent Inspector Assistant Inspector
(College graduates) Commissioner Assistant Commissioner Chief Superintendent
I CAN HELP YOU OUT IF YOU WANT...
It's such a waste...
NO, I'M GOING TO WORK.
WHY?!
I WANT TO BE A COP, TO WORK WITH THE COMMON MAN ON THE FORCE.
I DON'T GET IT.

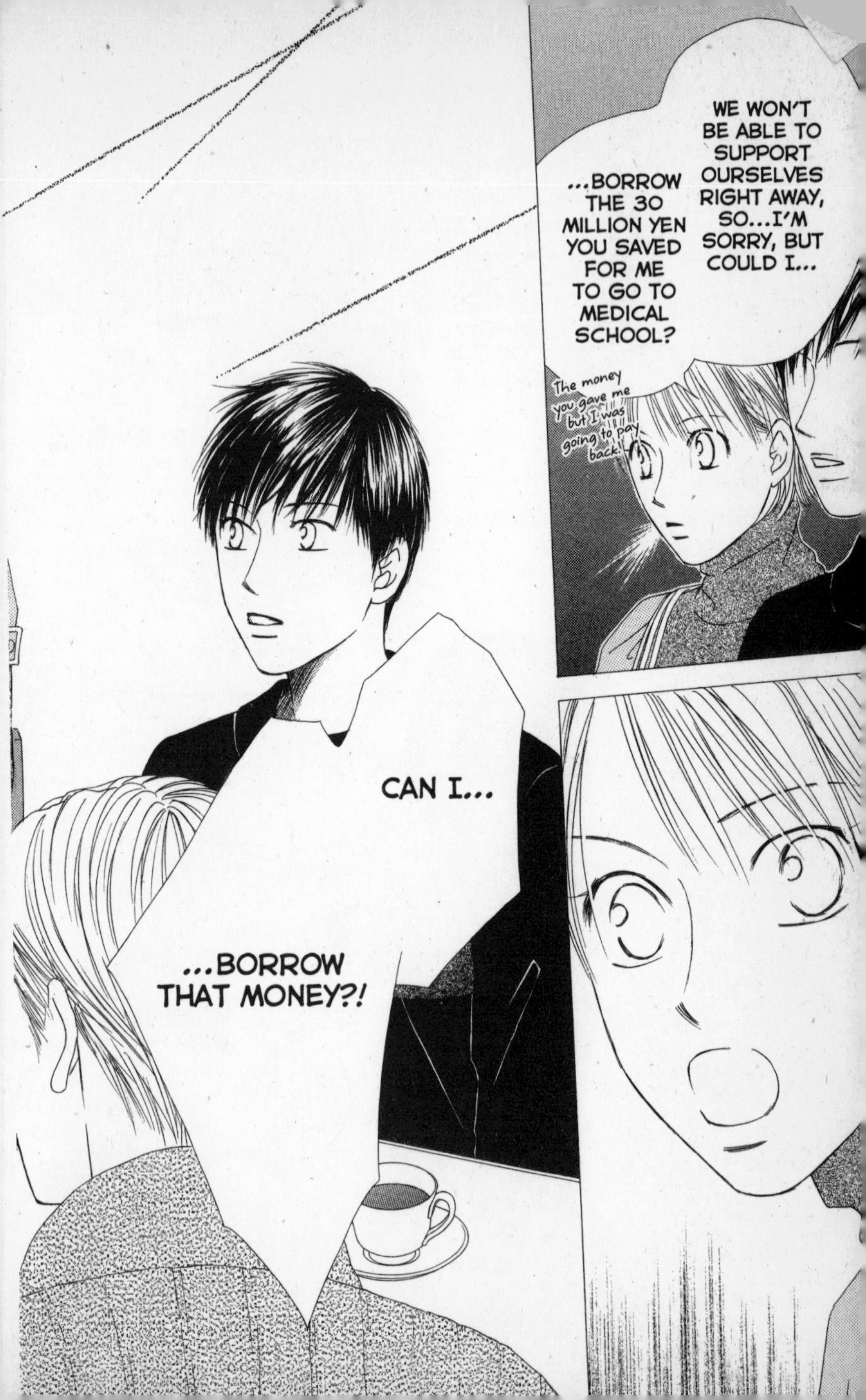
WE WON'T BE ABLE TO SUPPORT OURSELVES RIGHT AWAY, SO...I'M SORRY, BUT COULD I...
...BORROW THE 30 MILLION YEN YOU SAVED FOR ME TO GO TO MEDICAL SCHOOL?
The money you gave me but I was going to pay back.
CAN I...
...BORROW THAT MONEY?!

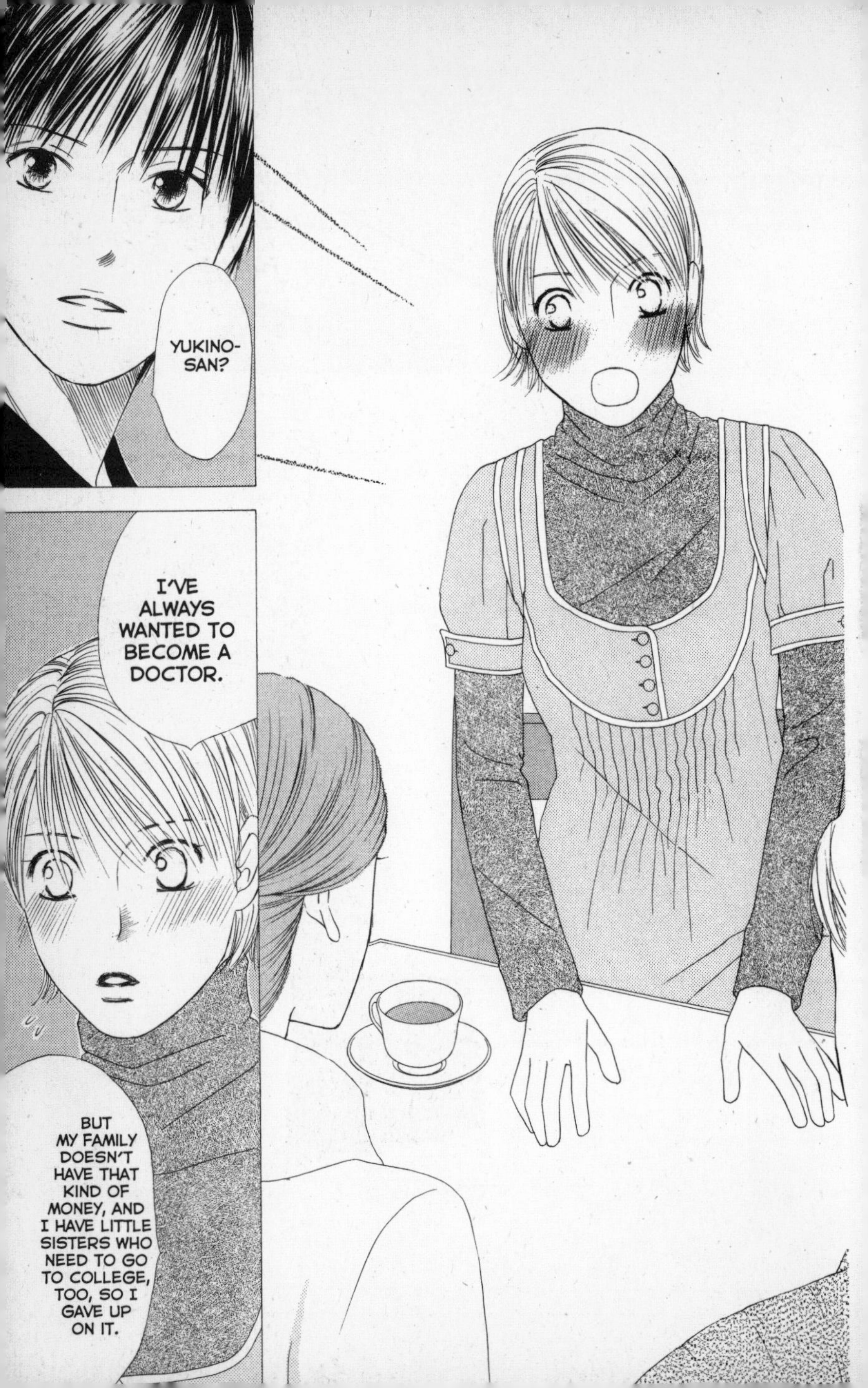
YUKINO-SAN?
I'VE ALWAYS WANTED TO BECOME A DOCTOR.
BUT MY FAMILY DOESN'T HAVE THAT KIND OF MONEY, AND I HAVE LITTLE SISTERS WHO NEED TO GO TO COLLEGE, TOO, SO I GAVE UP ON IT.

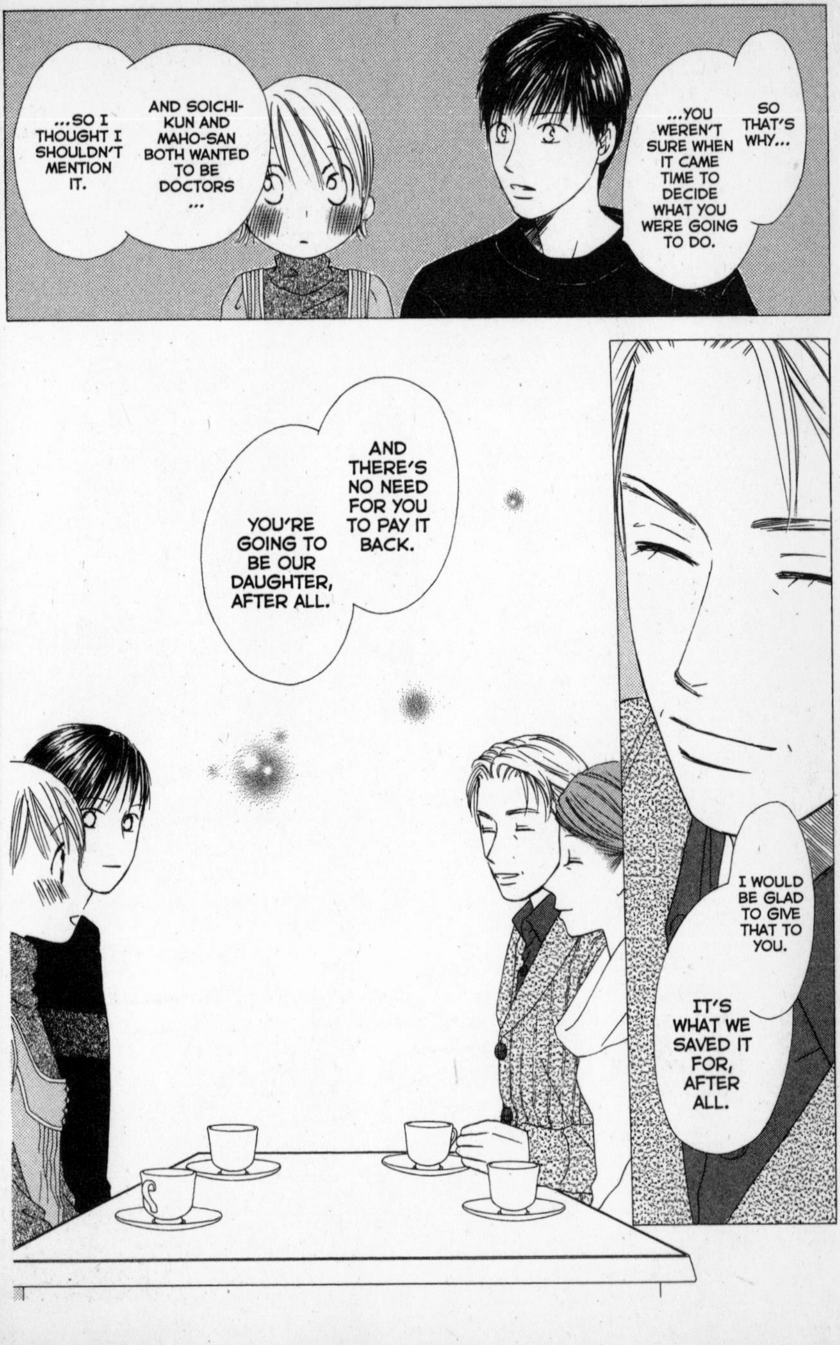
SO THAT'S WHY...
...YOU WEREN'T SURE WHEN IT CAME TIME TO DECIDE WHAT YOU WERE GOING TO DO.
AND SOICHI-KUN AND MAHO-SAN BOTH WANTED TO BE DOCTORS ...
...SO I THOUGHT I SHOULDN'T MENTION IT.
I WOULD BE GLAD TO GIVE THAT TO YOU.
IT'S WHAT WE SAVED IT FOR, AFTER ALL.
AND THERE'S NO NEED FOR YOU TO PAY IT BACK.
YOU'RE GOING TO BE OUR DAUGHTER, AFTER ALL.

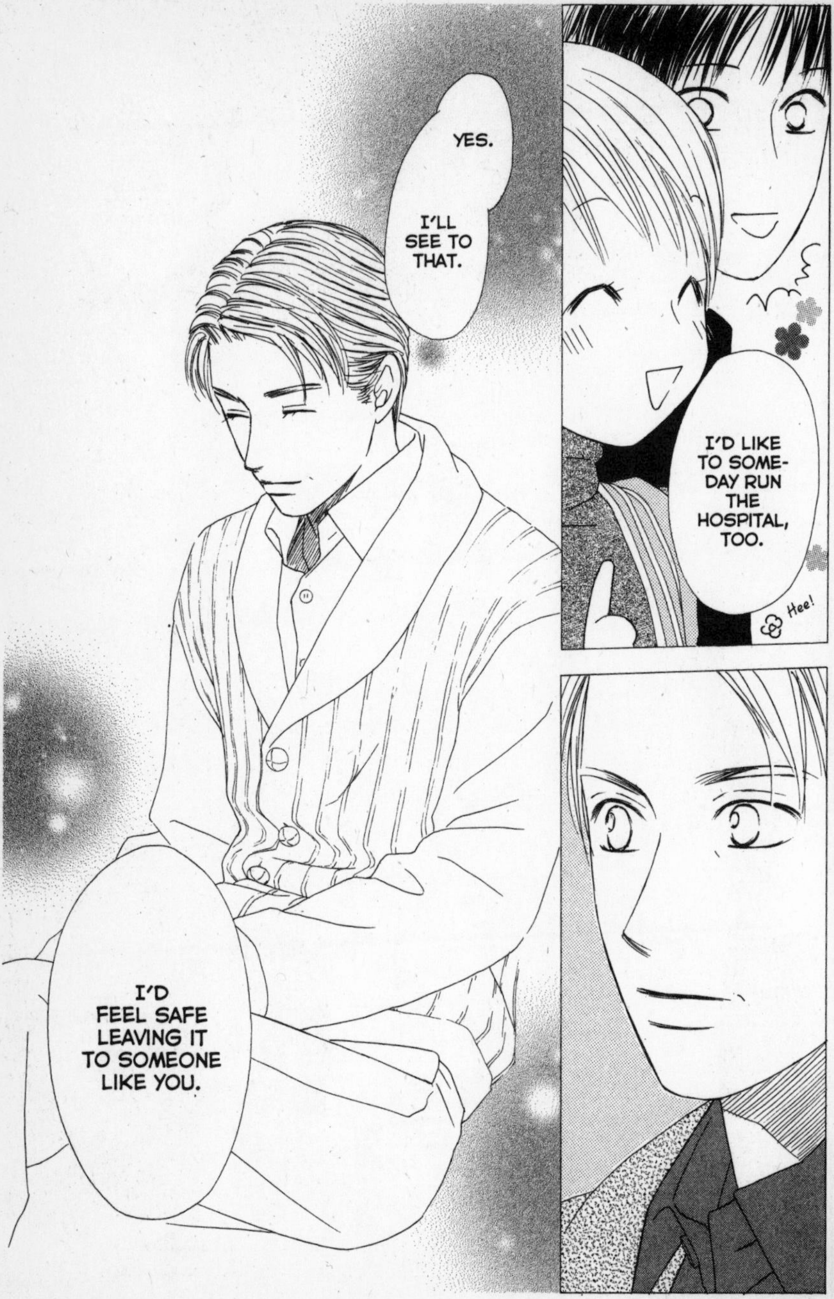
I'D LIKE TO SOME-DAY RUN THE HOSPITAL, TOO.
Hee!
YES.
I'LL SEE TO THAT.
I'D FEEL SAFE LEAVING IT TO SOMEONE LIKE YOU.

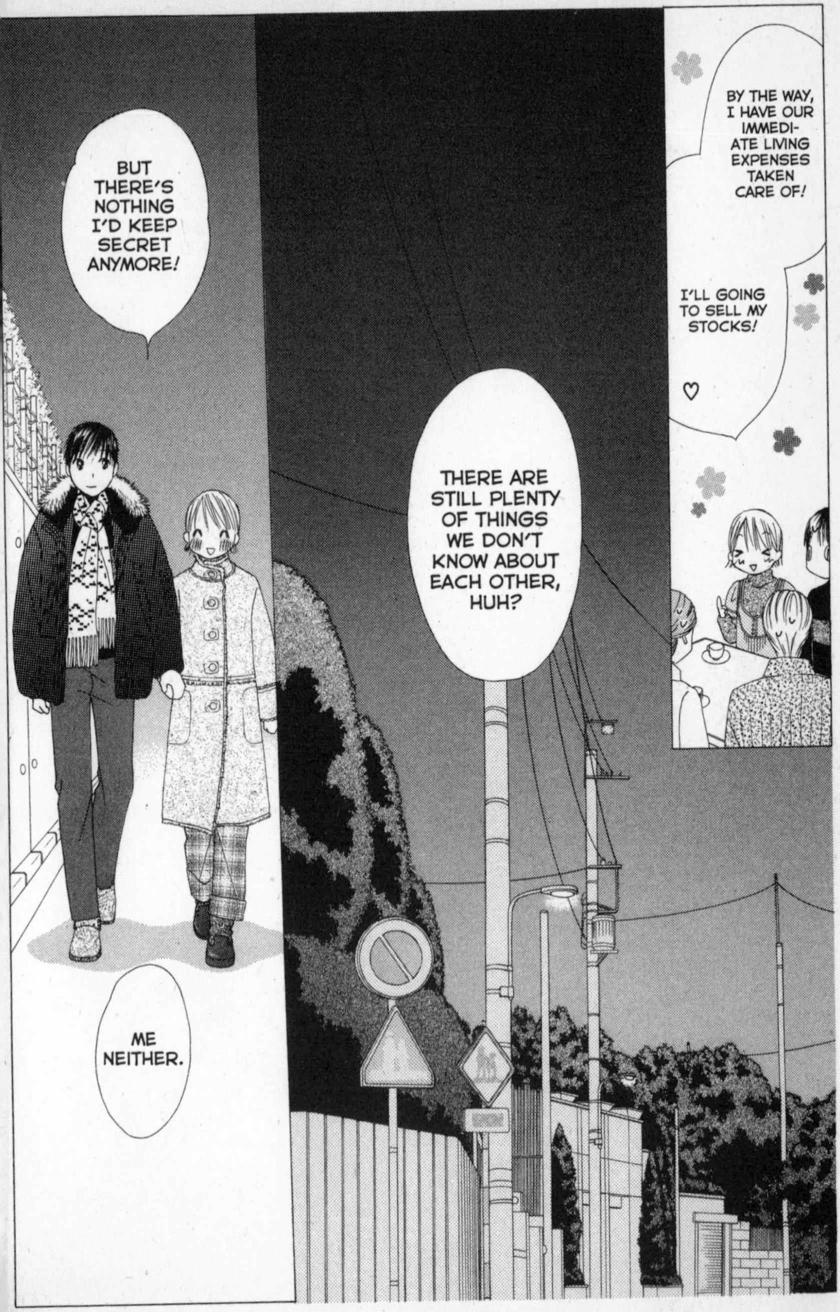
BY THE WAY, I HAVE OUR IMMEDI- ATE LIVING EXPENSES TAKEN CARE OF!
I'LL GOING TO SELL MY STOCKS! ♡
THERE ARE STILL PLENTY OF THINGS WE DON'T KNOW ABOUT EACH OTHER, HUH?
BUT THERE'S NOTHING I'D KEEP SECRET ANYMORE!
ME NEITHER.

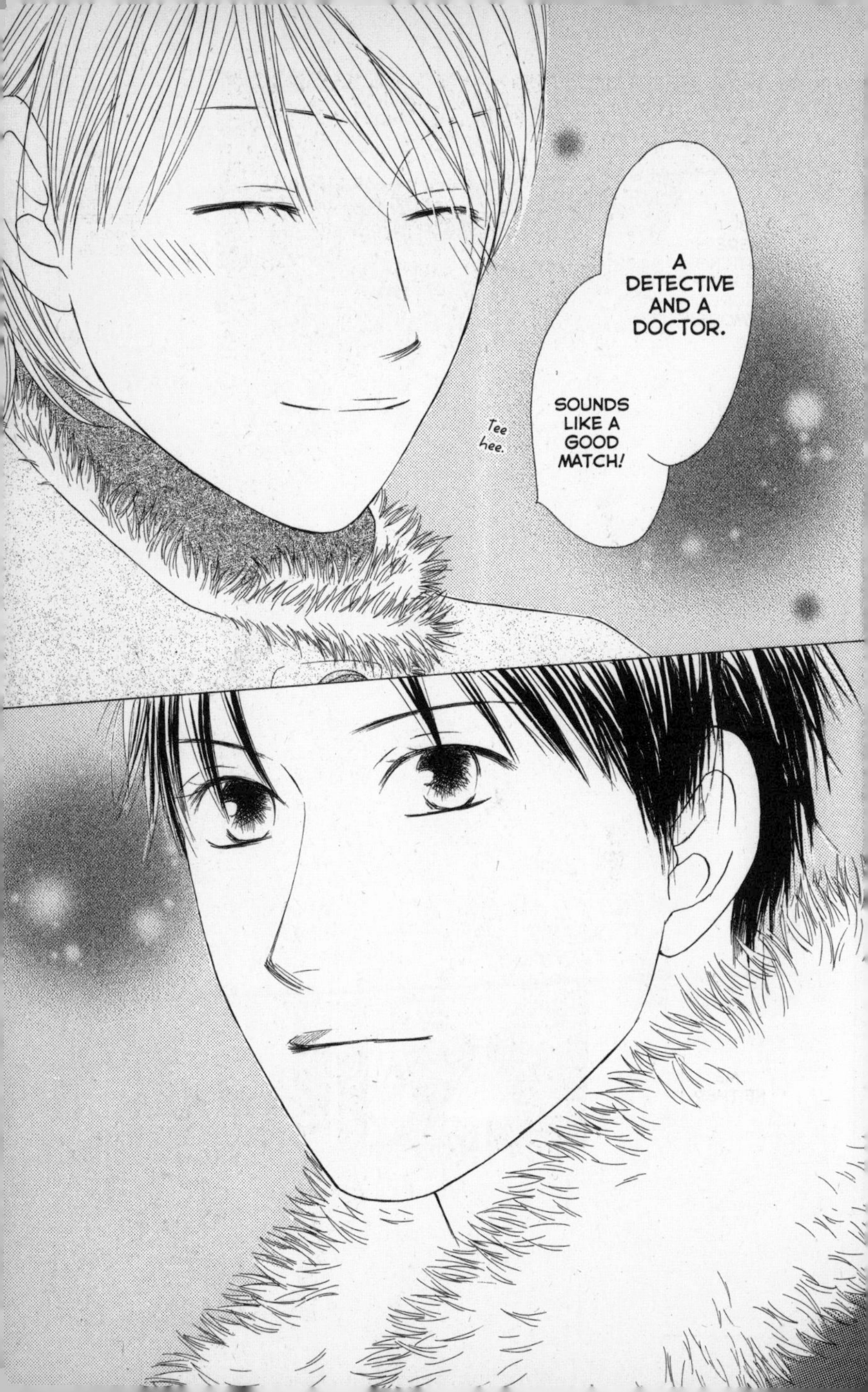
A DETECTIVE AND A DOCTOR.
SOUNDS LIKE A GOOD MATCH!
Tee hee.

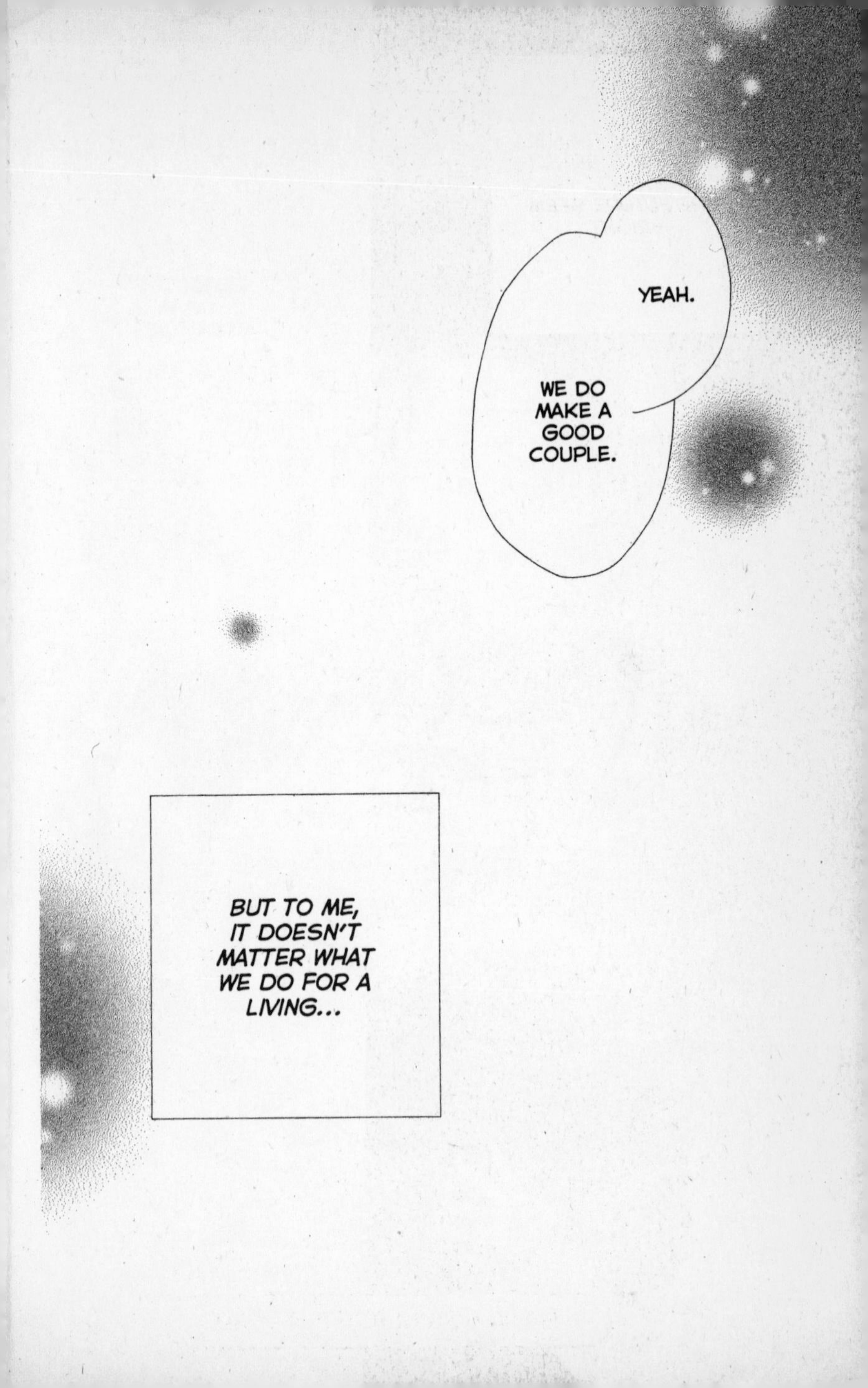
YEAH.
WE DO MAKE A GOOD COUPLE.
BUT TO ME, IT DOESN'T MATTER WHAT WE DO FOR A LIVING...

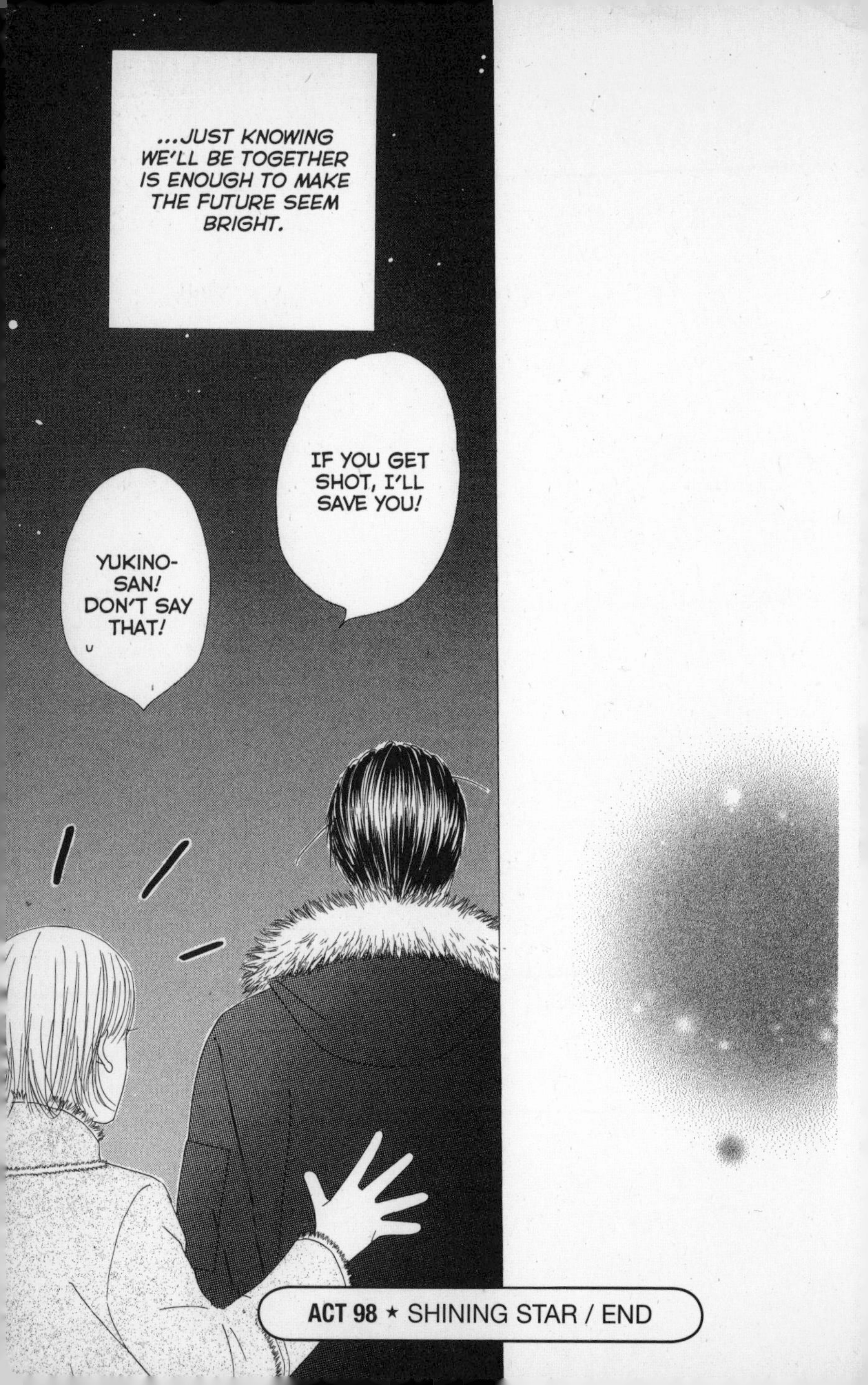
...JUST KNOWING WE'LL BE TOGETHER IS ENOUGH TO MAKE THE FUTURE SEEM BRIGHT.
IF YOU GET SHOT, I'LL SAVE YOU!
YUKINO-SAN! DON'T SAY THAT!

ACT 98 ★ SHINING STAR / END

coming soon

kare kano

his and her circumstances

volume twenty-one

As Yukino and Soichiro prepare to graduate, it looks like their future is finally sealed...but there still are a few surprises in store. Don't miss the final volume of Kare Kano, where you'll catch a glimpse of the whole gang, sixteen years in the future!

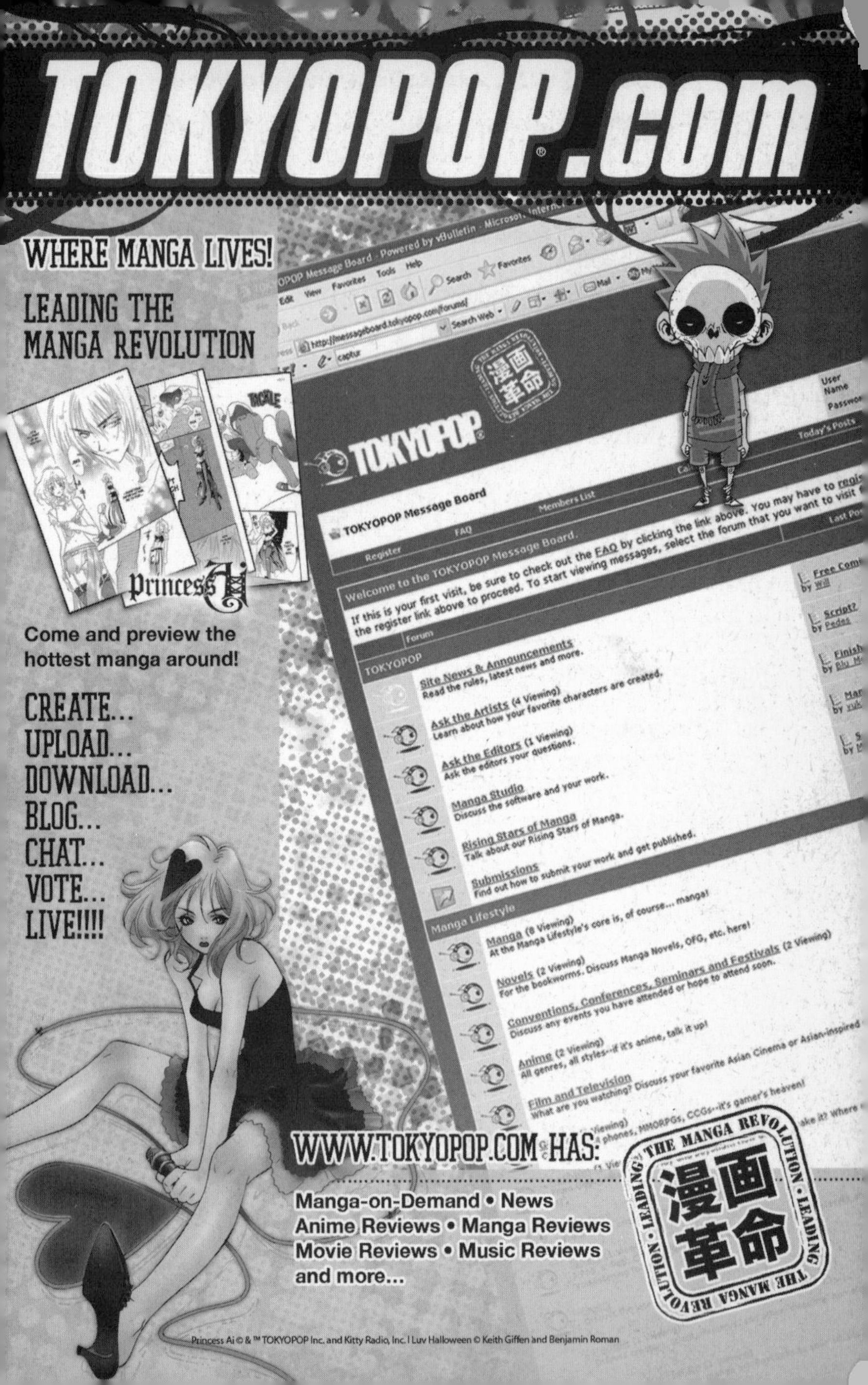
TOKYOPOP®.com
WHERE MANGA LIVES!
LEADING THE MANGA REVOLUTION
Princess Ai
Come and preview the hottest manga around!
CREATE...
UPLOAD...
DOWNLOAD...
BLOG...
CHAT...
VOTE...
LIVE!!!!
TOKYOPOP Message Board
Welcome to the TOKYOPOP Message Board.
Site News & Announcements
Ask the Artists
Ask the Editors
Manga Studio
Rising Stars of Manga
Submissions
Manga Lifestyle
Manga
Novels
Conventions, Conferences, Seminars and Festivals
Anime
Film and Television
WWW.TOKYOPOP.COM HAS:
Manga-on-Demand • News
Anime Reviews • Manga Reviews
Movie Reviews • Music Reviews
and more...
LEADING THE MANGA REVOLUTION
漫画革命
Princess Ai © & ™ TOKYOPOP Inc. and Kitty Radio, Inc. I Luv Halloween © Keith Giffen and Benjamin Roman

Jim Henson's

RETURN TO LABYRINTH™

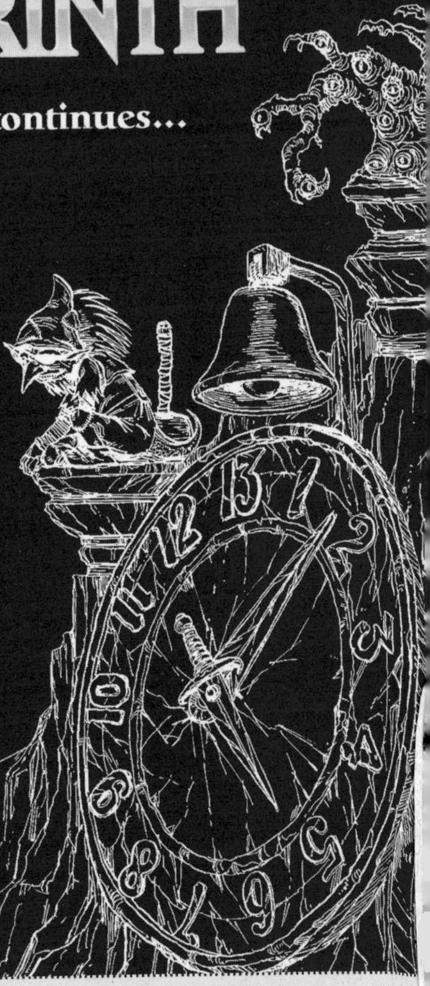

im Henson's classic continues...

he Goblin King has kept a watchful ye on Toby: His minions secretly uiding and protecting the child... egions of goblins working behind he scenes to ensure that Toby has hatever his heart desires... reparing him for the day when he vill return to the Labyrinth and take is rightful place beside Jareth as the eir to the Goblin Kingdom.

hat day has come...

.but no one has told Toby.

3y Chris Lie
ınd Jake T. Forbes

FANTASY
T TEEN AGE 13+

FOR MORE INFORMATION VISIT: WWW.TOKYOPOP.COM

STOP!

This is the back of the book. You wouldn't want to spoil a great ending!

This book is printed "manga-style," in the authentic Japanese right-to-left format. Since none of the artwork has been flipped or altered, readers get to experience the story just as the creator intended. You've been asking for it, so TOKYOPOP® delivered: authentic, hot-off-the-press, and far more fun!

DIRECTIONS

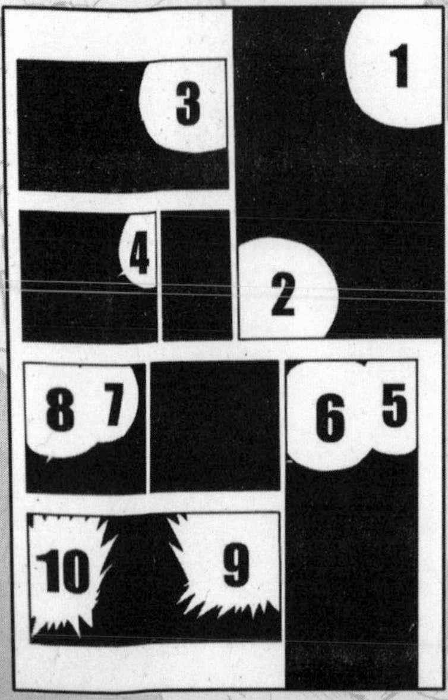
1
2
3
4
5
6
7
8
9
10

If this is your first time reading manga-style, here's a quick guide to help you understand how it works.

It's easy... just start in the top right panel and follow the numbers. Have fun, and look for more 100% authentic manga from TOKYOPOP®!

100% AUTHENTIC MANGA